Sustainability of
Thailand's
Competitiveness

Based in Bangkok since 2001, the **Research Institute on Contemporary Southeast Asia** (USR 3142 - UMIFRE 22 CNRS MAEE) focuses its activities on the political, economic, social and environmental evolutions of the eleven countries of the region. As a member of the network of research institutes of the French Ministry of Foreign Affairs and a Research and Service Unit of the French National Research Agency (CNRS), IRASEC has been tasked with the analysis of the major developments that affect, together or separately, Brunei, Burma, Cambodia, Indonesia, Lao, Malaysia, the Philippines, Singapore, Thailand, Timor Leste and Vietnam.

IRASEC promotes a variety of approaches by calling experts and specialists from all academic fields and teaming them up as required. Comparative approaches and transversal studies are favoured as much as possible. The institute endeavours to view and present each theme in its true historical and geographic dimensions.

IRASEC's research output consists of highly scientific synthetic works whose accessibility should not be restricted to experts only. The institute stresses the quality of presentation and didactic features of the books it offers to the public. It has developed a dynamic editorial policy with a variety of partners.

The **Institute of Southeast Asian Studies (ISEAS)** was established as an autonomous organization in 1968. It is a regional centre dedicated to the study of socio-political, security and economic trends and developments in Southeast Asia and its wider geostrategic and economic environment. The Institute's research programmes are the Regional Economic Studies (RES, including ASEAN and APEC), Regional Strategic and Political Studies (RSPS), and Regional Social and Cultural Studies (RSCS).

ISEAS Publishing, an established academic press, has issued more than 2,000 books and journals. It is the largest scholarly publisher of research about Southeast Asia from within the region. ISEAS Publishing works with many other academic and trade publishers and distributors to disseminate important research and analyses from and about Southeast Asia to the rest of the world.

Sustainability of Thailand's Competitiveness

The Policy Challenges

Edited by
Patarapong Intarakumnerd
and **Yveline Lecler**

IRASEC

INSTITUT DE RECHERCHE SUR L'ASIE DU SUD-EST CONTEMPORAINE
RESEARCH INSTITUTE ON CONTEMPORARY SOUTHEAST ASIA

BANGKOK

ISEAS

INSTITUTE OF SOUTHEAST ASIAN STUDIES
SINGAPORE

First published in Singapore in 2010 by
ISEAS Publishing
Institute of Southeast Asian Studies
30 Heng Mui Keng Terrace
Pasir Panjang
Singapore 119614

E-mail: publish@iseas.edu.sg
Website: <http://bookshop.iseas.edu.sg>

Co-published with
IRASEC
Research Institute on Contemporary Southeast Asia
29, Sathorn Tai Road
10120 Bangkok
Thailand
www.irasec.com

The responsibility for facts and opinions in this publication rests exclusively with the authors and their interpretations do not necessarily reflect the views or the policy of the publishers or its supporters.

ISEAS Library Cataloguing-in-Publication Data

Sustainability of Thailand's competitiveness : the policy challenges / edited by Patarapong Intarakumnerd and Yveline Lecler.
1.   Industrial promotion—Thailand.
2.   Competition—Thailand.
3.   Thailand—Economic conditions.
4.   Thailand—Economic policy.
I.   Patarapong Intarakumnerd
II. Lecler, Yveline.
HC445 Z9I53S96   2010

ISBN 978-981-4279-47-5 (soft cover)
ISBN 978-981-4279-48-2 (E-book PDF)

Typeset by Superskill Graphics Pte Ltd
Printed in Singapore by Utopia Press Pte Ltd

CONTENTS

Part III: Firms and Government New Initiatives:
The Industry Analysis

PREFACE

This book is a product linked to a collective research project titled, "Industrial Clusters in Asia: Old Forms, New Forms", funded by the French Ministry of Education and Research and the Region Rhône-Alpes Assembly (France) which brought together in the course of four years some twenty researchers and PhD students from France, Japan, China, Vietnam, and Thailand, under the coordination of two French research units of the University of Lyon: IAO (Institute of East Asian Studies, CNRS, ENS-LSH) and MODYS (World and Dynamics of Societies: CNRS).

An international workshop was held in Lyon from November–December 2006 where preliminary results were discussed, leading to the writing of a first, general collective book. To extend further and deepen the research on the Thai case, a complementary funding was proposed by the "Institut de Recherche sur l'Asie du Sud-Est Contemporaine" (IRASEC). The present book although integrating the issue of cluster which was at the core of the general research project it is based on takes a different approach while aiming to answer an important question for Thailand: Is its industrial development sustainable for the next decade? Most contributors were also engaged in the larger research programme, but some others have also been specifically included in because of their knowledge on relevant points that are central for Thailand but had not been given enough attention.

Before presenting the findings of this research, we would like to thank IRASEC, without which this book would not exist. We also want to express our gratitude to all persons who gave us time and helped us gather the necessary and up to date information: firms, administration executives, and university colleagues not involved in the project. They are too numerous to name here, but without them this book would not exist either. The opinions expressed in each chapter remain, however, the author's.

After giving a general overview of Thai development in three main areas — foreign investments, national innovation system, and education — which point out strengths and weaknesses and also make recommendations, we discuss the role of Thai institutions before illustrating the general findings of the study of three major industries concretely. By doing so, we hope that this book will be useful not only to policymakers and executives involved in economic or industrial development, but also to researchers and students who want to learn more about Thailand and emerging countries.

Patarapong Intarakumnerd and Yveline Lecler
February 2009

ABBREVIATIONS

AAT	AutoAlliance Thailand
AFTA	ASEAN Free Trade Area
AIT	Asian Institute of Technology
ASEAN	Association of Southeast Asian Nations
ATC	Agreement on Textiles and Clothing
BOI	Board of Investment
BOT	Bank of Thailand
BUILD	BOI Unit for Industrial Linkage Development
CAD/CAM	Computed Aided Design/Computed Aided Manufacturing
CDA	Cluster Development Agent
CELS	Centre of Education and Labour Studies
CEO	Chief Executive Officer
CIS	Commonwealth of Independent States
CNC	Computer numerically controlled
CNRS	Centre National de la Recherche Scientifique (National Centre of Scientific Research)
DIP	Department of Industrial Promotion
EE	Electrical and Electronic (industries)
EEI	Electrical and Electronics Institute
ENS-LSH	Ecole Normale Supérieure – Lettres et Sciences Humaines
EPZ	Export Processing Zone
EXIM	Export and Import (Bank of Thailand)
FDI	Foreign Direct Investment
FTA	Free Trade Agreement
FTI	Federation of Thai Industry
GATT	General Agreement on Tariffs and Trade

GC	Growth Contribution
GDP	Gross Domestic Product
GER	Gross Enrolment Rate
GFCF	Gross Fixed Capital Formation
GM	General Motors
GMS	Global Manufacturing System
GNP	Gross National Product
GPI	Gender Parity Index
HDD	Hard Disk Drive
HGA	Head Gimbal Assembly
HGSP	Hitachi Global Storage Products
HGST	Hitachi Global Storage Technology
HMMT	Honda Motor Manufacturing Thailand
HRM	Human Resource Management
HS	Harmonized System (nomenclature)
HSA	Head-Stack Assembly
HTTI	HDD Technology Training Institute
I/UCRC	Industry/university Collaborative Research Centre
IAO	Institut d'Asie Orientale (Institute of East Asian Studies)
IBRD	International Bank for Reconstruction and Development
ICs	Integrated Circuits
IDEMA	International Disk Drive Equipment and Material Association
IDF	Innovation Development Fund
IE	Industrial Estate
IEA	Evaluation of Educational Achievement
IEAT	Industrial Estate Authority of Thailand
IFC	Institute for Collaboration
IFCT	Industrial Finance Corporation of Thailand
ILO	International Labour Office
IMD	International Institute for Management Development
IMF	International Monetary Fund
IMMT	Isuzu Motor Manufacturing Thailand
IMT	Indonesia-Malaysia-Thailand (Growth Triangle)
IMT-GT	Indonesia-Malaysia-Thailand – Growth Triangle
IMV	Innovative International Multipurpose Vehicle

IRASEC	Institut de Recherche sur l'Asie du Sud-Est Contemporaine (Research Institute on Contemporary Southeast Asia
IRD	Institut de Recherche pour le Développement (French Research Institute in Development Studies)
IRP	Industrial Restructuring Plan
IS	Innovation system
ISCED	International Standard Classification of Education
ISI	Import-Substitution Industrialization
ISMED	Institute for SME Development
ISO	International Organization for Standardization
iTAP	industrial Technology Assistance program
JETRO	Japan External Trade Organization
JICA	Japan International Cooperation Agency
JODC	Japan Overseas Development Corporation
JPPCC	Joint Public-Private Consultative Committee
KICOX	Korea Industrial Complex Corporation
KMUTL	King Mongkut's University of Technology Ladkrabang
KMUTT	King Mongkut's University of Technology Thonburi
LEPII	Laboratoire d'économie de la production et de l'intégration internationale (Research Centre in Economy of production and Regional Integration)
M and A	Mergers and Acquisitions
M/D	Import/domestic demand
MAI	Market for Alternative Investment
METI	Ministry of Economy Trade and Industry
MEXT	Ministry of Education, Culture, Sports, Science and Technology
MFAs	Multi Fibre Agreements
MITI	Ministry of International Trade and Industry
MMC	Mitsubishi Motors Corporation
MMRC	Manufacturing Management Research Center
MNC	Multinational Corporation
MODYS	Mondes et Dynamiques Sociales (Worlds and Dynamics of Societies)
MOI	Ministry of Industry
MOU	Memorandum of Understanding

MSCI	The Management System Certification Institute
MTEC	(National) Metal and Materials Technology Center
MVA	Manufacturing Value-Added
NAIC	New Agro-Industrial Country
NBC	New Basic Car
NCP	National Competitiveness Plan
NEC	New Entrepreneurship Creation
NECTEC	National Electronics and Computer Technology Center
NESDB	National Economic and Social Development Board
NFI	National Food Institute
NGO	Non-Governmental Organization
NIC	Newly Industrialized Country
NIDA	National Institute of Development Administration
NIEs	New Industrial Economies
NIEs	Newly Industrializing Economies
NIS	National Innovation System
NSO	National Statistics Office
NSTDA	National Science and Technology Development Agency
NUMMI	New United Motor Manufacturing Inc.
OBM	Original Brand Manufacturing
ODA	Official Development Assistance
ODM	Original Design Manufacturer
OEC	Office of the Education Council
OECD	Organization for Economic Cooperation and Development
OEMs	Original Equipment Manufacturers
Off-JT	Off the Job Training
OIC	Organization of Islamic Conference
OJT	On the Job Training
OPV	Observation Post Vehicle
OSPUE	Operating Surplus of Private Unincorporated Enterprises
OTOP	One Tambon One Product
PICS	Productivity and Investment Climate Survey
PISA	Programme for International Student Assessment
PPP	Purchasing Power Parity

PPV	Pick-up Passenger Vehicle
PR	Public Relations
PTT	Petroleum Authority of Thailand
R&D	Research and Development
RIS	Regional Innovation System
RTOs	Research Technology Organizations
S and T	Science and Technology Policy
SALS	Structural Adjustments Loans
SET	Stock Exchange of Thailand
SICGC	Small Industry Credit Guarantee Corporation
SIFC	Small Industry Finance Corporation
SITC	Standard International Trade Classification
SMEs	Small and Medium Enterprises
STI	Skill Technology Innovation
SUV	Sport Utility Vehicle
TAI	Thai Automotive Institute
TCC	Thai Chamber of Commerce
TFP	Total Factor Productivity
TGI	Thai-German Institute
TIMSS	Trend in International Mathematics and Science Study
TISI	Thailand Industrial Standard Institute
TLO	Technology Licensing Organization
TMC	Technology Management Center
TMEC	Thai MicroElectronic Center
TMT	Toyota Motor Thailand
TNCs	Transnational Corporations
TPI	Thailand Productivity Institute
TPS	Toyota Production System
TSP	Thailand Science Park
TTI	Thai Textile Institute
TV	Television
TVCA	Thai Venture Capital Association
UIL	University-Industry Linkages
UIS	UNESCO Institute for Statistics
ULC	Unit Labour Cost
UMR	Unité Mixte de Recherche (joint affiliated research unit)

UNCTAD	United Nations Conference on Trade and Development
UNESCO	United Nations Educational, Scientific and Cultural Organization
UNIDO	United Nations Industrial Development Organization
VAT	Value-Added Tax
VC	Venture Capital
VCR	Video Cassette Recorder
WD	Western Digital
WEF	World Economic Forum
WTO	World Trade Organization
X/S	Export/domestic production
Y/K	Capital output ratio

CONTRIBUTORS

Natacha Aveline-Dubach joined the French National Center for Scientific Research (CNRS) in 1993, and became CNRS research director at the Institute of East Asian Studies in Lyon (ENS-LSH, CNRS, Lumière Lyon2 University). She currently holds the position of director of the CNRS regional office in Japan. She has spent more than eight years in Japan, and published various books on the globalization of property markets and its impact in Northeast Asia. Her recent research interests are in urban transport, regional land-use and cemetery development/funeral services in Asia.

Audrey Baron-Gutty is a PhD student in Political Science at the University of Lyon, Institute of East Asian Studies (ENS-LSH, CNRS, Lumière Lyon2 University). She has done research on regional development and educational issues, particularly in Thailand. She is now studying the impact of globalization on national educational and training policies. Supported by a scholarship from IRASEC, she has conducted extensive field work in Thailand (2007–2009).

David Hoyrup is consulting economist, formerly affiliated with LEPII-CNRS Grenoble. He conducted field research on economic growth in Southeast Asia and completed his doctoral dissertation on ASEAN emerging economies. He was post-doctoral fellow at IRASEC, Bangkok and contributed to several books on emerging Asian economies.

Patarapong Intarakumnerd is Lecturer at College of Innovation, Thammasat University. He was a project leader of Thailand's National Innovation System Study at the National Science and Technology Development Agency. He was previously a visiting fellow at the Centre of

Southeast Asian Studies at Kyoto University. His research interests include national innovation systems and clusters in developing countries, technology and innovation policies, the role of intellectual property right in economic development, university-industry linkages, and the strategies and evolution of latecomer firms.

Bruno Jetin is assistant professor in economics at Centre d'Économie de Paris Nord (CEPN, France). At the time this research was done, he was researcher at the Institut de Recherche pour le Développement (IRD, French Research Institute in Development Studies) affiliated to the Center for Education and Labour Studies (CELS, Chiang Mai University). His research areas are macroeconomics, applied industrial economics and labour economics in developing countries. He is now engaged in research on regional integration in Southeast Asia.

Yveline Lecler is presently Senior Research Fellow at Maison Franco-Japonaise (Tokyo), UMIFRE 19, and invited researcher at the Institute of Social Science, University of Tokyo, on a two years' leave from University of Lyon, Institute of Political Studies (IEP) and Institute of East Asian Studies (ENS-LSH, CNRS, Lyon2 University). She studied firms' agglomeration, SMEs, subcontracting and the international division of labour of Japanese firms, mainly in ASEAN. Her current research focuses on regional innovation policies and SMEs in Japan and Thailand.

Shinya Orihashi is Professor of Management at Tohoku Gakuin University. He is also Project Researcher at the Manufacturing Management Research Center (MMRC), University of Tokyo. He has studied the transfer of Japanese production and management systems, as well as the capability-building process at Japanese overseas subsidiaries. His major research field is Japanese automobile industries in Southeast Asia and in the rest of the world.

Akira Suehiro is Professor and Director of Institute of Social Science, University of Tokyo. His publications include *Family Business: The Agent of Late Industrialization* (2006, in Japanese) and *Catch-up Industrialization: The Trajectory and Prospects of East Asian Economies*. His current research interests are social security system in East Asia and new interaction between China and ASEAN.

Jean-Christophe Simon is senior economist at the Institut de Recherche pour le Développement (IRD, French Research Institute in Development Studies). He has worked for 25 years on development issues, currently as Research Fellow at UMR 201 Développement et Sociétés, and associated to LEPII-CNRS Grenoble. He has contributed to field research and public consultancy on overall planning, industrial development and entrepreneurship in African and East Asian countries. He currently teaches applied development economics at universities in Grenoble and Paris and contributes to research programmes on industrializing/emerging economies, climate change mitigation, and sustainable development.

INTRODUCTION

Patarapong Intarakumnerd and Yveline Lecler

The competitiveness of a country is not a given that lasts forever. Staying competitive requires continuous upgrading and, sometimes, even major transformation. Factors that used to underpin competitiveness in the past might turn to be ones reducing competitiveness in the future. Therefore, the ability of a country to learn to create new factors is very important for it to maintain its position in global competition. Thailand, which was once successful in catching up and competing with others, is now facing problems in maintaining its position and upgrading to the next stage of development.

COMPETITIVENESS, A KNOWLEDGE-BASED AND LEARNING ECONOMY, AND THE SIGNIFICANT ROLES OF INSTITUTIONS

A country's competitiveness and ability to catch up rely very much on its embedded "national" characteristics or so-called "national innovation system" or NIS. The roots of innovation systems (IS) concepts are based on Schumpeterian economics, which emphasize innovation and entrepreneurship, combined with the essence of Charles Darwin's evolutionary theory. The emergence of NIS concepts, particularly in industrialized countries in the northern hemisphere, can be traced back to the work of Lundvall (1988, 1992) on national systems of innovation or national policies of innovation, and other works (see Freeman 1987; Nelson 1988) started in the mid-1980s. NIS is an interactive system involving existing "institutions", private and public firms (either large or small), universities and government agencies, which aimed at the production of science and technology within national borders. Interaction among these units may be technical, commercial, legal, social, and financial, and the goal of the interaction may be development, protection, financing, or regulation of new science and technology (Niosi et al. 1993).

Institutions should be understood as encompassing "the basic rules of the game", the broad legal regime and the way it is enforced, widely held norms that constrain behaviour, and so on (North 1990). The norms, habits, and rules that are deeply ingrained in society play a major role in determining how people relate to one another, and learn and use their knowledge (Johnson 1992). The term "institutions" can also be associated with customs, and standard and expected patterns of behaviour in particular contexts (Hodgson 1988, 2006; Veblen 1899). The concept, therefore, covers both broad rules and governing structures that constrain behaviour, and the ways things are done. In an economy characterized by ongoing innovation and fundamental uncertainty, the institutional setting will have a major impact on how economic agents behave, as well as on the conduct and performance of the system as a whole.

One of the crucial institutions is the way firms interact with one another and with other players in innovation systems. Scholars and policymakers at present are quite interested in the geographical agglomeration of firms and the "cluster" concept. Studies of clusters have a long history. Alfred Marshall's famous *Principles of Economics* in 1890 is a cornerstone in this literature although he used the label "industrial districts". Marshall theorizes and emphasizes the dynamics of external economies associated with learning, innovation, and increased specialization. The research on districts reached a larger audience when Piore and Sabel (1984) published their seminal book, *The Second Industrial Divide,* and with the numerous works of Italian scholars (Beccatini 1990–92, among others). Nonetheless, it was the management guru Michael Porter who recently made the concept of cluster popular. According to Porter (1998), industrial clusters are geographical concentrations of interconnected companies, specialized suppliers, service providers, firms in related industries, and associated institutions (for example, universities, standard agencies, and trade associations) that combine to create new products and/or services in specific lines of business. Clusters emerge and develop because geographical proximity among firms promotes interactive and collective learning and generates positive externalities for participating actors. These benefits attract similar and related firms and other actors because they also want to participate in the interactive learning that takes place in these circumstances.

Today we are living in a world of globalization, where goods, services, capital, labour and information can move across national boundaries freer than before. We are also entering the era of the knowledge-based and learning economy. What is new in this era is neither information nor knowledge, which had been the core of economic activity since the industrial revolution in the eighteenth century. Still, knowledge is now the only meaningful factor in production. Other traditional factors in production, namely, natural resources, labour, and capital are secondary and can be obtained easily, as long as there is knowledge (Drucker 1993). However, knowledge can get obsolete very quickly. Therefore, what is important is not only "knowledge" in itself, but also the "learning" capability of an economy, that is, the ability to create, diffuse, and use new knowledge (Lundvall 2002).

In this era, NIS and its supporting institutions described above are obviously even more important than before. As stated by Lundvall, Intarakumnerd and Vang (2006), coping with globalization makes it necessary to understand the "historical" development of a country's innovation system, learning capability, and policy formulation processes. The development and competitiveness of a nation are path dependent. History does really matter in determining the present and the future.

THAILAND: A COUNTRY IN A MAJOR TRANSITION?

Thai economic development was drastically accelerated during the second half of the 1980s and all through the 1990s. The Asian Crisis led to a deep recession in 1997 and a few years following that. However, recovery was rather quick and the country seems to be progressing again. The success of Thailand in the past relied on two factors: foreign direct investments (FDIs) and low-cost competition. Thailand began its industrialization process with an import substitution strategy in the 1960s and 1970s. During this era, FDIs were rather limited and focused only on producing consumer goods to replace foreign imports. But in the 1980s, a major policy change to an export-led industrialization strategy was initiated. The Board of Investment (BOI), for instance, gave attractive fiscal incentives to foreign investors. The Thai government also created modern infrastructure such as "Industrial estates" first in the Bangkok Metropolitan Area. It then extended these facilities to more distant areas with the aim of wealth distribution. The result was a substantial increase in FDI in the second half of the 1980s and 1990s. Moreover, there was a positive change in terms of the development of agglomerations of firms in some provinces close to Bangkok such as Chonburi, Rayong, and Ayuthaya.

The underlying rationale behind the aforementioned FDI strategies is that it will automatically lead to the technological upgrading of local industries through the process of technology transfer from multinational corporations to local firms. Therefore, in the view of policymakers, this strategy should have led Thailand to successful industrialization and long-lasting competitiveness.

This is not really the case. Of course, foreign investors transferred technology to their subsidiaries. But this transfer often remained limited to production technologies. A number of subsidiaries progressively upgraded their production process technology and became able to assimilate and improve on these technologies eventually. However, most of them did not gain the knowledge to design or innovate new processes or products. In terms of the spillover impact to local firms, the situation is even worse. The transfer of technology, both embodied and disembodied, was substantially constrained within the boundaries of the network of MNCs' subsidiaries. Also, the development of a pure, Thai supporting industry that the government was anticipating as a kind of by-product of attracting FDI did not work in Thailand as it worked in Singapore or in Malaysia for instance as far as electronics are concerned. In fact, even though there is no one single path or one best way to enhance capability building, it seems that if incentives are not put on the agenda of public policies, technology transfer remains limited to what corresponds to MNCs own strategies. Some, willing to go further, may successively transfer more up to date technologies, but even if there are some exceptions, few are transferring designing or research and development (R&D) capabilities (see, for instance, Hobday, Bessant, and Rush 2007).

The economic crisis in 1997 and the subsequent downturn of sectors that used to be exporting stars, such as textiles and garments, are the wake-up calls to policymakers that previous policies are no longer supportive in the new competitive paradigm. Labour costs, which underpin Thailand's comparative advantage, have increased substantially. Thailand is, therefore, losing its competitiveness in attracting FDI to labour-intensive industries. At the same time, unlike East Asian Newly Industrializing Economies (NIEs) such as Korea (Amsden 1989; Chang 1994; Kim 1997), Taiwan (Hou and Gee 1993), and Singapore (Wong 1996), it fails in upgrading its industries in the global value chain.

What appears equally important at present is the emergence of a "new" competitiveness paradigm. This "new" paradigm is needed because of two factors: first the expansion of globalization and the knowledge-based and learning economy, as mentioned earlier, and second the emergence of strong regional competitors. These factors were not so relevant in the 1980s and early 1990s, when Thailand was successfully catching up. Big countries having huge surplus labourers such as China and India, or even a smaller nation such as Vietnam, have now joined the global and regional competition and there is no way Thailand can compete against them using a low-labour-cost strategy. As a result, Thailand is at a crossroads, and can be considered an economy in transition. The level it has reached in terms of development is too high for it to pursue a strategy based on its former comparative cost advantage, but its capability achievements are still too low for it to become an advanced economy, unless it addresses its own weaknesses and develop new capabilities to seize new opportunities and overcome threats generated by the globalization process and the emergence of its new competitors.

OBJECTIVE, APPROACH, AND MAIN FINDINGS OF THE BOOK

The purpose of this book is to explore the strengths and weaknesses of Thailand's industrial development and to point out what the challenges are that policymakers have to address to make this sustainable for the next decade and beyond. This book will not enter directly into theoretical debates concerning all the issues mentioned above, but will shed useful light on related aspects. All chapters will touch on these issues in one way or another.

To meet such an objective, the book will take a twofold approach: thematic and by industry. The study aims to identify the relevant issues that might be responsible for the difficulties Thailand has in increasing its international competitiveness, just like other Asian countries have done before when they reached the development level Thailand is now experiencing.

The main findings are as follows: Thailand has internal problems in pursuing an effective industrial upgrading strategy. First, its national innovation system is weak and fragmented. Actors such as government agencies, private firms, universities, research organizations, and so on are not so efficient in performing their supposed roles. For example, Thai private firms were not active in upgrading their technological capabilities. Unlike their counterparts in Japan and East Asia, their capabilities in reverse engineering and industrial design, which are the basis for technological learning of successful latecomer firms, are limited. Most policymakers subscribed to the so-called "linear model of innovation". They paid more attention to enhancing R&D capabilities of public organizations, namely universities and public research institutes, and hoped that these organizations would automatically transfer the results of R&D to the private sector. Equally important, actors in the innovation system here are not working together like a system, which leads to the enhancement of a country's competitive advantage.

Second, education is a major problem. Education in Thailand was designed to produce people who could work efficiently in production processes. It focused mainly on building workers' ability to work according to instructions given by their superiors or blueprints. Therefore, it was suitable for the period when the country's industry was in the early catching up phase and most local firms were either imitators of foreign products, or original equipment manufacturers (OEMs) of multinational corporations. When a country is attempting to move up the value chain and its firms are changing from imitators to innovators, the education system must be able to produce persons with creativity and high learning ability. This is unfortunately not the case in Thailand. The study shows that Thailand is losing part of its competitiveness because of a mismatch between increases in real wages and increases in labour productivity. The increase in the latter is lower due to Thailand's underachievement in education, compared with its Asian neighbours. Furthermore, the quality and quantity of science and engineering graduates here are inadequate. This is a serious problem for a country that aspires to be a learning and knowledge-based economy.

Last but not least, explicit and effective upgrading policy formulation and implementation are very much needed. In the Thai case, this has not happened. More strategic policies that try to strengthen the micro (firm-level) and meso (industry and cluster level) foundations of competitiveness were initiated recently. But the implementation of these policies have largely been compromised and fallen by the wayside because of the lack of genuine political will and the vested interests of various political groups, including politicians who initiated those policies. The mindsets and understanding of policymakers in the middle and low levels can prohibit fruitful implementation of well crafted policies agreed at the higher levels. There are several examples along this line. For instance, the cluster concept initiated by topic policymakers was understood and implemented differently by middle and lower rank bureaucrats and others. As a result, the introduction of the concept in Thailand, despite the good intention behind it, did not lead to a real change in terms of policy for upgrading industry. Policymakers have also capability problems in adjusting their policy in accordance with the fast changing global situation. Frequent political disruptions and short-lived governments are also major obstacles to the continuation of serious policy implementation.

The set of policy measures in Thailand is also limited. Unlike Japan and East Asian NIEs, most policy measures here are fiscal incentives. There are very few financial incentives such as grants and loans and, if any, ineffective. This is because the level of trust in Thailand is very low. Financial incentives, especially grants, are considered by policymakers as means that could possibly lead to nepotism and cronyism.

CONTENT OF THE BOOK

The book is divided into three separate, but connected parts. It will start with a broad review of the country's FDI, national innovation system, and industrial and education upgrading in general. After this overview, it will closely examine "specific" policies and strategies for industrial upgrading: industrial restructuring, and industrial estate policies and implementation. Finally, three case studies of the country's leading industrial sectors (automotive, textile and garment, and hard disk drive) will be provided to demonstrate Thailand's competitiveness clearly, and the evolution and effectiveness of Thailand's industrial upgrading at the sector level. A summary of each part and chapter is as follows:

Part I will provide a general view of Thailand's competitiveness, especially in terms of its industrial upgrading. The main focus will be on the three general factors shaping the country's competitiveness: foreign direct investment, national innovation systems, and education upgrading.

This part will provide the background for the rest of the book, which will focus more on key supporting elements of Thailand's competitiveness, namely the roles of institutions, strategies of firms, and government policies.

Chapter 1. David Hoyrup and Jean-Christophe Simon take a longitudinal approach on Thailand's foreign direct investment (FDI). They analyse historically, the relationship between the development process and the diversification of activities induced by foreign direct investment over the past four decades of Thailand's industrialization. They put emphasis on the interaction between growth, the international opening-up of the economy, and public policies. Their analysis of the impact of FDI on industrial development and sector diversification will describe the general landscape and point out weaknesses that will be further addressed in other chapters. Their conclusion is that although FDI inflows to Thailand remain strong, the country is facing serious challenges regionally from China and other Asian neighbours, and domestically by the inability of the state to formulate better supporting policies.

Chapter 2. Patarapong Intarakumnerd examines Thailand's industrial development from the national innovation system (NIS) perspective. He analyses whether the Thai NIS has helped the country catch up technologically with more advanced economies, or make the country fall behind others. He carefully investigates the evolution of roles and capability building of key actors, namely, the government, private firms, universities, knowledge intermediaries, financial markets, and institutions such as trust, entrepreneurship and so on. Moreover, the interactions among these actors and the process of systemic learning have been critically assessed. He illustrates that Thailand's national innovation system is in transition from one with a long-standing character of weak, fragmented, and slow-learning, to one that will be stronger, coherent, with more active learning. This happened because of two reasons. First, there has been a significant change in the behaviour of a key actor, the government. This change has brought about positive changes in other actors. Second, external factors, namely, the economic crisis of 1997 had cross-cutting effects on all actors in the system. It also induced changes. Nonetheless, these positive changes are just the "light at the end of tunnel". It remains to be seen over a longer time period whether they can create genuine and sustainable positive outcomes.

Chapter 3. Bruno Jetin provides a very critical analysis of the symbiotic relationship between Thailand's industrial upgrading and its educational upgrading. Like others, he acknowledges that Thailand is in a very difficult and challenging position. Its more labour-abundant Asian neighbours can offer cheaper labour, and similar or even better tax incentives for attracting FDI. At the same time, developed countries are better equipped with much better knowledge, productive organization, and infrastructure. Education is one of the most important vehicles for getting the country out of this situation. However, its education system has both quantitative and qualitative problems due to several reasons such as social inequality, a shortage of skilled teachers, the lack of the promotion of creativity and critical thinking in teaching, especially in the scientific areas, and the absence of a long-term education policy and continuous and well executed education reform. As a result, the country fails to provide a supply of qualified scientists, engineers and other types of human resources for industrial upgrading and the strengthening of its national innovation system.

Part II focuses on the role of Thai institutions in the development process of industries. It aims to explain policies implemented to support industrial competitiveness, whether through the attraction of FDI, or the promotion of SMEs. Analysing the changes that have occurred in policies formulation, objectives, and strategic orientation, depending on the successive governments, and the related outcomes, this part shows how private interests or corporate strategies are increasing their domination; in other words, how the government is losing part of its autonomy.

Chapter 4. Akira Suehiro first analyses Thailand's industrial promotion policies before the Asian crisis. With this background in mind, he then concentrates on two major plans implemented after the crisis by the successive governments: the Industrial Restructuring Plan (IRP, 1997–2000) based on Japanese experience and assistance, which emphasizes the promotion of supporting industries and SMEs in priority industries, and the National Competitiveness Plan (NCP, 2001–06), relying on Porter's work which refers to American management textbooks and is based on the cluster approach. Comparing these two plans in relation to the national and international contexts that determined their orientation, he examines the process of policies formulation, their respective objectives and means, and the major players involved. While both plans aimed, albeit through different approaches, at promoting good cooperation between the government and the private sector, the lack of institutional framework and capacities to support the cooperation produced rather poor policy outcomes. The dual-track policy of the Thaksin government and clusters implementation did not prevent local firms from being driven into labour-intensive or natural resources-based industries, while foreign firms increased their domination. Noting that the latter develop their activities in accordance with region-wide corporate strategies rather than with government industrial policies, A. Suehiro concludes that Thailand is losing its autonomy in policymaking and depends crucially on the corporate strategy of foreign firms. The country now has to improve its national competitiveness urgently at the microeconomic level, but also needs sound economic management at the macroeconomic level.

Chapter 5. Natacha Aveline examines the industrial estates policy of the Thai government which appears to be rather specific compared with those of other Asian countries. The Industrial Estate Authority of Thailand (IEAT), created in 1972 to regulate industrial development in close relation to environment protection, established industrial estates (IE) provided with modern infrastructure and a large range of services suited to foreign manufacturers' needs. This was attractive, but always led more to their concentration around Bangkok. The creation of IEs in more distant provinces was on the agenda, but the Asian crisis stopped the implementation of this. The Eastern Seaboard Development Plan gave a new impetus and led private entrepreneurs into getting interested and engaging in huge urban projects associated with IE creation. Considering that changes of policy with the Thaksin government which based its growth strategy on clusters did not led to the emergence of new forms of industrial agglomerations in IE, Natacha Aveline discusses the reasons Thailand could not achieve a rather balanced regional development like Korea did. Introducing the concept of Regional Innovation System, the chapter points out several elements such as, the cluster policy which Thailand relies more on an industry-wide approach than a geographical one; the lack of industry-specific policies until recently; or the weak urban framework, to explain comparatively why although IE still have a role to play, Thailand has difficulties relying on them to create true poles of innovation at the regional level.

Part III addresses transversally most of the issues already tackled in the two previous parts and chapters, taking an industry approach. Three relevant industries: automotive, textile and garment, hard disk drive (HDD), are studied in-depth. By emphasizing past developments and the present characteristics of each industry, taking into account a region-wide dimension, the chapters aim at illustrating concretely what is now at stake for Thailand to ensure its future competitiveness, whether through firms' strategies or government policies. These illustrations finally confirm at an empirical level the main findings of former parts.

Chapter 6. Shinya Orihashi focuses on the automotive industry, comparing both the strategies of car manufacturers before and after the Asian Crisis, and the Japanese and American ones. Through the analysis of the evolution that has occurred, namely the shift from a local market dedicated production to an export-oriented one, he shows how Thai subsidiaries were forced to implement structural reforms to enhance their international competitiveness. This gave them the opportunity to change their positions within their parent companies' global strategy. The Asian Crisis finally served as an impetus for them to invest in human resources development, and to increase production and quality capabilities. Thanks to these changes, the industry grew rapidly, leading to some difficulties that appeared recently such as the shortage of supporting industries with local first-tier suppliers falling down to second-tier, the lack of an engineering workforce reactivating the staff mobility etc. The export oriented strategy, for its part, is threatened by the higher appreciation of the baht, and also by the emerging excess production capacity in China and the commencement of the China-ASEAN Free Trade Agreement which strengthens competition. But this might be also seen as a new chance for the Thai automotive industry to improve its capabilities further.

Chapter 7. Audrey Baron-Gutty investigates the textile industry's long history from its traditional rural forms of development to its urban concentration in specialized districts to exports. She emphasizes the role played in each period by different actors, depending on industrial policies changes and foreign multinationals' investments, which have made the Thai textiles and garments industry a heavyweight in the national economy, and exports sector. Focusing on the present situation which is characterized by a loss in competitiveness, she points out the relevant issues at stake: rising labour costs, the higher baht, utility costs increases in the Bangkok area where the industry is concentrated, a non-supportive financial system, a lack of industrial strategy, etc. Thailand is now unable to compete in world markets through costs, and the industry absolutely needs to move up the value chain and engage in more innovative, technical, and quality productions. After describing some measures taken at the policy level, such as the Chaiyaphum cluster programme, she concludes by stressing the importance of long-term policies to promote research and enhance workers' capabilities in other words, defining a strategy articulating efficient and quality education and labour.

Chapter 8. Yveline Lecler takes a historical and region-wide approach to explain how Thailand recently became world number one in HDD production and exports. But to maintain such a position in the vertically integrated intraregional network that American and Japanese multinationals progressively built, at the very time when its comparative advantages are eroding, the country has to address new challenges: technology upgrading, supporting industry development, technician and engineers training. To succeed in having the whole value chain of HDD, including the most sophisticated components which are not yet produced, located in Thailand, the country is now turning to the building of more competitiveness-based advantages. The government has implemented new policies — for the first time sector specific, and correlating qualitative criteria — that are better for addressing the needs of both champion industries such as HDD, and foreign manufacturers involved. The HDD cluster programme recently launched is highly appreciated by firms, even though some doubts remain concerning the execution of actions decided, which are often too slow to be undertaken. Its detailed study shows that, although recent measures are going in the right direction, success will strongly depend on the ability of the country to catch up with its rivals by upgrading its education system, and linking industry and research institutions to innovate, without forgetting to upgrade the capabilities of Thai SMEs.

LIMITATIONS OF THE BOOK

It is our intention to cover all the important factors contributing to Thailand's competitiveness, but the book has limitations nonetheless. Firstly all chapters (with some exceptions) basically examine Thailand from 1960s onwards. There might be some phenomena which had happened before, which somehow affected the country's process of building up its competitiveness later, for example, the golden era of state enterprises in the late 1940s and 1950s. Secondly, some institutional factors have been neglected, for example, land reform (one of the major factors contributing to later success in the industrialization of Asian NIEs), the evolution of power relations among key actors (the royalty, bureaucrats, business people, the middle class, and the poor), and some laws and regulations (competition laws, laws and regulations on metrology and standard, environmental protection, and so on) and logistic problems. Lastly the book, to a considerable extent, pays attention to the competitiveness of the manufacturing sector, although agriculture (including the agro industry) and services (tourism, health, restaurants, and so on) are the competitive strength of Thailand. We certainly acknowledge these limitations. Nonetheless, most of them have been largely studied and published elsewhere and they are beyond the scope of the book, which focuses primarily on policy challenges for Thailand's competitiveness in light of the historical developments of East Asian NIEs, as well as present and future fiercer competition from other countries catching-up, especially in the manufacturing sector.

References

Amsden, A. *Asia's Next Giant: South Korea and Late Industrialisation*. New York: Oxford University Press, 1989.

Beccatini, G. "The Marshallian District as a Socio-Economic Notion". In *Industrial Districts as Inter-Firms Co-operation in Italy*, edited by F. Pyke, G. Beccatini, and W. Senbengerber, pp. 37–51. Geneva: ILO, 1990.

Becattini, G. "Le district industriel: milieu créatif". *Espaces et sociétés*, no. 66–67 (1992): 147–63.

Chang, H. *The Political Economic of Industrial Policy*. London: Macmillan, 1994.

Drucker, P. *Post Capitalist Society*. New York: Harper Collins, 1993.

Freeman, C. *National Systems of Innovation: The Case of Japan Technology Policy and Economics Performance: Lessons from Japan*. London: Pinter Publishers, 1987.

Hodgson, G. "The Approach of Institutional Economics". *Journal of Economic Literature* 36 (1998): 166–92.

———. "What Are Institutions". *Journal of Economic Issues*, XL (2006): 1–26.

Hou, C. and S. Gee. "National Systems Supporting Technical Advance in Industry: The Case of Taiwan". In *National Innovation System*, edited by R. Nelson, Oxford: Oxford University Press, 1993.

Johnson, B. "Institutional Learning". In *National Innovation Systems: Towards a Theory of Innovation and Interactive Learning,* edited by B.-Å. Lundvall. London: Pinter Publishers, 1992.

Kim, L. *Imitation to Innovation: The Dynamics of Korea's Technological Learning*. MA: Harvard Business School Press, 1997.

Lundvall, B.-Å. "Innovation as an Interactive Process: From User-Producer

Interaction to the National Systems of Innovation". In *Technical Change and Economic Theory*, edited by G. Dosi et al. London: Pinter Publishers, 1988.

————. *National Systems of Innovation: Towards a Theory of Innovation and Interactive Learning*. London: Pinter, 1992.

Lundvall, B., P. Intarakumnerd, J. Vang, eds. *Asian Innovation Systems in Transition*. Cheltenham, U.K., and Northampton, U.S.: Edward Elgar, 2006.

Nelson, R. "Institutions Supporting Technical Change in the United States". In *Technical Change and Economic Theory*, edited by G. Dosi et al. London: Pinter Publisher, 1988.

Niosi, J. et al. "National Systems of Innovation: In Search of a Workable Concept". *Technology in Society* 15 (1993): 207–27.

Piore, M. J., C. F. Sabel. *The Second Industrial Divide: Possibilities for Prosperity*. New York: Basic Books, 1984.

Porter, M. E. "Cluster and the New Economics of Competition". *Harvard Business Review* 76, no. 6 (November–December 1998): 77–90.

Rush, H., J. Bessant, and M. Hobday. "Assessing the Technological Capabilities of Firms: Developing a Policy Tool". *R&D Management* 37, no. 3 (June 2007): 221–36.

Veblen, T. *The Theory of the Leisure Class: An Economic Study of Institutions*. New York: Macmillian, 1899.

Wong, P. *National Systems of Innovation: The Case of Singapore*. Korea: Science and Technology Policy Institute, 1996.

Part I
Thailand's Industrial Development: General Views

1

FDI IN THAILAND
The High Road to Industrial
Diversification Revisited

David Hoyrup and Jean-Christophe Simon

INTRODUCTION

This chapter will consider the relationship between the development
process and the diversification of activities induced by foreign direct
investment (or FDI) over the past five decades of industrialization. Our
analysis will emphasize the interaction between growth, the international
opening up of the economy, and public promotion policies. It will consider
the regional context for FDI attractiveness in the ASEAN area, the impact
of FDI on industrial development, and sector diversification through
empirical data and policy analysis. Three phases will be defined, based on
industrialization dynamics and growth patterns: First the founding decades
(1959–85), then the period of FDI take-off-cum-export-led growth (1986–
96), and finally, the crisis years and the post-crisis period since 1997. The
conclusion, considering the situation in the present decade, addresses the
issue of the "uncertainty of FDI": Inflows remain strong amid a challenging
regional and domestic environment but China's position in the regional

arena both as a large market for inputs produced by neighbours, and as a recipient of FDI more than a significant investor — is ambivalent. Meanwhile competition from neighbouring ASEAN member countries is on the increase, and public policies look both erratic and lacking in consistency. Thailand's competitive advantage is indeed at stake and the reconstruction of this is a major challenge.

GROWTH AND INDUSTRIALIZATION

Thailand's growth pattern over the past decades is well analysed in economic literature, with major contributions from political economists (Hewison, Pongpaichit), mainstream economists (Warr, Krongkaew), and others (Simon, Suehiro). Thailand's case was also considered relevant in the controversial World Bank report on Asian Miracle economies (World Bank 1993). Thailand's industrialization is indeed a very good example of long-term growth-cum-development, a stage-based process sustained through time, with a strong transition of economic structures. Figure 1.1 offers an overview of this industrialization process — with three phases identified through three decades of development: 1970–85 when industry equals, then overtakes, agriculture in GDP; 1986–96, the golden decade in terms of growth and FDI inflows; and 1998–2005 with the aftermath of the Asian crisis.

The country can indeed be cited as a particularly telling case of a rapidly industrializing emerging economy on several counts:

- Accumulation through exploitation of natural resources, and diversification in primary processing. Over the past half century it exemplifies the growth pattern of those few developing economies that have actually benefited from mineral and agricultural exports to world markets.
- The country benefited from sustained and steady growth, avoiding the drastic effects of major systemic crises that struck most other developing countries (oil crises, structural adjustments). Opening up and export-led growth boosted overall development through two decades from the mid-seventies.
- Rapid industrialization was firmly grounded in both primary processing and labour-intensive assembly activities, which allowed for a progressive and highly diversified export mix.

Figure 1.1
Thailand's Overall Economic Performance since 1970

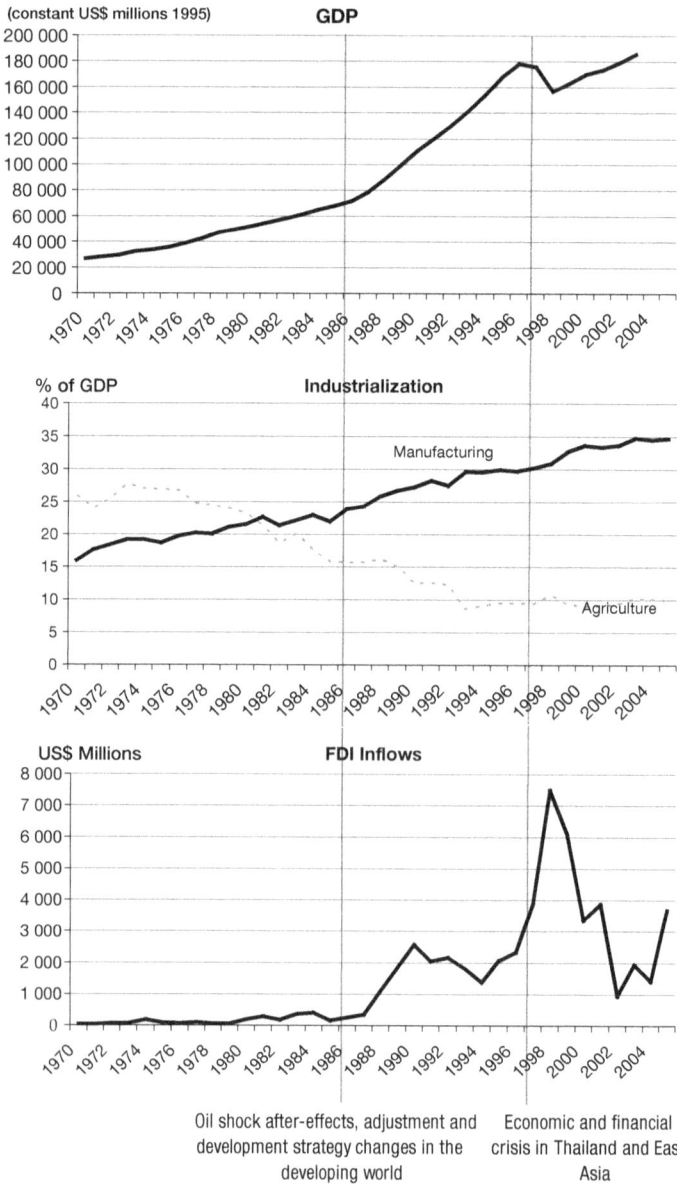

(constant US$ millions 1995)   **GDP**

% of GDP   **Industrialization**

Manufacturing

Agriculture

US$ Millions   **FDI Inflows**

Oil shock after-effects, adjustment and   Economic and financial
development strategy changes in the   crisis in Thailand and East
developing world   Asia

Sources: World Bank, Asian Development Bank and UNCTAD.

- State intervention can be labelled low-key over most of the past five decades. Although some governments favoured strong intervention in development, the Thai developmental state was much less proactive than that in Korea or Malaysia.
- Thailand established a central position in continental Southeast Asia in the late 1980s, thanks to peace and relaxed regional diplomacy. A regional productive system gradually emerged, backed by trade with neighbours and increasing industrial complementation supported by FDI.

FOREIGN DIRECT INVESTMENTS' CONTRIBUTION TO GROWTH

Economic analysis has focused increasingly on FDIs as a special component of economic growth. An abundance of literature still discusses factors and causality of FDI flows in relation to a country's opening up and development. In the context of an emerging economy, beyond the direct effects on capital formation and employment, FDI is assumed to generate new trade channels and bring in technologies, knowledge, and managerial experience.

- In Thailand, the contribution of FDI to overall growth can be labelled moderate (see Table 1.1). FDI was negligible in the first decades of development, and FDI promotion lagged behind that in other large ASEAN economies, particularly in the 1960s and 1970s when it represented a low proportion of capital formation investment.
- The unexpected FDI boom in the late 1980s was the result of external shock — although public policy created a favourable climate, with Thailand rapidly enhancing its promotion efforts.
- Foreign firms were welcome for specific activities, which originally took the form of setting up local trading and sourcing firms, as well as activities geared towards the domestic market — particularly by American and Japanese firms.
- Multinationals deciding to invest in Thailand had two motivations: accessing local markets (circumventing strong protection, as in the case of textiles, chemicals, or cars) and tapping resources and infrastructure provisions to establish a strong export base (petrochemicals, garments, or electronic components).

Table 1.1
FDI's Role in East Asian Growth

Cumulative FDI stock/GDP	1980	1985	1990	1995	2000	2005
China	3	3.4	7.0	19	18	14
Indonesia	13	28	34	25	16	8
Korea	2	2.3	2.1	1.9	7	8
Malaysia	20	23	23	32	58	36
Philippines	4	8.5	7.4	8	17	14
Singapore	52	73	83	78	121	158
Taiwan	6	4.7	6.1	6	6	12
Thailand	3	5.1	9.6	10.4	24	33

Source: UNCTAD World Investment Report 2005.

- FDI was instrumental in the economy's diversification thanks to local legislation favouring joint ventures, and local entrepreneurship capabilities which made the most of foreign companies' willingness to establish themselves in the country.

1. FDI IN THAILAND'S DEVELOPMENT PROCESS: FROM A LOOSELY EXPLOITED RESOURCE TO STRONG ASSET FOR INDUSTRIALIZATION OVER THE PERIOD 1955–85

Thailand established itself as a steadily developing country in continental Southeast Asia over three development decades, starting in the 1950s. First it had to strengthen its foundation through the modernization of its public administration and expansion of its infrastructure to cope with the growing needs of a large and growing rural population. It capitalized on active trading based on the exploitation of natural resources — whether mineral, forest, or agro-based; generating export; foreign currencies; and fiscal resources. Then, in the 1970s, new opportunities arising from world economic trends were snapped up: world demand and prices for commodities rose as the internal market expanded slowly. The industrial transition gained impetus with increasing contributions from export-oriented manufacturing activities to both the national value added and trade balance.

1.1 FDI as Both a Negligible and Overlooked Growth Factor: 1959–70

This decade was a time of state-led development, with countries needing to establish the base and infrastructure for economic take-off. Thailand benefited from easy financing from international and bilateral cooperation. The private sector steadily and discreetly asserted its role in the economy, through trading, financing (including an increasingly active Chinese diaspora network) and domestic market-oriented industries. In this context though, FDI did not receive much consideration for political reasons, and was minimal in value terms.

Growth and Development — First Stage

Regular growth was sustained with GDP growth in the 6–8 per cent per annum range throughout the 1960s, which is comparable to that in many other developing countries at that time, and was a rate needed to match rapid population growth. During the late 1940s and 1950s, agriculture asserted itself as the top contributor to overall growth. This is reflected in its share of about 30–35 per cent of GDP, and about 70–80 per cent of export value.

Agricultural performances were crucial for the well-being of the rural population and the rest of the economy in terms of trading, export, and fiscal revenue. The rice-producing sector was still of paramount importance, but a steady diversification took place with cassava, sugar cane, kenaf, and corn production mobilizing more land, attracting investment, and generating good export opportunities through active networks of planters, millers, middlemen, and traders.

Industry and trading activities interacted closely with agriculture — supplying of inputs, and providing downstream processing and trading activities. Local industries focused on semi-processing, and many manufactured goods were imported. New infrastructures (transport and irrigation) were planned and designed, but suffered from slow implementation due to the lack of capital and management capacity of the state.

Public Policy and Government Economic Intervention

Thailand's public policy framework benefited from a well established and heavily centralized state administration since the nineteenth century. This required upgrading after the Second World War though, as the preceding decades saw major shake-ups in Siamese institutions: the transition to constitutional monarchy, the nationalist regime of Field Marshal Pibulsongkram, and the Japanese Occupation. After the war, following a period of disappointing growth, the Thai government rolled out its first economic development plan, advised by the International Bank for Reconstruction and Development (IBRD)/World Bank, and implemented some basic measures and principles to modernize Thailand's economy in the 1960s. It was to repel the principle of the state as main producer/ entrepreneur, and encourage sector diversification.

The new framework for public intervention followed three main lines: stricter budget management, trade taxation (particularly on rice exports), plus tapping of foreign resources (particularly aid from the United States), and public service/infrastructure provision. In the area of basic industries development, this was the time for an import substitution policy, like in other developing economies. It aimed at maximizing domestic value added, supply, and linkage. In Thailand it was not very effective, although the local market gained in size and impetus. In addition, government-owned companies remained poorly managed and they did not play a strategic role in fostering new activities or back up new ventures initiated by increasingly active Sino-Thai entrepreneurs.

Industrial Development, Public Policy and Investment Promotion

Industrial expansion took place mostly through projects initiated by members of the Sino-Thai business sector. They were eager to seize emerging opportunities in manufacturing and international trading, thanks to abundant financial resources derived from local trade and investments from the Chinese diaspora/groups in Hong Kong, Taiwan, and Southeast Asia. They established flourishing ventures thriving on the steadily expanding local market for domestic goods, construction materials, and light equipment. A key to their success was their alliance with bureaucrats, particularly those in high civil service and military elite, who were invited to join company boards. Another positive element was business links with foreign partners, which gave them access to both brand, through licensing, and equipment/technology transfer (see Box 1.1 for more details).

The institutional context changed considerably too. Although the first legislation to promote industrial investment was promulgated in 1954, it came to full bloom in the following decade which marked a new era with

---

Box 1.1
Kingdom of Siam as an Hospitable Economy

The kingdom of Siam had a long-standing tradition of allowing in foreigners on its soil. Over the XIXth and XXth centuries many foreign migrants who came in as labourers from southern China and India turned first into traders or shopkeepers (which local subjects of the monarchy were not allowed to be). They were keen to settle in major provincial towns, and they established strong networks between the capital city and remote rural areas. They also managed export-oriented businesses such as rice or sugar mills or trading companies to direct primary products from Siam to foreign markets. Many established new family roots in the kingdom, and some ended up as the cornerstone of the business establishment — this being evidence of their successful integration into civil society. This partly accounts for the fact that Thailand as a developing country did not suffer from a dearth of local entrepreneurs.

Since the trade opening forced upon Siam by Great Britain, a couple of Western businessmen became active too in the kingdom: these long term residents held positions in finance, trade, and industry. They were mostly British and Americans, but some eminent entrepreneurs from Germany or Denmark left their marks too. Westerners, however, played a very modest role compared with the offspring of the Chinese diaspora. On a separate note, expatriates from Japan became active in the 1920s [sic] and then again in the 1970s–80s, developing a very tightly knit business community with activities ranging from banking to trading and manufacturing.

(For a more detailed analysis see I. Brown, *The Elite and the Economy in Siam* [Oxford University Press, 1991; K. Hewison, *Industry before Industrialization in Thailand*, 1992).

---

a benevolent state that was less suspicious of private business and profits. In the 1950s, state intervention was a deterrent to private investment (fear of nationalization, competition from state enterprises). Economic analysis, particularly studies for the first Plan (1961–66) showed a drastic need for increasing private investment. Thailand created an investment promotion scheme as early as 1959 in order to attract and facilitate foreign investment in local projects. In 1960 an Industrial Promotion Act was introduced that was later revised in 1962. The Board of Investment (BOI), as a government agency under the Office of the Prime Minister, was put in charge of promoting private business to serve overall growth.

Regulations were designed to promote target sectors for industrial policy, and deter foreign intervention in activities for which this was considered inappropriate. The investment promotion scheme presented no bias in favour of foreign investment, although several activities, including agricultural plantations, were not open to foreign investment in order to protect national assets. In addition, joint ventures were mandatory for all projects that were not mainly export-oriented. The promotional package included a series of legal protections (against nationalization or competition from public enterprises) and a set of tax exemptions (concerning both input imported for production and profit tax holiday).

The first period of industrial promotion was described by some economists as "Wisely designed/Poorly supervised policy" as the BOI did not have the capacity to select, prioritize, or supervise projects efficiently (Siamwalla 1975[1]). This resulted in lack of targeting, lack of integration, and weak linkages. In that context, FDI remained a badly identified and poorly tapped resource. It did not seem relevant for a country faced with several challenges such as a large traditional agricultural sector, a limited local market, or regional trading opportunities.

1.2 1970–85: Take-off Stage for an Aspiring NIC (Newly Industralized Country)

The strengthening of Thailand's development process through sustained growth and diversification of the economy coincided with increased internationalization of the world economy. The country succeeded in consolidating major institutional mechanisms and transforming the economy. Progress was made in the 1970s despite a shaky regional environment (last leg of the war in Indochina), an unstable domestic political situation, and poor interaction between the public and private actors. At that time Thailand, although valued by Japanese investors, was not seen as a particularly good target for FDI and MNC strategies, compared with Asian free market places such as Hong Kong, Singapore, or the increasingly recognized Malaysian manufacturing base located in Penang.

A New Economic Era: 1973–85

A new world economic context offered more opportunities for Thailand and this was reflected in its regular growth and an increasing trade opening ratio (Table 1.2). Increasing energy cost caused by the first oil shock was offset by a short-lived raw material boom.

Table 1.2
Change in Thailand's Economic Structure Since 1970s

%	1970–79	1980–89	1990–99	2000–2005
Manufacturing / GDP	18	22	24	23
Trade opening	33	55	80	105
Manufacture / exports	15	38	75	83
FDI stock / GDP	2	5	10	22

Source: World Bank-NESDB.

The domestic macroeconomic situation shows agriculture on a par with industry (around 18–22 per cent of GDP) but was then overtaken by manufacturing activities in the early 1980s. The concept of a Newly Industrialized Country was then discussed for Thailand — with suggestions that the country should be labelled "NAIC" (with "AI" referring to "agro-industrial" to account for the strong contribution of these activities).

Public Policy Adjustments

Public policy was subjected to government instability and frequent changes: the domestic scene was shaky, marked by political and social struggles. Macroeconomic management and development management had to face major challenges: on the external front, there was a raw materials boom, followed quickly by a bust, with increasing energy costs; and on the domestic front, the agricultural sector lagged as the country transited to a newly industrialized economy, with the result that the rural population under strong demographic pressure.

The country's development strategy focused on answering the needs of a rapidly growing rural population. The national strategy favoured the supply of infrastructure to improve the people's well-being and facilitate economic transformation — transport with improved road networks, communication, irrigation, and electricity.

The implementation of these programmes absorbed a substantial proportion of the country's funds and energy, which led to structural adjustment constraints in the early 1980s. The structural adjustment programme had serious consequences on public policy, particularly, the industrialization strategy, over the period 1979–85, although it went smoothly compared with most other developing economies:

- Macroeconomic management focused on adjustment: the government budget and public borrowing were tightened, depressing public spending. A double devaluation took place, which briefly shook the economic climate, which was later restored, thanks to expanding export opportunities.
- The aborted big push delayed or cancelled major public investment in strategic projects and industries. This structural adjustment related measure prevented Thailand from following Malaysia and Indonesia in terms of expansion of big projects and national industries (from fertilizers to automobiles or aeronautics). It created private investment opportunities and paved the way for innovative schemes (such as the build-operate-transfer projects) that were fully tested later.

FDI as a Growing and Dynamic Asset

In the early 1970s Thailand embarked on the first phase of export promotion, through the adoption of a more liberal policy towards foreign business. FDI volumes remained limited, but gave a decisive impetus to export-oriented manufacturing, which consisted mainly of primary agricultural processing and garments. The country's industrial policy remained poorly focused, and was subject to various business interests in targeting priority industries (Simon 1996, Tambunlerchai 1993[2]). In the late 1970s the idea of designing new public-sponsored and owned infrastructure for industries was floated, but did not materialize. The aim was to imitate neighbouring countries, such as Indonesia and Malaysia, where such grand schemes benefited from oil revenues to foster growth and enhance attractiveness. The example of the Industrial Estate Authority, created in 1972 (see Chapter 5), shows that beyond promulgating new regulations, the Thai administration lacked experience, efficient regulations, and was thus slow to act: public-led industrial zones took a full decade to take root and contribute to manufacturing development. Two features marked that decade:

- The increased role of joint ventures resulting from strategies of firms, particularly transnational corporations (TNCs) to tap domestic and exports markets. This was largely based on the holy alliance of Sino-Thai capitalists and foreign investors. Local business elites were not short of capital, but needed access to markets and technology.

- The decisive role of Japanese firms was more conspicuous, as global investment from Japan overtook FDI from the United States in the period 1969–80 (an average of 520 million baht annually versus 490 million baht for the United States).

The Thai government promulgated amendments on investment promotion rules in 1977 to strengthen the BOI's promotional package. The BOI revised a list of priority activities in which companies, either local or foreign, would receive special privileges; the tools used to stimulate investment included exemptions on import duties, income tax holidays, and some exemption on foreign equity restrictions. More projects with export emphasis were approved.

Seed for a New Boom Era?

In the early 1980s, although growth was sustained and adjustment relatively smooth compared with many other developing countries, Thailand faced a confidence crisis and viewed its future as uncertain: It was exposed to the oil shock and world rice prices still kept a strong bearing on the domestic mood. Furthermore, it had missed the big industrial investment wave experienced by neighbouring Malaysia (which proved to be a blessing later), while political life was still marred by government instability and military coups. The other side of the coin was a country with solid institutions, led by a respected monarch (a far cry from the situation prevailing in the Philippines), an educated population, and a pacified countryside, as the economy diversified and opened up to the world. Indeed the country was ready to make the most of an unexpected new economic situation and advertise itself as an "open society and dynamic economy", the motto coined to advertise in roadshows in foreign countries in the late 1980s.

2. FDI BOOM IN THE LATE 1980s: WINDFALL, TIMING, AND EXPLOITATION

Economic performances recorded by the Thai economy during this decade (1986–96) led some observers to speak about an "economic miracle". At that time, the idea of "miracle" was justified, because of the rapid "double-digit" growth and robust industrialization achieved. With the benefits of hindsight, however, one could speak rather of a "good combination" of sound macroeconomic policy, an exceptional international and regional environment, and adequately well timed FDI regulation changes. It can also be argued that performances recorded in this era resulted from the previous decade of strong investments and industrial development. In addition, it cannot be overlooked that weaknesses accumulated in the period 1986–96, particularly with regard to institutions and regulatory procedures, were certainly at the root of the severe crisis that hit the country in 1997.

2.1 A Positive International and Regional Context

Most emerging Asia economies, particularly the bigger countries of ASEAN (Indonesia, Malaysia, Thailand, the Philippines) faced adjustments, debt management challenges, and cyclical downturns in the early and mid-1980s; nevertheless, they avoided the downward spiral, hyperinflation, and being "lost decade for development" that mark most parts of Africa and Latin America at that time. Thailand for its part progressed relatively smoothly through government-managed adjustment, largely because it was not overexposed internationally or heavily indebted, and was open enough to make the most of the new international economic situation. Two related and connected elements shall be included here. First the emergence of the East Asian economic powerhouse, and secondly the globalization of the world economy.

Japan's and East-Asia's Rising Power, The Plaza Agreements, and the Endaka

The rising power of Japan led to huge imbalances in its trade relationships with Europe, and particularly the United States, in the early 1980s. A major international negotiation (the so-called "Plaza Agreement") between the United States, Europe, and Japan, led to the strong appreciation of the yen (also known as endaka) from 1985 onwards. Subsequently, Japanese companies faced increasing competition exporting from their domestic base. Many of those firms, especially the biggest companies in the automotive or electronic sectors, began to look for places abroad where they could produce more cheaply. This was a major turn in the repositioning of Asia Pacific in the world economy.[3]

The same can be said about the four Asian NIEs (the "dragons" — Hong Kong, Taiwan, Singapore, and South Korea). After two decades of rapid economic growth, wages were on the rise, weighing down the competitiveness of low value-added products. As they also recorded trade surpluses vis-à-vis the United States, the American government decided to withdraw the special access to the U.S. market they enjoyed. Their currencies appreciated, and their manufacturers faced similar difficulties to those of Japanese companies in trying to remain competitive in exports. They also looked for cheaper new production locations in order to produce low value-added products. Therefore, in the late 1980s many famous East Asian firms invested heavily in Thailand — many to establish an export base, and others to take hold of a rapidly emerging local market (see changes of sources of FDI in Annex 1.1).

The Quickening of Industrial Globalization and the Washington Consensus

The quickening of the globalization process (Figure 1.2), highly visible when we look at the FDI and international trade picture, began in the mid-1980s. Of course, the bulk of FDI was directed towards advanced countries. But during the 1980s and 1990s, some companies began to relocate their activities in low-cost countries in order to reduce costs. The trend of relocating low value-added activities was also made possible because of innovative products, based on new productive processes. The best example lies in the electronic industry, where products such as videotape recorders and television sets, which could easily have parts produced in different countries, and then assembled in others.

Firms involved in this process were not interested in sloppy Africa or crisis-prone Latin America. Therefore, FDI was looking for countries which could combine several advantages: trade openness, access to international commercial lanes, cheap labour, an educated and dedicated labour force, and hospitable regulations for FDI. This new regional and international division of productive processes had a strong impact on Southeast Asian emerging countries such as Thailand. In this context, successive Thai governments acted to meet these conditions. They proved very successful as both MNCs and medium-sized foreign firms from various countries decided to set up in Thailand. Besides Japanese and Northeast Asian companies, American and European companies

Figure 1.2
Globalization Take-off: World Trade and World FDI Stocks, 1960–2004 (US$ millions)

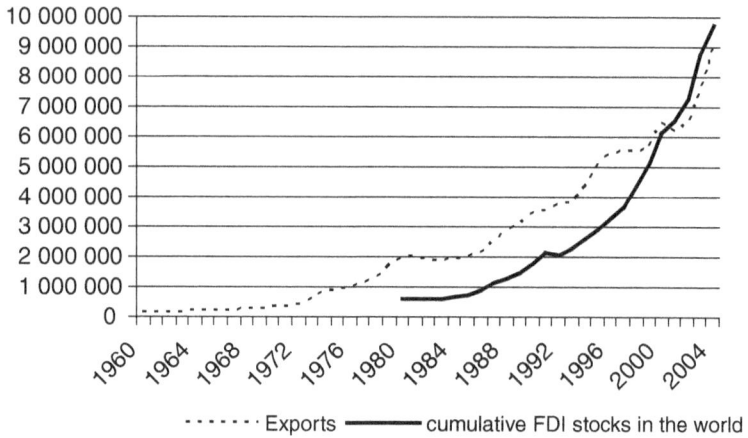

Source: UNCTAD.

established subsidiaries in the form of greenfield investments, frequently in joint ventures with local partners. Major world institutional actors for development, such as the World Bank and the IMF, backed up these moves with policy recommendation guidelines for liberalization, privatization, openness, and deregulation.

2.2 A Major Turn in Development Strategy: Export-led Growth and FDI Promotion

The mid-eighties witnessed a major change in Thailand's development pace and strategy, especially in the field of trade and investment regulation.[4] The change towards a new development strategy was rather smooth, not a *coup d'état* or sudden ideological shift. Reforms in the mid-eighties resulted more from a continuous process of adaptation to the changing regional and international setting. This "management of economic opening" can be compared to the "governing the markets" observed by Wade in Taiwan.[5] Moreover, unlike most developing countries which embarked on the liberal development strategy path, these reforms were not prescribed by the IMF or the World Bank as a condition for helping the government.

The New Path to Industrialization:
Privatization, Openness, Liberalization

Because of the growing fiscal deficit, the government decided first to proceed with fiscal changes. Besides revenue measures (reorganization in the administration and tax collection, introduction of new taxes, and a broadening of the tax base), most of these efforts were directed towards expenditures. The tools used comprised a conservative wage policy, reduction in capital expenditure, price increases, and investment reduction by public companies. As fiscal deficit was still a problem in 1984–85, the government proceeded to make major changes in the budgetary process, by underestimating revenues — correcting a tendency to overestimate them. Robinson et al. (1991)[6] characterized the fiscal policy of the 1980s as countercyclical. Results were encouraging, as the deficit of 5 per cent of GDP in 1984–85 was transformed into a surplus of 5 per cent in 1989–90. Besides those direct fiscal effects, reforms set the tone for the role of the public sector in the next decade.

A second area of reform was trade policy. The first step of the new trade policy was to reduce non-tariff barriers to trade (limiting goods subject to import restrictions). In this first step, the only measure affecting nominal tariffs was the setting of a ceiling of 60 per cent to tariff rates. Therefore, the overall tariff level remained unchanged, but its dispersion declined. Tariff barriers, previously affecting mainly exporters, were offset more and more in the late 1970s and 1980s by various export promotion measures: duty drawback schemes, export criteria used in determining the distribution of investment promotion, institutional support to exports. Export promotion became fully effective in the early 1990s with major tariff reforms. In October 1990, the government decided to reduce tariffs on capital goods used in manufacturing from 20 per cent to 5 per cent. The change was completed by a second tariff reform in 1991, which saw a reduction of tariffs on raw materials, some capital goods, and intermediate products.

Besides fiscal orthodoxy, the various Thai governments opted to peg the baht to the dollar or a currency basket dominated by the dollar. It also liberalized interest rates progressively, in order to enable commercial banks to adjust to a more flexible interest rate system. Foreign exchange transactions, as well as current account transactions were also liberalized between May 1990 and April 1991. These measures were especially welcomed by foreign companies, as it allowed the repatriation of investment funds without prior approval from the Bank of Thailand. The process of financial liberalization was coupled with the restructuring of commercial banks (widening of the scope of business, reduction of entry barriers), and the strengthening of prudential supervision (which proved to be insufficient a few years later!). In the mind of policymakers, these moves were destined to help the country become the main financial hub in Southeast Asia, ahead of Singapore and Malaysia. The Anand Panyarachun government introduced a major reform in this direction, with the launch of the Bangkok International Banking Facility in 1992. Under this scheme, local and foreign banks were allowed to put down deposits, borrow in foreign currencies from abroad, and lend money both in Thailand and abroad.

Change in FDI Regulation: Surfing on the New Investment Wave

In order to boost economic activity, more foreign businesses were allowed to enter the Thai market. As part of the global shift towards an export led growth strategy, FDI legislation was reformed in the middle of the eighties.[7] Foreign equity limits were relaxed in most sectors. The negative list was revised, and activities forbidden to FDI were restricted to media, defence, and weapons production.

In the early 1990s, the Board of Investment, remaining under the direct supervision of the Prime Minister's Office, strengthened its leading role as the promoter of both pro-FDI and regional development oriented policies, as part of the Seventh National Plan (1992–96).

On the one hand, promotion rules were amended (1993–95) to increase the scope of foreign investments, alongside other reforms to deregulate foreign investment in financial services and banking.

On the other hand, taking into account strong imbalances in regional development resulting from rapid industrialization (Parnwell 1996; Simon 1996), new investment policy guidelines integrated criteria based on regional areas. This was to widen decentralization for new projects or relocations beyond the Greater Bangkok and lower central region (Zone I: Bangkok and five provinces). It set a three-tier promotion package whereby projects were encouraged to locate in distant provinces, that is, Zone II (thirteen provinces), and Zone III (fifty-eight provinces). Under the new regulations, manufacturing ventures producing for the local market could be foreign owned if located in provinces distant from the Bangkok metropolis, and the same applied to those exporting more than 80 per cent of their production, independent of their location. The major exceptions to this scheme were industrial estates developed by, or in cooperation with, the Industrial Estate Authority of Thailand. The role and effectiveness of these zones in attracting foreign companies have been widely debated.[8] Nonetheless, political choices and measures of various governments at the end of the 1980s and the beginning of the 1990s were clearly pro-business and pro-growth. Coupled with the positive environment described in the previous section, this macroeconomic and regulatory environment transformed the country into a very strategic location for TNCs.

2.3 Economic Performances: The Miracle Decade and Its Limits

The "miracle decade" can easily be characterized by the usual indicators, related either to FDI or industrialization. Besides the sheer magnitude over a short period, the question of causality in the relationship between FDI and growth arises; this is a well-debated point in economic literature on export-led growth strategies. When we consider the subsequent crisis and competitiveness issues of the late 1990s in Thailand, it is worth addressing the issue here.

FDI Surge in Thailand

The surge in FDI inflows beginning in 1987–88 was really amazing compared with previous trends (Figure 1.3). From US$163 million in 1985, FDI inflows surged to US$2,575 million in 1990. FDI represented 7.5 per cent of Gross Fixed Capital Formation (GFCF) in the peak year 1990 and averaged over 3 per cent in the following years — before the 1997 crisis.

During that period, most FDI came from Japan, as Japanese corporations were intensively relocating low value-added manufacturing activities (see the case of automobile industry in Chapter 6). Japanese firms were followed by Korean, Hong Kong, Taiwanese, and Singaporean companies, and by American ones too. European TNCs came somewhat later, at a slower pace, partly because the business opportunities and environment of Southeast Asia were underestimated, and also because of the greater focus on the opening up of Eastern Europe.

Figure 1.3
FDI Inflows and Origin

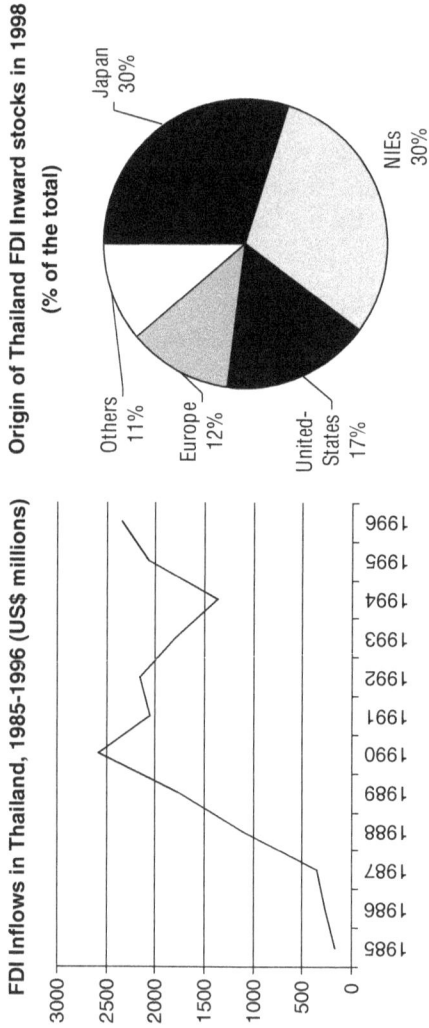

Origin of Thailand FDI Inward stocks in 1998
(% of the total)

FDI Inflows in Thailand, 1985-1996 (US$ millions)

Source: UNCTAD and Bank of Thailand.

Most of these investments were in manufacturing: 44 per cent of total inflow went to the manufacturing sector during the 1985–90 boom,[9] compared to only 30 per cent during the 1970s. Light and labour-intensive industries, such as food processing, clothing, toys, and light electrical apparatus were preferred by TNCs. Later, they invested in more complex industries, such as the electronic and electrical industries, even if the assembly activity of these new firms was still a low value-added part of the process.

The surge of FDI inflows shows that Thailand, already open to foreign trade and companies, became a very attractive place for TNCs in the mid-1980s. Thailand was then ranked top among developing economies for both its economic environment and flexibility of doing business by several studies on FDI localization.[10] While Thailand attracted only 0.7 and 1.1 per cent of total FDI inflows in the developing world and in Asia respectively in 1982, these weights improved to 7 per cent and 10.7 per cent in 1990 respectively. The figures for 1996 (2.5 and 1.6 per cent of the developing world and Asia respectively), the year before the crisis, showed that the relative share of Thailand in world and Asian FDI inflows declined quickly. This decline can probably be attributed in part to competition from other major emerging countries, especially in Asia, notably the rising China (India was not a serious competitor at that time). But this trend also reflects a deterioration of the domestic economic environment and Thailand's attractiveness. These limits will be reviewed later.

FDI Consequences on Industrialization: Diversification for a New Specialization

FDI inflows, by entering so quickly and so massively in an emerging country, contributed to major changes in its economic structure, as can be seen through several indicators. The GDP growth rate rose steadily. The ten years following the 1983–85 reforms witnessed a mean annual growth rate of 9.7 per cent. This growth was combined with structural changes, with a shift from an agrarian economy towards an industrialized one. The manufacturing sector's share of the GDP rose from 21.9 to 28.2 per cent between 1985 and 1996. Manufacturing growth was fuelled by intermediaries (rubber, glass, minerals) and equipment goods (transport machinery, professional equipment, electrical, and non-electrical machinery). The textile and clothing sector remained very dynamic (see

Chapter 7), and the agro-industry, albeit less dynamic, was still quite strong in 1996. Thailand also entered into a high-investment era, as the share of investment (GFCF) in the GDP went from 28.2 per cent in 1985 to 42.8 per cent in 1991, and stayed above 40 per cent during the 1990s.

In terms of external relationships, exports climbed seven to eight times during the decade, from US$7.1 billion in 1985 to US$56.4 billion in 1996. The export ratio (exports over GDP) almost doubled, from 18.3 to 33.6. Thailand also diversified significantly its export structure with manufactures jumping from 30 per cent in 1984 to 70 per cent ten years later. The surge was driven by light industry (agro-industry with seafood, fruits, and textiles, plus leather and jewelry industries), and by assembly industries such as electric and electronic products (notably cathode ray tubes, VCR, TV monitors and household appliances), and automotive parts and components.

The consequences of FDI on the Thai economy and on industrialization now have to be reviewed and some further analysis can be applied for assessment. Firstly, what are the main conclusions of theoretical and empirical literature on the FDI-overall growth nexus, and do they apply to Thailand? Secondly, what do econometrical tests reveal about the causality between FDI and growth of the Thai economy?

Positive Consequences of FDI on Industrialization. Economic literature often stresses three kinds of benefits arising from attracting FDI and TNCs. At one level, FDI makes a similar potential contribution to development as any other form of capital flows by channelling resources into a developing country. It provides more capital than the country can muster by saving, even a high-investing country such as Thailand. Moreover, FDI is much more resilient to economic fluctuations than short-term capital flows (portfolio investments) and does not generate any debt, as loans would do. In Thailand, foreign companies contributed massively to the national financing of investments, and in a more reliable way than portfolio capital inflows.

Secondly, some argue that FDI, provided the economic environment is not biased towards import-substitution, can foster exports, which in turn benefits the exporting country. In the case of Thailand, like in neighbouring countries, electrical and electronic products, largely dominated by TNCs and relocated firms from East Asia, account for one-third of total exports. FDI has probably helped Thailand to boost exports and diversify its production. In addition, TNCs usually control extended commercial networks, which means that attracting TNCs helps the economy's integration into world markets.

Thirdly, TNCs, through FDI, bring various technological inputs into the host country, either in terms of engineering, managing, or marketing capability. Several studies though, question that contribution. One reason lies in the fact that technology transfers is far from automatic. On the one hand, TNCs are often reluctant to transfer their knowledge. They frequently transfer outdated or basic technologies. On the other hand, host developing countries face difficulties in adopting and retaining technology and knowledge. In Thailand, particularly, problems of education, qualification, and institutions too have hampered the absorption of foreign technology.[11] Moreover, the expansion and success of Special Economic Zones or closed industrial estates mean that TNCs locate mainly in these enclaves, developing few links with local firms (details of linkages will be elaborated on in the Chapters 6–8). Several case studies in Thailand show different linkage patterns: small and medium foreign firms are keen to access the local market (including export-oriented firms), but the biggest companies establish themselves in the country to produce for exports (as seen in the production of security helmets or sports goods). The former often have a local partner and are involved in joint ventures, whereas the latter are more isolated in special zones and tend to keep their original suppliers from abroad. There are a few brilliant exceptions, from Japanese or European firms, whose large companies sought local partners in order to maximize market penetration and establish a high standard of industrial operation.

The Causality Question. Regarding the second question, the literature on this has been more careful in recent years. FDI is often considered as an engine of growth.[12] Some studies have shown that the positive effects of FDI are not systematic.[13] Some authors argue for a different causality scheme: high economic growth attracts foreign companies and thus induces FDI. In any case, we are still at an "inconclusive stage" (Mainguy 2004[14]). In the case of Thailand, econometric tests offer several lessons. Firstly, Thomsen[15] is of the opinion that FDI played a positive role on exports and economic growth, but admits that exports would have risen even without the FDI surge, and that FDI did not contribute much to technological transfers. Secondly, Kohpaiboon shows that if FDI contributed to GDP growth, it was mainly because the FDI surge was coupled with export expansion. He, therefore, thinks that FDI liberalization and trade openness were both engines of growth. Finally, Tanna and Thopaibul[16] take a diametrically opposite view and argue that there is almost no support for a strong FDI-led growth hypothesis. Growth is better explained by domestic investment and exports. They consider FDI's somehow limited impact to be mainly due to low human capital stock which limits the country's technology absorbing capacity.

Dynamism, Openness, and Beyond?

Nonetheless it might be considered that to some extent surge in FDI inflows during the 1980s and 1990s had positive effects. It brought capital to help finance the development process, and fostered exports, which in turn, transformed Thailand into one of the most dynamic emerging countries. Even if growth and structural changes are not to be solely attributed to FDI and TNCs, the foreign component was clearly part of Thailand's economic success.

However, attractiveness was on the decline even before the 1997 crisis, especially because the Thai economy was not able to overcome bottlenecks, particularly in infrastructure or education, and did not succeed in integrating foreign firms efficiently into the local production fabric, and maximizing linkages between sectors. How the country managed to adjust from the crisis and remain attractive is, therefore, a topical question that bears on development strategy and perspective, as will be seen in the next section.

3. THE PAST DECADE: FROM CRISIS ADJUSTMENT TO CURRENT UNCERTAINTIES FOR FDI AND COMPETITIVE STRATEGIES IN THAILAND

The past decade offers a picture of contrasts: the first part epitomized by the Asian Economic Crisis of 1997–98 that originated in Thailand, and the recent years showing "new growth" in Asia, although with a distinctively ambiguous regional context. Indeed emerging Asian economies have been competing among themselves, while facing dual leadership or influence from East Asia powers-to-be: Japan on the economic front, and China in political or diplomatic terms.

It is also worth considering the context of the 1997 crisis for Thailand and the diverse and sometimes conflicting analyses on it, to stress the regional dimension, the role of subsequent national policies for restoring growth and competitive advantage, and also the new opportunities for FDI, and M&A (mergers and acquisitions) resulting from companies' adaptation of local regulations. Strikingly, FDI in Thailand, at least its volume, was not affected by the crisis as such. Growth resumed with the domestic market orientation of the Thaksin government policies in the years 2001–06. Foreign investors have increased their activity too, but Thailand's national attractiveness, seen in a regional context, is being questioned as some neighbouring countries such as Vietnam continue to sharpen their competitive edge.

3.1 From Crisis to Adjustment: Lessons from a Difficult Period for Thailand and Southeast Asia

Over the past decade the regional scene has gained relevance — not so much as the area of a crisis that was specific to Asian tigers among emerging economies, but rather as the framework of an increasingly complex economic system. The so-called "factory Asia" is indeed showing increasing potency, with growing interactions between sites of production located in about ten countries along a path of the world containing major shipping lines and cargo airlines (see Chapter 8 for illustration). This dynamism has strengthened in spite of the slow implementation of mechanisms and institutions such as trade agreements or legal protections to make it function more smoothly.

From a National to a Regional Crisis

A brief characterization of the 1997–98 crisis in Thailand, with reference to particularly abundant literature, suggests the following salient features:

- Thailand was in dire straits even before the early months of 1997: it experienced a slowing down of export growth in 1996, suffering among other things from sluggish Japanese markets and a downturn of electronic goods sales.
- Public policies, regulations implementation, and supervision capacities were weakened too; a brain drain from senior civil service

to a dynamic private sector affected several departments and agencies (from Bank of Thailand to the Ministry of Finance); immature reforms in the corporate and finance sectors resulted in shaky deals and company failures (such as Finance One in 1996), and there were also supervision problems and wrongdoings on the Security Exchange of Thailand.

- Over the first semester of 1997, the government's management of the crisis was appalling, with the government losing credibility progressively, leading to the July devaluation of the baht.
- The monetary turmoil contagion then struck all kinds of economies in the region — from insular financial centres such as Singapore to industrial giants such as Korea.

The severe crisis that followed the baht's drastic devaluation from July 1997 raised some doubts about the global development strategy, particularly, the role of foreign companies in the development process. It was argued that the rapid and huge liberalization process, of which FDI deregulation was only a part, was at the root of the crisis — the East Asian area became even more attractive to investors as other emerging countries in Latin America had experienced their own monetary crises earlier. The openness to foreign capital made a country such as Thailand very sensitive to investors' perceptions. After 1994, the increasing borrowings in U.S. dollar-denominated markets, competition from other emerging nations (especially China), and the changing trend in the dollar-yen exchange rates contributed to the perception that the positive performances would not be sustainable. Of course, with hindsight, this crisis arose as a result of rapidly increasing and poorly managed international exposure. The problems of Thailand were attributable more to hot money and overinvestment in unproductive activities (particularly real estate) than to openness towards FDI in manufacturing as such. Nevertheless all types of foreign investment were viewed with critical eyes at the time.

The crisis extension to other Asian economies — with drastically differing economic fundamentals (particularly for Malaysia or Korea) — followed a classical scenario of contagion and confidence gap, aggravated by short-term investors and speculators. At any rate the problem did not stem from unbalanced government budgets but from the piling up in private sector debt. These debts themselves resulted from a reluctance of family controlled firms to open the capital of companies to foreign shareholders —

which raises questions on the rationale of corporate governance in most emerging Asian economies and the scope for evolution. Finally, the debate among prominent economists focused on the appropriateness of IMF-led policies to contain the so-called "financial crisis" and supervise adjustments in the most affected Asian economies. It was generally agreed that poor diagnosis and badly formulated recipes from the World Bank and IMF (promoters of the so-called Washington consensus) were instrumental in shutting out credit supply to the private sector and placing excessive and inadequate constraints on government budgets.

Adjustment on the Eve of the New Century

National policies of East Asian countries for facing the crisis were diverse in relation to various macroeconomic situations, well beyond some simple "Washington Consensus" erroneous doctrine: they ranged from the isolated — though eventually effective — position of Malaysia tightening short-term capital flows, to the tragic acceptance of IMF-led package by Indonesia. Thailand, for its part, albeit the source of the storm, benefited from generous help (including substantial Asian countries' contribution) and gentle supervision — which led to slow financial company restructuring. Korea was much more proactive in that respect. Interestingly, both countries had to amend their commercial and investment promotion legislations in order to allow larger foreign ownership in the corporate sector.

Industrial restructuring and changes in regulations largely explain the FDI surge following the crisis in several Asian countries: in Thailand several major companies were on the verge of bankruptcy due to the drying up of the domestic market and they turned to foreign partners to open up their capital base or increase foreign equity share. This was the case in the automobile sector and the retail business. It was also a golden opportunity for major MNCs to set foot in sectors which had been restricted before.

A final element to be mentioned concerns regional interactions among Asian economies. Firstly, the "shared" monetary-financial crisis made countries aware of a common issue, namely, the peg to the U.S. dollar and the lack of regional information and a coordination mechanism. This resulted in an idea put forward by Japan of an "Asian monetary fund" — first discarded under IMF pressure and recently revived — but also to pragmatic steps such as the Chiang Mai initiative which took place in 2001 for Asian economies to organize a framework for future bilateral financial cooperation. Secondly the crisis years revealed the growing relevance of production and market connections among Southeast Asia, East Asia, and China, with this new regional dimension emerging with a bearing on both public policies and strategies of private firms.

3.2 Thailand's Strategies for Growth Renewal and FDI Policy in 2000

In the present decade Thailand has shown both resilience in growth, despite the severe recession of 1997–99, and some progress in overall development. It maintains a good standing among major ASEAN countries' manufacturers. Nevertheless it has been giving mixed signals in its international economic relations — from stronger bilateralism to some ambiguous attitudes towards FDI in the earlier years or first period of Prime Minister Thaksin Shinawatra's government, which were corrected later. Then the 2006 coup triggered additional political instability, with a deterioration of Thailand's image and standing in the international business community.

A New Macro Economic Management

Although the 2006 coup put an end to the experience of Thaksin Shinawatra's government, the policies adopted between 2001 and 2006, also labelled "Thaksinomics" (see Chapter 4), left their mark as they were mainly focused on expanding internal demand through publicly sponsored infrastructure projects and reviving private consumption with generous credit and public funds allocation. In addition, a new doctrine was put forward to instill ideas of corporate governance and entrepreneurship into various ways of social and administrative life, and this is possibly still influencing many attitudes and policies.

Part of the lasting effect can be attributed to the implementation of populist policies: they targeted promotion of small-scale production, particularly in poorly developed districts — the OTOP programme (One Tambon One Product), which aimed at fostering entrepreneurial spirit in local villages and communities. Public policies and substantial funding were geared towards improving education and medical care. "Thaksinomics" was also concerned with backing the Thai corporate system — not least, Shinawatra family's own assets. This was made possible, thanks to generous public spending on local strategic projects — particularly infrastructure, and soft negotiations for the financial restructuring of companies following the crisis. In the area of FDI and investment, promotion policies were ambiguous.

In another area worth considering, namely regional economic relations, "Thaksinomics" showed proactive endeavours on all sides, particularly in the Asia region: it is noticeable that Thaksin could court China as well as seek new relations with India, while looking for inspiration from Singapore too — particularly in the field of bilateral relations, concluding as it did bilateral agreements with Australia and New Zealand. Its negotiations with the United States are not finalized yet and are being put on hold because of the 2006 coup.

Unstable Framework for FDI Promotion

FDI inflow experienced a strong increase after 1998–99, largely because of the opportunities for acquisition of shares in ailing companies in both finance and industry. It kept a sustained pace after 2002 alongside overall growth of the world economy and sustained activity in East Asia (see Annex 1.2).

Following the Asian crisis, the framework for FDI in Thailand was made more favourable, as the BOI policy was revamped, notably in 2000 and 2002: some provisions concerning sector or zoning restriction were further relaxed while new opportunities were created for 100 per cent foreign ownership in companies that were non-export-oriented. All in all, the Thai package was said to be as generous as its neighbours and could be negotiated on a case-by-case basis (for a more comprehensive analysis, see Brimble 2002, Rochanonda 2006).

On the other hand, the FDI policy suffered from the first years of "Thaksinomics" — at the time there was some debate on the appropriateness of backing some new privatization schemes or participating in the expansion of public infrastructures. Apprehensions have been alleviated since, and more explicitly welcoming messages have frequently been expressed by both the public financial authorities and the investment promotion agency. Thus, Thailand has benefited again from substantial FDI, largely due to the generous supply of long-term capital on world markets translating into large inflows targeting industry and services over the past years.

FDI as a Tool to Address Emerging Issues

Thailand was still one of the major recipients of FDI in ASEAN in the period 2000–05 (third behind Singapore and Malaysia), with Vietnam close behind. In 2006, approved investment in Vietnam was higher than similar figures for Thailand. But major uncertainty comes from competition with China — a formidable challenge. Over the 1990s several analyses concluded that ASEAN countries did not suffer from China's appetite for FDI (see Wu 2003), as Southeast Asia enjoyed a global surge in world FDI flows, and this diagnosis is likely to be valid in the present decade too.

The current wave of investment confirms some trends of the late 1990s: Japanese firms are at the forefront of manufacturing FDI, largely because of their activities in the automobile sector, but also in light electronics and communication equipment. Other sectors such as construction material, metal, chemicals, and pharmaceutical industries have also benefited recently from strong FDI (see other chapters for manufacturing activities). A significant move gathered strength in the service sector with foreign distribution giants expanding their network. Beyond this, two areas will likely be of interest for future projects, particularly in joint ventures: the promotion of local brands and standards to make them reputable beyond Thailand's border, and industrial projects aimed at improving sustainability and preservation of natural resources.

These sectors' expansion do contribute to building a new national competitive advantage, but some challenging issues remain for further industrial development. Two areas in particular remain critical:

- Manpower training and improvement are still lagging behind. Vocational/technical education has not matured enough to back up industrial activities, and privatization has induced an inflation of degrees poorly supervised.
- Linkage between firms, whether vertical or horizontal, remains limited, but for a few exceptions in sectors such as auto parts, furniture, or agricultural equipment. Few clustering experiences seem to flourish to their full scale. In addition, interaction between firms and technical and scientific research is minimal.

Although these issues were already identified as priorities in the early 1990s, little progress has been achieved by public intervention until now. This is in spite of targeted efforts by several public agencies. For example, the BOI placed emphasis on the BUILD programme established in 1992 to create or strengthen linkages between manufacturing firms, and on STI or "Skill Technology Innovation" (see Chapters 2 and 8), implemented since 2003, to encourage projects that promote human resource and skills, or have a high technological content (equipment or software design or production). The Ministry of Science promoted funds for applied research involving the private sector, as a complement to the efforts of specialized agencies, such as National Science and Technology Development Agency, which also addresses innovation and the networking of firms (see Chapter 2).

CONCLUSION: FDI AND CONSTRUCTION OF A NEW COMPETITIVE ADVANTAGE

Finally, through the experience of Thailand, it is worth revisiting several fundamental questions regarding FDI in a long-term growth-cum-industrialization process, with the benefit of hindsight over several decades of growth.

Firstly is FDI conducive to the diversification of economic activities? The case of Thailand clearly suggests a positive answer. Not only did FDI contribute to the comprehensive tapping of fundamental resources — from agricultural processing to unskilled manpower mobilization — but it also accompanied the maturation of industrial sectors as shown in the chemical, automobile, and computer parts sectors, and even beyond into various services such as transport and tourism.

A second aspect is related to its national policy and setting — whereas the literature on this remains inconclusive on the correlation between FDI and opening of the economy, there is little doubt that Thailand benefited from its ASEAN location for both waves of Japanese investment and integration in the productive networks of automobile and electronics industries (see Chapter 4). It did so in two ways: first, positively, by upgrading its promotion efforts and publicizing coherent regulations. It also established its position in contrast with neighbouring countries whose attractiveness was dubious at times (such as the Philippines in the 1980s or Indonesia after the 1997 crisis) or whose policies were more restrictive (such as Malaysia). In addition, the country played its cards well to be among the leaders of an ASEAN regional productive system in the automobile and consumer electronics sector, capitalizing on its stability to foster the trust of flagship MNCs.

Third, what are the prospects for a new wave of FDI? As its past shows, new ventures in Thailand can tap some substantial national assets such as a stable demographic trend with a growing number of middle-class consumers, in a country that feels prosperous, and enjoys excellent livelihood conditions by the standards of emerging countries. These days, fears of the relocation of some labour intensive, low-skilled activities to other countries are rising as some large plants curtail their activities in the garment or sport shoes sector. This would justify strengthening the national competitive advantage of tourism and related services requiring a more complex mix of labour and specialized services (conventions, medical care, retirement).

Another potential area gaining relevance lies in the continental subregional market where projects are set to multiply over the next few years. Thailand's "central position" means it is actually facing both South China and Vietnam, and the increasing economic relevance of the Greater Mekong area will see its rapid transformation through a new wave of investment by the end of this decade. On a larger scale, the regionalization process will also affect future FDI: the time is probably ripe for large ASEAN countries to highlight their position relative to those of Asian giants such as China and India. In the past decade, the ASEAN group had difficulties standing out as a dynamic economic area, but recent actions (such as the ASEAN+3 initiative) and tighter production networks could validate a new, promising scenario.

To make the most of these opportunities will no doubt require more political maturity from the Thai state — and its citizens too. The environment for FDI has to show transparency and stability. In the years to come there is still room for public promotion policies but they will probably have to be more targeted, and take advantage of the existing production system, its potential linkages, and spillover effects. A new assertiveness, or even a new vision, is needed to overcome many lagging issues ranging from the management of natural resources to skill generation with the upgrading of local educational standards and the building of an authentic National Innovation System; this in turn would contribute to strengthening the framework for further investment, as the following chapters will discuss.

Annex 1.1
Thailand: Trends in FDI by Source

Share of total FDI (% 5-year average)	1980–85	1986–90	1991–95	1995–2005
Japan	17%	41%	15%	26%
Europe	14%	8%	11%	12%
United States	18%	12%	11%	10%
ASEAN	5%	10%	9%	16%
Other Asia	4%	12%	13%	30%

Source: Bank of Thailand.

Annex 1.2
FDI in Asian Emerging Economies

FDI inward flow/gross capital formation	1971–75	1976–80	1981–85	1986–90	1991–95	1996–2000	2001–05
China	nc	0.0	1.1	2.8	11.2	13.0	9.3
Indonesia	15.5	4.1	1.1	2.4	5.2	−1.0	3.2
Korea	4.9	0.6	0.6	1.3	0.6	4.6	2.7
Malaysia	14.0	12.8	11.0	10.8	19.7	16.9	0.3
The Philippines	2.6	1.7	0.7	6.8	8.4	9.4	12.4
Singapore	16.9	16.9	18.4	38.3	29.3	41.6	5.8
Taiwan	1.8	1.3	1.5	3.7	2.2	3.6	55.4
Thailand	3.2	1.5	2.6	5.1	3.8	15.4	6.8

Source: UNCTAD.

Notes

1. A. Siamwalla, "Stability, Growth and Distribution in the Thai Economy", in *Finance, Trade and Economic Development in Thailand*, edited by Puey Ungphakorn (Sompong Press, 1975).
2. J-C. Simon (1996); S. Tambunlerchai (1993).
3. Pasuk, Phongpaïchit, *The New Wave of Japanese Investment in ASEAN* (Singapore: Institute of Southeast Asian Studies, 1990).
4. Peter G. Warr and Bhanupong Nidhiprabha, *The East Asian Miracle: Economic Growth and Public Policy* (New York: Oxford University Press, 1993, 1996).
5. R. Wade. *Governing the Market* (Oxford University Press, 1992).

6. Robinson David et al., "Thailand: Adjusting to Success", IMF Occasional Paper, No. 85, August 1991.
7. This is well documented, see Suphatchalasai (1995), and also Heather Smith (1995).
8. See also the contribution by N. Aveline, Chapter 5. Regarding EPZ policies refer to "Economic and Social Effects of Multinational Enterprises in Export Processing Zones", Working paper of International Labour Organisation and United Nations Centre on Transnational Corporations (Geneva, ILO).
9. Archanun Kohpaiboon (2003).
10. See, for example, information compiled in websites such as <http://www.doingbusiness.org/>.
11. Laurids S. Lauridsen (2002); Brimble (2002). See contribution by B. Jetin on education and manpower skill, in Chapter 3.
12. Organization for Economic Cooperation & Development (OECD), "Foreign Direct Investment and Recovery in Southeast Asia" (Paris: OECD, 1999).
13. Sanjaya Lall, "Changing Perceptions of Foreign Direct Investment in Development", in *International Trade, Foreign Direct Investment and the Economic Environment*, edited by P.K.M. Tharakan and D. Van Den Bulcke (London: Macmillan Press, 1998), pp. 101–34.
14. Claire Mainguy, "L'impact des Investissements Directs Étrangers sur les Pays en Développement", Région et Développement, no. 20, pp. 64–89.
15. Stephen Thomsen, "Southeast Asia: The Role of Foreign Direct Investment Policies in Development", Working Papers On International Investment, No. 1, 1999.
16. Sailesh Tanna and Kitja Topaiboul, "Human Capital, Trade, FDI and Economic Growth in Thailand: What Causes What?", DEGIT Conference Papers, No. c010_046, June 2005; available at <http://www.ifw-kiel.de/VRCent/DEGIT/paper/degit_10/C010_046.pdf>.

References

Akrasanee, Narongchai and A. O. Krueger. *Trade and Employment in Developing Countries*. University of Chicago Press, 1980.

Akrasanee, Narongchai and S. Naya. *Thai-Japanese Economic Relations: Trade and Investment*, p. 103. Bangkok: Publ. Ecocen – Jetro, 1974.

Bénassy-Quéré Agnès et al. "Institutional Determinants of Foreign Direct Investment". *World Economy* 30, no. 5 (2007): 764–82.

Brimble, Peter. "Foreign Direct Investment: Performance and Attraction. The Case of Thailand", p. 26. Bangkok: Brooker Group, 2002.

Chirathiwat, Suthiphand. "Global and Regulatory Change in FDI in ASEAN Countries" (Chapter 9). In *Regional and Global Regulation of International Trade*, edited by F. Snyder, p. 304. Hart Pub., 2001.

Healey, Derek. *Les Exportations Japonaises de Capitaux et le Développement Économique de l'Asie*, p. 268. Paris: OCDE, 1996.

Kohpaiboon, Archanun. "Foreign Trade Regimes and the FDI-Growth Nexus: A Case Study of Thailand". *Journal of Development Studies* (December 2003).

Lall, Sanjaya. "Changing Perceptions of Foreign Direct Investment in Development". In *International Trade, Foreign Direct Investment and the Economic Environment*, edited by P.KM. Tharakan and D. Van Den Bulcke, pp. 101–34 (London: Macmillan Press, 1998).

Lauridsen, Laurids S. "Coping with the Triple Challenge of Globalisation, Liberalisation and Crisis: The Role of Industrial Technology Policies and Technology Institutions in Thailand". *The European Journal of Development Research* 14, no. 1 (2002): 101–25.

————. "Foreign Direct Investment, Linkage Formation and Supplier Development in Thailand during the 1990s: The Role of State Governance". *European Journal of Development Research* 16, no. 3 (2004): 561–86.

Maximin, Bertrand. "L'enjeu de L'investissement Direct International en Thaïlande. L'émergence d'un N.P.I. de la Seconde Génération". *Mondes en développement*, T. 22, no. 86 (1994): 9–22.

Mainguy, Claire. "L'impact des Investissements Directs Étrangers sur les Pays en Développement". *Région et Développement*, no. 20 (2004): 64–89.

Nomura Research & ISEAS. *The New Wave of Foreign Direct Investment in Asia*, p. 277. Singapore: Institute of Southeast Asian Studies, 1995.

OECD. *Foreign Direct Investment and Recovery in Southeast Asia*. Paris: OECD, 1999.

Okuda, Satoru. *Industrial Linkage and Direct Investment in APEC*. Tokyo: IDE-JETRO, 2000.

Oman, Charles P. et al. *Investing in Asia*, p. 248. Paris: ADB & OECD, 1997.

Parnwell, Michael. *Uneven Development in Thailand*. London: Avebury Publishing, 1996.

Ramstetter, Eric D. "International Trade, Multinational Firms and Regional Integration". In *Multinationals and East Asian Integration*, edited by W. Dobson and C.S. Yue. Singapore: Institute of Southeast Asian Studies, 1997.

Robinson, David et al. "Thailand: Adjusting to Success". *IMF Occasional Paper*, No. 85, August 1991.

Rochanonda, Chadin. "Tax Incentives and FDI in Thailand". International Symposium on FDI. Public School Hitotsubashi University, Tokyo, 2006.

Siamwalla, Ammar. "Stability, Growth and Distribution in the Thai Economy". In *Finance, Trade and Economic Development in Thailand*, edited by Puey Ungphakorn et al. Sompong Press, 1975.

Simon. J-C. "Trade and Investment links between Europe and Asia: Long Term Trends and Post Crisis Adjustments — with special reference to industries in Korea and Thailand". *European Journal of East Asian Studies* 1, no. 3 (2001).

———. "Transformations et Industrialisation en Thaïlande: Croissance et Développement Économiques à Travers Cinq Décennies". In *Thailande Contemporaine*. Paris: IRASEC-L'Harmattan, 2002.

Smith, Heather. "Industry Policy in East Asia". *Asian-Pacific Economic Literature* 9, no. 1 (1995): 17–39.

Suehiro, Akira. *Capital Accumulation in Thailand*. Center for East Asian Cultural Studies, 1989.

———. "Social Capabilities for Industrialization. Government Policies Technology Formation and Small Business". In *Asian Pacific Economies and Small Business*, edited by Nakaoka et al. Osaka University of Economics, 1995.

Suphatchalasai, Supat. "Export-Led Industrialization". In *Thailand's Industrialization and Its Consequences*, edited by M. Krongkaew. New York/London: St Martin's Press/Macmillan Press, 1995.

Tambunlertchai, Somsak. "Manufacturing". In *The Thai Economy in Transition*, edited by P.G. Warr, pp. 118–50. Cambridge: Cambridge University Press.

Tanna, Sailesh and Kitjia Topaibul. "Human Capital, Trade, FDI and Economic Growth in Thailand: What Causes What?". DEGIT Conference Papers, No. c010_046, June, available at <http://www.ifw-kiel.de/VRCent/DEGIT/paper/degit_10/C010_046.pdf>.

Thomsen, Stephen. "Southeast Asia: The Role of Foreign Direct Investment Policies in Development". Working Papers on International Investment, No. 1 (1999).

Warr, Peter G. and Bhanupong Nidhiprabha. *Thailand's Macroeconomic Miracle: Stable Adjustment and Sustained Growth*. Kuala Lumpur: Oxford University Press, 1996.

Wu, Friedriech, and Kok Keong Puah. "Foreign Direct investment to China and Southeast Asia: Has ASEAN been Losing Out?". *Journal of Asian Business* 19, no. 1 (2003): 89–105.

2

CATCHING UP OR FALLING BEHIND
Thailand's Industrial Development from the National Innovation System Perspective

Patarapong Intarakumnerd

INTRODUCTION

What were and presently are the kinds of institutional structures and policies that facilitate technological learning and mastery across the broad front needed for industrial development? This is one of the central questions for researchers in several fields of economics, especially, development economics, institutional economics, and economics of technical change and innovation. Understanding differences across countries in their level of development and the reasons for backwardness was, of course, a central concern of the great classical economists, particularly Adam Smith. But these questions gradually moved to the periphery of the field. The question came back into focus after World War II. That the development problem was a catch up problem was put forth explicitly in Alexander Gershenkron's *Economic Backwardness in*

Historical Perspective (1951), which considered the policies and new institutions of the states of continental Europe during the mid and late nineteenth century as they strove to catch up with the United Kingdom, and reflected on the present day relevance of this experience. Moses Abramowitz's propositions (1986) about the institutional and political conditions explaining why countries catch up, forge ahead, and fall behind clearly had this orientation. Nonetheless, we need a "holistic" view to understand a country's industrial development and the underlying reasons behind successful catching up or falling behind. One useful and practical concept is the national innovation system (NIS).

The emergence of the NIS concepts, particularly in the industrialized countries in the northern hemisphere, can be traced back to the work of Lundvall on the national system of innovation or national policies of innovation, and other works (see Freeman 1987, 1988; Nelson 1988) started in the mid-1980s. NIS is the interactive system of existing institutions, private and public firms (either large or small), universities and government agencies, which aim at the production of science and technology (S&T) within national borders. Interaction among these units may be technical, commercial, legal, social, and financial, and the goal of the interaction may be development, protection, financing, or regulation of new science and technology (Niosi et al. 1996, p. 139).

This chapter tries to analyse Thailand's industrial development by using the perspective of a national innovation system. It will focus especially on the evolution of actors, and their linkages and learning processes in the Thai NIS.

In 1997, Thailand had the worst economic crisis in forty years. Apart from other causes such as untimely financial liberalization and the burst of the bubble economy (as was also illustrated in Chapter 1), diminishing international competitiveness was also a major reason. A strong evidence of this is the very low growth rate of Total Factor Productivity (TFP), which explains other reasons for a country's economic growth apart from the growth of capital, labour, and land. There are education system, progress of science, technology and innovation, and other social, capital, and institutional factors. Even in the period of high growth between 1987–95 when the economy in general grew at a rate of almost 10 per cent, the TFP growth rate was only around 1.5 per cent. During the crisis (1997–98), TFP's growth was even more negative than the overall growth of GDP (see Table 2.1).

Table 2.1
Growth Rates of GDP and Contributing Factors
(In %)

Period	Economic Growth	Labour Factor	Land Factor	Capital Factor	TFP
1982–86	5.37	0.74	0.02	4.71	−0.09
1987–95	9.92	0.66	0.01	7.70	1.55
1996	5.90	0.17	0.01	6.94	−1.22
2 years during crisis (1997–98)	−5.94	−0.48	0.00	1.48	−6.95
3 years after crisis (1999–2001)	3.79	0.75	0.01	0.91	2.11
2002–05	5.81	0.80	0.02	1.99	3.00
Average 1982–2005	6.03	0.60	0.01	4.73	0.70

Source: Adapted by the author from data in National Economic and Social Development Board (2007), National Productivity Enhancement Plan presentation on 26 January 2007.

The loss of international competitiveness leading to the economic crisis arose from the weak and fragmented NIS (see details in Intarakumnerd et al. 2002). In turn, the crisis also affected the actors of the Thai NIS. This will be discussed in detail later.

Here, we attempt to analyse the national innovation system of Thailand in a broad perspective by examining the evolution of roles, capabilities, and the linkages of the following actors: government, university, private firms, private bridging organizations (industry, trade, and professional organizations), financial intermediaries/markets, and institutional context.

Taking into account idiosyncratic differences in terms of historical, institutional, cultural, and international contexts, the study, to some extent, analyses the evolution of Thai NIS in comparison with that of leading East Asian countries (namely, Japan, Korea, and Taiwan) in order to shed light on the strengths and weaknesses of the Thai NIS.

As already mentioned, together with the existing literature on Thailand's NIS and those of the aforementioned countries, the main source of information for our study is the R&D/Innovation Survey, carried out twice — in 2000 and 2002. The survey in 2000 was the first of its kind in Thailand and it covered both R&D and other technological innovation activities only in the manufacturing sector. The second survey, in 2002, included the service sector for a better understanding of the nature and differences of R&D and innovation activities in both manufacturing and services.[1] The survey adopted definitions and methodologies used by the Frascati Manual and the Oslo Manual of the Organization for Economic Cooperation and Development (OECD), and was in line with those used in several countries in Asia (such as Singapore and Malaysia).

1. ACTORS AND LINKAGES OF THAILAND'S NATIONAL INNOVATION SYSTEM

1.1 Government

Up to the time of the government of Prime Minister Thaksin Shinawatra (January 2001–September 2006), the scope of Science and Technology (S&T) policy in Thailand was rather narrow. It covered only four conventional functions, namely, research and development, human resource development, technology transfer, and S&T infrastructure development. This narrow scope of S&T was very much based on the perception that private firms were "users" of S&T knowledge mainly produced by government agencies and universities (see Arnold et. al. 2000). There was no articulated national innovation policy. Though the word "innovation" was mentioned in several national plans, it was not whole-heartedly incorporated into the scope of S&T policies (see Lauridsen 2002). In addition, unlike in Japan, Korea, and Taiwan, S&T elements were not part of broader economic policies, namely, industrial policy, investment policy and trade policy, and, to the lesser extent, education policies (see Intarakumnerd et. al. 2002).

The industrial policy of Thailand did not pay enough attention to the development of indigenous technological capability as an integral factor in the process of industrialization (Sripaipan, Vanichseni, and Mukdapitak 1999, p. 37). As pointed out in Chapter 1, investment policy, especially the promotion of foreign direct investment (FDI), aimed primarily at generating inward capital flows and employment. Unlike in Singapore where FDI was specifically used to upgrade local technological capability (see Wong 1999), there was no explicit and proactive link between the promoting of FDI and the upgrading of local technological capability in Thailand. Trade policy, of which the most important instrument in Thailand was the tariff, was not used strategically to promote technological learning like in newly industrializing economies (NIEs) (see Amsden 1989; Chang 1994; Lall 1996). Instead, trade policy was very much influenced by macroeconomic policy, for instance, reducing domestic demand for imports when there was a balance of payment deficit. The Ministry of Finance, the dominant agency which controlled the policy, had little knowledge or experience of industry and industrial restructuring (Lauridsen 2000, pp. 16–20).

Moreover, industrial policy in Thailand was limited to so-called "functional" intervention, such as promoting infrastructure building, general education, and export push in general. There were virtually no selective policy measures, such as special credit allocation and special tariff protection targeting particular industries or clusters. The exception was the local-content requirement in the automobile industry, which was rather successful in raising the local contents of passenger vehicles to 54 per cent in 1986 (see Doner 1992). Interestingly, with the exception of the automotive industry, there was no reciprocal performance-based criteria (such as export and local value added and technological upgrading targets) set to provide state incentives like in Korea or Japan (see Johnson 1982; Amsden 1989; Evans 1989, 1998; Chang 1994; Lall 1996). Investment promotion privileges, for example, were given away once an investment was approved. The aim of attracting foreign direct investment and promoting exports overshadowed the need to develop local initiatives and indigenous technological capabilities. As a result, linkages between multinational corporations and local firms were also weak. Unlike in Taiwan, the governmental protection and promotion, without strengthening the absorptive capabilities of Thai suppliers, left a profound impact on the weak technology and supplier network of industries. (Vongpivat 2003)

A major change in policy came recently under the Thaksin government. A dual track policy was the main thrust of the new policy. The government tried to enhance the international competitiveness of the nation by strengthening the "external" side of the Thai economy, namely, exports, foreign direct investment, and tourism. At the same time, it attempted to increase the capabilities of domestic and grass root economies by implementing projects such as the Village Fund (one million baht to increase the local capabilities of each village), a three-year debt moratorium on farmers' debt, the One Tambon[2] One Product Project (supporting each tambon in having a product champion), and the People Bank, which gives loans to underprivileged people without the requirement of a collateral (see more details in Chapter 4). Some academics and politicians from opposition parties branded these new grass root supporting policies as "populist policies" aimed at winning votes from the rural poor.

The Thaksin government, unlike its predecessors which paid more attention to macroeconomic stability, focused more on enhancing meso- and micro-level foundations for Thailand's international competitiveness. The high priority of the "competitiveness" issue on the government's agenda was illustrated by the establishment of the National Competitiveness Committee chaired by the prime minister himself. It was the first time that the Thai government had serious "selective" policies addressing specific sectors and clusters. The government declared five strategic clusters which Thailand should pursue: the automotive industry, food, tourism, fashion, and software. Clear visions were given to these five clusters: Kitchen of the World (food cluster), Detroit of Asia (automotive cluster), Asia Tropical Fashion, World Graphic Design and Animation Centre (software cluster), and Asia Tourism Capital. Building the innovative capabilities of the nation was highly regarded as a very important factor in increasing and sustaining Thailand's international competitiveness. "Innovative nation with wisdom and learning base" was one of seven Thailand's Dreams projected by the government. To make this dream come true, several strategies were devised. These include continuous investment in R&D and technology; a good environment for attracting and stimulating innovation; high accessibility to knowledge and information across the nation; having Thai people use English fluently as a second language, and showing strong learning basis such as a passion for reading, better accessibility to cheap but good books, thinking school with innovations (see Phasukavanich 2003).

Equally important, the new ten-year Science and Technology Strategic Plan (2004–13) places the concept of national innovation system and industrial cluster at its heart. The scope of the plan is much broader than the aforementioned four functional areas. Measures to stimulate innovations and strengthen the national innovation system and industrial clusters are explicitly highlighted.

The National Economic and Social Development Board (NESDB) has been implicitly responsible for the overall cluster policy of the country. It has made significant attempts to diffuse the concept to various government and private-sector agencies by organizing cluster seminars and workshops in the main regions of Thailand. It also commissioned a study to create a "cluster mapping" of Thailand, that is, the identification of significant agglomerations of firms that function or have the potential to function as clusters in various geographical locations throughout the country. Several implementing government agencies such as the Department of Industrial Promotion and sector-specific institutes under the Ministry of Industry (Thai Automotive Institute, Thailand Textile Institute, National Food Institute, Electrical and Electronics Institute, and so on), the National Science and Technology Development Agency under the Ministry of Science and Technology, the Office of SMEs Promotion, and others tried to develop their own cluster projects in their responsible areas (Intellectual Property Institute 2006).

The Board of Investment (BOI) has substantially changed its policy by paying more attention to issues underlying long-term competitiveness of the country, namely, the development of indigenous technological capability and human resources. A special investment package promoting "Skill, Technology and Innovation or STI" has been initiated. Firms can enjoy one or two years of extra tax incentives, if they do at least one of the following during the first three years after acceptance: spend at least 1–2 per cent of their sales on R&D or design activities; employ scientist or engineers with at least a bachelor's degree as at least 5 per cent of their workforce; spend at least 1 per cent of their payroll on training of their employees; and at least 1 per cent on training the personnel of their local suppliers. The flourishing of the cluster concept also affected investment policy. In 2004 BOI initiated new investment packages for specific strategic clusters such as the hard disk drive (see more details in Chapter 8) and semiconductor sectors. Eligible firms in these sectors are not only final product makers, but also suppliers in the value chain. This indicates a transformation of the focus of investment policy measures from giving incentives to individual projects, which might not be related to one another, to using incentives to strengthen the cluster as a whole.

The cluster concept was used as a main industrial policy of the Thaksin government at the national, regional, and local levels. At the national level, it was used to strengthen advance industries, both in the service and manufacturing sectors, such as automotive, textile (see more details in Chapter 7) and garment, software, and tourism, in order to create coherent and innovative "industrial clusters". At the regional level, Thailand was divided into nineteen geographical areas. Each area had to plan and implement its own cluster strategy, focusing on a few strategic products or services. It was supervised by the so-called "CEO Governors", who are given the authority by the central government to act like provincial Chief Executive Officers (CEOs). At the local level, the cluster concept was applied to increase the capacity of grass root economies known as "community-based clusters", and especially to help the "One Tambon-One Product" project succeed.

1.2 Private Firms

Several studies of Thai firms conducted since the 1980s state that most firms have grown without deepening their technological capabilities in the long run, and their technological learning has been very slow and passive (see Bell and Scott-Kemmis 1985; Chantramonklasri 1985; Thailand Development Research Institute 1989; Dahlman and Brimble 1990, Tiralap 1990; Mukdapitak 1994; Lall 1998). The recent World Bank's study (see Arnold et al. 2000) confirms this long-standing feature of Thai firms. Only a small minority of large subsidiaries of transnational corporations (TNCs), large domestic firms, and SMEs has capability in R&D, while the majority is still struggling with increasing their design and engineering capability. For a very large number of SMEs, the key issue is much more concerned with building up more basic operational capabilities, together with craft and technician capabilities, for efficient acquisition, assimilation, and incremental upgrading of fairly standard technology. The slow technological capability development of Thai firms is quite different from what characterized Japan, Korea, and Taiwan. Firms in these countries moved rather rapidly from being mere imitators to innovators. As early as the 1960s, Japanese firms became more innovative, invested heavily in R&D, and relied less on importation of foreign technologies (Odagiri and Goto 1993, also described in Chapter 4). In general, firms in Korea and Taiwan, where industrialization (beginning with import substitution) started more or less in the same period as in Thailand, were more successful in increasing absorptive capacity (of foreign technology) and deepening indigenous technological capabilities in several industries (see, for example, Amsden 1989; Kim 1993; Lall 1996; Hobday 1995; Kim 1997). In the electronics industry, for instance, Korean and Taiwan firms were able to climb technological ladders (from simple assembly to own design and R&D) by exploiting institutional mechanisms such as OEM and ODM[3] to help latecomer firms in those countries acquire advanced technology and access demanding foreign markets (see Hobday 1995).

A comparison of the Thai and Korean innovation surveys, both conducted in 2002, illustrates the differences of these two countries in terms of innovative capabilities. Companies in Thailand lag far behind companies in Korea with respect to innovation. More than 40 per cent of Korean firms carried out innovations against just above 10 per cent in Thailand. It is striking that a much higher number of companies in Korea carry out product innovations. This could be an indication that Thai companies are at the stage where they would rather use their resources to improve production processes rather than the product itself, which in turn could hint at a rather OEM-oriented economy. At the same time very few companies in Thailand do both product and process innovations, which are very common in Korea. This reflects the more advanced innovation behaviour of Korean companies.

1.3 Universities and Government Research Technology Organizations (RTOs)

From the Thai R&D/Innovation Survey 2002 and Korean Innovation Survey 2002, it can be seen that universities and research institutes were regarded as a much more important source of information by Korean firms than by Thai firms (see Table 2.2).

Technological activities of public research technology organizations (RTOs)[4] mainly focused on R&D and on providing technical services such as testing and calibrating. Those organizations did not particularly assist firms in building up their "internal" technological capabilities especially "non-R&D" capability such as technology assimilation, adaptation, designing, and engineering. These capabilities are the technological thresholds typically faced by most Thai firms. In this aspect, Thai RTOs behave differently from those in Japan and East Asian NIEs, when their levels of development were more or less at the current level of Thailand.

A recent study done by Schiller (2006) illustrates that linkages between universities and industry in Thailand are mostly limited to consulting and technical services (this is also emphasized in Chapter 7), hampered by mutual distrust, and maintained for those involved to receive an extra personal income. At present, most linkages are based on personal contacts

Table 2.2
Importance of External Information Sources
(Percentage of firms receiving information from the following sources)

Thailand	%	Korea	%
Clients	77.4	Customers	77.7
Internet	63.0	Competitors	69.3
Parent/ associate company	61.2	Exhibition	65.5
Locally-owned suppliers	59.9	Internet	64.9
Specialist literature	56.6	Component suppliers	61.7
Professional conference & meetings	55.2	Patents	59.8
Foreign-owned suppliers	54.8	Equip. suppliers	57.7
Fairs and exhibitions	53.1	Universities	53.6
Competitors	42.1	Enterprise within the group	52.9
Technical service providers	40.2	Public Research Inst.	52.6
Universities or other higher education institutes	35.8	New personnel	51.9
Business service providers	33.1	Trade Associations	44.2
Patent disclosures	32.0		
Gov. or private non-profit research institutes	29.5		

Source: Composed by the author from data in Thailand R&D/Innovation Survey 2002 and Korean
          Innovation Survey 2002.

and operate without an elaborate institutional framework. Genuine research linkages are lacking. There is also a lack of confidence-building communication among players.

1.4 Private Bridging Organizations

This section analyses the roles and capabilities of non-profit organizations, such as trade and industrial associations, in supporting the technological capability development and innovation activities of firms. With regard to innovation support, there are just a small number of these organizations disseminating knowledge and promoting the innovation capability of firms.

In Thailand, the Federation of Thai Industry (FTI) and Thai Chamber of Commerce (TCC) are the most powerful private-sector organizations. Their influence is strong on the government's economic policies. They can pressure the government to induce policy changes. Most of their activities, however, aim at the protection of their short-term interests and gaining leverage in negotiations with government (Laothamatas 1992; Phongpaichit and Baker 1997a, p. 150), on matters such as export quotas, import levies, and tax regime. They are not very active in promoting the innovation capability of Thai firms. History does matter as well. Their members come from the commercial capital, rather than the industrial capital (Samudavanija 1990, p. 275). Therefore, they pay more attention to short-term commercial gains rather than long-term capability development.

The FTI and TCC voiced their needs and concerns in the Joint Public-Private Consultative Committee (JPPCC) in an attempt to gain investment privileges and commercial advantages (Phongpaichit and Baker 1997b). The role of this committee was very prominent in the mid-1980s when the idea of "Thailand Inc.", aspired to by the government during that period, was popular. Since then, both the FTI and TCC have represented the interests of the private sector in several national-level committees. The importance of JPPCC, nonetheless, has later declined substantially.

There is a small range of activities of the FTI and TCC that aim to encourage the diffusion of technological knowledge among their members. Examples are management consulting services, promotion of ISO certification and clean technology, and training programmes in energy saving, sanitary standards, entrepreneurial management, design, and technological skills upgrading ("Federation of Thai Industries", n.d.). These activities are more active in the "strategic" sectors designated by the government. Firms in these industries are more open to change. Some sectoral groups within the FTI are more enthusiastic about change than others, especially those having explicit concerns over the loss of national competitiveness in comparison with other latecomer countries.

Where trust building among members is concerned, which is itself a kind of social infrastructure for knowledge diffusion and innovation, the role of FTI and TCC is not very impressive. They could create a certain level of trust among members through congregation, exchanges of ideas and opinions, and the sharing of information among members. Trust mostly emerges gradually from joint activities such as marketing campaigns and trade fairs. However, the internal organizations of FTI and TCC are politically divided. For example, ever since the TCC expanded with a growing number of provincial members, the organization has been more divided and fragmented because of regional power politics (Phuchatkan November 1992, pp. 14–15). The provincial chambers made the criticism that Bangkok-based business groups manipulated the TCC (Chotiya 1997, pp. 258–59).

1.5 Financial Intermediaries/Markets

Like those in Japan and Korea, Thailand's financial system supporting industrial development is bank based. The commercial banks are the ones to finance most of the private sector investments in Thailand. Many entrepreneurs in Thailand develop innovative projects that require external financing, but face the problem of not knowing where they should go for funds. According to the survey carried out by the Ministry of Industry, the major problem that limits entrepreneurial firms in taking up innovative activities is the lack of capital funding (see Advance Research 1997). Moreover, while the entrepreneurs want to tap the money from financial institutions, they face difficulties obtaining a bank loan. Banks are conservative in granting loans and would generally not support risky businesses. Most start-up firms face many years of negative earnings and are unable to make the interest and principal payments that would be required on a bank loan.

Several industrial development banks were set up to provide long- and medium-term financing, and the four most important ones among those are the Industrial Finance Corporation of Thailand (IFCT), SME Bank, Small Industry Credit Guarantee Corporation (SICGC), and Innovation Development Fund (IDF). Some of these financial institutions are not well known to private firms, and they are not operating efficiently because of chronic bureaucratic red tape. While the maximum loan limit under the programmes is rather low, the interest rates claimed are not so different from those charged by commercial banks. The application processes are complicated and time-consuming. Processing the loan, in most cases, takes several months. This discourages firms, especially SMEs, from seeking institutional loans and forces them to take loans from informal sources where they can get credit more quickly (*The Nation* — various issues; *The Bangkok Post* — various issues). Some institutions such as the IDF were rather restrained in providing the necessary funds to firms with innovative projects as their project evaluators, mainly university professors, lack the understanding of innovation processes and had limited business capability (Turpin et al. 2002, p. 73). However, the IDF has performed very well as a pioneer in "non-financial issue", that is, encouraging an "innovation culture" in the private sector and the Thai society at large through innovation awards, for example.

As for a capital market, Thailand has no stock market especially established to promote such high-tech start-ups such as those in Japan (JASDAG, NASDAQ-Japan, and MOTHERS), Korea (KOSDAQ), and Taiwan (TAIDAQ and TIGER). The Market for Alternative Investment (MAI) is a business unit of the main market, the Stock Exchange of Thailand (SET). It was set up in 1999 as a new secondary market for trading SME shares. MAI's requirements for initial public offerings have been adjusted to allow SMEs flexibility in entering the capital markets. However, this market is not specifically aimed at promoting knowledge-intensive start-ups. In practice, MAI attracts little interest from SMEs because the founding shareholders are reluctant to initiate common stock rights issues that would effectively dilute their stakes in the listed companies. Since most SMEs are family controlled, this reduces the willingness to enact equity issues (for fear of diluting levels of ownership and control). Therefore, the capacity of MAI as a conduit for small businesses is constrained. Moreover, many SMEs find that MAI requirements tend to disqualify most small- and medium-sized enterprises, as they fall below the minimum capitalization level required. As a result, there are too few outstanding shares to trade adequately on the market (Freeman 2000).

In 1994, the Thai Venture Capital Association (TVCA) was set up because of the realization of the importance of setting up macroeconomic fundamentals to provide firms with access to finance. At present, approximately half of the Thai Venture Capital Association's (TVCA) members, that is, the ordinary members, are Thai and international venture capital and/or private equity fund management firms. The other half, the extraordinary members, operate businesses related to venture capital (VC) or private equity, such as financial advisory firms, accounting firms, legal firms, securities firms, and finance companies. Understanding the policies to supply the venture capital finance, the Thai government has supported several VC funds, such as the SME Venture Capital Fund (1 billion Thai baht), the Thailand Equity Fund (US$50 million), and the Thailand Recovery Fund (US$250 million). The government also considers giving tax incentives to promote more VC investment in Thailand.

Compared with Taiwan, Thailand's venture capital sector is lagging in terms of its growth and has far less impact on financing innovation and the emergence of knowledge-intensive start ups. Unlike Taiwan, in Thailand venture capitalists tend to finance firms at an expansion or mezzanine stage, rather than in the early start-up phase (see "Taiwan Venture Capital Association", n.d.).

2. INSTITUTIONAL CONTEXT

The aforementioned actors operate in the specific Thai institutional context. Now we examine entrepreneurship, attitude to failure, and trust as they influence the innovativeness of firms in Thailand.

Like the economy in Indonesia, the Thai economy is also different to others in Southeast Asia because no class of indigenous, big business entrepreneurs exists. Even smaller businesses in Bangkok, especially in retailing, are mostly owned and operated by Sino-Thais (East Asian Analytical Unit 1995, p. 78). The dominance in Thailand of family-owned enterprises established by immigrant Chinese entrepreneurs has long been ingrained into Thai business norms and culture. Therefore, historically and culturally, entrepreneurship in Thailand is not much different from that in Chinese-dominated countries such as Taiwan.

In terms of trust, Chinese-owned businesses tend to be built as family-affiliated corporations that have ownership- and kinship-led rather than skill-based, management. This "family-ownership-control-type business" (Suehiro 1992, p. 392), characterized by low stock-ownership diffusion and more family-related CEOs, has led to business and joint investment cooperation among different companies within the same family affiliates, but little cooperation with various enterprises of other families (Suehiro 1992, p. 390; and East Asian Analytical Unit 1995, p. 78). Although many Chinese-run firms have grown into big conglomerates covering many business areas, the founding family still holds the ultimate rein. Later, firms under the same family umbrella overlap and compete, leading to intrafamily conflicts. In short, cooperation is less likely to happen in interfamily businesses, but more likely to take place in intrafamily enterprises, although this might also create difficulties because of family complexities and contentions.

One characteristic of the Chinese-Thai entrepreneurship is its negative attitude towards failure and this provokes two contrasting views. While the first view sees the Sino-Thai influence as a threat to innovation, because of its low acceptance of failure and its lack of merit-based management, the second view sees the Chinese-Thai business culture as a positive condition that tolerates risky ventures needed for long-term planning and investment.

First of all, due to the fact that Chinese-run enterprises expand their businesses for the main purpose of increasing the "total fortune of the family" (Suehiro 1992, p. 403), they advance into areas such as finance and real estate. This evidence shows they are risk-averse when doing businesses. Upfront profit from trading and the property business is far more attractive than expensive technology-intensive manufacturing that will only earn longer-term gains. As a result, technological development or long-term sustainability is not much of a concern. Political capability in terms of gaining access to lucrative, oligopolistic sectors seems more important than technological capability in this case.

The structural and political context also affect the behaviour of Sino-Thai firms. The main rationale for their domestic expansion and diversification is the fact that they can take advantage of the government's industrial promotion and other tax incentives while diversifying into foreign ventures for scale and scope, given the limited domestic market and intensive local competition (Suehiro 1992, p. 400). Therefore, the liberalization and high industrial growth of the 1980s, together with many favourable conditions outside that are unrelated to the fundamental capability of Thai industries, lured Thai conglomerates into diversifying in new areas technologically unrelated to their original businesses. In order to do that, the underlying capability these firms accumulated is the capability to establish and maintain political connections with government authorities, rather than technological and innovation capabilities (see Intarakumnerd et al. 2002).

The second view, however, sees Chinese-Thai entrepreneurship positively. The fact that "Sino-Thai families traditionally were reluctant to relinquish ownership and management of their companies..." (East Asian Analytical Unit 1995, p. 80) allows them to create long-term visions for their own family businesses. While some list their assets in the stock market, many still prefer to raise capital conservatively through loans and offshore bonds issued with a chance for them to benefit from different international interest rates. The continuing vision from fathers to children protects them from the short-term concerns of stock prices or the threat of acquisition. The deep-rooted corporate culture and tacit learning of family members create a qualified decision base for risky projects (Intarakumnerd 2000, p. 16). Therefore, they are capable of embarking on risky ventures with the expectation of future success without being distracted by stockholders.

Entrepreneurship in Thailand has experienced interesting changes. The attitude to and behavioural changes of entrepreneurship in Thailand come from exposure to modernism, innovative culture, and new technologies of the West that have infiltrated through because of the overseas education of some members of the younger generations. This factor is where the two contrasting views of Sino-Thai business culture finally merge. The combined traits of making fast decision and long-term planning will create a condition that allows Thai business to grow both horizontally and vertically. It will likely create a business structure, which while remaining family-run, becomes increasingly innovative and adaptive to the changing environment. The attitude that favoured kinship rather than managerial skills has also started to change. The professionalism of management has grown despite tight family control (see Intarakumnerd 2000), allowing for better prospects for competency building and technology development.

The innovation surveys show that the attitude of accepting failure rose from 10.5 per cent in 2000 to 19.5 per cent in 2002. As many as 63.5 per cent of the firms, surveyed in 2002 considered establishing long-term strategic partnerships with other firms as rather important or important. There was also a positive change in other attitude indicators, such as openness of customers to innovation. This indicates a better innovative environment in Thailand.

Furthermore, the Thaksin government had tried very hard to make Thai society more entrepreneurial. It encouraged the Thai people to change their attitude from wanting to be employees of the government or big corporations, to wanting to be self-made entrepreneurs. The Ministry of Industry had the strong intention to produce 5,000 new entrepreneurs a year. As a result, financial incentives, technical supports, and training courses were provided by government agencies and education institutes to individuals and start-up businesses.

3. LEARNING PROCESS IN THAILAND'S NATIONAL INNOVATION SYSTEM

The Thai national innovation system evolved over time due to the impact of systemic learning. It has been moving from a "weak and fragmented" system to a "stronger and coherent" one. Learning processes were caused by two key reasons. One was the interaction between actors in the system. Another was the change in external environment that affected the whole system.

As mentioned in section 1, the emergence of the Thaksin government had made significant changes in the policy paradigm of the government sector. Moreover it had made an impact on other actors interacting with the government. The roles of business associations, for example, has been affected. The Thaksin government thought that the Joint Public-Private Consultative Committee (JPPCC) was rather passive and finally, changed its style of operation from large assemblies happening sporadically to less formal meetings every Friday. This new form of informal meetings between the prime minister and the private sector led to clearer national strategic goals, with more up-to-date concepts such as supply chain management and industrial clustering, being introduced. Business associations began to acknowledge the importance of clusters and tried to use the cluster concept to formulate and implement their strategies. The Thai Chamber of Commerce and Federation of Thai Industries started to carry out their activities on a cluster basis and reorganized their internal organizations according to clusters (Intellectual Property Institute 2006).

Similarly, public RTOs and universities were also under pressure from the Thaksin government and the Budget Bureau to increase their revenue, and hence reduce their reliance on the national budget. They were forced to become more relevant to industrial needs in order to earn extra income. In the past few years, some Thai public universities have attained autonomous status. The idea was to take them out of the red tape bureaucratic system and let them enjoy more freedom financially. Most of their budget is still subsidized by government, but they are expected to generate relatively more income from other sources, especially from the private sector. Therefore, they have to conduct research and other activities which are more relevant to industry. Recently, universities have increasingly tried to increase industry sponsorships and forge links with industry through establishing collaborative R&D, training activities, and linkage mechanisms, namely, technology and business incubators, technology transfer departments, technology licensing offices (to license out their intellectual properties which are products of their research), and science parks (see College of Management 2003; Schiller 2006).

The emergence of the Thaksin government and its interaction with other actors of the NIS could have inspired systemic learning, that is, changes in the behaviour of these actors. Nonetheless, the implementation of the aforementioned policies was far from successful. For example, there were several shortcomings in implementing the cluster concept:

(a) Confusion of the cluster concept. Different government and private-sector agencies had a different understanding of the cluster concept. Some considered a cluster to be an industrial sector with no specific geographical concentration in mind (see Chapter 5). For them, a sector covering the whole country was a cluster. As a result, each agency implemented a cluster strategy according to its understanding.

(b) Fragmented implementation. Cross-ministerial policy coordination has been a major problem in Thailand. Though clustering was assigned as a strategic government policy, and the NESDB oversaw the supposedly integrated national cluster strategy, its implementation was still incoherent.

(c) Lack of champions and trust in the private sector. Firms in the same cluster usually saw others as competitors, making it quite difficult for them to collaborate. The overseas Chinese-Thais, the dominant group of entrepreneurs in the country, collaborated more with firms in the same family clans than with outsiders (see Intarakumnerd 2006).

(d) Limited support from the local governments. Unlike in other countries, the local governments in Thailand have a short development history. Until recently, local governments had very limited roles and budgets. Later, even though their role and budgetary authority expanded, administrators of local governments had neither any understanding of, nor paid attention to, the cluster concept.

(e) Limited linkages between universities and public research institutes as knowledge providers, and private firms. The relationship between universities and public research institutes, and firms in Thailand, was relatively weak. It was based on private relationships rather than organizational ones. Most of them were ad hoc and concentrated on training and consultancy rather than long-term collaborative R&D. Therefore, universities and government research organizations were not usually agents in clusters. The knowledge flows from them which could help to revitalize firms in clusters were quite limited.

The Thaksin regime also had negative impacts on innovation system, the major one is pervasive corruption. It did not only increase the scale of old types of corruption such as bribery, but also induced new ones such as "policy corruption" (implementing government policies that are beneficial to the ruling party's financiers), corruption involving conflicts of interest (such as concluding trade agreements that benefited businesses owned by core party leaders or their relatives), "access corruption" (unequal access to government data and state mechanisms which are used to benefit politicians' cronies), and others (Boonmi 2006). The corruption allegation was very much believed and it appalled many people, especially the middle class. The military subsequently used it as a pretext to oust the Thaksin government in September 2006. Therefore, unlike the experiences of East Asian NIEs, changes under the Thaksin era failed to instil an effective learning process that led to successful catching up.

Another cause of systemic learning is the change in the external environment. The economic crisis in 1997 was a major shock to the Thai economy and a wake-up call to all actors in the Thai NIS, especially private sector firms which had to face strong international competition. More intense competition in the global market and the economic crisis in 1997 have, to some degree, led to a change in behaviour among Thai firms. The first innovation survey indicates that more than 80 per cent of R&D performing firms expressed strong interest in increasing their spending in the following three years. This finding is supported by studies of Thai firms after the 1997 economic crisis (see, for example, Thailand Development Research Institute 1998; Arnold et al. 2000). It shows a few interesting phenomena:

(a) Several large conglomerates recently increased their R&D activities. After the crisis they changed their long-standing attitude of relying on off-the-shelf foreign technologies, to developing in-house R&D capabilities.

(b) A number of smaller companies recently increased their technological efforts by collaborating with universities' R&D groups in order to stay ahead in the market or enter a more profitable market sector.

(c) Recently, several subcontracting suppliers in the automobile and electronics industries were forced by their TNC customers/partners to increase their efforts in modifying product design and improving efficiency, and were able to absorb the design and know-how from foreign experts.

(d) There were emerging new start-up firms (with fewer than fifty employees) relying on their own design, engineering, or development activities. These companies were managed by entrepreneurs having a strong R&D background from studying or working abroad. Many of them were "fabless" (no fabrication activities) companies.

A more recent study by NSTDA's researchers also indicates the positive change of Thai firms. Several locally owned OEM manufacturers experiencing external pressure, especially from foreign customers that adopted global sourcing strategies, started to develop products through their own designs and brand names (see Intarakumnerd and Virasa 2002).

4. CONCLUSION

In conclusion, one cannot argue that Thailand has succeeded in catching up with the forerunner countries in terms of industrial development. It has also fallen behind other Newly Industrializing Economies in Asia. From the innovation system perspective, the reason for its unsuccessful catching up is the country's long-standing weak and fragmented national innovation system. The learning process in the system is very slow in moving towards a stronger and more coherent one.

Nonetheless, the learning process has started and Thailand's national innovation system is in transition. The passive and slow technological learning of firms, ineffective and incoherent government policies, isolated education and training institutes, technologically unsupportive and risk-averse financial institutions, incompetent trade/industry associations, and an unfavourable institutional context have been perpetuated circumstances for the past fifty years of Thailand's industrialization. These have begun to change. One of the main actors of the NIS — the government — spearheads the change. Though it has several drawbacks, a major shift in government policies and practices encourages and pressures other actors of the system to change as well. The economic crisis in 1997 can be considered a blessing in disguise as this enormous external shock stimulated positive changes in the behaviour of actors in the NIS. A certain number of private firms in particular started to change their views on technology accumulation and have started putting more effort in developing their indigenous technological capabilities, which is the foundation for catching up.

However, the transformation of Thai NIS is slow and difficult. The coup in late 2006, in a way, demonstrates the resistance from the "long-established" parts of the actors in the NIS. Coup leaders and sympathizers (the military, government officials, old-family business elites, university professors, and NGOs leaders) are the ones who have been pressurized to change under the Thaksin era.

Notes

1. For the first survey, a total of 2,166 firms were selected, using stratified random sampling based on firm size and industry, from the top 13,450 companies by revenue in 1999. It basically included all firms with total revenues of over 12 million baht as reported to the Commercial Registration Department. Of the 2,166 firms sampled, a total of 1,019 completed questionnaires were received — a 47 per cent response rate. Of these, 223 firms carried out innovation activities. For the second survey, the sampling framework of firms was drawn up based on the first survey plus firms with annual revenue of at least 12 million baht. The sampling frame in the manufacturing sector consisted of 14,870 firms (including 1,019 manufacturing firms which responded to the first survey). For the service sector, a total of 6,082 firms were selected from 26,162 firms. The overall response rate received for both sectors is 37 per cent with 2,246 completed questionnaires returned. Of these, 261 carried out innovation activities.
2. The tambon is a unit of local government administration. One tambon comprises several villages.
3. OEM and ODM are specific forms of subcontracting. Under Original Equipment Manufacture (OEM), a latecomer firm produces a finished product to the precise specification of a foreign transnational corporation, which will market under its brand name via its own distribution channels. Under Original-Design Manufacturer (ODM), a latecomer firm carries out most or all product design (Hobday 1995, p. 37).
4. These include National Science and Technology Development Agency, Thailand Institute of Scientific and Technological Research, Synchrotron National Research Laboratory, National Institute of Metrology, and Geo-Informatics and Space Technology Development Agency.

References

"About Kenan Institute Asia 'Your knowledge partner'". (n.d.). Available at <http://www.kiasia.org/aboutus/index.html> (accessed 24 July 2003).

"About TPA". (23 July 2003). Available at <http://www.tpa.or.th/newtpa/about/main_about.html>. Accessed 24 July 2003.

Advance Research. *The Study of SMEs in Thailand*. Report submitted to the Department of Industrial Promotion, the Ministry of Industry, Thailand, Advance Research, 1997.

Altenburg et al. "Strengthening Knowledge-Based Competitive Advantages in Thailand". GDI Working Paper 1/2004, German Development Institute, Bonn, Germany, 2004.

Amsden, A. *Asia's Next Giant: South Korea and Late Industrialisation*. New York: Oxford University Press, 1989.

Amsden, A. and T. Hikino. "Borrowing Technology or Innovating: An Exploration of the Two Paths to Industrial Development". In *Learning and Technological Change*, edited by R. Thomson. New York: St. Martin's Press, 1993.

Arnold, E. et al. "Enhancing Policy and Institutional Support for Industrial Technology Development in Thailand: The Overall Policy Framework and the Development of the Industrial Innovation System". World Bank, 2000.

Bell, M. "Learning and Accumulation of Technological Capacity of Developing Countries". In *Technological Capability in the Third World*, edited by M. Fransman and K. King. London: Macmillan, 1984.

―――. "Knowledge-Capabilities, Innovation and Competitiveness in Thailand: Transforming the Policy Process". A report for the National Science and Technology Development Agency (Thailand). World Bank, 2002.

Bell, M. and D. Scott-Kemmis. "Technological Capacity and Technical Change". Draft Working Paper No. 1, 2, 4, and 6. Report on Technology Transfer in Manufacturing Industry in Thailand, Science Policy Research Unit, University of Sussex, the United Kingdom, 1985.

Boonmi, T. " 'Thaksinocrony' Rules Thailand". *The Nation*, 24 March 2005, p. 23.

Brooker Group Public Company Limited. "Technology Innovation of Industrial Enterprises in Thailand". Final Report submitted to National Sciene and Technology Development Agency, September 2001, Thailand.

Brooker Group Public Company Limited. "Thailand's 2nd R&D/Innovation Survey in Manufacturing and Service Sectors and Database Development". Final Report submitted to National Sciene and Technology Development Agency, May 2003, Thailand.

Chang, H. *The Political Economic of Industrial Policy*. London: Macmillan, 1994.

―――. "Institutional Structure and Economic Performance: Some Theoretical and Policy Lessons from the Experience of the Republic of Korea". *Asia Pacific Development Journal* 4, no. 1 (1997): 39–56.

Chantramonklasri, N. "Technological Responses to Rising Energy Prices: A Study of Technological Capability and Technological Change Efforts in Energy-Intensive Manufacturing Industries in Thailand". Unpublished D.Phil. thesis., Science Policy Research Unit, University of Sussex, Brighton, U.K., 1985.

Chotiya, P. "Changing Role of Provincial Business". In *Political Change in Thailand*, edited by K. Hewison, pp. 258–59. London: Routledge, 1997.

College of Management. "S&T Needs and Production of Manpower in the Manufacturing Sector". Draft Final Report submitted to National Science and Technology Development Agency, Thailand (in Thai), June 2003.

Dahlman, C. and P. Brimble. "Technology Strategy and Policy for Industrial Competitiveness: A Case Study of Thailand". Paper prepared for the World Bank, World Bank, the United States, April 1990.

Dahlman, C. et al. "Technology Strategy and Policy for Industrial Competitiveness: A Case Study of Thailand, in Decision and Change in Thailand: Three Studies in Support of the Seventh Plan". World Bank's Report, World Bank, the United States, 1991.

Doner, R. "Politics and the Growth of Local Capital in Southeast Asia: Auto Industries in the Philippines and Thailand". In *Southeast Asian Capitalists, Southeast Asia Program* (SEAP), edited by R. McVey. New York: Cornell University Press, 1992.

East Asia Analytical Unit. *Overseas Chinese Business Networks in Asia*. Department of Foreign Affairs and Trade, Australia, 1995.

Evans, P. "The Future of the Developmental State". The *Korean Journal of Policy Studies* 4, no. 2 (1989): 129–46.

———. "Transferable Lessons? Re-examining the Institutional Prerequisites of East Asian Economic Policies". *Development Studies* 34, no. 6 (1998): 66–86.

Federation of Thai Industries. Available at <http://www.fti.or.th/nfti/org/index.html> (n.d.; accessed 24 July 2003).

Freeman, N. *Constraints on Thailand's Equity Market as an Allocator of Foreign Investment Capital: Some Implications on Post-Crisis Southeast Asia*. Singapore: Institute of Southeast Asian Studies, 2000.

Goto, A. "Cooperative Research in Japanese Manufacturing Industries". In *Innovation In Japan*, edited by A. Goto and H. Odagiri. Oxford: Oxford University Press, 1997.

Government Information Office. "Taiwan's Educational Development and Present Situation". Available at <http://www.gio.gov.tw/taiwan-website/5-gp/yearbook/chpt17.htm>. Accessed 24 June 2003.

Hobday, M. *Innovation in East Asia: The Challenge to Japan*. Aldershot, UK: Edward Elgar, 1995.

Hou, C. and S. Gee. "National Systems Supporting Technical Advance in Industry: The Case of Taiwan". In *National Innovation System: A Comparative Analysis*, edited by R. Nelson. Oxford: Oxford University Press, 1993.

Intarakumnerd, P. "Thai Telecommunication Business Groups: An Analysis of the Factors Shaping the Direction of their Growth Paths". Unpublished D.Phil. thesis. Science Policy Research Unit, University of Sussex, Brighton, the United Kingdom, 2000.

Intarakumnerd, P. et al. "National Innovation System in Less Successful Developing Countries: The Case of Thailand". *Research Policy* 31, nos. 8–9 (2002): 1445–57.

Intarakumnerd, P. and T. Virasa. "Taxonomy of Government Policies and Measures in Supporting Technological Capability Development of Latecomer Firms". A paper presented at the 6th International Conference on *Technology Policy and Innovation*, August 2002, Kansai, Japan, 2002.

Intellectual Property Institute. "Science and Technology Policy in Thailand". A report to the Ministry of Science and Technology, Bangkok, Thailand, 2003.

"Invigorating Thai Business-ITB". (n.d.). Available at <http://hypershop.tripod.com/itbproject.html> (accessed 24 July 2003).

Johnson, C. *MITI and the Japanese Miracle: The Growth of Industrial Policy*, 1925–1975. California: Stanford University Press, 1982.

Kim, L. "National System of Industrial Innovation: Dynamics of Capability Building in Korea". In *National Innovation System: A Comparative Analysis*, edited by R. Nelson. Oxford: Oxford University Press, 1993.

———. *Imitation to Innovation: The Dynamics of Korea's Technological Learning*. Cambridge, US: Harvard Business School Press, 1997.

Kim, L. and R. Nelson, eds. *Technology, Learning, and Innovation: Experiences of Newly Industrializing Economies*. Cambridge: Cambridge University Press, 2000.

Lall, S. *Learning From the Asian Tigers: Studies in Technology and Industrial Policy*. London: Macmillan Press, 1996.

———. "Thailand's Manufacturing Competitiveness: A Preliminary Overview". Unpublished Paper for Conference on Thailand's Dynamic Economic Recovery and Competitiveness. Paper for Session 4, Bangkok, 20–21 May 1998.

Laothamatas, A. *Business Associations and the New Political Economy of Thailand: From Bureaucratic Polity to Liberal Corporatism*. Boulder, CO: Westview Press, 1992.

Lauridsen, L. "Policies and Institutions of Industrial Deepening and Upgrading in Taiwan III-Technological Upgrading". International Development Studies Working Paper No. 13. Roskilde University, Denmark, 1999.

———. "Industrial Policies, Political Institutions and Industrial Development in Thailand 1959–1991". International Development Studies Working Paper No. 21. Roskilde University, Roskilde, Denmark, 2000.

———. "Coping with the Triple Challenge of Globalization, Liberalization and Crisis: The Role of Industrial Technology Policies and Technology Institutions in Thailand". *European Journal of Development Research* 14, no. 1 (June 2002): 101–25.

Ministry of Science and Technology (MOST), Republic of Korea. "Science and Technology Policy in Korea: Vision and Strategies for the 21st Century". Available at <http://unpan1.un.org/intradoc/groups/public/documents/apcity/ unpan008041.pdf>. Accessed February 2003.

Mukdapitak, Y. "The Technology Strategies of Thai Firms". Unpublished D.Phil. thesis. Science Policy Research Unit, University of Sussex, Brighton, the United Kingdom, 1994.

Odagiri, H. and A. Goto. "The Japanese System of Innovation: Past, Present and Future". In *National Innovation System: A Comparative Analysis*, edited by R. Nelson. Oxford: Oxford University Press, 1993.

Phasukavanich, C. "The Pace of Thailand through the Year 2020". Powerpoint presentation, Bangkok, Thailand, 20 May 2003.

Phongpaichit, P. and C. Baker. *Thailand: Economy and Politics*. Singapore: Oxford University Press, 1997*a*.

———. "Power in Transition: Thailand in 1990's". In *Political Change in Thailand*, edited by K. Hewison. London: Routledge, 1997*b*.

Phuchatkan (Thai daily economic newspaper), 14–15 November 1992, p. 4.

Samudavanija, C. *State and Society: Triple Characteristics of Thai State in a Plural Society* (in Thai). Bangkok: Chulalongkorn University, 1990.

Schiller, D. "The Potential to Upgrade Thai Innovation System by University-industry Linkages". *Asian Journal of Technology Innovation* 14, no. 2 (2006): 67–92.

Science and Technology Policy Institute. "Review of Science and Technology Policy for Industrial Competitiveness in Korea". A report prepared by Science and Technology Policy Institute, Seoul, South Korea, 1995.

Science and Technolog Policy Institute. "Korean Innovation Survey: Manufacturing Sector". A report prepared by Science and Technolog Policy Institute, Seoul, South Korea, 2002.

Sripaipan, C., S. Vanichseni, and Y. Mukdapitak, eds. *Technological Innovation Policy of Thailand, Bangkok* (Thai version). Thailand: National Science and Technology Development Agency, 1999.

Suehiro, A. "Capitalist Development in Post-war Thailand: Commercial Bankers, Industrial Elite, and Agribusiness Groups". In *Southeast Asian Capitalists*, edited by R. McVey. New York: Cornell University Press, 1992.

———. "Family Business Reassessed: Corporate Structure and Late-starting Industrialisation in Thailand". *Developing Economies* 41, no. 4 (1993): 378–407.

Taiwan Venture Capital Association (TVCA). Available at <http://www.tvca.org.tw/> (accessed 24 July 2003).

Thailand Development Research Institute. "The Development of Thailand's Technology Capability in Industry". Reports Volumes 2–5, Bangkok, Thailand, 1989.

———. "Effective Mechanisms for Supporting Private Sector Technology Development and Needs for Establishing Technology Development Financing Corporation". A report submitted to National Science and Technology Development Agency, Bangkok, Thailand, 1998.

Tiralap, A. "The Economics of the Process of Technological Change of the Firm: The Case of the Electronics Industry in Thailand". Unpublished D.Phil. thesis. Science Policy Research Unit, University of Sussex, Brighton, the United Kingdom, 1990.

TPA News Services. (23 July 2003). Available at <http://www.tpa.or.th/newtpa/services/main_services.html>. Accessed 24 July 2003.

Turpin, et al. "Improving the System of Financial Incentives for Enhancing Thailand's Industrial Technological Capabilities". A report prepared for the World Bank, Washington D.C., the United States, June 2002.

Vongpivat, P. "A National Innovation System Model: An Industrial Development in Thailand". Unpublished Ph.D. thesis, The Fletcher School of Law and Diplomacy, Tufts University, Cambridge, the United States, 2003.

Wong, P. *National Systems of Innovation: The Case of Singapore*. Seoul: Science and Technology Policy Institute, 1995.

———. "National Innovation Systems for Rapid Technological Catch-up: An Analytical Framework and a Comparative Analysis of Korea, Taiwan, and Singapore". A paper presented at the DRUID's summer conference, Rebild, Denmark, 1999.

3

INDUSTRIAL UPGRADING AND EDUCATIONAL UPGRADING
Two Critical Issues for Thailand

Bruno Jetin

Thailand can no longer rely on cheap labour and fiscal incentives to maintain a continuous flow of foreign direct investment (FDI) which, as Chapter 1 has shown, has been one of its major engines of growth. In neighbouring Asian countries, multinational firms can find cheaper labour and more tax exemptions, while developed countries offer better competitive advantages in terms of knowledge, productive organization and infrastructure. To free itself from being sandwiched, Thailand must upgrade its industrial base and improve its productivity. But this is only possible if Thailand upgrades its education and scientific systems at the same time and combine them in a coherent way, which is not the case today. Primary education is now universal, but not secondary education, and higher education does not play the role that one could expect in developing scientific capabilities. What is worse, the problem is not only quantitative, but also qualitative. The quality of education in Thailand is poor for a number of reasons among which are social inequalities, too much emphasis given to learning by rote of past and sometimes dogmatic knowledge, a shortage of skilled teachers, and above all, the lack of critical thinking and initiative, which are so important for creativity, and in particular, scientific creativity. The education system also suffers from an institutional disorganization that the ongoing decentralization reform will worsen. Much the same can be said of higher education. The absence of a long-term policy on the part of the ministry of education and the ministry of science, and the excessive importance placed on the autonomy of universities make it nearly impossible to organize a coherent and national supply of scientists and engineers capable of satisfying the needs of private companies and contributing to the accumulation of scientific knowledge for converging towards the establishment of the kind of national innovation system discussed in the previous chapter. This does not mean that Thailand cannot change the present situation. Fortunately, Thailand is not an overly indebted country and has the fiscal means for an ambitious education and scientific policy. The issues at stake are essentially a question of public policy. But as education was not put on the agenda early enough, industrial upgrading did not reach the expected level.

This chapter will be organized as follows: Section 1 will assess the achievements of the Thai education system from an international perspective, and the education and skill levels of the workforce. For this purpose, we will use national and international data series extensively. The main lesson here is that Thailand lags behind compared with Asian countries and has to improve its quality of education. Section 2 makes an assessment of the present state of the Thai industry and productivity. The main lesson here is that the contribution of productivity to industrial growth has been low and sometimes even negative. One way to improve this poor score is to strengthen labour productivity through the incorporation of better educated and higher skilled workers.

1. UPGRADING THE EDUCATION SYSTEM

Thailand, like other medium-income countries in Asia, has successfully achieved universal primary education. For these countries, the focus now has shifted to secondary education for a number of reasons. First, some of the children who completed primary education are now seeking secondary education to get access to better jobs. Second, because of the ICT revolution and increased competition due to globalization, economies increasingly need a more sophisticated labour force, equipped with new knowledge that cannot be obtained in only primary school or low-quality secondary school programmes. Good quality and complete secondary education is now the minimum standard for entering the labour market. Third, secondary education is also a bridge to tertiary education and the key building block of national technological capabilities.

Thus, for all these reasons, secondary education has turned critical and justify a special emphasis in our evaluation of the Thai education system. In the Thai context, upgrading education means increasing dramatically the number of students who complete upper secondary education, and improving the quality of secondary education.

This has not been the case until now. Unlike OECD countries and many East Asian countries that have followed a pyramid pattern,[1] Thailand took a different path. The big push towards universal primary education took place only as recently as the eighties and completed in the nineties. But then, the focus shifted towards tertiary education, at the expense of the expansion of secondary education (De Ferranti et al. 2003). This means that distribution of educational attainment was squeezed in the middle. The consequence is a lack of skilled workers and a shortage of good students for tertiary science education.

Productivity and Investment Climate Surveys (PICS) conducted by the World Bank show that in Thailand 75 per cent of the workers in the manufacturing sectors are unskilled workers and only 11 per cent are skilled workers, compared with 49 per cent and 31 per cent respectively in Malaysia (World Bank 2006a, p. 98). Again, this is characteristic of the present stage of the Thai industrialization process that relied merely on the incorporation of unskilled rural workers migrating to the cities. But if Thailand wants to go beyond the assembly stage and escape from competition from lower-cost assemblers, such as China and Vietnam, it will have to increase the size and quality of its labour force.

1.1 The Thai Education System from an International Perspective

Thailand has achieved remarkable success in attaining universal primary education. More generally, it can be said that the objectives of "Education for all" that corresponds to the "Millennium Development Goals" are already fulfilled. Table 3.1 shows how Thailand compared with other Asian countries at different development stages for the year 2004, according

Table 3.1

Education System and Background Characteristics of Selected Asian Countries, Reference Year 2004

Countries and regions	Background Population in million 2004	Background GNP per capita (PPP) 2004	Adult Literacy[1] Total	Adult Literacy[1] GPI (F/M)	Primary GER (%) 2004	Primary GPI (F/M) 2004	Secondary GER (%)	Secondary GPI (F/M)	Tertiary GER (%)	Tertiary GPI (F/M)	Teaching Staff Primary school teachers, female % 2001	Teaching Staff Pupil/teacher ratio in primary schools	Finance Total public expenditure on education as % of GDP	Finance Total public expenditure on education as a % of total government expenditure
East Asia														
Cambodia	14,071	2,423	73.6	0.76	137	0.92	44	0.74	3	0.46	41	53	1.9	14.6
China	1,307,989	5,003[3]	90.9	0.91	118	1.00	73	1.00	19	0.85	53	21	3.2[6]	13[2]
Indonesia	222,781	3,361[3]	87.9	0.90	116	0.98	62	0.99	16	0.80	52	20	0.9[3]	9[4]
Hong Kong	7,040	30,822	n.a	n.a	108	0.94	85	0.97	32	0.97	78	19	4.7	23.3
Japan	128,085	29,251	n.a	n.a	100	1.00	102	1.00	54	0.89		20	3.6	9.8
Korea	47,817	20,499	98	0.98	105	0.99	91	1.00	89	0.61	72	30	4.6	16.5
Laos	5,924	1,954	66.4	0.72	116	0.88	46	0.76	6	0.63	44	31	2.3	11.7
Malaysia	25,347	10,276	88.7	0.93	93	1.00	70	1.11	29	1.29	67	19	6.2	25.2
The Philippines	83,054	4,614	92.6	1.02	113	0.99	84	1.10	29	1.28	87	35	2.7	16.4
Thailand	64,233	8,090	92.6	0.95	99	0.96	77	1.00	41	1.17	58	21	4.2	27.5
Vietnam	84,238	2,490[3]	90.3	0.93	98	0.93	73	0.95	10	0.77	78	23	3.2[3]	12.6[3]
East Asia and the Pacific Average	2,086,748	5,354	92	0.93	113	0.99	73	1.0	23	0.89		22		
South Asia														
Bangladesh	141,822	1,870	41.1	0.62	109	1.03	69	1.19	7	0.28	36	55	2.5	14.2
India	1,103,371	3,139	61	0.65	107	0.94	70	0.82	11	0.67	40	41	3.8	10.7
Nepal	27,133	1,490	48.6	0.56	113.9	0.88	44[7]	0.77[7]	6	0.40	30	40	3.4[2]	14.9[3]
Pakistan	157,935	2,225	41.5	0.53	82	0.73	32	0.70	3	0.80		37	2	10.9
Sri Lanka	20,743	4,390	92.1	0.95	102	0.99	98	1.00				23	3.1[5]	
South and West Asia Average	1,528,108		59	0.66	110	0.91	51	0.83	11	0.7		39		
World average			82	0.89	106	0.94	65	0.94	24	1.03		26		

Notes: 1. 2000–2004 Average   2. 2 data for 1999   3. data for 2003   4. estimation by ISU for 2002   5. data for 1998   6. estimation by OECD for 2001   7. average of 2003–2005, based on UNESCO data.

Source: Computed by the author from data of UNESCO database (several years) and from data in UNESCO 2005, UNESCO 2006.

to several indicators that were deemed relevant by the United Nations Educational, Scientific and Cultural Organization (UNESCO) for the completion of "Education for all" goals and for the quality of education (see UNESCO 2005). It can be seen that there is a clear pattern of educational achievements according to the level of income per capita. East Asia in general fares much better than South Asia in terms of adult literacy and education enrolment because South Asia is much poorer. Nearly all East and South Asian countries had gross enrolment rates (GER)[2] close or superior to 100 per cent which means that they had achieved universal access to primary education.[3] For secondary education, gross enrolment rates are significantly below 100 per cent for Cambodia, China, Indonesia, Laos, and South Asian countries (with the exception of Sri Lanka). Universal access to secondary education in these poorer countries is far from being achieved. For tertiary education, the differences in GER are even higher. Gender discrimination, measured by the Gender Parity Index (GPI)[4] is interesting because there is no real universal education without the eradication of gender discrimination, but also because gender discrimination is generally an indicator of the poor quality of education (UNESCO 2005). A majority of countries still has not achieved gender parity in primary education, and the situation is usually worsen in secondary and tertiary education. The percentage of female teachers and the pupil/teacher ratio in primary education are also indicators of quality. According to UNESCO (2005), female teachers in primary schools have a positive influence on education scores, especially for female students. With some exceptions, one can see that richer countries usually have a higher percentage of female teachers in primary schools. Things are more complex with the pupil/teacher ratio. Theoretically, a low ratio is better for the quality of education, and a very high ratio, like in Bangladesh, India, Nepal, Pakistan, Cambodia, or the Philippines, signals a poor quality of basic education. However the corollary is not true. A low ratio may be preferable, but is not the guarantee of good education if it reflects the predominance of rural schools where the number of pupils is low, but school conditions are also usually bad. Keeping this in mind, one can see that East Asian countries in general have a lower ratio than South Asian countries, which creates good conditions for good quality education. Finally, public spending on education shows that richer countries tend to spend more on education (as a share of GDP) and some of them such as Hong Kong, Malaysia, and Thailand dedicate a large share of total government expenditure to education, signalling that it is a national priority.

How does Thailand score against this regional background? It can be seen that in 2004, Thailand had a high level of adult literacy (92.6 per cent), had completed universal primary education, and had a high gross enrolment rate in secondary education (77 per cent), which is slightly higher than the regional average (73 per cent) but inferior to the most advanced Asian countries such as Japan, Korea, and Hong Kong, or even the Philippines. In tertiary education, the gross enrolment rate is among the highest in the region, putting Thailand ahead of competitors with comparable GDP per capita, but with it still below Japan and Korea. At all levels, discrimination against girls is low (GPI close to 1), and there are even more female students than male students at the tertiary level.[5]

These goods results are recent and need qualifications. First, until 1977, Thailand only had four years of compulsory education (until Grade 4 in primary school). From 1978 until 1992, compulsory education was extended to six years (until Grade 6 or the entire primary school education). From January 2003, a new compulsory Education Act adopted in 1999 requires all children aged from seven to sixteen to be enrolled in basic education institutions, except for those who have already completed Grade 9 at age fifteen. Actually Grade 9, which corresponds to the end of lower secondary education, is presently the end of compulsory education, which has been extended to nine years of schooling (from Grade 1 to Grade 9). To help families comply with the law, the Thai state in October 2002 granted, for the first time in Thai history, free access for all students to "basic education", which covers six years of primary and six years of secondary education.

As of May 2004, this subsidy was extended to two years of pre-primary schooling so by now the provision of free basic education has been extended to fourteen years.

These institutional evolutions help explain why the progress in education through the generations has been slow. Most Thai people have the level of education required by law at the time they were in school. And because complete primary education was made mandatory only as late as in 1998 without subsequent extensions until 1992, secondary education enrolment stagnated throughout this period.

This explains why, despite recent improvements, the legacy of the past is still dragging Thailand backward. Figure 3.1 shows that in the fifties Thailand was counted among the countries which had the lowest enrolment in secondary school (6 per cent), together with China, Malaysia,

Figure 3.1
Gross Enrolment Ratio (GER) in Secondary Education in Middle-income Asian Countries

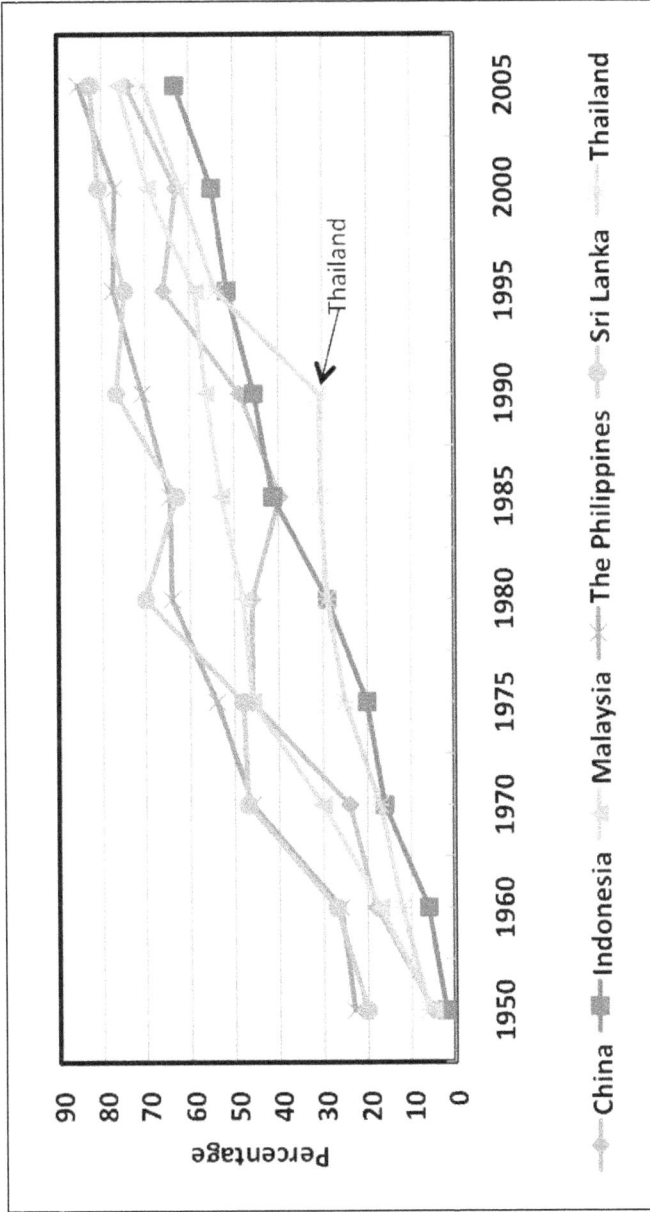

Source: Computed by the author from World Bank's "Edstats", UNESCO data center, and other sources, see annex 1.

Indonesia, and below all the other lower middle-income countries.[6] However, the gap with the other countries was not important and could have been filled in subsequent years. But this has not happened, on the contrary, Thailand's lag has worsened in the sixties and seventies, and especially the eighties. Indonesia overtook Thailand in 1980 and Thailand became the lower middle-income country with the lowest enrolment ratio in secondary education. In the eighties, this ratio remained constant at around 30 per cent while in all other comparable countries it was above 40 per cent and rising. The eighties can be deemed the "lost decade" for Thai secondary education. The absence of the extension of compulsory education to secondary education is to blame for this stagnation.

This situation was not a fatality due to poverty. In the Philippines and Sri Lanka, enrolment in secondary education had always been higher and even reached 70 per cent in 1990, 40 per cent higher than the Thai level. Economic reasons cannot be invoked because these countries were not richer than Thailand. The real reason is simply that education was not a political priority in Thailand for a long time. Because universal primary education became mandatory only after 1977, secondary school generalization suffered a historical delay in Thailand compared with other Asian countries at the same development stage. It was only in the nineties, after the extension of mandatory school to nine years in 1989 (until Grade 9), that enrolment in secondary education jumped to 50 per cent by 1995 and then 70 per cent by 2005.[7] Thai enrolment in secondary schools has now converged with the average of low middle-income Asian countries. But the initial delay in generalizing secondary education in the eighties still takes its toll.

Figure 3.2 adapted from the World Bank (2006c) shows the level of education of the adult working population (twenty-five to sixty-five years) for the period 1999–2004, according to country.[8] With an average of 7.1 years of education in 2002, Thailand ranked among the lowest, on a par with Indonesia (7.2 years), which has less than half the GDP per capita of Thailand, and below Vietnam (8.8 years), with a GDP per capita that is more than three times lower. Only Cambodia fared worse. Clearly, the level of education in Thailand is not as high as its level of development would enable it to have. Figure 3.3 shows that 50.5 per cent of the Thai adult working population has not even completed primary education, and 16.4 per cent has completed only primary education. The contrast with Vietnam, one of Thailand's newest competitors in the region, is

Figure 3.2
Average Years of Education among the Adult Working Population

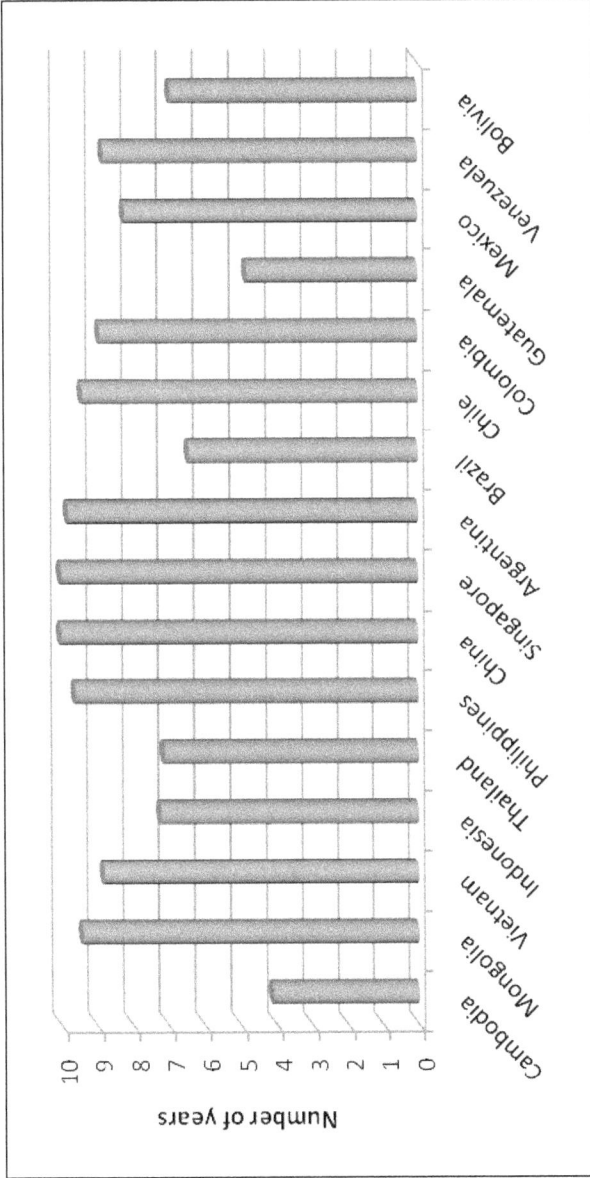

Source: Adapted by the author from World Bank, 2006c, based on various household surveys in the period 1999–2004.

Figure 3.3
Stock of the Working Population with No Education or with Primary Education Only

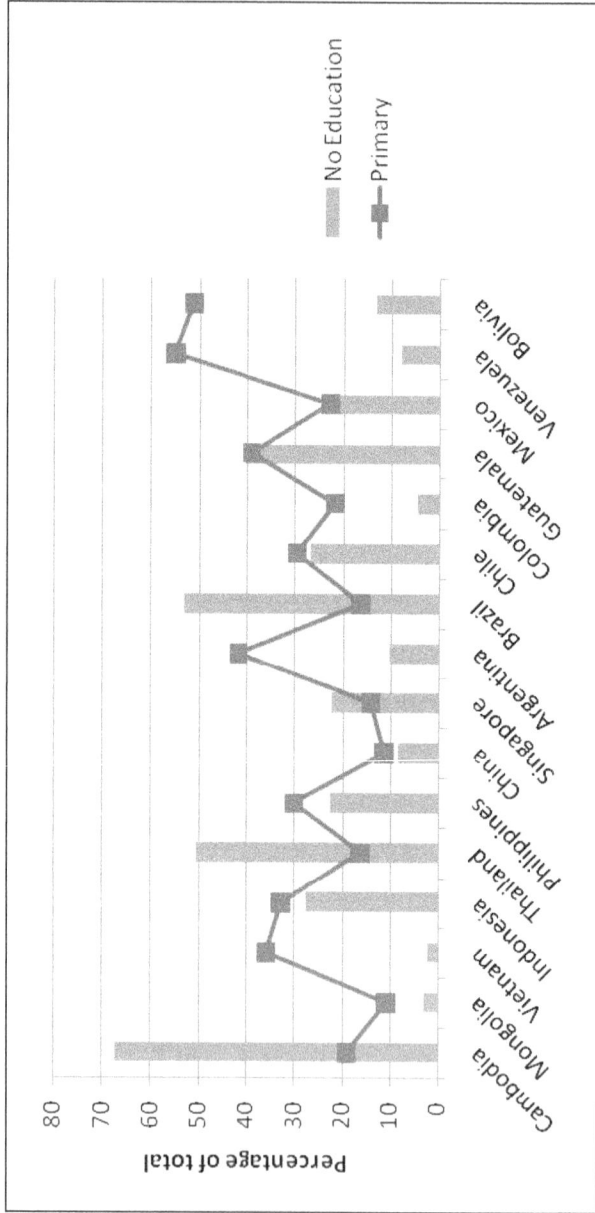

Source: Adapted by the author from World Bank, 2006c (Table 2.2, p. 47), based on various household surveys in the period 1999–2004.

striking. Only 2.2 per cent of the adult working Vietnamese has not completed even primary education, and 35.8 per cent has completed primary education.

Figure 3.4 shows that Thailand has one of the lowest percentages of adult working population having completed lower secondary education (LSEC, until Grade 9) and fares even worse for upper secondary education (USEC). For instance, 32.4 per cent of Chinese working population has achieved LSEC to be compared with 9.4 per cent only in Thailand. In Indonesia, 14.5 per cent of working population has completed USEC, almost double the share of Thai workers (7.5 per cent). Tertiary education shows a similar situation (see Figure 3.5). In the Philippines, 25.7 per cent of workers have tertiary education compared to only 10.4 per cent of Thai workers.

1.2 The Quality Problem

Measuring the quality of education is a complex task. It presuppose an agreement on the purposes of education and on the learning process, which seldom exists. For some, education should focus on preparing young people to get a job. This narrow definition limits education to the acquisition of what is thought to be useful knowledge. For others, education should also prepare the young to become independent citizens able to live in society. This broader definition of the purpose of education makes the assessment of the quality of education in a purely quantitative way more difficult. For instance, according to UNESCO (2005) "learning to know, learning to do, learning to be together and learning to be" are the four principal concepts that define the quality of education. This implies cognitive and non-cognitive skills, the latter being difficult to quantify by essence. The same difficulty holds true for learning. If we define learning in a very narrow way as the transfer of explicit knowledge by teachers to passive students who have to memorize it, then the scope of quality assessment will be very limited. If learning means acquiring explicit and tacit knowledge in a personal and collective way,[9] then the quality of an education system should be judged by its capacity to enable students to progress in the acquisition of knowledge so defined. And this is difficult to assess.

These are the reasons tests scores which are usually considered for international comparisons of education quality must be interpreted with

Figure 3.4
Stock of Secondary Education among the Adult Working Population

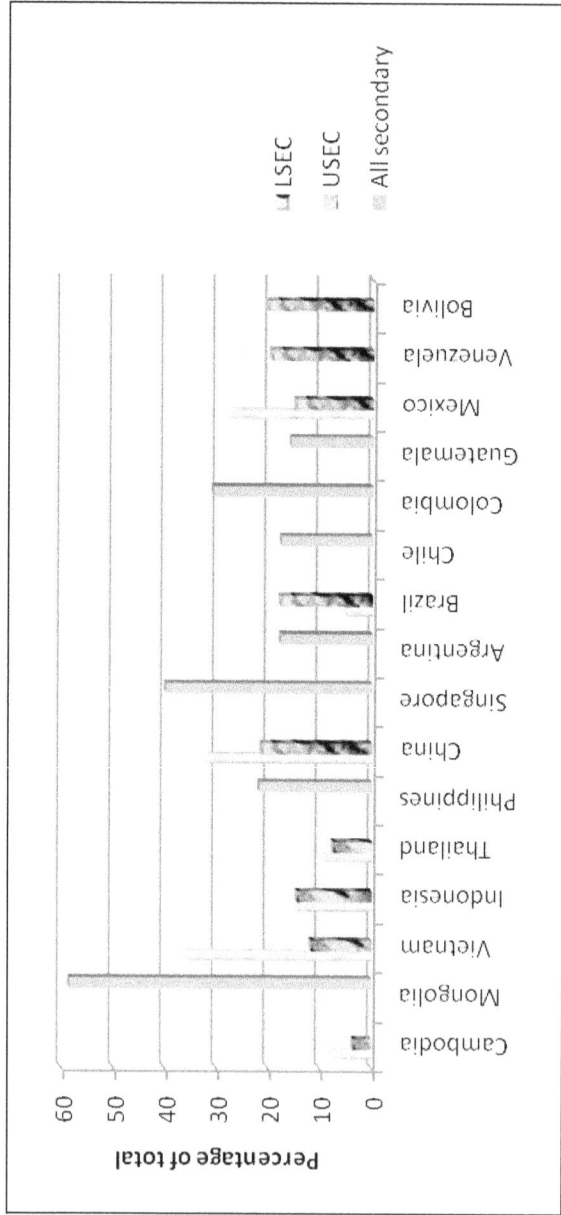

Source: Adapted by the author from World Bank, 2006c, based on various household surveys in the period 1999–2004.

Figure 3.5
Stock of Vocational and Technical and Tertiary Education among the Adult Working Population

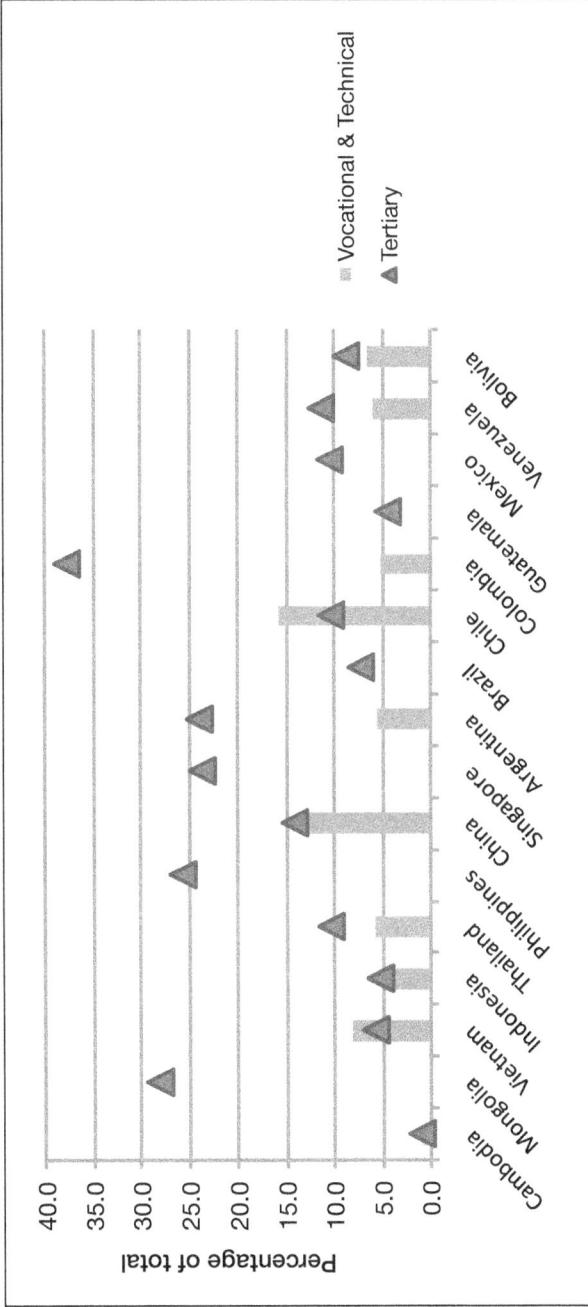

Source: Adapted by the author from World Bank, 2006c, based on various household surveys in the period 1999–2004.

precaution. They provide useful information about how well items in the curriculum are being learned and understood by students. "But they tell nothing about values, capacities or other non-cognitive skills that are also important aims of education" (UNESCO 2005, p. 46). In themselves, they also tell us nothing about the underlying causes of the registered results. What are the reasons for bad scores? Poor capabilities of students; poor quality of schools; or poor social conditions of students and their families? A combination of several elements, but which ones? To be useful, tests have to be confronted with relevant indicators that describe the main social features of students, their families, and their schools.

In the case of Thailand, two international tests are regularly performed: the PISA[10] and TIMSS[11] tests. When compared with other countries at similar income levels,[12] Thailand registers higher scores, which is a good point. But a comparison with the most successful East Asian countries shows how much Thailand has a lot more to improve (World Bank 2006*b*, p. 54). For PISA, 2003 scores in mathematics, Thailand, with 417 points ranks thirty-nine among forty-six countries above Brazil, Mexico, and Indonesia, but below the OECD (Organization for Economic Cooperation and Development) average (500 points) and far behind its Asian counterparts, Japan (553), Hong Kong (550), and Korea (542). There is a real quality gap among these countries. Moreover, very few Thai children score in the top proficiency levels. "For PISA, less than 10% of students scored beyond levels 4 in mathematics or reading (among six levels). This is in stark contrast to all three participating East Asian upper-income countries, where roughly 50% of students in mathematics and 40% in reading scored above this level". Worse, "a very large share of students is performing below acceptable proficiency level. Thailand has roughly 40% of students performing at or below the PISA level one (among 6 levels) in literacy and over 50% at or below level one in mathematics. To sum up, a vast proportion of students are functioning at, or below, the most basic level of language, mathematics and science ability" (World Bank 2006*b*, p. 59). The same holds true for TIMSS.

The bad quality of education in Thailand is the result of several factors, which the socio-economic features of the family stand prominently with teacher quality, the pedagogy used, and school characteristics. For instance, according to the Ministry of Education, only 4 per cent of teachers in lower secondary schools had a Master's degree and 11 per cent for upper secondary schools. For some, these Master degrees were obtained in "open universities" whose quality is dubious. In terms of pedagogy, section 22 of the 1989 educational reform promoted innovative ways of learning, centred on "self-development enabling learners to develop at their own pace and to maximise their potential" (OEC 2004, p. 75). In reality, these measures were not systematically applied. "Rote learning is pervasive even in the best schools, and innovative forms of learning are confined only to small segments. Vocational schools lack equipment, and teachers lack motivations" (S. Khoman 2005, p. 259). As for school characteristics, the lack of educational resources (computers, library material, multimedia resources, science laboratory equipment, and facilities for the fine arts) appear as the most important obstacles to student achievement.

More broadly, Ashvin Ahuja et al. (2006) have analysed PISA 2003 results for mathematics in Thailand to understand how school, family, and student characteristics interact and produce cognitive achievements.[13] 5,236 fifteen-year old students from 175 schools around Thailand have been tested. Students are divided into quintiles based on their mathematical scores, with 564 points for the top quintile, 328 points for the bottom quintile and an average of 423 points. Students from the bottom 20 per cent usually go to smaller schools (1,471 students on an average), where there is a higher students per teacher ratio (25.2) than in bigger schools (2,785 students on an average) frequented by students in the top 20 per cent (21.6 students per teacher). Figure 3.6 shows that more of those in the bottom 20 per cent study in small villages and small cities while more of students in the top 20 per cent study in big cities. Those in the first group have less qualified teachers in mathematics than those in the top 20 per cent and also lack an "adequate library" in their schools. Their family factors reveal that only 8 per cent have one parent with a university degree against 42 per cent of the top 20 per cent students. About half of the bottom 20 per cent have at least one parent working in a full-time job, which means that for the other half, neither the father nor the mother has a full-time job. They tend to have fewer books and to live a more isolated way than the top 20 per cent students. Their personal characteristics and attitudes complete the picture. They spent around half the time the top 20 per cent students spent at homework, more frequently arrived late at schools and had spent less time in kindergarten. Finally, 49 per cent thought that "school is a waste of time" against 27 per cent of the top 20 per cent.

Figure 3.6
Differences in Characteristics of Top/Bottom Performers in PISA Mathematics Test Scores (%)

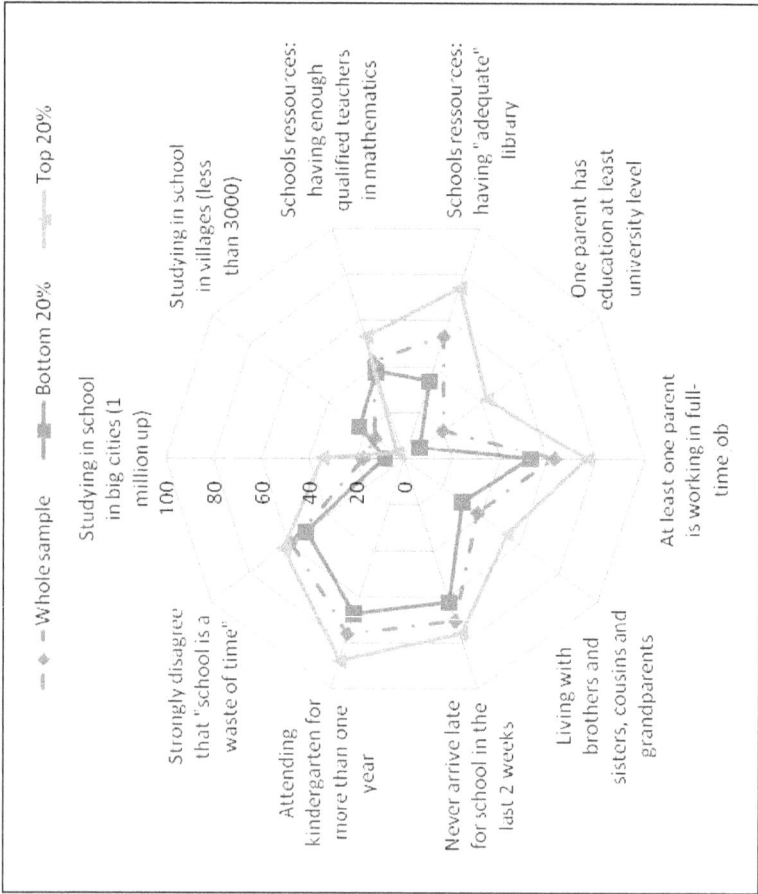

Source: Adapted by the author from Ahuja et al. (2006) with PISA 2003 data.

All these social characteristics converge to the conclusion that those who have the worst results in the PISA test suffer from social handicaps due to poverty and the geographical isolation that usually go together. This is confirmed by the fact that the cost of education remains the main obstacle to access to secondary education. Despite the government's commitment to twelve years of free education, non-tuition costs such as library fees, exam levies, and access to computers, meals, and transportations costs create too heavy a burden for poor families. The cost of school tuition and textbooks which are covered by the government for poor families represented only 19 per cent to 25 per cent of the total cost of sending a child to lower or upper secondary school (NSO 2002). The same survey pointed to the inability to pay the direct costs of education as the overwhelming reason for children completing an educational cycle (for instance, lower secondary) not progressing to the next educational level. According to the World Bank (2006b), the average expenditure per student at the secondary level was equal to about 2,300 baht in 2002 (US$65), but with those in the poorest quintile spending only 860 baht compared with 6,800 baht by those in the richest quintile, or close to eight times as much. This gap appears to have widened over time since in 1994 the gap was only four times as much. More recent data confirm this trend. According to A. Ahuja et al. (2006), sending children to public high school would cost a family around 2,500 baht per month directly and indirectly, from about 1,500 baht per month for lower secondary school. This is the major reason poor families decide to stop sending their children to school after compulsory education ends at Grade 9.

1.3 The Need for Scientific and Research Capabilities

History shows that countries that have climbed up the industrial ladder and caught up with more advanced countries had at least two things in common: One is the "rapid increase in the level of education and an emphasis on higher education in science and engineering. Another is the creation of public institutions to conduct research and provide services to industrial firms (UNIDO 2005). The reason is that innovative capabilities imply the practise of research which mobilizes both explicit and tacit knowledge.[14] Because tacit knowledge and a good part of explicit knowledge are "people embodied", the education system has an important role to play in producing skilled workers and researchers. In other words, as already stated in Chapter 2, creating a true National Innovation System (NIS) coherent with the education system is now a high priority on Thailand's agenda. Due to the cumulative nature of learning, the sooner a country starts increasing the level of education and building scientific capabilities, the higher its chances of engaging in a sustained catching up process. In this regard, Thailand's scores are mixed.

Several studies (Intarakumnerd et al. 2002; T. Altenburg et al. 2004; World Bank 2006*a*) point to the same hurdles in the creation of an efficient NIS in Thailand and the successful upgrading of its industries. First, the aggregate spending in Thailand on R&D as a percentage of GDP is low, and rising only slowly from a low base. "Most Thai firms, even large corporations, have a deep rooted attitude of not developing their own indigenous technological capabilities" and "want to rely on off-the-shelf imported technology mostly in the forms of machinery, and turn-key technology transfer from abroad or joint venture with foreign partners" (P. Intarakumnerd et al. 2002). Second, "foreign companies have transferred amazingly little tacit knowledge and technology, as evident from a handful of companies setting up research establishments in Thailand and from the scope of research undertaken" (World Bank 2006*a*). Third, there is no global and coherent scientific and industrial policy, but a multitude of ministers and institutions in charge of different aspects and sectors, with overlapping functions and weak coordination. Fourth, there is not enough linkage between public research institutes and universities, and private companies (Schiller 2006) and between companies themselves (Dhanani and Scholtès 2002).

International comparisons with other Asian, Latin American, and developed countries, are instructive. Figure 3.7 compares total expenditures on R&D as a percentage of GDP of selected countries, ranked by their GDP per capita in U.S. dollar at PPP (purchasing power parity) rates in 2003. The objective is not to prove a strict causality between GDP and R&D expenditures, which in the long-term work both ways, but to situate Thailand on an international scale.

Thailand dedicates 0.3 per cent of its GDP to R&D, which is very low and only slightly higher than Vietnam's expenditure (0.2 per cent), although its GDP per capita is about three times higher. One would expect Thailand to spend as much as one of its main competitors, Malaysia (0.7 per cent). The announcement by the Thai government in June 2007 to nearly double the budget of state-run R&D institutes over the next three years will raise

Figure 3.7
Total Expenditure on R&D as % of GDP in Selected Countries

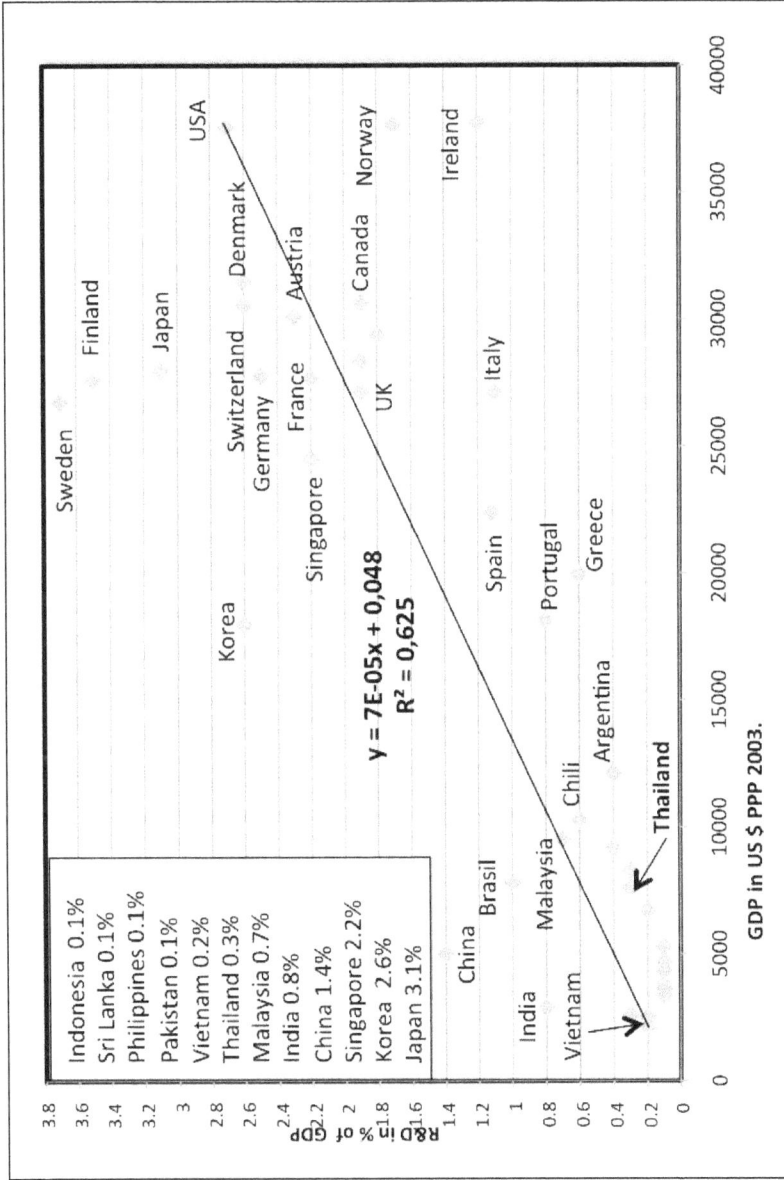

	R&D in % of GDP
Indonesia	0.1%
Sri Lanka	0.1%
Philippines	0.1%
Pakistan	0.1%
Vietnam	0.2%
Thailand	0.3%
Malaysia	0.7%
India	0.8%
China	1.4%
Singapore	2.2%
Korea	2.6%
Japan	3.1%

$y = 7E\text{-}05x + 0{,}048$
$R^2 = 0{,}625$

GDP in US $ PPP 2003.

Source: Computed by the author from UNESCO data.

the R&D spending to 0.5 per cent (*The Nation*, 11 June 2007). If successfully executed, this decision will put Thailand in the R&D spending trend that can be expected from a country that has reached a certain stage of development. But that may be not enough. Countries that are catching up, such as China, are spending much more (1.4 per cent) than the average. Those which have already achieved a high level of development (Singapore and Korea) are also spending much more than the average (2.2 per cent and 2.6 per cent respectively). The same is true as far as science and engineering are concerned. Thai research output has specialized in agricultural sciences, life sciences, and medical sciences, and to a lesser extent, engineering sciences (see Figure 3.8).[15] The specialization in agricultural science is comparable to that in the other second-generation Newly Industrialized Countries (NICs) and fits well with the strong exports of agricultural and food products evidenced in section 1. But Thai specialization in life sciences and medical sciences is not seen either in first-, or second-generation NICs. There is a potential there which is not matched by enough strong industrial companies that could turn it into an export advantage.

However, the specialization in engineering is rather weak unlike in China and first-generation NICs. As have been said previously, countries that have caught up have invested heavily in science and engineering education. For instance, in 2000 the share of natural science and engineering degrees among total first degrees in China was around 53 per cent, against 17 per cent for Thailand, even though the Thai GDP per capita was 1.7 times higher than the Chinese GDP per capita (UNIDO 2005, p. 45). If Thailand wants to upgrade its industry with more local R&D content to go beyond the assembly stage, it has to increase dramatically the number of graduates and PhD holders in sciences and engineering, just as Taiwan and Korea did and as China is presently doing.

Increasing spending in R&D and the number of students in science will prove insufficient if universities, as institutions, are not reformed so as to increase their research activities. According to Schiller (2006), "most of University-Industry linkages (UIL) in Thailand are mainly limited to services without deeper research involvement and to linear modes of knowledge transfer. Half of the UIL projects comprise consulting services". Technical services and informal contacts are the second most important modes of cooperation and the third is based on teaching. Research-based and interactive modes of cooperation have been included in less than

Figure 3.8
Index of Specialization for "Science Citation Publication" (SCI) of Asian Countries

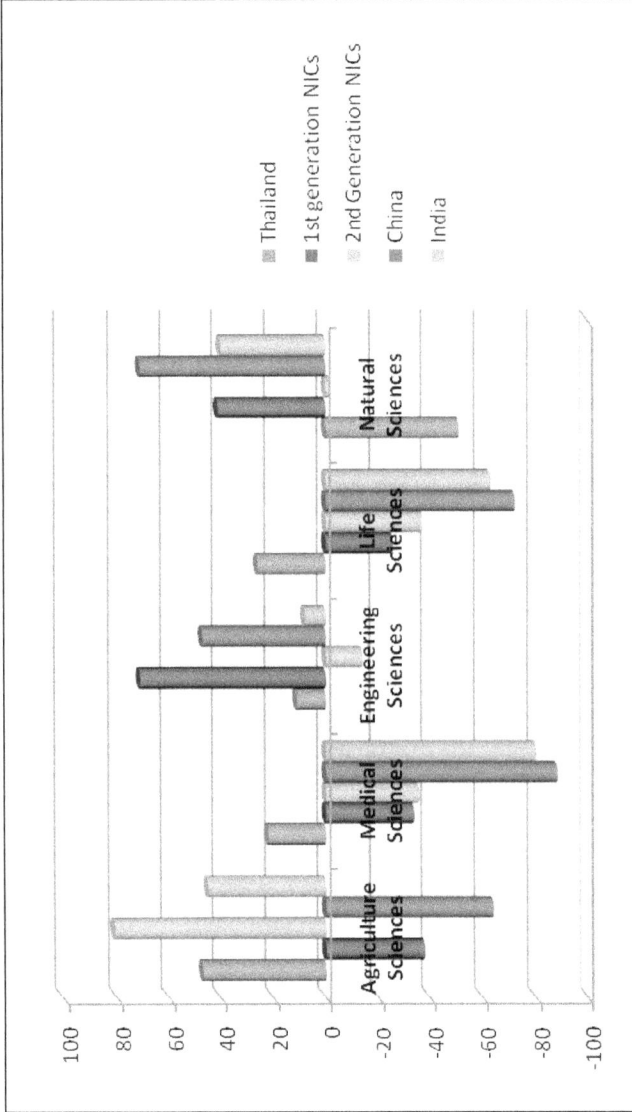

Source: Adapted by the author from Schiller's calculations (2006), p. 76, based on SCI EXPANDED, NIW et al. 2002.

10 per cent of cooperation projects. The supply of consultancy and other services lead Thai scholars to spend more time for projects outside the university (8.9 hours per week) at the expense of their time committed to research (5.11 hours per week) (Sharma et al. 2004, p. 71). The most important reason is that scholars are looking for additional personal income to supplement their wages which are too low. For engineers, the wage premium in the private sector is estimated at about 500 per cent of the corresponding wage in the public sector.

Another factor which accounts for the low research activities of Thai universities is that teaching and administrative work are often considered as important as research work for advancement in the career path. The consequence is that scholars tend to teach a lot at the expense of research activities, not only because it increases personal income, but also because it is positively appreciated by the hierarchy when it comes to promotions.

The first consequence of this is that few universities are capable of keeping pace with the growth of modern industries and the quick evolution of technology. They are, therefore, unable to take advantage of, and promote the technical progress and research capabilities of private firms. The second consequence is that the link between research and the teaching curriculum is weak. Most scholars cannot easily transform their research results into lecture content because their research activity is insufficient. This leads to a lack of curriculum updating and dynamism, and to overdependence on foreign research results and foreign textbooks. A subsequent effect is that the secondary school curriculum and teachers cannot only rely on research results provided by Thai universities to keep themselves updated and renovate their courses.

Developing its educational level and technological capabilities became such an urgent task for Thailand that it started to diversify its production system and specialize at the sector level for a few export-oriented activities. Indeed, the success of this incipient structural change now depends on Thailand's capacity to go beyond the assembly stage (see Chapter 8, for example). To upgrade these industries, Thailand has relied mainly on off-the-shelf foreign technology products and licences, and technology transfers by multinational firms. This allowed the country to develop to a certain extent, but, as we shall see in the next section, did not guarantee a productivity increase sustainable enough to avoid difficulties as soon as labour costs grew faster.

2. A NECESSARY INDUSTRIAL UPGRADING

Five major growth cycles have marked the Thai economy in the post-war era (Mallikamas, Rodpengsangkaha, and Thaicharoen 2003), as well as one dramatic crisis in 1997–98 (–6.1%). Figure 3.9 shows that the growth cycle 1987–96 with an average annual growth rate of 9.5 per cent, has been by far the most important one in both, amplitude and duration. The sluggish recovery that has followed since the crisis (4.7 per cent in the period 1999–2008) raises the question of whether or not this boom period was truly exceptional for structural reasons that have changed since then. Among these reasons were an exceptional mobilization of the labour force and a high rate of capital accumulation, but without the proportionate productivity gains. This is characteristic of an essential take-off phase of industrialization which cannot be sustained in the long run. Once the labour force is fully engaged in the production process and huge investments made, it becomes necessary to shift to an intensive growth regime based on higher productivity and endogenous technical progress. There are reasons to think that this step is necessary, but has not yet been taken in Thailand. This can be observed in the evolution of the interrelationships between Thailand's international trade and the growth process.

2.1 Thai Competitiveness Before and After the Crisis

Much-publicized survey-based indicators of competitiveness show that Thailand occupies an intermediate or even a good ranking position but at the same time suggest the need for urgent progress in technology development and innovation. The World Economic Forum's competitiveness index in 2007–08 ranked Thailand twenty-eighth behind twenty-first-ranked Malaysia and eleventh-ranked Korea. IMD world competitiveness index placed Thailand in thirty-second place in 2006, a small drop from the thirtieth spot in 2003. The World Bank's Doing Business Survey for 2007 ranked Thailand eighteenth among 175 economies, while A.T. Kearney's Global Services Location Index for 2005 ranked Thailand sixth among forty countries. But the World Bank's Knowledge Economy Index gave Thailand a rating of 4.88 in 2006, against 8.12 for Taiwan (China) and 8.20 for Singapore.

These publications try to capture the various aspects of competitiveness which is indeed a multifaceted and complex phenomenon. But because

Figure 3.9
Real GDP Growth Rate in Thailand (1952–2008)

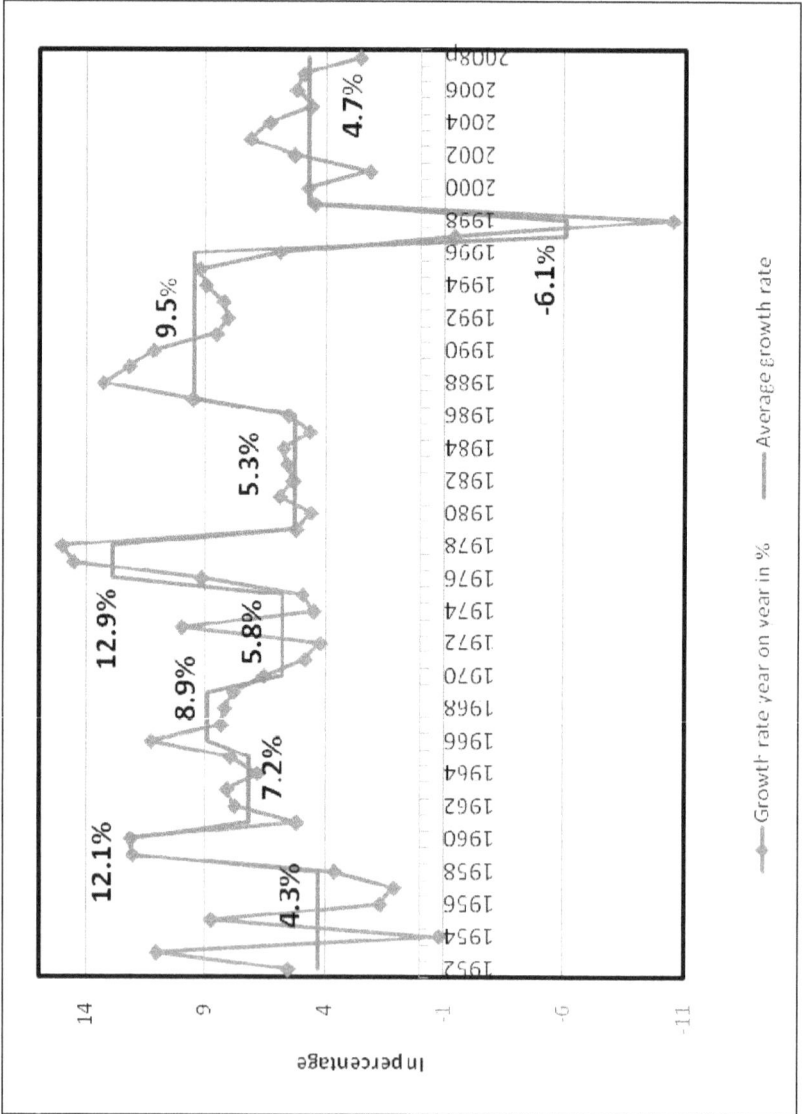

Source: Author's calculations with NESDB data. Constant GDP, 1988 prices.

our purpose is to analyse the link between labour and competitiveness, it is useful to observe the evolution of Unit Labour Cost (ULC). ULC is the ratio of total labour costs to real output.[16] As such, ULC is a reflection of cost competitiveness. This does not mean that other input costs, particularly capital costs, are not important. But usually the share of labour cost is large relative to other inputs, and hence provides useful information on cost competitiveness. ULCs have another advantage. If we divide the numerator (nominal labour compensation) and the denominator (real output) by the number of workers we obtain a measure of the cost of labour per capita (on the numerator) and a measure of labour productivity (on the denominator). We, therefore, have a direct link between labour productivity and the cost of labour used in generating output.

If labour productivity rises faster than labour costs per capita, unit labour cost decreases and competitiveness improves, and vice versa. This means that cost competitiveness does not only depend on low labour cost, but can be improved by raising productivity to create more output. In Thailand, labour cost per employee was initially very low (24,156 baht on average in 1980), below the value of labour productivity (32,905 baht).[17] It only tended to increase at a higher pace than productivity in the final years of the boom period (1987–96) (see Figure 3.10).

In 1996, one year before the crisis, it caught up with the level of labour productivity. Meanwhile, Thai employers have enjoyed a long period of low unit labour cost, which means that Thai workers were producing a higher value than they cost. It is remarkable that after the crisis, the level of productivity stayed below the level of labour cost. In the long run, this pattern is not sustainable. Labour productivity has to improve in order to match the growth rate of labour cost at least.

This evolution explains why the domestic unit labour cost (in baht) has increased in the long run, exerting a negative pressure on cost competitiveness (see Figure 3.11). But this loss of cost competitiveness did not materialize until 2005. Thanks to a 60 per cent devaluation of the baht vis-à-vis the U.S. dollar during the 1997–98 crisis, cost-competitiveness improved sharply until 2005. This is why the unit labour cost converted into US$ at PPP foreign exchange rates[18] exhibits a downward trend. This favourable period may be over. Due to a surplus in the balance of payments and the accumulation of foreign reserves, the baht has strengthened recently against the U.S. dollar. The appreciation against the U.S. dollar has been particularly strong in 2006 and 2007,

Figure 3.10
Determinants of Unit Labour Costs in Thailand

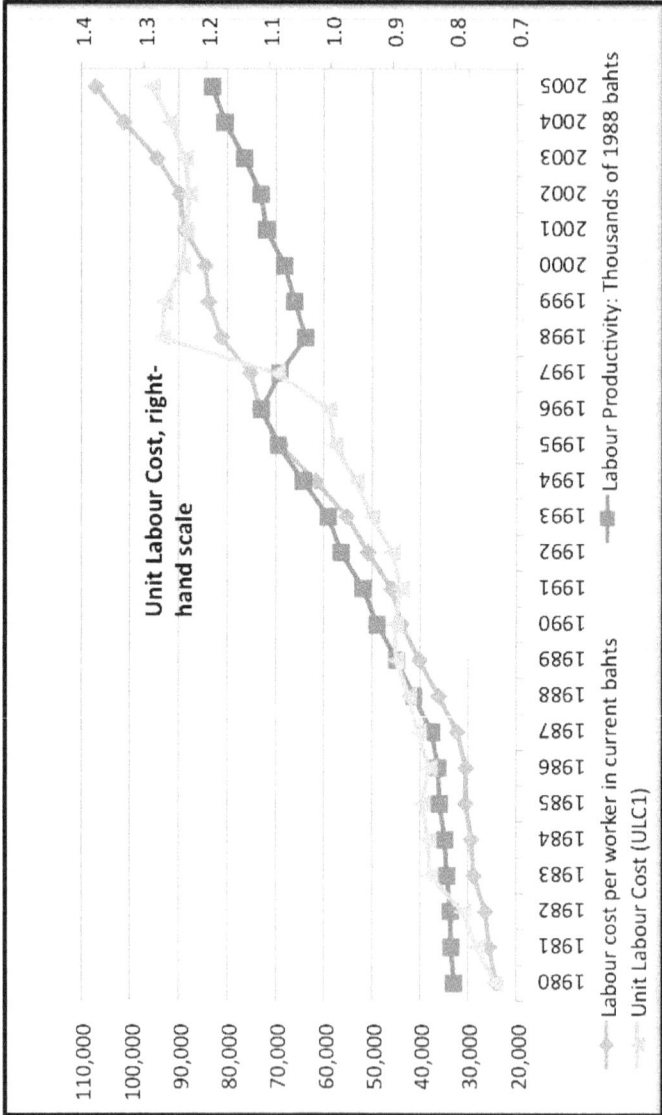

Unit Labour Cost, right-hand scale

Labour cost per worker in current bahts

Unit Labour Cost (ULC1)

Labour Productivity: Thousands of 1988 bahts

Source: Author's calculations based on NSO, NESDB and BOT data.

Figure 3.11
Thai Competitiveness Before and After the Crisis

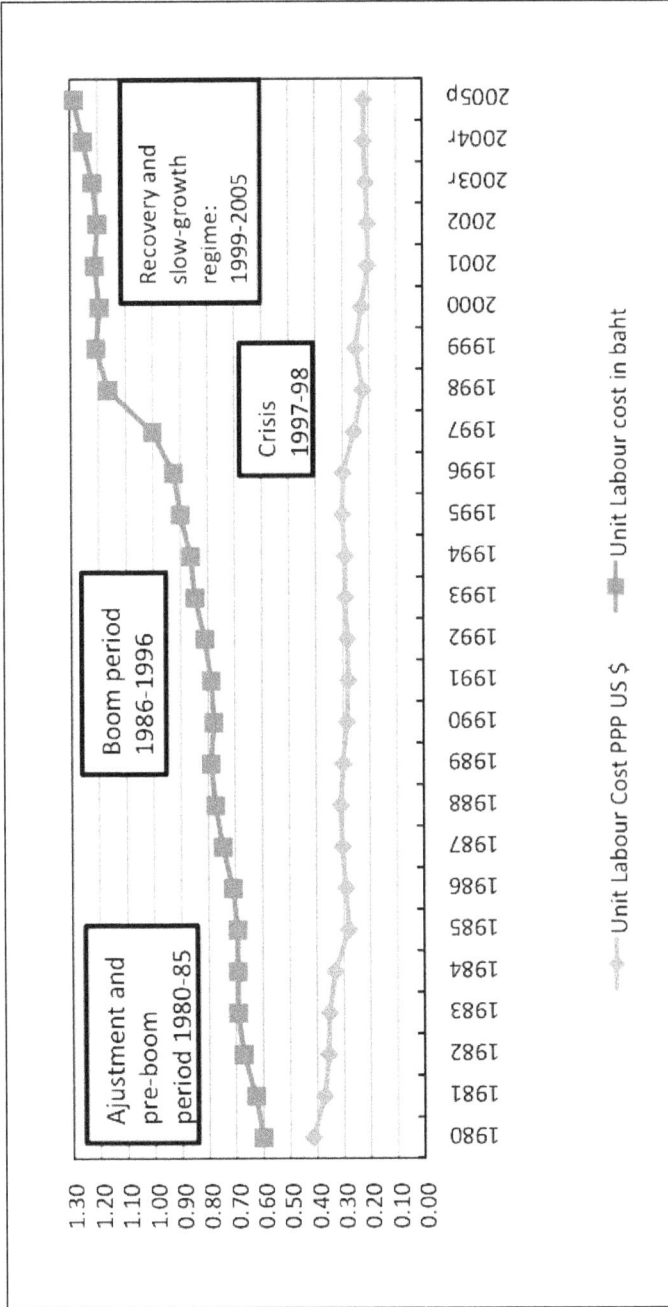

Source: Author's calculations based on NSO, NESDB, BOT, and the World Bank.

putting Thai competitiveness under pressure.[19] Like many other countries, Thailand will have to learn to compensate currency appreciation either with higher productivity or lower wages.

The sustainability issue of the Thai growth regime that was already apparent in 1996 is back again. The long-term solution cannot be permanent wage restraint or the systematic devaluation of the baht (which would be difficult anyway due to the excess in the balance of payments), but enhancing productivity and upgrading industry. This has to be done in conjunction with increasing the local content of FDI-based exports and by diversifying the industrial base to produce more differentiated products. This is the only way for it to become less dependent on low labour cost for competitiveness. Thailand has made some progress in this direction and now produces more scale-intensive and high-tech intensive products. But similar progress in local value-added and local technological capabilities remains to be seen.

2.2 Structural Change in Production and International Trade

In the past two decades, Thailand has turned into a relatively successful industrial country. According to UNIDO (2005), which measures the overall industrial development of a country by its "Manufacturing Value-Added (MVA) per capita", Thailand comes in at forty-fourth place in 2002, up from the sixty-second in 1990, from a world sample of 156 countries. This puts Thailand in the second quarter of countries behind Malaysia (34th), Taiwan (16th), Korea (14th) and Singapore (9th) but in front of China (75th), Indonesia (82nd) and the Philippines (84th). In terms of exports of manufactured goods per capita, Thailand ranked 43 in 2002 up from 47 in 1990 within a similar hierarchy of East Asian countries. It can be said that Thailand has reached an intermediate level of industrialization.

Despite this relative success, Thailand has not earned much foreign exchange through international trade. On the contrary, Thai international trade in products overall, but also in manufactured products, systematically had been in deficit until the 1997–98 crisis (see Figure 3.12). The deficit in manufactured products was stable around US\$3 billion during the cycle 1980–86, but widened during the boom cycle to reach the unsustainable level of around US\$16 billion in 1996. The import of machinery, technology, and intermediate products due to Thailand's rapid industrialization during the boom cycle (1987–96) was the main cause of this deficit.

Figure 3.12
Trade in Manufactured Goods (US$ billion/year)

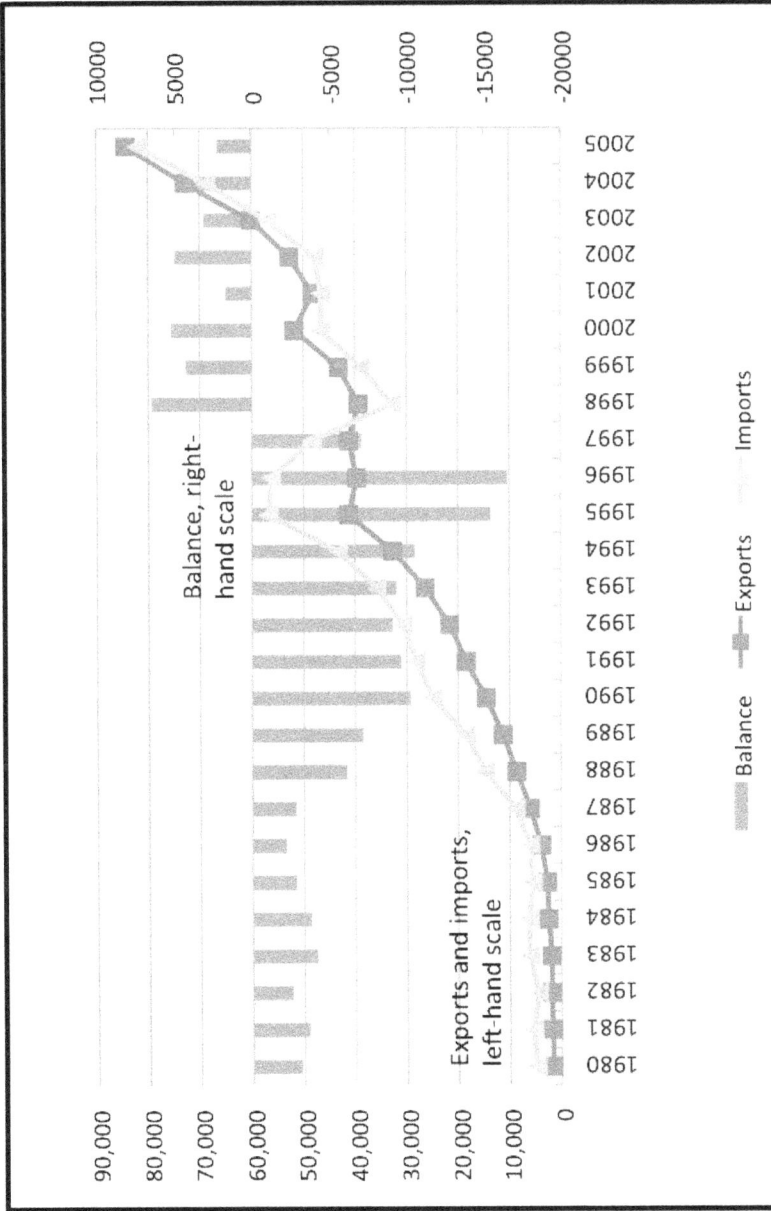

Source: Computed from WTO databank, SITC Rev. 3 classification.

Agricultural products and food were among the few products to generate a surplus, but this was insufficient to compensate for the deficit in manufacturing. It was only after the crisis that trade in manufactured products posted a surplus of US$2.8 billion on average for the period 1999–2005. This is a significant change that deserves closer scrutiny. One explanation is the slowdown in economic growth and private investment which reduced imports of capital and intermediate goods. In this sense, the surplus in manufactured products was fragile.

A second explanation was the significant progress in the technological upgrading of Thai industrial output since the mid-seventies. As quoted by Dhanani and Scholtès (2002, p. 18):

> The share of resource-based industries, including food, wood and paper resources, halved from 50% to around 25% of total manufacturing value-added between 1975 and 1998.... Labour-intensive industries increased their share from around 20 to 30% until 1990, and then declined to around 25% by 1998. The share of scale-intensive industries, including basic chemicals, fertilizers, refineries, cement and iron and steel remained stable at 18–19%. The technologically more-advanced differentiated industries, including machinery, consumer electronics and motor vehicles, doubled their share from 8 to 17 % by 1995, while the share of science-based industries, including medicines, office and computing equipment, and precision goods, increased their shares more rapidly, from 3 to 8% by 1995, and to 13% by 1998.

The evolution of Thai exports mirrors this structural change in the production system. Agriculture which represented 16 per cent of total exports in 1995 now accounts for only 10 per cent, while manufactured exports now represent 83 per cent of total exports (see Figure 3.13). The technological level of manufactured exports seems to have improved a lot during the 1990s. The share of labour-intensive manufactures has decreased from 19 per cent in 1995 to 9 per cent in 2006 while resource-based manufactures have remained constant at around 10 per cent. High-tech intensive manufactures have increased from 47 per cent in 1995 to 64 per cent in 2006.

A closer look at manufactured exports (see Figure 3.14) reveals that while traditional labour-intensive products such as garments, footwear, and leather products are really declining or even disappearing (see chapter 7 for textiles), three high-tech intensive products, non-electrical machinery, and parts (HS 84), electrical machinery and equipment (HS 85), and vehicles

Figure 3.13
Technology Level of Thai Manufactured Exports (and their % of total exports)

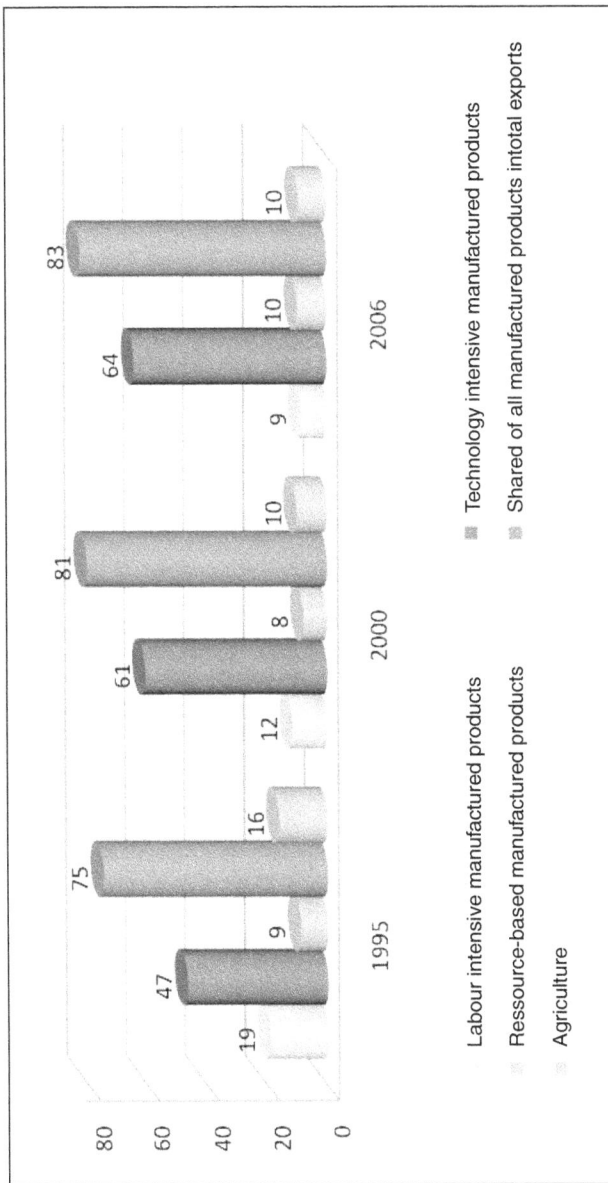

Source: Author's calculations from economic and financial statistics, Bank of Thailand, various issues.

Figure 3.14
Thailand's Exports of Manufactured Products (% of total exports)

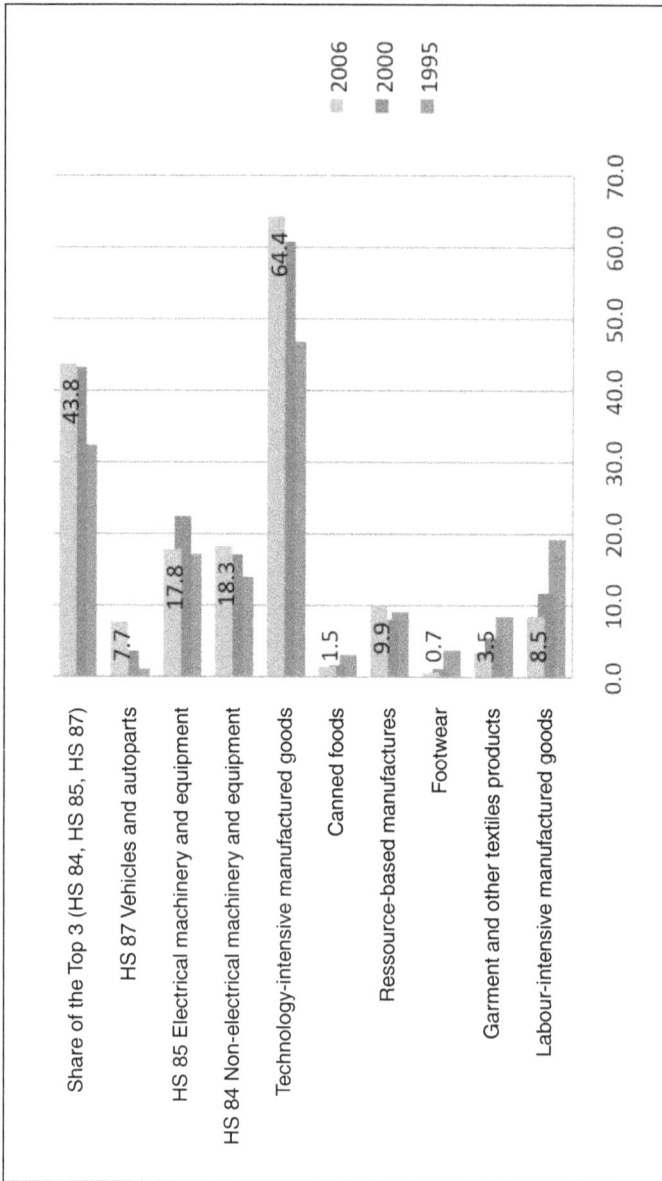

Source: Author's calculations from economic and financial statistics, Bank of Thailand, various issues.

and automobile parts (HS 87) are now the top three export products, accounting for 44 per cent of total exports in 2006.[20]

This shows an increasing concentration on too few products and a potential fragility in case of a decline in the demand for these products in foreign markets.

To sum up, Thailand is apparently moving from resource-based and labour-intensive specialization to technology-intensive specialization in keeping with the most dynamic sectors of international trade.

The point is that most of these technology-intensive exports have a high import content which creates a problem for trade balance and indicates that the local value-added is low. One can get a clearer view of the importance of local assembly of imported components and raw materials by looking at the import to export ratio at the sector level and the contribution of these sectors to growth. Patrawimolpon and Pongsaparn (2006) classify Thai manufacturing sectors into two main groups: low import to export ratio (<100 per cent) and high import to export ratio (>100 per cent) that impose a burden on the current account. Their growth contribution is measured based on data provided by the input-output tables of 2000, and compared with the median contribution to growth as a benchmark. Their results show that sectors with a low import to export ratio are usually resource-based and labour-intensive such as processed food, rubber, textile, footwear, leather, ceramic, furniture, wood and paper, jewellery, and non-metallic products.

In particular, textiles, processed food, and more recently, wood, are traditional products which have low import content and a high contribution to growth. Sectors with a high import to export ratio are usually the most technological and capital-intensive ones such as vehicles, plastic, petroleum, and chemical products, although the ratio may decline over time.

This is especially the case for vehicles which have turned into high contributors to growth over time, but were still net importers in the period 1995–2000 while machinery has already turned into a high contributor to growth with a low import to export ratio. These sectors are where FDI inflows are concentrated and where the import content was initially high, limiting technological spillover. A decrease in the import content signals an improvement in local capabilities to master a bigger part of the supply chain. To confirm these evolutions we have calculated using WTO data the net exports of the important category "machinery and transport equipment" (SITC section 7), and two of its main sub-categories, "office and telecommunications equipment" (which includes computer and related products and components), and "automotive products".

Figure 3.15 shows that after the crisis, the category "machinery and transport equipment" sector has turned into a net exporter with a surplus of about US$2.5 billion per year, except for a short period during the world economic slowdown during 2001–02. This slowdown had a dramatic impact on exports of "office and telecom equipment", which accrued a deficit of US$10 billion while "automotive products" were not seriously affected. Since 2002, there has been a spectacular turnaround. The surplus in "office and telecom equipment" is US$5 billion on average. It remained strong in 2006–07. The automobile industry has also turned into a net exporter after the crisis and has reached the surplus record level of US$3.6 billion in 2005, in sharp contrast with the 1990s.

This result is achieved in the context of a regional division of labour organized by multinational companies that has contributed to a diversification of export destinations. In 1995, Thailand was dependent on just three countries for 49 per cent of its exports, namely the United States (18 per cent), Japan (17 per cent), and Singapore (14 per cent) (See Table 3.2). In 2006, the situation improved. These three countries now account for only 36 per cent of Thailand's total exports. Japan's share, in particular, has lost 4 per cent to the benefit of China (9 per cent), while ASEAN's and the European Union's share remained globally stable. On the import side, the decline of Thailand's traditional trading partners is confirmed (Japan, Singapore, the European Union and the United States) to the benefit of ASEAN and China. This evolution reflects the growing inscription of Thailand in the regional division of labour. For instance, Southeast Asian countries were the major importers of Thailand's vehicles and parts'exports (HS87), accounting for 24 per cent of its total vehicle exports in 2006, followed by the European Union with 17 per cent. Thai exports of electrical machinery and equipment (HS85) to China is another case in point. About 39 per cent of the HS85 exports to China were electronic integrated circuits (HS8542) which were assembled in China before being exported to the third markets. Vehicle parts (HS8708) account for 75.5 per cent of total Thai automobile exports to China. India is still a marginal trade partner, but in the future, it can turn into an important one if the project of a free trade zone between ASEAN and India succeeds, and if more multinational companies are willing to extend their regional division of labour from Southeast Asia to South Asia, as some are already doing.

Figure 3.15
Net Exports of Machinery and Transport Equipment (SITC 7)

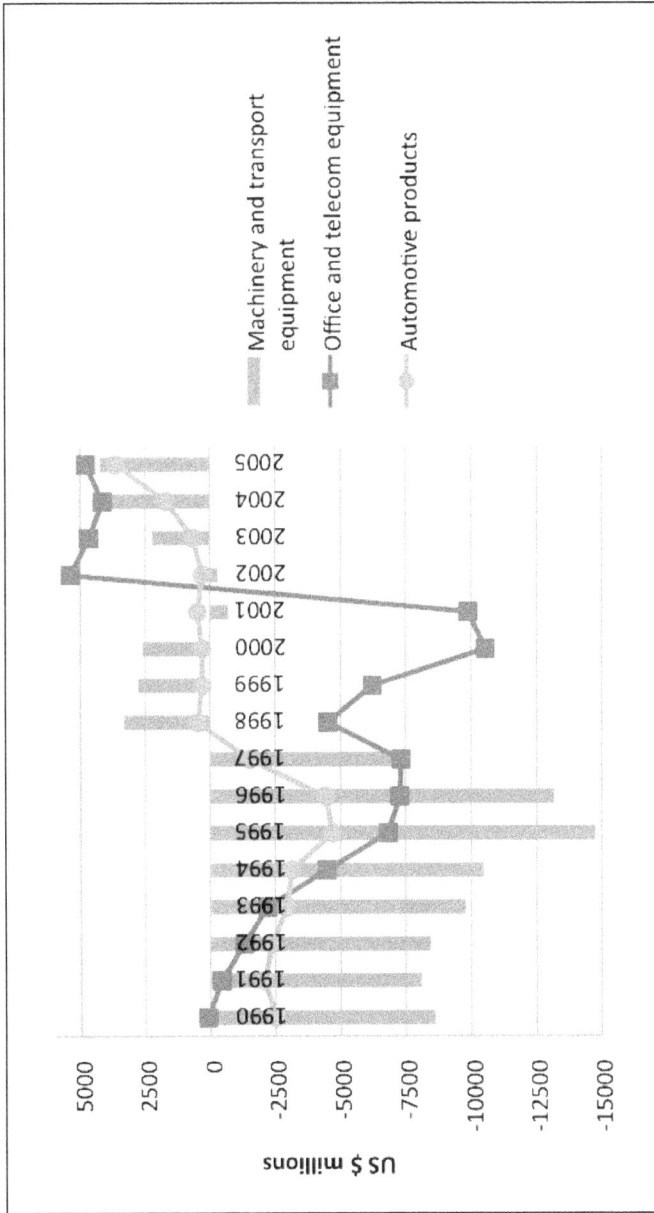

Machinery and transport equipment

Office and telecom equipment

Automotive products

Source: Author's calculations from WTO database, SITC Rev. 3 classification.

Table 3.2
Thai Exports and Imports

Thai Exports by destination, in %			
	1995	2000	2006
Japan	16.8	14.7	12.7
Singapore	14.0	8.7	6.4
ASEAN	19.1	19.4	20.9
China	5.2	4.1	9.0
India		0.8	1.4
The United States	17.8	21.3	15.0
The European Union (15)	15.1	15.8	13.0
Total exports	100.0	100.0	100.0
Thai Imports by destination, in %			
	1995	2000	2006
Japan	30.5	24.7	20.1
Singapore	5.9	9.7	4.5
ASEAN	12.6	16.6	18.4
China	3.0	5.4	10.6
India		0.1	1.3
The United States	0.0	0.1	1.3
The European Union (15)	0.0	0.0	0.0
Total imports	14.5	10.2	8.4

Source: Author's calculations with WTO data.

To sum up, since the crisis, Thailand has made some progress in terms of a better trade balance, more diversified exports, and more diversified customers. But it remains to be seen if these progress are sufficient to reduce its sensitivity to adverse foreign demand shocks.

Furthermore, these significant improvements in the structure of production and trade do not mean that Thailand has succeeded in establishing an integrated and sophisticated production system involving innovation and design. The technological upgrading has not been as important and fast as the above figures suggest. The point is that the classification used is based on the technological level of the final product, and not on the technological level of the production process itself, and the value-added it incorporates into the product. In fact, the import content of differentiated and science-based products is high, indicating that Thai industries are still more specialized in the low-skilled assembly stage of imported complex components than in the production phase of manufacturing. One has to nuance this assertion because the situations change a lot according to the industry. The chemical industry, for instance, requires a high proportion of skilled and highly skilled workers. The automobile industry relies on a lot of assembly tasks, but these now imply a high level of organizational and behavioural skills on the part of the workers and the local content is now high (see chapter 6). This is probably less the case in most of the electronic industry segments in Thailand where mere assembly of imported components explains why employers prefer to recruit young, low-skilled female workers.

The problem is that the assembly process of imported components is clearly less productivity-enhancing than more integrated processes with higher local content. This makes a difference at the macro level for the dynamics of productivity and growth. This is what we are trying to catch by turning now to a macroeconomic approach.

2.3 Growth and Productivity

Several studies have analysed the factors in Thailand's growth in order to measure the respective contributions of capital, labour, and land (for agriculture), and the so-called "total factor productivity". The basic idea is that economic growth is explained by the use of increasing volumes of capital, labour, and land and by their increasing productivity due to technical progress, education and skills, and fertility respectively. Their combined productivity is called "Total Factor Productivity" (TFP). Studies differ in terms of theoretical approach, methodology, scope, and time period. An in-depth survey is beyond the scope of this chapter. Suffice it to say that some studies rely on a production function, usually a Cobb-Douglas one that presents the disadvantage of supposedly restrictive hypotheses such as constant returns to scale, perfect substitution between labour and capital and declining marginal productivity. The growth accounting approach, on the other hand, does not rely on any of these assumptions. In the case of Thailand, this second strand of studies leads to the following conclusions:

The most important factor of growth has been the accumulation of capital, followed by the mobilization of labour, while TFP has played a modest role, albeit a significant one. But, most of TFP growth in the past has come from the migration of workers from agriculture which has low productivity, to industry, which has a higher one. However, productivity increases arising from inside the industrial sector and, therefore, depending on innovation, were rather rare. For the whole period of 1977–99, Chandrachai, Bangorn, and Chockpisansin (2005) found that the migration from agriculture to industry represented 72.4 per cent of TFP (see p. 316). This so-called "productivity bonus" is bound to disappear in the coming years when most of rural workers will have migrated. In 2006, agriculture's share of the labour force had already dropped to 37 per cent of the total labour force, down from 50 per cent in 1996. Unless we hypothesize that this share may gradually fall to less than 10 per cent, which is not plausible, the shift bonus can no longer be an important source of productivity in the coming decades. It is especially the case if most of the rural workers find a job in the services sector where productivity is low, rather than in manufacturing, where productivity is higher.

The most recent growth accounting exercise conducted by the World Bank (2006a) covers the period 1977–2004. It shows that in the period prior to the financial crisis (1977–96), capital contributed 4 per cent out of an average output growth of 7.7 per cent, labour contributed to 2 per cent, and TFP growth contributed 1.6 per cent. In itself this level of TFP is not negligible, but if we take into account that most of this TFP stems from the migration of rural workers to industry, this means that endogenous TFP, the one that comes from technical and organizational innovations has in fact been very low. During the recovery period (1999–2004), the rate of growth (5 per cent) did not fully recover and stayed under its historical trend. Capital accumulation fell (0.9 per cent) and TFP improved (2.1 per cent). It remains to be seen whether this improvement in TFP signals a long-term change, or is due to a short-term effect of an intense, industrial restructuring as a result of the crisis.

A decomposition of the contribution of labour into a quantitative effect (employment) and a qualitative effect (progress in the level of education of employees) reveals that education has always been a minor source of growth at 0.3 per cent during 1977–96, while employment (1.6 per cent) has played a major role. The most recent period (1999–2004) shows only a slight improvement of the contribution of the level of education (0.4 per cent).

This tends to prove that even if the young generations are much more educated, the effect of their better education is still not perceptible in the growth rate. This is due to the fact that the bulk of the labour force remains poorly educated (see section 1). Even in 2004, 59.4 per cent of the labour force still had less than secondary school education, a slight improvement from 78.3 per cent in 1994. The delay in improving education in Thailand has had a long-lasting effect on growth.

At the sector level, we observe that this global pattern also prevailed in the manufacturing sector. In particular, the TFP and the "quality of labour" effect (the effect of the level of education) had almost been the same (1.3 per cent and 0.4 per cent respectively in 1977–96), which indicates that manufacturing has not been significantly more efficient than the whole economy, even during the high-growth period. In the last period (1999–2004), the contribution of capital (0.8 per cent) dropped more sharply because manufacturing was the most affected by the fall in investment. As a consequence, the strong increase in TFP from 1.3 per cent to 2.7 per cent reflects more the elimination of excess capacity and the search for rationalization, rather than the incorporation of technical progress through investment in a new generation of equipment. In agriculture in the whole period (1977–2004), about two-thirds of output growth was due to capital,[21] all other factors playing a reduced role, in particular, education. Services is the only sector where labour played a more important role than capital, and where TFP is negative in the long run, which is explained by the severity of the crisis. It is also the only sector where the contribution of education was the highest (13 per cent from 1977–2004)[22] and improving during the recovery period. This may be explained by the fact that the new educated generations prefer to work in services rather than in manufacturing.

To sum up, Thailand is now confronted with the necessity to increase intrasector productivity which means that education and technological performance must improve substantially. This in turn implies, among other things, establishing a National Innovation System as already discussed in Chapter 2 and improving education and skills, the lack of quality of which was clearly emphasized in the first part of this chapter.

CONCLUSION

In conclusion, we would like to draw the lessons of our analysis and present three policy recommendations.

The first concerns the necessary industrial upgrading. Few foreign companies and even fewer private Thai firms engage in R&D activities because they are not convinced that innovation is necessary for their operations in Thailand. Up to now, firms in Thailand have been able to compete and achieved expected profit, thanks to low labour cost and labour-intensive technology requiring few local adaptations. But this golden age for private firms is bound to an end in the medium term because unit labour costs are rising in Thailand and new low-labour costs countries are emerging. Investing in R&D to improve and differentiate existing products and create new ones and to improve productivity to lower unit labour costs is unavoidable. But this is easier said than done. The Thai government is trying to convince foreign firms, for instance, in the electronic industry, to locate more R&D activities in Thailand, with fiscal incentives and a better supply of skilled workers. This runs counter to the international tendency of multinational firms to create global supply chains in which each function is located in different countries, according to their relative advantage, and to diversify risks. Why would multinational firms locate R&D activities or the production of high value-added products in the present Thai environment? Fiscal incentives are insufficient to convince these firms to change their global supply chain. The alternative would be to rely on Thai private firms. But here lies another structural problem of Thai capitalism. For historical reasons, there are not enough big and strong Thai industrial private firms that could take the lead in transforming Thailand into an innovative country. There is no equivalent of the big Indians firms such as Tata, or of Korean chaebols such as Samsung, LG, or Hyundai, or of the Taiwanese Acer and innovative SMEs.[23] Deprived of these alternatives, we think that Thailand would be best with an active policy of using state companies as the major vector of R&D activities. This may seem old-fashioned in these times of free trade and market-friendly policies, but historical evidence shows that developing countries that have created and accumulated R&D capacities have relied extensively on state companies (Katz 2004). State companies have played the role of incubators for private companies because they have provided jobs to newly graduated scientists and engineers. They have achieved R&D, which although not on the forefront of technical progress laid the foundations for further endogenous progress. This possibility has not been explored sufficiently in Thailand and because Thailand is not an over-indebted country, there is no strong financial constraint that would make it impossible. This new active public policy could be combined with other measures such as public financing of start-ups in technology-intensive projects. At the present moment, there is no public development bank able to finance start-ups, or mechanisms to provide newly graduated Thai entrepreneurs with collaterals that would make them eligible for credit banking, as Chapter 2 has explained.

The second recommendation concerns universities. Thai universities are divided into two broad categories: "Teaching universities" and "research universities". Although scholars in "research universities" do more research than those in "teaching universities", they dedicate only 18.1 per cent of their estimated hours per week during the teaching period to research and thesis supervision, against 30 per cent in Australian universities for instance (Sharma, Thasnapark, and Launglaor 2004). This is clearly not enough. Research should be made a clear priority in terms of time dedicated and status, and all universities should be standardized under the same legal status of "research universities". Not only should scholars be better paid, but research should become the first criterion for promotion. At the same time scholars' activities should become more transparent and they should be accountable and allowed no sideline jobs, especially teaching in private universities. A unique and stringent legal status for universities would avoid the present situation where tertiary education has become a business. New private universities are opening up every year, which provide a poor quality of education, but deliver degrees easily. These low quality diploma mills serve neither the national interest nor even individual interests because they sap the necessary confidence in diplomas, and private firms learn to distinguish between them. This supposes a radical reform of Thai universities that is yet to come.

The third recommendation concerns secondary education. Secondary education must progress quantitatively and qualitatively to provide the skilled workers that Thailand needs and more and better future students for tertiary education, especially in scientific fields. The only way to achieve this is to remove the current financial obstacle by guaranteeing effectively, totally, and not partially, free secondary education for poor households. Given the growing inequality of revenues in Thailand, this means that only a minority of rich households should have to pay for the cost of education. More broadly, positive discrimination for rural schools should be developed beyond the present stage, because this is where the majority of pupils leaving school after Grade 9 are located. The fact that the number of pupils in rural areas is falling creates good conditions for improving the quality of education, in particular, by implementing innovative pedagogy, provided that schools have the appropriate equipment and teachers feel the support of the whole institution for innovative teaching.

But education upgrading cannot be achieved by the education system alone. Without a strong commitment from the government to the reduction of social inequalities, the quality of education cannot be significantly improved, because schools can only partially compensate for social handicaps. But without industrial upgrading, education upgrading makes no sense. What's the point in being better educated if there are no better jobs enabling a better life? The promise of higher wages and better work conditions are also strong incentives for becoming more educated. In this respect, Thailand still has a lot to improve on. Wages only really start to rise for those who have a university degree, while students who have completed secondary schools do not receive significantly more than those who only have primary education. Climbing up the development ladder truly relies on decent jobs.

To achieve the objectives listed above, a comprehensive and consistent industrial, as well as science and technology, policy is needed. Of course, Thailand has developed such policies over time, but as the next chapter will show, some shortcomings remain.

Annex 1 relative to Figure 3.1

The following sources have been used to construct Figure 3.1. "Edstats", the World Bank's data base that compiles a variety of national and international data sources (such as UNESCO Institute for Statistics (UIS) and OECD) and the World Bank data on pertinent education topics. The data retrieved from Edstats for gross enrolment rate in secondary education goes from 1970 to 2005 and generally comes from the UNESCO data base, UIS. For previous years we have used the following publications that relied on various issues of UNESCO statistical yearbook: Donald Adams, David W. Chapman (1998), Clementina Acedo, Mitsue Uemura (1997), A. Deolalikar, R. Hasan, H. Khan, M.G. Quibria (1997), W.O. Lee (1998), Keith M. Levin (1997), A. Mingat, and J. P. Tan (1996).

Annex 2 relative to Figure 3.10 and 3.11

Compensation of employees is a statistical term used in national accounts and balance of payments statistics. It is defined as "the total remuneration, in cash or in kind, payable by an enterprise to an employee in return for work done by the latter during the accounting period". It also includes "other costs of labour that are paid by employers such as contributions to social security and pension schemes (whether public or private)". (B. Van Ark, E.J. Monnikhof [2000]).

The problem with the compensation of employees is that it relates to public and private wages earners and does not take into account the income of self-employed workers in urban and rural areas such as farmers and their employees and "own-family workers". Their income is called "Operating Surplus of Private Unincorporated Enterprises (OSPUE) in national accounts. They are usually part of the informal economy. Sociologically, these workers are much closer to wage earners than to employers of big formal firms. In Thailand, the NESDB measures this part of income as "Income from Unincorporated Enterprises". OSPUE should be counted as labour income, but it is in fact a mixture of labour income and profit. Simply adding OSPUE overestimates the share of labour income in GDP, but leaving it out underestimates it. To make things clear, the average proportion of the compensation of employees in Thailand to GDP in 1980–2005 was 36 per cent of GDP, while the average proportion of the compensation of employees, plus the income of unincorporated enterprises to GDP amounted to 80 per cent of GDP. The solution proposed by D. Gollin (2002) consists of two adjustments and then taking the average of the two. Adjustment 1 is calculated as following: (Compensation of employees + Income from Unincorporated Enterprises)/(GDP at factor cost) to one. This adjustment treats all OSPUE as labour income. Adjustment 2 is calculated as following: (Compensation of employees)/(GDP at factor cost — Income from Unincorporated enterprises) to one. This adjustment takes into account wage earners only and excludes completely OSPUE from labour income. It is obvious that this or any other procedure involves an element of subjectivity given the issue at hand. It is not claimed that this newly calculated share is absolutely correct as it is impossible to know this. However, it seems much more reasonable than the original one calculated by simply dividing labour compensation by GDP. The sources used are the Thai national accounts provided by the National Economic and Social Development Board (NESDB) from 1980 to 2005, and the "Labour Force Survey" of the National Statistical Office (NSO) for data on employment for the same period. The unit labour cost is then calculated as the ratio of the nominal labour income per worker previously calculated, divided by labour productivity. Labour productivity is calculated as the quantity of output per worker. The quantity of output is defined as the GDP at factor cost at constant 1988 prices. The nominal exchange rate and the Purchasing Power Parity exchange rate are taken from the IMF data base.

Notes

1. Primary education is universalized first, then secondary education, followed by an expansion of tertiary education.
2. The Gross Enrolment Rate is the "number of pupils enrolled in a given level of education, regardless of age, expressed as a percentage of the population in the theoretical age group for the same level of education. For the tertiary level, the population used is the five-year age group following on from the secondary school leaving age". (UNESCO 2006).
3. Because the Gross Enrolment Rate (GER) does not take age into account, children older than the theoretical grade age and repeaters push the GER above 100, which, in some cases, signals a bad quality of education and bad social conditions for the population. Net Enrolment Ratios are preferable because they do take age into account, but data is missing for a number of countries such as Thailand because there is no system of students repeating a grade. All children go to the upper grade at the end of the year whatever their scores.
4. The GPI is calculated as the GER of female students divided by the GER of male students.

5. The Gross Parity Index (GPI) divides the Gross Enrolment Rate (GER) of female students by the GER of male students. A GPI equal to 1 means that there are as many female students as male students. A GPI superior to 1 means that there are more female students.

6. We use the World Bank classification. Countries are classified as low income, lower middle income, upper middle income, and higher income according to their GNP per capita in 2005. In Figure 3.1, Malaysia is the only upper middle income country while all the others are lower middle income countries.

7. The GER for secondary education for Thailand in Figure 3.1 for 2005 (70 per cent) is below the GER presented in Table 3.1 (77 per cent), although both data comes from UNESCO. The reason is unknown because both series use the International Standard Classification of Education (ISCED97). The problem is not so important because we are more interested in the relative position of each country than the exact level.

8. Source: World Bank 2006c based on the following surveys: Cambodia (Socio-economic Household Survey 2004), Vietnam (Living Standards Survey 2002), Indonesia (Susenas 2003), Thailand (Socio-economic Survey 2002), the Philippines (Annual Poverty Indicator Survey 1999), China (Economic, Population, Nutrition, and Health Survey 2000), Singapore (Labour Force Survey 1998), Argentina (INDEC 2003), Brazil (PNDA 2001), Chile (ECSN 2003), Colombia (ECV 2003), Guatemala (MECOVI 2000), Mexico (ENIGH 2002), Venezuela, R. B. de (EHM 2002), Bolivia (MECOVI 2002). All surveys are nationally representative except for China's Health and Nutrition Survey, which represents only nine of twenty-two provinces in China.

9. For more details, see Jetin (2006).

10. PISA has been set up by the OECD in 1998 and is now covering fifty-nine mainly industrialized and middle-income countries, among which is Thailand. PISA measures content "literacy", a concept that encompasses how fifteen year old students apply knowledge and skills: how they identify, solve, and interpret problems; and how they analyse, reason and communicate. It also covers reading literacy.

11. The Trend in International Mathematics and Science Study (TIMSS) was created in the late 1950s by the International Association for the Evaluation of Educational Achievement (IEA). By 2000, some fifty countries were participating in surveys covering mathematics and science, reading and other subjects. TIMSS is a curriculum-based test administered to eighth-grade students, typically fourteen to fifteen years of age.

12. These countries are Brazil and Indonesia which together with Thailand, belong to the category of "lower income countries" defined by the World Bank. Mexico and Uruguay were also participating but belonged to the upper-middle category. Japan, Korea, and Hong Kong also participated but important countries of interest, such as China, India, and Malaysia, did not.

13. The variables in PISA encompass not only students and family characteristics,

but also include data on schools characteristics and resources as well as students' attitudes towards learning.

14. Tacit knowledge is one dimension of knowledge along with explicit knowledge (Polanyi 1966). While explicit knowledge can explain why it is scientifically possible to ride a bicycle, it cannot teach a novice how to actually ride a bicycle. Riding a bicycle can only be learnt by personal experience, even if advice can help. The same applies to a great variety of economic and scientific activities. For example, most of the knowledge required by venture capital and private equity companies is tacit (Nelson 2003). Reproducing successfully a scientific experience implies personal tacit knowledge of the scientist and not only a scientific publication demonstrating the result.

15. Figure 3.8 shows an index of specialization which expresses the share of a scientific field in one country in relation to the share of this field in the world. The transformed values range from –100 to +100. Positive values indicate a specialization above the world average.

16. The labour cost is usually defined as "the compensation of employees", who are, by definition, wage earners, and this is derived from national account statistics. The advantage of using national accounts is that the definition of compensation includes social contributions and is hence more comprehensive. However, it does not include the compensation of self-employed workers, which combines labour and capital income and is often called "mixed revenues". This is a major problem for the analysis of developing countries where the share of self-employed workers in the workforce is usually 50 per cent or more. The risk is that the major part of labour income is not taken into account in unit labour cost. To address this problem, we have applied Gollin's (2002) methodology. Basically, we first estimate the labour income share in GDP of wage earners to get a low estimate. Then we calculate the labour income share of wage earners plus self-employed in GDP to get a high estimate. Finally the "adjusted labour income" is calculated as the average of the two estimations. See the methodological annex 2 for further details.

17. Labour productivity is calculated as the GDP at factor cost at 1988 prices divided by total employment (farm and non-farm employment). Data are taken from National Accounts, computed by NESDB, and the Labour Force Survey, computed by the NSO, and can be retrieved at their respective website.

18. The Purchasing Power Parity (PPP) rate is the rate at which the currency of one country (for instance, the Thai baht), would have to be converted into that of another country (usually the U.S. dollar) to buy the same amount of goods and services in each country. PPP rates are much more stable and enable comparison of labour cost levels across countries because they make sure that the same volume of production is taken as a benchmark.

19. In 2006, the annual average baht to the U.S. dollar exchange rate was Bt37.88 compared with an average rate of Bt40.22 in 2005. The real effective exchange

rate also appreciated by 8 per cent in 2006. Agriculture and labour-intensive industries are the most sensitive to this appreciation.

20. Because databases do not provide updated information on all aspects, and differ from country to country, and from one international institution to another, we have to combine different ones. In this case, the product code comes from the Harmonized System nomenclature (HS) of the United Nations database COMTRADE. Source <http://www.trademap.net/Thailand>.

21. This proportion is calculated by dividing the contribution of capital (1.9 per cent) by the real output growth (2.9 per ent) in the period 1977–2004.

22. We divide the contribution of the qualitative effect of labour (0.7 per cent) by the real output growth (5.4 per cent) for the period 1977–2004.

23. For further developments on this issue, see P. Intarakumnerd's chapter in this book.

References

Acedo, Clementina and Mitsue Uemura. *Education Indicators for East Asia and the Pacific*. Washington, D.C.: World Bank, 1997.

Adams, Donald and David W. Chapman. "Education and National Development in Asia: Trends and Issues". *International Journal of Educational Research* 29 (1998): 583–602.

Ahuja, A., T. Chucherd, and K. Pootrakul. "Human Capital Policy: Building a Competitive Workforce for 21st Century Thailand". Bank of Thailand discussion paper, DP/07/2006, BOT, Thailand, 2006.

Altenburg, T., M. Gennes, A. Hatakoy, M. Herberg, J. Link, and S. Shoengen. "Strengthening Knowledge-based Competitive Advantages in Thailand". Reports and working papers 1/2004, German Development Institute, 2004.

Chandrachai, A., T. Bangorn, and K. Chockpisansin. "Total Factor Productivity Growth : Survey Report. Part II- National Reports, Thailand". APO 2004, Tokyo.

Deolalikar, A., R. Hasan, H. Khan, and M.G. Quibria. "Competitiveness and Human Ressource Development". *Asian Development Review* 15, no. 2 (1997): 131–63.

De Ferranti, D. et al. *Closing the Gap in Education and Technology*. Washington D.C.: World Bank, 2003.

Dhanani, S. and P. Scholtès. "Thailand's Manufacturing Competitiveness: Promoting Technology, Productivity and Linkages". Small and Medium Enterprises Technical Working Papers Series, UNIDO, Vienna, 2002.

Gollin, D. "Getting Income Shares Right". *Journal of Political Economy* 110, no. 2 (2002): 458–74.

Intarakumnerd P., P.A. Chairatna, and T. Tangchitpiboon. "National Innovation

System in Less Sucessful Developing Countries: the Case of Thailand". *Research Policy* 31 (2002): 1445–57.

Jetin, B. "The Cognitive International Division of Labour Hypothesis: What Possible Effects for Thai Labour and Education?". *Journal of Education* 33, nos. 1–2 (January–December 2006), Chiang Mai, Thailand.

Katz, J. "The Limits of the Prevailing Orthodoxy. Technology and Education as Restrictions to Productivity Growth and International Competitiveness in Latin America". Communication presented at the DRUID Summer Conference 2004 on Industrial Dynamics, Innovation And Development, Elsinore, Denmark, 14–16 June 2004

Khoman, S. "Education: The Key to Long-term Recovery? ". In *Thailand beyond the Crisis*, edited by P. Warr. New York: Routledge Curzon, 2005.

Lee, W.O. "Equity and Access to Education in Asia: Leveling the Playing Field". *International Journal of Educational Research* 29 (1998): 667–83.

Levin, Keith M. "Education Development in Asia: Issues and Planning, Policy and Finance". *Asian Development Review* 15, no. 2 (1997): 86–130.

Mallikamas, P.R., D. Rodpengsangkaha, and Y. Thaicharoen. "Investment Cycles, Economic Recovery and Monetary Policy". Discussion paper, Monetary Policy Group, Bank of Thailand, 2003.

Mingat, A. and J.P. Tan. "The Full Social Returns to Education: Estimates based on Countries Economic Growth Performance". Human Capital Development Working Paper No. 73. Washington, D.C.: World Bank, 1996.

Nelson, R. "Physical and Social Technologies and Their Evolution". *Économie Appliquée* 56, no. 3 (2003): 13–29.

NSO. "Children and Youth Survey (CYS) of 2002". National Statistical Office, Bangkok, 2002.

OEC. "Education in Thailand". Office of the Education Council, Ministry of Education, Thailand, 2004.

Patrawimolpon, P. and R. Pongsaparn. "Thailand in the New Asian Economy: The Current State and Way Forward". Bank of Thailand Discussion Paper, DP/04/2006, BOT, Thailand, 2006.

Pholphirul, P. "Competitiveness, Income Distribution and Growth in Thailand: What does the Long-Run Evidence Shows?". International Economic Relations Program, Thailand Development Research Institute, Bangkok, May 2005.

Polanyi, M. *The Tacit Dimension*. New York: Doubleday, 1996.

Schiller, D. "The Potential to Upgrade the Thai Innovation System by University-Industry Linkages". *Asian Journal of Technology Innovation* 14, no. 2 (2006).

Sharma, R., U. Thasnapark, and W. Launglaor. "A Comparative Analysis of Thai Research University's Academic Staff Perceptions of their Work and Related Issues in Research and Other Universities". *Journal of Institutional Research South East Asia* 2, no. 2 (June 2004).

UNESCO. "Global Education Digest 2006. Comparing Education Statistics Across the World". UNESCO, Paris, 2006.

———. "Education for All: The Quality Imperative". The EFA Global Monitoring Report Team, UNESCO, Paris, 2005.

UNIDO (United Nations Industrial Development Organization). "Industrial Development Report 2005. Capability building for Catching-up: Historical, Empirical and Policy Dimensions". UNIDO, Vienna, 2005.

Van Ark, B., E.J. Monnikhof. "Productivity and Unit Labour Cost Comparisons: A Data Base". Employment Paper, No. 5, ILO, Geneva, 2000.

World Bank. "Thailand Investment Climate, Firm Competitiveness and Growth". Report No. 36267-Th, Poverty Reduction and Economic Management Sector Unit, East Asia and Pacific Region, Washington, D.C., 2006a.

———. "Thailand Social Monitor: Improving Secondary Education". Thailand Social Monitor Series. Washington, D.C., 2006b.

———. "Meeting the Challenges of Secondary Education in Latin America and East Asia. Improving Efficiency and Resource Mobilization", edited by Emanuela di Gropello. World Bank. III. Series: Directions in Development, Washington, D.C., 2006c.

Part II
The Roles of Institutions: Clusters and Industrial Estates

4

INDUSTRIAL RESTRUCTURING POLICIES IN THAILAND
Japanese or American Approach

Akira Suehiro

1. INTRODUCTION

East Asian governments seem to have adopted three different types of policies on industrial promotion when doing national planning for economic development in the past. (Suehiro 2008, Ch. 6).

The first type is an industry-specific policy, in which the government intentionally selects several industries and promotes them by employing trade restrictions on imported goods, and providing government subsidies, tax incentives, and loans. The main policy objective is to create national or indigenous industrial entrepreneurs who will compete with foreign firms advancing into domestic market. Typical of this kind of policy is strategic promotion of industries such as machinery and electronics goods in Japan in the 1950s and the 1970s, and in South Korea and Taiwan between the 1960s and the 1980s (Hashimoto et al. 1998; Wade 1990).

The second type is a more moderate industrial promotion policy, in which the government provides a set of policy incentives to local and foreign companies in promoted industries. Compared with the first type in which the governments preferred an industry-specific approach and a policy of loans, the second type covers a wider rage of industries, and offers tax incentives rather than loans. At the same time, foreign investors are usually granted the same privileges or incentives as local ones to serve as important contributors to industrial development. Unlike in Japan, South Korea, and Taiwan, the principal purpose of this policy is to promote import-substitution type of industrialization of the country rather than foster local industrial firms (Somsak 1981). For this reason, foreign firms have frequently played an essential role in the development of major industries. Typical cases can be seen in the experiences of Thailand and Indonesia between the 1960s and 1980s, or Malaysia, before the government decided to adopt a comprehensive policy in favour of a group of *bumiputera* in 1981 (Gomez 1997).

The third is a non-interventionist type policy, in which governments have no intention to control directly the economy, and attempt instead to guarantee a free market for the private sector regardless of the type or nationality of industry. They confine their roles to providing indirect support to industrial development such as public occupational training, the improvement of productivity, and the promotion of R&D in high-tech industries.[1] These services are principally given to private firms through government agencies, research institutes, and national universities with the public financial support. Typical cases may be observed in Hong Kong and Singapore between the 1970s and the 1980s. The main policy objective is not to promote import substitution, but to enhance the international competitiveness of the national economy under the free market mechanism.

Any single country in East Asia, however, does not always stick to a particular type of policy. And there are many variations among countries in the same category even in the same period, or within the same country in different periods. For instance, the South Korean government adopted restrictive policies on foreign direct investment in strategic industries, while the Taiwanese government gave similar opportunities to foreign firms as long as they entered a form of joint venture with local partners. The Philippines and Indonesia started industrial promotion of the second type, but later switched to the first type or industry-specific policies to promote heavy and chemical industries. Examples are the "Eleven Strategic Industries Promotion Plans" under the Marcos regime in the Philippines at the end of 1970s, and the "Ten Strategic Industries Development Plans" under Bacharuddin Jusuf Habibie, then Minister of Research and Technology in Indonesia at the end of 1980s.

What is important here is to identify the similarities and the differences in industrial policies among countries in East Asia. In order to do this, I have selected five major elements as key indicators for characterizing industrial policies. These five are: (1) main policy objectives addressed by the government; (2) significant means of implementing policies to be adopted (or available means under the *given* conditions); (3) major players, including both the government sector and private sector in implementing policies; (4) policy results in terms of economic performance in promoted industries; and (5) changes in international economic environment, in particular, globalization, and increasing external pressure on economic liberalization.

This chapter aims to examine the experience of Thailand by comparing two different types of industrial policies after the Asian currency crisis in 1997, namely, the Industrial Restructuring Plans (IRP) under the Chuan Leekphai administration (1997–2000), and the National Competitiveness Plans (NCP) under the Thaksin Shinawatra administration (2001–06).[2]

In the initial stage of economic development, Thailand had adopted a moderate industrial policy of the second type, in accordance with its five-year national economic and social development plans. However, in the mid-1990s, the government began to reconsider conventional policies, and in 1998 switched its policy objective to restructuring *targeted* industries, including small and medium-sized enterprises or SMEs (Ministry of Industry 1999; JETRO 1999). This switch is closely related both to the economic difficulties caused by the Asian crisis and to the policy suggestions given by the Japanese government. Indeed, when the Ministry of Industry of Thailand formulated IRP, they accepted Japan's technical cooperation, and imported some significant ideas from the Japanese experience (Suehiro 2000*b*; JETRO 1998). But the Thaksin administration, which seized power in 2001, abruptly decided to abort IRP. Instead the new government invited Michael Porter, who is a professor of Harvard Business School, as a special policy advisor to the prime minister (Porter 2003), and replaced Japan-oriented IRP by America-oriented NCP.

Because of the differences of the two external policy advisor teams in their approaches to industrial policies, the two major plans, IRP and NCP, show an interesting contrast. IRP principally focused on *international competitiveness at the workplace level* and proposed the promotion of *supporting industries* (SIs), as well as SMEs as key players in SIs, while NCP focused on *innovation-driven development* beyond the workplace and proposed the development of *industrial clusters*, including the non-manufacturing sector. Thereafter, the two major plans seem to provide us with good examples when we discuss the perspective of industrial policies in East Asia in the new era of globalization and economic liberalization.

This chapter consists of six parts. Following this introduction, I will do an overview of industrial policies of Thailand prior to the Asian crisis in section 2. In sections 3 and 4, I introduce the more detailed story of IRP and NCP, referring to the background, the process of policy formulation, and outline of the projects. In section 5, on the basis of these fact-findings, I compare the two plans with reference to policy objectives, policy means, responsible agencies and major players, and international conditions, to determine the policy direction. Section 6 is a temporary conclusion derived from my study of these two plans.

2. OVERVIEW OF INDUSTRIAL PROMOTION POLICIES IN THAILAND

Objectives, Means, and Responsible Agencies

Between 1939 and 1959, the Thai government had adopted a state interventionist approach in industrial promotion. They, in fact, established many state enterprises in major manufacturing industries, and otherwise also controlled directly rice exports, sugar refining, and commercial banking (Suehiro 1989, Chs. 4 and 5). At the same time, they also restricted the free entrance of foreign firms into the domestic market because of the state ideology of economic nationalism. It was only after 1960, when the government started the first Six-Year National Economic Development Plan (later changed to the Five-Year Plan) that they eventually switched their economic policy from state-led development, to a private sector-based development (see Table 4.1).

From the 1960s, three government agencies were mainly responsible for industrial promotion in Thailand. They were the National Economic and Social Development Board (NESDB) for economic development planning; the Board of Investment (BOI) for investment promotion for local and foreign firms; and the Ministry of Commerce (MOC) for trade policy. Compared with the cases of Japan and South Korea, we see several

Table 4.1
Regulations and Liberalization of Industrial Sector in Thailand, 1960–97

Year/Month	Major Industrial Policies
1961/01	The first National Six-Year Economic Plan started (later changed to the Five-Year Economic & Social Development Plan)
1962/01	Industrial Promotion Act B.E. 2505 (1962) was enacted under the auspices of the Board of Investment (revised in January 1966 and June 1968)
1969	Committee for Automobile Industry Development formed in Ministry of Industry
1969–77	BOI (Board of Investment) promotes feed milling and agro industry
1971	Restrictions on new construction or expansion of spinning and weaving factories (later partially lifted for export-oriented factories; fully liberalized in 1991)
1971	Restrictions imposed on a number of car models; locally-manufactured auto parts promoted
1972/10	Investment Promotion Act was revised in favour of some types of export-oriented industries
1972/12	Restriction on the type of occupations where foreigners can work
1977	New Investment Promotion Act enacted to promote fully export-oriented industries such as agro-industry
1978	Ban on car imports; procurement of locally-manufactured auto parts reinforced
1978	Petroleum Authority of Thailand (PTT) set up (using natural gas discovered in 1973)
1980/09	The Committee to Develop Basic Industries on the Eastern Seaboard was established to promote heavy and chemical industries (Rethinking Committee was set up due to economic recession in November 1985)
1981	Joint Public and Private Sector Consultative Committees (JPPCCs) set up to tackle prolonged economic recession
1982–83	World Bank provides Structural Adjustment Loans (SALs) to the Thai government
1984	National Petrochemical Corporation established (public enterprise)
1989	Japan International Cooperation Agency (JICA) and Ministry of International Trade and Industry (MITI) proposed promotion of supporting industries to the Thai government according to the "New AID Plan" (ODA based policy recommendation)
1989	Sahaviriya group granted monopoly rights for integrated steel plants (fully liberalized in 1994)
1990/05	Oil refining industry deregulated; Caltex Oil (Texaco Group) approved as the fifth company
1990/07	Import ban on cars under 2300cc lifted; reduction of import duties on automobiles
1991/04	Cement industry fully liberalized

continued on next page

Table 4.1 — *cont'd*

Year/Month	Major Industrial Policies
1992/08	Petrochemical industry liberalized (PE, PP, PVC)
1993/11	Automobile assembly fully liberalized
1994	Export and Import Bank of Thailand (EXIM) established
1995/05	Petrochemical industry fully liberalized
1996/05	Bureau of Supporting Industry Development established
1996/09	Five-Year Master Plan for Electronics Industry Development formulated
1996/11	Master Plan of Industrial Development of Thailand formulated
1997	National Industrial Development Committee set up to promote industrial restructuring

Sources: Arranged by the author from his data base and Suehiro (2008, Ch. 6).

similar characteristics of industrial policies in Thailand in both its policy objectives and means.[3]

Firstly, the Thai government aimed at the promotion of import-substitution type of industries (ISIs) *in general* rather than the promotion of particular industries. In Japan and South Korea, the government had frequently selected particular industries such as machinery and electrical/electronics as *strategic* industries, and formulated five-year development plans for each industry (Fukagawa 1989; Wade 1990; Hashimoto et al. 1998; Suehiro 2008, Ch. 6).

Contrary to such *industry-specific* policy, the Thai government attempted to cover a wider range of industries as their targeted ones. For instance, they listed as many as 123 types of industries in the Industrial Investment Promotion Act of 1962, which was the first comprehensive act for industrial promotion (this act was revised in 1966 and 1968) (Ministry of Industry 1966). In these acts, the government requested applying firms to meet the simple conditions of either a minimum size of initial investments (or employment size), or a minimum capacity of production to seek economies of scale. The BOI was responsible for the process of screening firms to be promoted in cooperation with the NESDB, and provided them with a set of privileges. Unlike in the previous period of economic nationalism, foreign firms were also given the same privileges as local ones as long as they were expected to contribute to the industrial development of Thailand.

Secondly, the government attempted to support firms promoted with tax incentives, not direct fiscal finance or loans. In Japan, the Ministry of Finance set up the Trust Fund Bureau (TFB) for the purpose of financing a national economic development plan. In addition to government bonds, the TFB pooled a huge amount of people's savings at nationwide postal offices and pension funds, and provided fiscal investment and loans (FILs) to firms promoted in strategic industries through the Japan Development Bank or JDB (Nippon Kaihatsu Ginko, established 1951). In South Korea, the government provided firms promoted with industrial credit through government-sponsored financial institutions.

In Thailand too, the Industrial Finance Corporation of Thailand (IFCT) was established by the Ministry of Finance in November 1959 to serve as a supplier of industrial credit. But IFCT could merely account for less than 1 per cent of the total outstanding bank loans, and its contribution to industrial investment was very limited. Instead the government preferred the provision of tax incentives to fiscal finance, which included the exemption of corporation tax and exemption of import duties on raw materials and machinery, for five to seven years. The BOI gave special treatment on electricity fees and water supply services. In the case of foreign firms promoted, they were also granted privileges in getting work permits and land holdings in spite of the fact that their ownership in joint ventures was restricted in favour of local partners after the 1970s.

Thirdly, in order to protect local infant industries, the government increased import duties on manufactured goods between 1962 and 1964. For instance, import duties on yarns and fabrics were increased from 20 per cent to about 60 per cent. Thus the combination of trade policy with investment promotion became the core means for import-substitution-oriented industrialization during the 1960s. What should be noted here is the fact that the investment promotion policy implied a discrimination one for firms not promoted in tax treatment, and inclined to produce lobbyist activities among private firms. At the same time, this policy hardly contributed to the improvement of management and productivity of firms promoted because they were automatically guaranteed tax privileges as long as they met the initial requirements of the BOI. The BOI was not empowered to supervise the business activities of firms promoted. In contrast, in Japan, the Ministry of International Trade and Industry (MITI) and Japan Development Bank (JDB) acted as supervisors through the strict process of screening firms promoted and granting loans. With MITI's technical advice and JDB's monitoring, loans seem to have served as an important instrument for modernizing production technology and the management of these firms (Freedman 1988; Nippon Kaihatsu Ginko 1993).

In the 1970s, two occasional events greatly affected the industrial promotion policies of Thailand. The oil shock or rapid increase of imported crude oils in 1973 made the government decide to shift its policy objective from import substitution to export promotion. The government was requested to look for new sources of foreign currency earnings to balance its increasing import value. Fortunately, the increase of crude oil caused a rapid increase of export unit price of other primary products such as rice, maize, natural rubber, and sugar. Consequently, the export-oriented agro-industry became one of targeted sectors in the New Investment Promotion Act enacted in 1977. In addition, in 1972, natural gas was occasionally discovered in the Gulf of Thailand. In order to utilize natural gas, the government launched ambitious projects for developing petrochemical and other heavy industries in Eastern Thailand (Industrial Development Plans on the Eastern Seaboard). Thus, Thailand had two major targets by the end of 1970s, namely, export promotion based on agro-industry, and the upgrading of its industrial structure based on domestic energy resources (Higashi 2000).

However, the second oil crisis in 1979 in turn produced negative effects on non-oil producing developing countries such as Thailand through a combination of declining demand for primary commodities in industrial advanced countries, and increasing interest rates in international financial markets. Indeed the annual growth rate of world exports dropped from 20 per cent in the 1970s to merely 6 per cent in the 1980s, while international interest rates jumped from 1 per cent to 6 per cent in the corresponding period (Suehiro 2000, p. 17). Immediately after the second crisis, Thailand experienced a long-term economic recession, and was forced to suspend the Eastern Seaboard Industrial Projects temporarily because the government depended heavily on external public debts. Finally, the government decided to call for IMF's standby credit and the World Bank's structural adjustment loans (SALs) between 1982 and 1983 (Chaipat 1992; Suehiro and Higashi, eds. 2000, chapter 1).

The economic recession of this period inevitably produced big conflicts about adequate economic policies to be adopted in Thailand. For instance, inside the NESDB, a conflict surfaced between a group who was pro-industrial promotion, in favour of the Eastern Seaboard projects, and a group who was anti-industrial promotion, in favour of rural development projects, while among those in the academic circle, a conflict was revealed as to the policy orientation between economic protectionism and economic liberalism.[4]

Similar to the situation in the 1970s, external events again determined the trend for the Thai economy, particularly a Plaza Accord concluded in September 1985. This international arrangement of foreign exchange rates among advanced countries (Group of Five meeting) caused rapid appreciation of the Japanese yen and the local currencies of East Asian NICs against the U.S. dollar. After the Plaza Accord, a great amount of direct investment from these countries/regions flowed into Southeast Asian countries, including Thailand (see Chapter 1). Surprisingly, the total net value of foreign direct investments which Thailand received in 1990 alone (64.7 billion baht) was equivalent to the aggregated amount for fifteen years between 1973 and 1987 (64.6 billion baht) (Suehiro 1998, p. 19). Such an investment boom developed into a construction boom, and then into a stock market boom. Owing to active investments from foreign and local firms, Thailand could enjoy unprecedented economic expansion between 1988 and 1996, which recorded an annual growth rate of 9.6 per cent on average in real GDP, 12.5 per cent in the manufacturing sector, and 19.1 per cent in export value, respectively (Suehiro 2006, p. 195; see also Figure 4.1).

In this period of economic boom, the government launched *new industrial policies* in addition to existing export promotion policies. Four policy agendas may be important in connection with our discussion in the next part. Firstly, the government announced the acceleration of industrial upgrading policies by fully supporting the Eastern Seaboards industrial projects (see Chapter 5). The Ministry of Finance lifted the limitation on external borrowings for these projects entirely, while the BOI provided a wider range of tax incentives for foreign and local firms that planned to invest in petrochemicals, steel, and automotives in Eastern Thailand (Higashi 2000).

Secondly, the government switched its basic investment policy from protection to liberalization, and decided to open the door gradually to local and foreign investors in important industries such as oil refining, cement, automotives, auto cycles, petrochemicals, and electrical/electronics between 1991 and 1995 (see Table 4.1). The shift to economic liberalization in selected industries was principally designed to adjust the conventional industrial investment policy to financial liberalization starting in 1990. In addition to this original purpose, it was apparent that the government also intended to attract more foreign investors into the Eastern Seaboard industrial projects (Suehiro and Higashi 2000, Ch. 3).

Thirdly, the Ministry of Industry (MOI) eventually started the decentralization of industrial sites from the Bangkok Metropolitan area to the countryside. For this purpose, MOI promoted the establishment of government-sponsored and private-owned industrial estates outside Bangkok (see Chapter 5), while appointing thirteen prefectures as "strategic industrial areas" in Central, North, Northeast and South Thailand in 1993 (Nipon and Fuller 1996). Supporting the MOI's decentralization policy, the BOI also announced a new category of the "Third Zone" to promote industrial investment in remote areas, and decided to reduce tax privileges in the First Zone (Bangkok) and the Second Zone (Eastern area, etc.) in April 1993 (Suehiro 1998, p. 24).

Finally, the MOI began to adopt a new strategy of developing particular industries. For instance, they approved the five-year development plan for the electronics industry in September 1996, as part of a master plan for the industrial development of Thailand which was announced in November 1996. The master plan was not only aimed at promoting heavy industries but also at developing supporting industries in conjunction with the development of the automotive and electronics industries. These plans were the first of such efforts in Thailand in the sense that the government formulated its policy on the basis of comprehensive field research on each industry (TDRI 1996).

Three agencies or institutions are basically responsible for the planning of these plans. They are the Department of Industrial Promotion of the MOI in planning a grand design, the NESDB in coordinating sectoral plans with the national economic and social development plans, and the Thailand Development Research Institute (TDRI), the most productive private think-tank, in research activity and policy suggestions. At the same time, Japan's MITI also cooperated with the MOI through JICA's technical assistance (Japanese ODA), particularly in drafting the development plan for supporting the automotive and electronics industries (Ministry of Industry 1995).

As the brief overview above suggests, Thailand has continuously changed its industrial policies from investment promotion of import substitution to a combination of export promotion with industrial upgrading, and then to a combination of accelerated industrial upgrading, introduction of economic liberalization, and construction of master plans for industrial sector. And major policy objectives were also changed from the protection of local infant industries in domestic markets to the enhancement of the industrial sector under the pressure of economic globalization. This being the case, what is the economic performance of Thailand under such policy shifts? And how can we evaluate the causality between the government policies and economic performance? This is the next question to be answered here.

Industrial Performance and Policy Evaluation

Figure 4.1 summarizes the long-term trend of the economic performance of Thailand between 1972 and 2005. Annual growth rates of real GDP, the manufacturing sector, and exports, are employed as indicators to show its economic performance. As the figure suggests, the Thai economy has experienced periodical fluctuations, or repetitions of boom and recession, in conjunction with such external shocks as the primary commodities boom, the second oil shock, and the investment boom. Nevertheless, from the long-term perspective, it is safe to say that Thailand has successfully achieved "stable growth" for the past three decades (Warr and Bhanupong 1996; Suehiro and Higashi 2000, Ch. 1).

Besides *relative* economic stability, the figure also informs us that the industrial sector has almost always exceeded real GDP in terms of annual growth rate, while export growth had exceeded industrial growth until the Asian crisis in 1997. These facts, consistent with the findings in Chapter 3, temporarily suggest to us that the economic growth in Thailand has been driven mainly by the industrial sector, based on export expansion in each period of economic boom. If this observation is acceptable, we must examine the next question, namely, whether or not economic stability and industrial growth can be attributed to the government policies, and we also need to answer another question, which is, whether or not government policies have transformed the Thai industrial sector into a competitive one in a globalized economy.

Regarding these questions, many scholars seem to share common views on the government's role in contribution. More exactly, they have frequently held positive views on the government's role in sound management at the *macroeconomic* level, in contrast with negative views on the role in industrial promotion at the *microeconomic* level. Typical work on this may be seen in the Warr and Bhanupong report which was published by the World Bank in 1996. This report was originally prepared as part of country-based background papers for the famous World Bank's report on

Figure 4.1
Economic Growth and Exports in Thailand, 1972–2005 (%, annually)

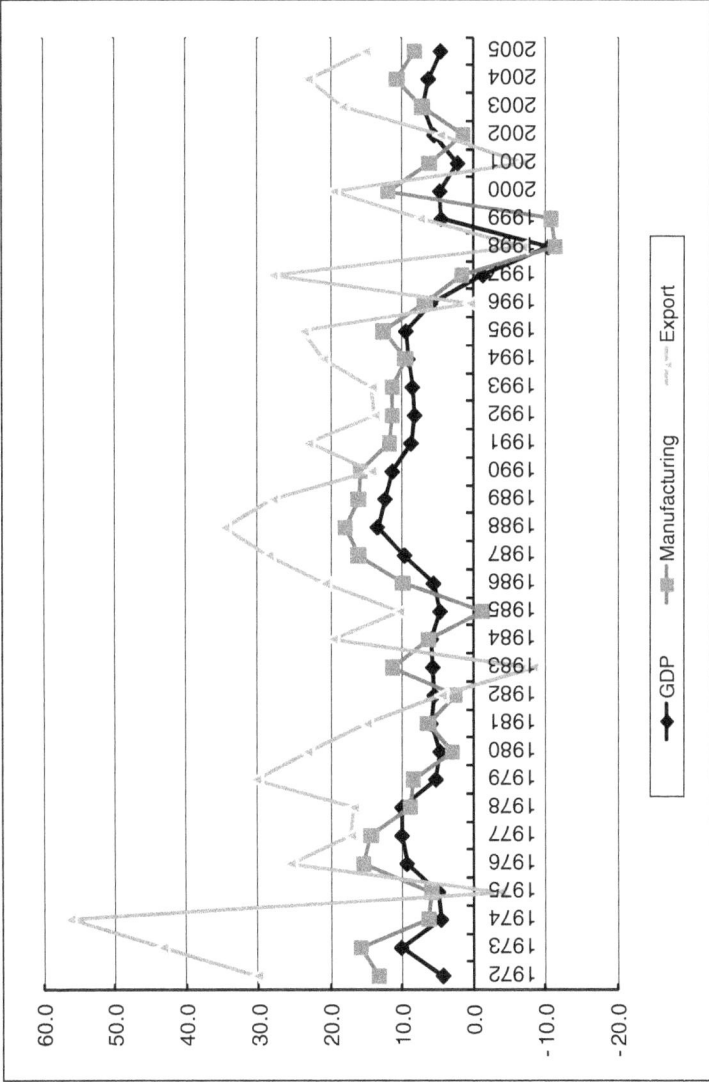

Notes: 1. Figures show actual ones; 2. Exports are computed on the basis of U.S. dollars.
Sources: 1972–95: NESDB, National Income of Thailand 1960–1995, revised edition; 1996–2005: Figures from the Bank of Thailand's homepage.

"The East Asian Miracle: Economic Growth and Public Policy" (World Bank 1993).

To meet the request of the World Bank, Warr and Bhanupong carefully analysed the interrelationship between Thailand's macroeconomic miracle and the government's role, and in particular, investigated the government's response (fiscal and monetary policies) to external shocks between the 1970s and 1980s. In this report, the authors were reluctant to appraise discretionary adjustment policies in the short run, and instead emphasized properties of automatic stabilizers in the market mechanism or long-term policy outcomes. They concluded that "Thailand's outstanding record of macroeconomic stability can be understood properly only when the long-term sources of policy stability are emphasized" (Warr and Bhanupong 1996, p. 232). On the other hand, "at the industry level, it is clearly the poor performers that are promoted by these measurements [protection, export promotion, tax incentives, etc.]. The political economy behind these results is presumably that industries that are well organized for lobbying purposes put proportionately more resources into the behavior that secures bureaucratic support than industries that are less well organized" (Warr and Bhanupong 1966, p. 81).

A similar argument is discovered in the paper of Christensen, Ammar, and Pakorn (1997) concerning the topic of "Institutional and Political Bases of Growth-Inducing Policies in Thailand". In this paper, the authors focused on the role of the state in fostering economic growth, looking in particular at the effectiveness of state intervention, and the issue of model transferability from South Korea and Japan. To meet this task, they presupposed two major hypotheses which are as follows.

"First, Thai economic policy has been most effective in maintaining a macroeconomic equilibrium conducive to trade, investment, and the growth of private firms. It has been least effective in either identifying or implementing sectoral objectives. Thai sectoral policies have not been guided by a "picking-winners" strategy and have been marked often by patronage and rent-seeking. And, second, regarding transferability, we argue that an activist state may require certain institutional capacities that, by many measures, have eluded Thai economic policy, notably sectoral policy. The stable macroeconomic environment, combined with the resources and entrepreneurial strategies of private firms, particularly in the banking sector, have helped overcome certain weaknesses on the sectoral side" (Christensen et al. 1997, p. 23).

Other scholars also arrive at the same conclusion that the Thai good economic performance, including industrial growth, has been supported by the government's conservative macroeconomic policies, particularly its fiscal and monetary policies, and a "pattern of predominantly company-led industrialization" (Lauridsen 1991, p. 43). Industrial growth and export expansion in Thailand, they insist, have been underpinned by long-term policy outcomes and activities of private firms. On the other hand, they show negative views on the direct policy effect at the level of particular industry or particular sector. As Lauridsen specifically noted, "the predominant pattern of structural change was that of diversification into a range of new industries (*widening*) rather than development of high-value added activities (*deepening*). Thailand generally failed to develop local capabilities in the manufacture of parts and capital goods production" (Lauridsen 1991).

In fact, such industrial weakness was revealed in the decline of manufactured exports, particularly the decline of exports of labour-intensive products from Thailand in 1995 and 1996, preceding the currency crisis. This export slump became a significant opportunity for the government to reconsider its conventional approach to industrial promotion after the crisis.

3. INDUSTRIAL RESTRUCTURING PLANS UNDER THE CHUAN ADMINISTRATION

Background of IRP and Its Objectives

In January 1998, or six months after the outbreak of the Asian crisis, the master plan of the Industrial Restructuring Plans (IRP) was approved by the cabinet (the Chuan Leekpai administration). In March of the same year, the Department of Industrial Promotion of the Ministry of Industry (MOI) formulated the IRP "strategic plans" in accordance with each targeted industry, while, in June, the MOI submitted to the cabinet a comprehensive "action plan" on the basis of the IRP master plan (Ministry of Industry 1999; Suehiro 2000b).

IRP was understood as a plan to be hastily prepared for the Chuan government to use up US$600 million from the Asian Development Bank, which was part of a total of US$17. 2 billion supplied as standby credits by the IMF and consortium members, including Japan, to rescue Thailand from the currency crisis in August 1997 (Suehiro 2000*b*, p. 42). However, the original idea of IRP may be dated back to the mid-1990s, when the MOI drafted a master plan for the development of the Thai industrial sector in a changing international economic environment. Therefore, we will examine the general background of IRP first.

Table 4.2 is constructed to indicate the export problems facing Thailand in 1995 and 1996. In addition to the ordinal classification of export products (agricultural, agro-industrial, industrial, and mineral goods), I have tried to reclassify major products into three main categories, according to the differences in both the commencement of their actual export, and their annual growth rates. The three categories are: (A) a group of traditional exportable products such as rice, natural rubber, and sugar, which were constantly declining in their proportions to total exports; (B) a group of labour-intensive type of products the export of which began to increase from the 1980s, including agro-industrial products, textiles and garments, footwear, leather products, gems and jewellery, and integrated circuits; (C) a group of newly emerging products the export of which rapidly increased after the 1990s, including electrical/electronics products, automobile parts, and plastic and chemical products.

In 1996, Thailand for the first time experienced a serious export slump (or the so-called *1996 export crisis*) during the economic boom. Examining carefully the export performance by employing the above three categories, we see that group B suffered an export decline of 14 per cent in 1996 against the previous year.[5] Contrary to government expectations, group C — which had enjoyed an export increase of 448 per cent between 1990 and 1995 — also saw its export growth rate decline to merely 4 per cent in 1996. When the National Industrial Development Committee (NIDC) was established in August 1997, its first task was not to promote "industrial development" in line with the economic boom, but to tackle "industrial restructuring" under the export crisis. More exactly, they were requested to look for a way to recover international competitiveness in *sunset* industries (namely, group B in Table 4.2), and then a way of enhancing international competitiveness in *growing* industries (group C) (Ministry of Industry 1998, pp. 1–4).[6]

In response to the NIDC's order to examine major causes behind the 1996 export crisis, the MOI reported the following points as serious problems facing the Thai industrial sector. They include: (1) lower management efficiency and higher production cost in manufacturing firms;

Table 4.2
Export Performance of Thailand by Type of Commodities 1990–97
(Unit: Million Baht)

Commodity Group/	Classification	1990	1995	95/90	1996	96/95	1997	97/96
Total Export		589,813	1,406,310	2.38	1,411,039	1.00	1,806,685	1.28
Agricultural products		132,837	231,417	1.74	230,659	1.00	257,562	1.12
Rice	A	27,770	48,627	1.75	50,735	1.04	65,094	1.28
Natural rubber	A	23,557	61,261	2.60	63,373	1.03	57,459	0.91
Frozen shrimps	B	20,454	50,302	2.46	43,045	0.86	47,185	1.10
Tapioca	A	24,465	18,253	0.75	20,651	1.13	22,466	1.09
Broiler chickens	B	7,590	9,662	1.27	9,398	0.97	11,272	1.20
Agro-industrial		73,521	132,132	1.80	142,030	1.07	170,500	1.20
Canned fish	B	21,623	33,295	1.54	34,244	1.03	49,309	1.44
Sugar	A	17,694	28,769	1.63	32,081	1.12	31,493	0.98
Industrial products		366,736	1,016,457	2.77	993,958	0.98	1,280,145	1.29
Computer goods	C	38,695	131,242	3.39	167,674	1.28	220,305	1.31
Garments	B	65,804	102,019	1.55	79,875	0.78	97,139	1.22
Intergrated circuits	B	21,581	58,182	2.70	58,539	1.01	75,838	1.30
Gems & jewellery	B	34,892	52,499	1.50	54,273	1.03	55,623	1.02
TVs and Radios	C	7,980	31,589	3.96	34,627	1.10	43,579	1.26
Footwear	B	20,220	53,778	2.66	33,544	0.62	35,306	1.05

Item	Class							
Automobile parts	C	—	12,638	—	15,630	1.24	32,616	2.09
Fabrics	B	12,746	23,051	1.81	21,712	0.94	28,272	1.30
Air conditioners	C	1,960	20,177	10.29	24,074	1.19	27,415	1.14
Plastic products	C	7,988	52,691	6.60	22,093	0.42	27,023	1.22
Plastic materials	C	1,090	10,889	9.99	10,664	0.98	23,981	2.25
Transformers	C	822	14,063	17.11	15,115	1.07	21,956	1.45
Video goods	C	11,751	23,270	1.98	16,516	0.71	21,686	1.31
Furniture	B	7,717	17,384	2.25	17,405	1.00	20,988	1.21
Chemical products	C	—	9,681	—	13,703	1.42	20,816	1.52
Printed circuits	C	1,252	13,887	11.09	11,673	0.84	19,929	1.71
Mineral goods		9,761	14,326	1.47	28,270	1.97	50,543	1.79
Tines	A	1,875	406	0.22	—	—	—	—
A Group	A	95,361	157,316	1.65	166,840	1.06	176,512	1.06
B Group	B	212,627	400,172	1.88	342,637	0.86	409,660	1.20
C Group	C	71,528	320,127	4.48	331,769	1.04	459,306	1.38

Note: Classification of commodities is made on the basis of the author's survey.
Sources: Ministry of Commerce, Trade Statistics and Economic Indicators of Thailand, various issues.

(2) lower level of production technology and dominance of low-end products in manufactured exports; (3) shortage of marketing know-how and no capacity to develop new markets; (4) lower level of workers' skill and their lower educational background; (5) the limited scope of supporting industries; (6) concentration of manufacturing firms in the Bangkok Metropolitan Area; (7) no adequate policy to manage industrial pollutions and other problems. All of these problems reflected more or less poor policy outcomes at the microeconomic level, and showed an industrial weakness tending towards industrial *widening*, rather than industrial *deepening*. In order to overcome these problems, the MOI proposed eight policy agendas as in the following (Ministry of Industry 1998, pp. 10–18).

(1) Improvement of management efficiency and reduction of production cost through the effort of productivity improvement.
(2) Introduction of modern machinery and equipment, by replacing old-fashioned ones.
(3) Skill development of production workers and provision of continuous occupational training.
(4) Promotion of SMEs and employment outside of Bangkok.
(5) Relocation of labour-intensive industries from Bangkok to the countryside and promotion of local economy in rural areas.
(6) Capacity building in manufacturing firms in developing new products, new design, and new markets.
(7) Active invitation of foreign investors to technology-intensive industries.
(8) Shift of pollution-type industries to remote areas and establishment of industrial waste control system.

As for the agencies engaged in each task, MOI and the Industrial Estate Authority of Thailand (IEAT) were appointed to be principally responsible for policy targets 1 to 5, while the Ministry of Commerce was responsible for 6, the BOI for 7, and the Ministry of Science, Technology and Environment for 8 (see Figure 4.2).

On the other hand, the MOI extended the scope of targeted industries from electronics and machinery in the 1996 Master Plan to *seven* industrial groups in the IRP temporary plan in September 1997 and further to *eleven* ones in the IRP final master plan in January 1998. These eleven industrial groups include: (i) textiles and garments; (ii) food processing; (iii) footwear

Figure 4.2
Organization Chart for the Industrial Restructuring Plan in Thailand, 1999

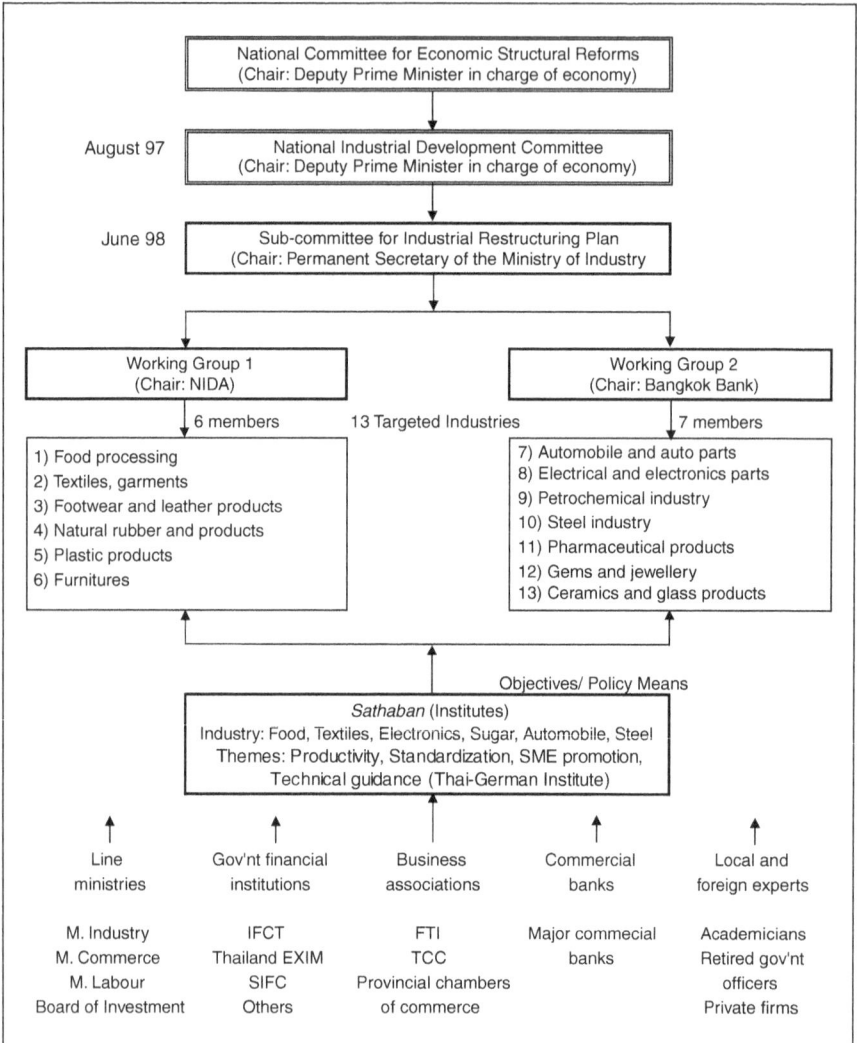

Notes: NIDA: National Institute of Development Administration; IFCT: Industrial Finance Corp. of Thailand; EXIM: Export and Import Bank of Thailand; SIFC: Small Industry Finance Corporation; FTI: Federation of Thai Industries; TCC: Thailand Chamber of Commerce.

Source: Made by the author on the basis on his research interview in Bangkok, August 1999.

and leather products; (iv) gems and jewellery; (v) electrical/electronics products; (vi) automobile products; (vii) furniture; (viii) ceramics and glass products; (ix) pharmaceutical and chemical products; (x) plastic products; and (xi) rubber products.

Among them, groups i to vi were already selected in the IRP temporary plan, while groups vii to xi were newly added in IRP final master plan.[7] However, the expansion of the scope of targeted industries did not end here. In the process of drafting a strategic plan (March 1998), another two industries, petrochemicals and steel, were also included in the IRP due to strong pressure from both business circles and local individual big firms.[8] These thirteen strategic industries in the long run are estimated to account for over 60 per cent of the total value added in the manufacturing sector in 1998. The matrix to show the interrelations between *eight* policy objectives and *eleven* (not thirteen) industrial groups are illustrated by the author in Table 4.3.

Japan's Policy Support and the *Sathaban* System

It is apparent that the IRP master plan partially succeeded in enhancing the assets of the MOI's existing industrial promotion policies introduced in the first half of 1990s (industrial relocation, etc.). But we should not overlook a new aspect of IRP, together with the direct and indirect assistance of the Japanese government to the MOI before the Asian currency crisis.

In Japan, from the mid-1980s, MITI started new technical cooperation projects for ASEAN countries under the name "New Asia Industries Development Plans" or "New AID Plans" to support industrial upgrading in the area. For Thailand, a big team of technical experts was dispatched twice by JICA, and they conducted intensive field studies in cooperation with the Department of Industrial Promotion of the MOI and the Metalworking and Machinery Industries Development Institute belonging to the MOI. The first team was sent to engage in field studies between 1987 and 1988 on selected export-oriented industries such as textiles/garments, gems and jewellery, toys and supporting industries such as dyeing and moulding (JICA 1991). The second team conducted field studies between 1991 and 1992 on two major industries, automobile and electronics, with a special reference to the situation of local industries supporting these two (JICA 1995).

But the reports of the Japanese expert teams, based on their field research, hardly attracted the real attention of the Thai government in an

Table 4.3
Eleven Targeted Industries and Eight Objectives of the Industrial Restructuring Plan 1997

Targeted industries	1 Improvement of productivity	2 Modernization of equipments	3 Skills development	4 SMEs promotion in rural area	5 New products development	6 Relocation of factories	7 Invitation of foreign firms	8 Control of pollution
1 Food processing	C	C	C		C		C	C
2 Textiles, garments	C	C	C		C	C		C
3 Sport shoes	C	C	C		C	C		
4 Leather products	C				C	C		
5 Plastic products	C	C			C			C
6 Gems and jewellery	C				C	C	C	
7 Ceramics, glass products	C				C			
8 Pharmaceuticals, chemical products			C	C	C			
9 Electronics parts	C	C	C	C		C	C	
10 Auto parts	C	C	C	C				
11 Other specific industries			CAM/CAD		Packaging		Rubber products	Plating

Note: C means that an objective covers a targeted industry.
Source: Made by the author from data of the Ministry of Industry (1998).

era of economic boom because a lot of Japanese firms including SMEs, occasionally advanced into Thailand to invest in petrochemicals, automobiles, electronics and related supporting industries. It was only after the 1997 currency crisis that the Thai government actually acknowledged the importance of Japan's reports, including their many policy suggestions.[9]

Apart from field studies through the "New AID Plans", Japan's MITI also started annual regular meeting from 1993 onwards with staff of the MOI to discuss problems facing the Thai industrial sector. At these meetings in Bangkok or Tokyo, MITI suggested that the MOI adopted Japanese models in designing Thailand's industrial promotion policies. In the Japanese experience, MITI always emphasized the necessity of promoting supporting industries (SIs) and SMEs in order to enhance the competitiveness of Thai industrial products in world markets. Therefore, just before the Asian crisis, MOI staff were already familiar with the Japanese approach and key concepts in Japanese-style industrial polices, such as productivity improvement at workplaces, SI promotion, and SMEs promotion. And these concepts were substantially incorporated into the IRP master plan in accordance with policy suggestions by Japanese technical experts dispatched after the crisis (JETRO 1998).

Another important characteristic in the IRP is observed in the role of unique responsible agencies. Before the crisis, government agencies such as NESDB, MOI, MOF, and BOI, were exclusively responsible for the industrial promotion policies in Thailand. However, full government involvement became more and more difficult partially because of the increasing pressure of economic liberalization and partially because of policy conditions laid down by the IMF and World Bank that the government downsize the number of both public agencies and government officers. For these reasons, the government needed to set up non-government institutions or *sathaban* to implement IRP.

Sathaban is a kind of independent institution which consists of three groups of staff — those recruited from the public sector, private sector, as well as local/foreign technical experts — and its activity is put under the auspices of an independent board of directors from the government. It is true that the government (or foreign aid agency) usually grants land, facilities and equipment together with initial working capital to a *sathaban*. But *sathaban* itself is expected to mobilize necessary funds from the private sector or the money market (issuance of bonds) to expand its activity (Ministry of Industry 1998).

A *sathaban* was established in accordance with two different criteria — the type of strategic industry (food processing, automobiles, etc.) it is in and the specific purpose of its activity (productivity improvement, industrial standardization, technological training, etc.). By the end of 1998, there were ten *sathaban* in operation under the supervision of MOI (see Table 4.4). According to the MOI policy, industry-specific type *sathaban* would cover all the thirteen strategic industries of IRP in the future, but this idea was finally abandoned by the Thaksin administration in 2002 (see section 4).

A prototype *sathaban* may be seen in the Thailand Productivity Institute (TPI), which was established as an independent institution in January 1994 to reorganize the former Productivity Division of the Department of Industrial Promotion of the MOI. TPI staff consisted of government officers, staff recruited from the private sector and Japanese technical experts dispatched by JICA and MITI-JODC (Japan Overseas Development Corporation). After the crisis, TPI quickly expanded its services owing to support from both the MOI and Japanese government. By 1999, TPI was reported to be employing 150 consultants and providing more than 1,000 clients (firms) with five major consulting services on the ISO 9000 series, promotion of the Kaizen activities, support of efficient handling of machinery, improvement on management of production processes, and human resources development (Suehiro 2000*b*, p. 49; Thailand Productivity Institute 2001).

The Thai-German Institute (TGI) followed the same pattern of a triple alliance between the public sector, private sector, and foreign (German) technical experts. TGI is mostly financed by the KfG Bank, a German international aid agency, and the German Development Cooperation (GTZ). TGI provides local skilled workers and technicians/engineers with various OJT-based services for automation production management, training of CAD/CAM, and teaching moulding and dyeing. Profits obtained from these services become a part of the funding to support the TGI activity, in addition to German public assistance (Thai-German Institute 1999).

Other *sathaban* on the basis of specific industry also employed a similar system as TPI and TGI to underpin their activities. For instance, the Thai Automotive Institute (TAI) recruited necessary staff from the public sector, the private sector, including the Federation of Thai Industries (FTI), and Japanese experts through JICA and JODC technical assistance (twenty-three Japanese staff in 2000) for the purpose of the

Table 4.4

The Industrial Restructuring Plan and *Sathaban* in Thailand as in October 1999

Sathaban (Institute)	Approval at the Cabinet Meeting Starting up	Objectives, Activities and Organization
Thailand Productivity Institute (TPI)	Jan 94	Reorganize the Productivity Division of Industrial Promotion Dept., Ministry of Industry into a *sathaban*.
	Jun 95	20 board members with 161 staff for 1,000 clients (firms)
Thai-German Institute (TGI)	Sept 92	Financial support from KfW Bank and Germany Development Corporation or GTZ.
	Nov 95	Providing On-the-Job Training (OJT) for local people in the fields of automation management, Computer Numerically Controled (CNC), Computer Aided Design/Computer Aided Manufacturing (CAD/CAM), and moulding and dyeing technology.
		12 board members, 79 local staff and 5 German experts
Thailand Textile Institute (TTI)	Oct 96	Set up by both Industrial Promotion Dept. and business associations.
	Jun 97	Four subcommittees in formulating master plan, product inspection, human resources development, and technology and environment problems.
National Food Institute (NFI)	Oct 96	Set up by both Industrial Promotion Dept. and business associations.
	Oct 96	Promotion of product inspection and food safety standards
		23 board members and 55 local staff
The Management System Certification Institute (MSCI)	Oct 97	Reorganize the Thailand Industrial Standard Institute (TISI) into a *sathaban*.
	Mar 99	Providing test, inspection and certification for product standard
		Diffusion and guidance of a series of ISO 9000
		14 board members and 55 local staff

Institution	Date	Description
Thai Automotive Institute (TAI)	Jul 98	Set up by Industrial Promotion Dept in collaboration with private firms.
	Apr 99	Planning of master plan, certification of product standards, human resources development, and improvement of technology and quality of auto parts
		Development of "supply chain" system
		20 board members with 28 local staff (later 23 Japanese experts)
Electrical & Electronics Institute (EEI)	Jul 98	Set up by Industrial Promotion Dept. in collaboration with private firms
	Feb 99	Planning of master plan, promotion of exports, certification of product standards, and Off-the-Job Training (Off-JT)
		Matching parts makers with assemblers
		29 board members with 28 local staff
Foundation for Cane & Sugar Research Institute	none	Reorganize the Sugarcane and Sugar Institute into a *sathaban*
	Apr 99	13 board members under the Permanent Secretary of the Ministry of Industry
Institute for SME Development (ISMED)	Apr 99	Copying the Japan's Small and Medium Business Institute
	Jun 99	Thammasat University serves as a core centre in collaboration with eight universities
		Teaching and training of owners of SMEs in the field of management and accounting
		Development of a *kigyo shindan-shi* system.
		21 board members, recruiting local staff
Iron & Steel Institute	Dec 98	Promotion of cartel in sale of steel products among four major steel firms
	n.a.	Under planning

Sources: Research interview by the author in Bangkok in November 1998 and in August 1999; documents compiled by the JETRO Bangkok Center.

capacity building of local auto parts manufacturers in both management and production technology.[10]

Policy Shift from SI Promotion to SMEs Promotion

In the process of implementing the IRP, however, the government had changed its policy priority from restructuring of targeted industries in line with the improvement of its international competitiveness, to the general promotion of SMEs. It is true that the MOI aimed to promote SMEs in the initial stage of formulating IRP. They principally looked at SMEs as main players in supporting industries (SIs) to enhance the cost performance of export-oriented industries such as electronics, and otherwise as main contributors in creating new employment outside of Bangkok. But political elements became a pressure for the Chuan government to change its policy objective from the promotion of SMEs in SIs through technical assistance, to the promotion of SMEs as a whole, through public financial support (Suehiro 2000b, p. 49).

More concretely, the Chuan coalition government reshuffled its cabinet in October 1998, and appointed Suwat Lippatapanlop as the new Minister for Industry. Suwat at the time was the secretary general of the Chart Patthana Party. It was reported that Suwat made a direct request to the prime minister for the post of Industry Minister to enhance the presence of his party in a coalition government. Immediately after the appointment, Suwat ordered MOI staff to accelerate the promotion of SMEs as the most urgent policy target in the IRP. In the same period, the Thai Rak Thai Party (TRT: Thai people loving the country of Thailand) led by Thaksin Shinawatra also appealed to the people with a set of policy agendas, including SMEs promotion. And between 6 and 8 November, the TRT organized a big open conference on SMEs at the Sirikhit Convention Hall (Suehiro 2000b, pp. 57–58).

In competing with these activities of their political rivals, Prime Minister Chuan and Finance Minister Tharin Nimmanhaeminda, who belong to the Democrat Party (core party of a coalition government), immediately adopted counterbalancing measures. On 23 November, Tharin met with Yosano Akira, a minister of MITI, in Bangkok and obtained a promise of technical and financial assistance for the promotion of SMEs from the Japanese government. At the same time, the Ministry of Finance in December provided the cabinet with an extra budget of

35 billion baht for the public support of SMEs, while in January 1999 Suwat and the MOI submitted to the cabinet the SME Promotion Act. Acceding to the requests of Suwat and Tharin, the MITI finally decided to dispatch a special mission led by Mizutani Shiro to Thailand in January 1999. The Mizutani mission visited Bangkok periodically until July, and served two ministers in two different tasks: technical support for the IRP for the MOI, and support of SMEs in the financial field for Tharin and the MOF (Suehiro 2000*b*, pp. 58–60).

Because of these political elements, the target of the IRP was now expanded to the promotion of SMEs on the whole, and the means of implementing this policy from technical assistance to thirteen strategic industries and SIs through *sathaban* to financial support to SMEs through government financial institutions such as the Small Industry Finance Corporation (SIFC) and Japan's ODA.[11] It is true that the MITI continued to give technical assistance to the MOI by employing Japanese model such as credit analyses of SMEs, advice for the modernization of production technology, and the establishment of the factory evaluation system through a scheme of on-the-job training. The last one is a scheme in which Japanese experts train local people, including the second generation of SMEs owners, as professionals (*kigyo shindan-shi*) for the sake of improving SME management at the workplace. But such activities has no effective linkage to the restructuring of strategic industries. Moreover, the financial support of the government tended to produce the traditional behaviour of rent seeking among SME owners in the same way as before (see section 2). Consequently, the original policy objective of IRP was eroded in exchange for political campaigning for the coming election, and the role of the Japanese model and the transfer of Japanese experiences in the IRP had become less important by 2000.

4. NATIONAL COMPETITIVENESS PLANS UNDER THE THAKSIN ADMINISTRATION

Thaksin's Reforms and Background of the NCP

The general election in January 2001 completely changed the political landscape in Thailand. The ruling party changed from the Democrat Party led by Chuan Leekpai and Tharin Nimmanhaeminda, to the TRT led by Thaksin Shinawatra, which won 248 out of 500 seats in the election.

Thaksin, who was appointed the new prime minister in February, had served as a government officer in the Computer Centre of the Police Department. In 1983, he started his own business of computer rental service for government agencies and universities. Thanks to a combination of his distinguished talents, the IT boom, and his connections with government agencies, he quickly expanded his business scope from rental and maintenance services of computers into the sale of mobile phones and satellite services. By mid-1990s, he had successfully developed his companies or the Shin Group into the largest conglomerate in the telecommunications industry of Thailand (Pasuk and Baker 2004).

Because of his unique career background, Thaksin attempted to introduce a business approach into the management of politics, under the slogan "a country is a company; a prime minister is the CEO of a country". At the same time, he challenged almost all sectors of the Thai economy and society to modernize the state in conjunction with new worldwide wave of globalization, liberalization, and IT revolution. His ambitious plan may be expressed in economic policies (the so-called *Thaksinomics*), or "dual-track policies" addressed in his policy speech in March 2001. As already mentioned in Chapter 2, the dual-track policies aimed at two different targets: the promotion of grass roots economy in rural areas by giving opportunities and necessary funds to the rural people, on one hand, and the promotion of private firms in urban areas on the other hand by providing incentives to local and foreign investors.

In 2001, however, the Thaksin administration placed stress on the first track, or the promotion of grass roots economy, in accordance with the TRT policy agenda in its election campaigns. These policy agendas include: (1) a village (*tambon*) fund scheme in which the government provides one million baht equally to all the villages (70,000 villages) and urban communities to create new projects; (2) a three-year moratorium on debt payment for peasants; (3) a "one village (*tambon*) one product" or OTOP movement in which the government encourages the development of specific products in local communities; (4) the establishment of the People Bank for small-sized own-account business owners; (5) a 30-baht healthcare service or a universal healthcare scheme; and (6) the promotion of SMEs through government-sponsored financial institutions. Needless to say, these policies were aimed at eliciting the support from the people for the new administration (Suehiro 2000c; Worawan 2003; Pasuk and Baker 2004, Chapters 4 and 5).

Entering 2002, in addition to such a populist-type approach, the Thaksin administration began to extend the scope of its policy agenda to the second target in its "dual-track policies". The core of the second target is the construction of national competitiveness or an "Outline of Competitiveness Development in Thailand", which was officially approved by the cabinet in April 2002. As far as industrial policy was concerned, the cabinet had already approved an action plan of "New Industrial Restructuring Plans" in December 2001. This plan was a revised version of the MOI's plan to adjust the previous IRP in line with the ninth Five-Year National Economic and Social Development Plan starting in October 2001.

But, in practice, Thaksin completely neglected the MOI's revised plan and ordered the NESDB to draft a new plan for industrial development. This is partially because Thaksin did not welcome the policy advantages in the Chuan administration, and partially because he needed a new state strategy corresponding to his four-year tenure, not an industrial policy, in corresponding to the Five-Year Plan. An "Outline of Competitiveness Development in Thailand" is thus a direct product of his top-down style of politics, and became the guideline for formulating the National Competitiveness Plan (NCP) in 2003.

In May, or the month following the approval of the outline, the government set up the National Competitiveness Committee as a core agency to discuss the NCP. At the same time, Thaksin eventually terminated the activities of the National Industrial Development Committee which had been responsible for the IRP in the Chuan administration. In June, he decided to allocate an extra budget of 16.6 billion baht for the FY 2003 for a feasibility study of the NCP. From October 2002, the NESDB started the joint work of drafting the NCP in collaboration with staff of SASIN (Graduate Institute of Business Administration of Chulalongkorn University). In May 2003, the government invited Professor Michael Porter from the Harvard Business School as a special policy advisor to the prime minister.

Finally, in October 2003, the NESDB submitted to the cabinet the final report on the "National Competitiveness Development in Thailand" (NESDB 2003a, 2003b). In order to gear up for the policy agenda included in this final report, Thaksin allocated a special budget of 75.5 billion baht for FY 2004 or 6.5 per cent of the total budget, and 23.4 billion baht for FY 2005 or 1.9 per cent of the total budget. As in the case of the 16.6 billion baht for FY2003, these funds came exclusively from the Central Fund

(*Ngop Klang*) which was put under the direct control of the prime minister.[12]

Porter's Diamond Model and Cluster-based Approach

Just like the case for the IRP, the external advisor group played an important role in determining the policy direction of the NCP. This means, the work of drafting the NCP was closely connected with the ideas and policy suggestions of Michael Porter. The reason the government selected him as a policy advisor was that Somkhit Jatuphithak, who was deputy prime minister in charge of economic affairs and finance minister at that time, was occasionally a translator of Porter's work (1990) into the Thai language. Somkhit introduced Porter's academic works to Thaksin, and Thaksin showed keen interest in Porter's Diamond Model while discussing state strategy. In any case, Porter came to live in Bangkok for two weeks and proposed the basic concepts for, and final direction of the new industrial policy to the government.

According to Porter's observation, Thailand was facing many problems in the industrial sector, particularly in its *productivity* (see Figure 4.3). As discussed in Chapter 3, the chart in Figure 4.3 clearly confirms that Thailand achieved by far the lowest performance in terms of labour productivity (GDP per person employed per hour) than Asian NICs such as Taiwan and Singapore, and was ranked in the lowest level in terms of the annual growth rate of labour productivity, even when with ASEAN countries and China.

In addition to such a poor performance in labour productivity, Porter also pointed out the weakness of the Thai industrial sector using his Diamond Model, which was originally constructed to identify a competitive advantage in a particular country, with reference to four fundamental conditions, which are factor or input, demand, context for firms' strategy and rivalry, and the development of related and supporting industries.[13] Each condition is interlinked to one another in determining the national competitiveness of the country concerned. Examining each condition one by one in the context of Thailand, Porter based his judgment of current Thai industrial competitiveness from a *regional* perspective.

For instance, with regard to the factor condition, he concluded that the general skill of the Thai labour force was low and communication networks were expensive outside Bangkok. Likewise, with regard to the development

Figure 4.3
Labour Productivity and Growth of Labour Productivity in East Asia: 1995–2000

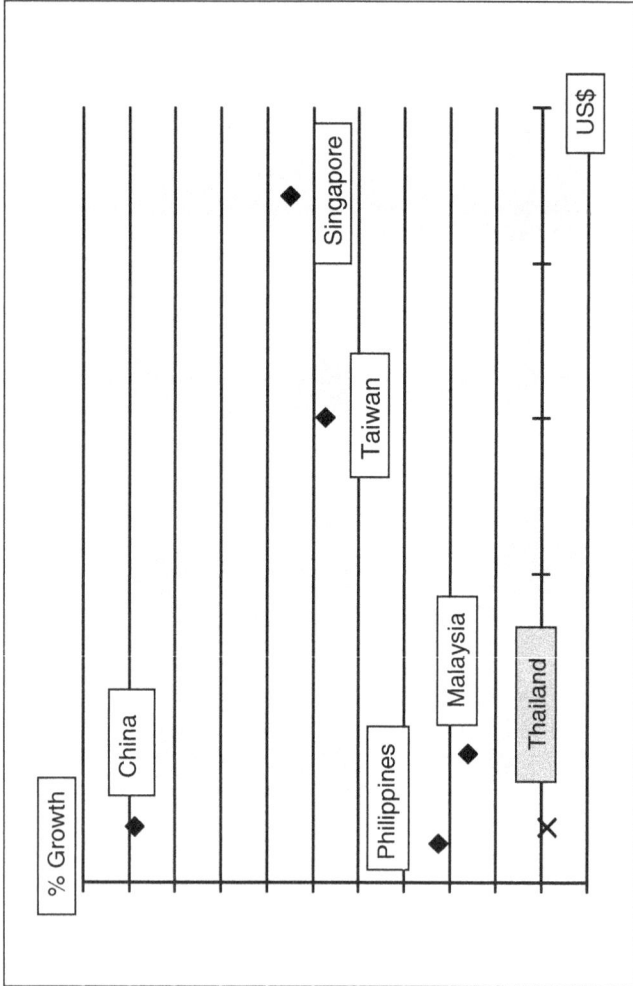

Sources: Made by the author on the bases of IMD (2001, p. 446) for GDP per person employed per hour (US$) and NESDB (2003a) for the growth of labour productivity between 1995 and 2000.

of supporting industries, he observed that Thai clusters were focused on a few labour-intensive stages of their industries' value chain and cluster organizations tended to be focused solely on lobbying. Over the long period, he gave a positive evaluation for merely four items (foreign investment, natural resources, infrastructure, and domestic market for pick-up trucks) out of fifteen selected items (see Table 4.5).

Based on such pessimistic observation, he emphasized that Thailand must move to *a new model of competitiveness*, in which the government is

Table 4.5
Porter's Diamond Model and Thailand's Weaknesses

Items	Weakness and Strength in Thailand	New Direction to be Adopted
Factor (Input) Conditions	(S) locations, natural resources, and physical infrastructure (roads).	presence of high quality, specialized inputs
	(W) low skill level; expensive communication network cost	human, capital and natural resources; various infrastructure
Demand Conditions	(S) pick-up truck is one of the most developed markets in the world	unusual local demand in specialized segments.
	(W) local demand is unsophisticated, not lead international trend.	sophisticated and demanding local customers
Context for Firm Strategy and Rivalry	(S) inward foreign investment raise the level of competition.	local context and rules that encourage investment and sustained upgrading.
	(W) firms compete on low input cost; bureaucracy and corruption	open and vigorous competition among locally based rivals.
Related and Supporting Industries	(W) focusing on a labour intensive stages of industries' values chain.	access to capable, locally based suppliers and firms in related fields.
	(W) cluster organizations tend to be focused solely lobbying.	presence of clusters instead of isolated industries.

Note: W is weakness, while S is strength.
Sources: Made by the author on the basis of NESDB (2003*a*; 2003*b*).

expected to gear up for the upgrading of the business environment rather than the promotion of targeted industries. He also claimed that "a sound macroeconomic, political, legal, and social context creates the potential for competitiveness, but is not sufficient. Competitiveness ultimately depends on improving the microeconomic capability of the economy and the sophistication of local companies and local competition" (Porter 2003, pp. 12–13). Until the Asian crisis in 1997, Thailand had gradually shifted the pattern of industrial development from factor-driven development to an investment-driven one. It was now necessary for Thailand to enter a new stage of *innovation-driven* development. *"Without an improvement in microeconomic fundamentals, current growth will be short-lived."* That was his conclusion.

Looking at the final report on the NCP in October 2003 (NESDB 2003*a*; 2003*b*), we can easily discover the strong influence of Porter's arguments, as well as his policy suggestions. Concerning major problems facing the Thai industrial sector, the NESDB summarized them into five points: (1) low labour skill and low potentiality in developing science and technology; (2) weakness of industrial linkage and lower cooperation at the business level; (3) ineffective legal framework and bureaucracy which hamper the improvement of competitiveness; (4) business strategy focusing on price competition in the short run rather than long-term investment plan to support company competitiveness in the future; and (5) the overall lack of sophistication of domestic demand. All these arguments overlap with Porter's presentation to the Thai government.

Based on these perceptions over the situation at the time, the NESDB's report selected five groups of industries to target, which, as already mentioned, are the food, automotive parts, fashion, tourism, and software. Of these five, the first four were already included in the strategically promoted industries in the "Mid-Term Economic Policy 2001–2006", which was approved by the cabinet in July 2001.[14] The method of targeting particular industries seems similar to the MOI style in drafting the IRP in 1998. Examining the final report of the NESDB carefully, however, we see substantial differences between the IRP and NCP in both policy objectives and means. In brief, NCP put stress on the *policy-agenda* approach based on the key concepts of cluster and innovation, rather than the *industry-specific* approach which the MOI had adopted in the IRP (see section 5).

The final report proposed that the government adopt two major groups of policy agenda, together with six more concrete strategies (NESDB 2003*b*).

The first group belonged to a policy agenda aimed at coordinating government policy with business (company) strategy. This group consisted of four strategies: (i) upgrading the business environment, including natural and human resources, infrastructure, science and technology, and investment incentives; (ii) active cluster development in association with government support in matching the business sector with the public sector and local research institutes; (iii) transforming company strategy from a short-run cost reduction policy to a more sophisticated one focusing on value-added creation and market segmentation; and (iv) leading a cross-national strategy through regional (Asian level) cooperation in the fields of information exchange, standardization of products, and regionwide market development.

The second group belonged to a policy agenda aimed at coordinating policymaking with effective policy implementation. The second group consisted of another two strategies: (v) redefining the roles of business and government in relation to the *cluster-based approach*, that is, shifting from the initiative of the government at the national economy level to cooperation between public sector, business sector, universities, and local research institutes at a *cluster level*; and (vi) decentralizing more economic policies to the regional (provincial) level and promoting the creation of region-based cluster outside Bangkok.

Obviously, these six concrete strategies also corresponded to the ideas given by Porter in his presentation. More precisely, the final report on the NCP is a product of the joint team of the NESDB and the SASIN (younger staff and graduate students) who simply adapted concepts and ideas of Porter to the state strategy outlined by Prime Minister Thaksin. All the agencies and experts related to the work of drafting the master plan of industrial development in 1996 and the IRP of 1998 were intentionally excluded from the present working team. Indeed, we cannot discover any contribution of the MOI and the Thailand Development Research Institute (TDRI) to the final report. The NCP final report did not refer at all to field studies conducted by the MOI, JICA, and TDRI in the past. Rather the NCP final report was garnished with a lot of terminology and concepts borrowed from American business school textbooks, and was a good contrast to the IRP, which mainly imported key concepts from Japan's experiences through Japanese experts. Next, let me move to the comparison of the IRP and NCP with reference to policymaking, policy objectives, means to implement policies, responsible agencies, and main players.

5. COMPARISON OF THE IRP AND NCP

As far as perceptions of major problems facing Thai industrial sector were concerned, both the IRP and NCP seemed to arrive at similar conclusions. They equally discovered fundamental problems in low labour productivity, low-level capacity in developing new production technology and new markets, and poor cooperation between the public sector and business sector. Both also addressed the necessity of changing policy direction from economic expansion (widening) to the improvement of industrial competitiveness (deepening), and from sound macroeconomic management to the creation of microeconomic competitiveness. The two plans also shared the basic idea that the public sector should cooperate with the private sector and other non-government institutions in response to the increasing pressure from economic globalization and liberalization.

The major differences between the IRP and NCP are policy targets, policy implementing means, and the role of the government. For policy targets, the IRP focused on the improvement of competitiveness *for the specific manufacturing industry* as well as *capacity building at the workplace* in each company or factory, while the NCP put the first priority on the improvement of competitiveness *at a cluster level*, including the non-manufacturing sector (R&D, legal services, and accounting services), as well as the *transformation of company strategy* in each firm in line with the development of the global value chain (GVC) based on information and communication technologies.

Such shift in policy targets corresponded to policy recommendations by economists in the World Bank who emphasized innovation-driven development and cluster-based approach for the crisis-hit East Asian countries. They argued that:

> innovation will be the engine of growth for much of East Asia now that the initial resource-intensive phase of industrialization is ending. Innovation in a broad range of area, from products to services and business organization, will be the principal source of increases in productivity and in export competitiveness.... Moreover, successful clusters rely on policies supporting openness, which encourage many-stranded links with other clusters worldwide. In other words, product and process innovation is a function not just of investment in R&D, but also of the clustering of networked firms in an open and competitive policy environment. (Yusuf and Evenett 2002, pp. 3–4).

More critical differences between the two plans may be seen in the major players and the role of government in implementing industrial policies. For instance, the IRP employed the *sathaban* as the significant instrument in achieving its targets, but it presupposed the initiatives of the MOI and the NESDB in the promotion of supporting industries and SMEs. For funding *sathabans*, the government continued to serve as the largest contributor, together with foreign aid. The IRP also continued to employ conventional policy measures. Although the IRP shifted its policy priority to strategic industries, the government still resorted to tax incentives through the BOI, public technical assistance through foreign economic aid, and fiscal support through line ministries. There was no effort made to develop new policy implementing means to achieve the IRP.

In contrast, the NCP restricted the government's overall support for state projects. Rather, Thaksin seemed to have defined the government role as coordinating multiple players to create a new business environment. He expected private firms and the stock market to play a more active role in supporting state projects. It is true that the Thaksin administration decided to allocate a huge amount of extra budget for the NCP in the first three years, which amounted to 115.5 billion baht. But all of this was aimed at supporting FS, the starting up of the projects, and the provision of seed money. After the initial three years, the government almost fully entrusted the projects to the private sector and leading private firms in targeted industries.

In the case of the development of the automotive industry, the Thaksin administration employed the Thai Automotive Institute (TAI) as the core agency in the initial stage. But three years later, he changed the policy to encourage foreign firms to offer direct support through BOI tax incentives, or otherwise to give indirect support to private initiated projects. The main projects in the development of the automobile industry were next transferred from the TAI to Japanese auto assemblers who had expanded production bases in Thailand according to their regionwide corporate strategies. At typical case may be seen in the Thailand Automobile Industry Development Plan starting in 2005 in which four Japanese leading firms (Toyota, Honda, Nissan, and Denso) jointly planned to train 1,000 competitive, local auto parts manufacturers in the Japanese production system in the next ten years.[15] Thaksin did not provide any more fiscal support any more to this giant project, except in the provision of visas and work permits.

The case of the fashion industry shows more clearly the policy direction of the Thaksin administration with regard to the relationship between the public sector and private firms. In order to promote this industry, Thaksin did not agree to set up a new *sathaban* because he himself viewed *sathaban* as ineffective agencies, excepting TAI and the National Food Institute. Instead, he appointed the president of the Association of Gems and Jewellery Exporters in Thailand, Thai owners of leading jewellery exporting companies, and owners of modern boutique shops, as chairpersons of seven subcommittees of an industrial cluster of the fashion industry. Major projects were planned by these firms, while the government contributed to coordination in international campaigns, the setting up of pavilions and the arrangement of exhibitions. As Christensen, Ammar and Pakorn (1997) already pointed out, industrial performance depends principally on "entrepreneurial strategies of private firms" rather than well-arranged government industrial policies.

6. CONCLUDING REMARKS

Frankly speaking, it is difficult for us to make a precise evaluation on the policy outcomes of the IRP and NCP. This is because that IRP was abruptly terminated by the Thaksin government after the general election in 2001, while the NCP was eventually suspended by the Surayut new government after the military coup in September 2006. Each plan could survive for merely four years, even if we include the period of policymaking (the IRP from 1997 to 2000, and the NCP from 2002 to 2005, respectively). Such time spans are too short to evaluate precisely the policy outcomes of each plan with reference to its original policy targets.

Rather it is worth noting that the two short-lived plans suggest to us the changes in environment that determined economic policymaking as well as the role of economic technocrats in Thailand. Two elements seem to influence economic policies decisively, including industrial policies. Firstly, economic liberalization meant that some policy instruments were taken off the hands of economic technocrats. Although the BOI still continued to provide firms promoted with tax incentives, the government could hardly employ other policy implementing means such as direct subsidies, protective import duties, fiscal finance, and favourable industrial credit under the strong pressure of international financial institutions. The government was now expected to play the role not of a conductor but of a coordinator in national projects according to the NCP.

Secondly, the change in power structure or the increasing power of elected politicians, political party leaders, and the prime minister inevitably narrowed the scope of authority of economic technocrats in decision making. In the era of military rule, political leaders gave technocrats some autonomy in policymaking as long as the former group was guaranteed benefits and political rent from state activities. However, after governments were established through periodical general elections, political party leaders became important players in policymaking. We see a typical case in the promotion of SMEs in the Chuan administration, in which the MOI was forced to shift major policy objectives in the IRP due to the political games inside the coalition government. Thaksin also changed the decision making system in economic policies. He neglected NESDB's Five-Year Plan and MOI's IRP, and replaced them by his own state strategies by using the Central Fund in national budgets. These facts suggest to us the limited role of economic technocrats in both economic planning and sectoral policy in contemporary Thailand.

Another notable characteristic observed in the two plans is the underdevelopment of institutional capacity for handling industrial policies in Thailand. As Japan's experiences suggest, adequate policy targets and effective policy implementation need some institutional factors, which include: (1) planning by able technocrats equipped with accurate industrial knowledge; (2) constant information exchange between the government and private sector through meetings of industrial councils; (3) a well-arranged monitoring system for firms promoted without political intervention; and (4) well-organized business associations which represent members' interests and national interests rather than the particular interests of individual firms.

In spite of the fact that the IRP and NCP attempted to look for good cooperation between the government and private sector, there is no institutional framework and institutional capacity to support such cooperation. Due to the lack of industrial knowledge and experience among technocrats, they must frequently depend on external advisors and foreign experts. Due to the lack of information exchange, the NCP directly imported basic ideas from American business school textbooks. Due to the lack of well-organized business associations, leading firms inclined to look after their own interests rather than national interests, which led them to rent-seeking behaviour. Such limitations in institutional capacity may be the most important element for the poor policy outcomes in the sectoral policies of Thailand.

Lastly, I would like to conclude this chapter by noting two major problems facing contemporary Thailand in the field of industrial development. Firstly, Thailand could achieve economic stability, industrial growth, and export expansion due mainly to the sound management of macroeconomics and the active response of private firms to changing environments. Sound management of macroeconomics has been underpinned by good cooperation among government agencies such as the NESDB, MOF, MOI, BOI, the Bureau of Budgets, and the Bank of Thailand. However, such cooperation was seriously damaged under the Thaksin administration, which resulted in economic instability since 2006. Of course, the further development of the Thai industrial sector presupposes economic stability at the macroeconomic level. Therefore, Thailand is now facing not only the improvement of national competitiveness at the microeconomic level, but also sound economic management at the macroeconomic level.

Secondly, the liberalization of industrial investment in the early 1990s made it possible for foreign firms to enter Thailand more freely. Foreign firms are no longer good partners for local firms in domestic protected markets, but have become strong competitors in liberalized markets. Foreign firms have been risen constantly increasing in size from the mid-1990s, and particularly after the Asian crisis. For instance, according to my original survey on the distribution of the 100 largest firms in terms of annual turnover, there were sixty-three Thai firms and thirty-seven foreign firms in 1994. In 2004, the figures reversed, with forty-five Thai firms and fifty-five foreign firms. If we choose manufacturing firms from the 100 largest firms, we see that thirty-three Thai firms accounted for 448 billion baht (62 per cent of aggregate total sales of manufacturing firms) against eighteen foreign firms with 276 billion baht (38 per cent) in 1994. In 2004, these figures changed to twenty-two Thai firms with 1,025 billion baht (34 per cent) against forty-nine foreign firms with 2,023 billion baht (66 per cent) (Suehiro 2006, p. 287).

As these figures show, foreign firms are increasing their dominant status more and more and this is particularly so in electronics, automobiles, petrochemicals, steel, and telecommunications. Local firms are being driven into labour-intensive or natural resources-based industries such as agro-industry, garments, furniture, and gems and jewellery. Foreign firms are now developing their production and marketing activities in only accordance with their regionwide corporate strategies, rather than with the government industrial policies of their host countries. They will go along with governments as long as they can obtain benefits from state policies such as the BOI tax incentives. This implies that Thailand is losing its autonomy in policymaking and must depend crucially on the corporate strategies of foreign firms. To use an expression of Lauridsen, Thailand is now experiencing a pattern of predominantly *foreign company*-led industrialization. This is a result of economic globalization and liberalization.

Notes

1. Masuyama calls this type "industrial policies in the entrepot NIEs" (Masuyama, Vandenbrink, and Chia 1997, Chs. 3 and 4). See also Suehiro (2008, Ch. 6).
2. For the process of formulating and implementing IRP, see Suehiro (2000*b*). There are no academic works concerning NCP excepting Oizumi (2004), but NESDB (2002, 2003*a*, 2003*b*) and Porter (2003) are fundamental documents for understanding NCP.
3. For industrial policies in Thailand between 1960s and 1980s, see Somsak (1981); Atchakan (1988); Suehiro (1989, Ch. 6); and Lauridsen 1991.
4. For instance, economists in the NESDB, regardless of their different stances on industrial promotion and rural development, appealed for the necessity of economic protection, while Dr Narongchai (advisor to the IFCT) insisted on economic liberalization (Narongchai 1982).
5. On export evolution, see also Chapter 3.
6. The NIDC was originally established to implement the 1996 Industrial Development Plan of the MOI. But ironically, before implementing this plan, the 1996 export crisis forced the NIDC to reconsider the plan, and to replace it by the Industrial *Restructuring* Plan.
7. In the IRP temporary plan, textiles and garments were classified separately, and targeted industries accounted for seven industries.
8. Major pressures came from industrial clubs of the Federation of Thai Industries (FTI) and leading local firms such as the Sahaviriya group, NTS group, and SSP group in the steel industry. Author's research interview conducted at the MOI in Bangkok in March 1999.
9. Japan's MITI dispatched Tanigawa Hiroya as a special policy advisor to the MOI from March to December 1998. Tanigawa cooperated in promoting supporting industries (SIs) in accordance with policy suggestions in the JICA report of 1995 (JETRO 1999).
10. Author's research interview conducted at TAI in August of 1999.
11. For the detailed story of Japan's support to SMEs in Thailand after 1998, see

Oki (1999). Oki is an expert dispatched by JICA to SIFC to design the framework of SMEs' finance.

12. The Central Fund is a special budget funding for extra national expenditure such as natural disasters, royal travels, additional compensation to government officers, and expenditure for government officers' pension. Traditionally, this central fund had accounted for around 10 per cent of the total budget allocation, while 80 to 85 per cent of the total budget was allocated to personnel and investment expenditure through line ministries. Thaksin changed the traditional system and utilized the Central Fund as a budget source to support his state strategies, such as village funds projects, the NCP, and the provincial cluster development strategy. Consequently, the percentage of the Central Fund to the total budget increased between 20 and 25 per cent in his administration.

13. Porter's Diamond Model is described in Porter (1990), and is summarized in Suehiro (2000a, Ch. 2; 2008, Ch. 2).

14. The mid-term economic policy, which strongly reflected the TRT policy agenda in the election campaign, classified industries promoted into three categories of the A type, with further promotion (industries using Thai traditional skills), the B type with priority given to the improvement of international competitiveness (food processing, automotive parts, textiles, and tourism), and the C type with new investment (bio, microchips, e-commerce). Apparently, the B type industries were automatically transferred to targeted ones in the NCP, although textiles were replaced by the fashion industry, including garments, leather products, and gems and jewellery.

15. Author's research interview with staff of Toyota Motor Thailand, conducted in Bangkok in August 2005.

References

Amsden, Alice H. *The Rise of "the Rest": Challenges to the West from Late-Industrializing Economies*. New York: Oxford University Press, 2001.

Anek Laothamatas. *Business Associations and the New Political Economy of Thailand: From Bureaucratic Polity to Liberal Corporatism*. Boulder: West View Press, 1992.

Atchakan Sibunruang. "Industrial Development Policies in Thailand". A Report prepared for the World Bank. Bangkok: Board of Investment, 1988.

Bangkok Post ed. "To Stay Competitive — Somphob: Five-Year Industrial Restructuring Plans". *Bangkok Post*, 6 October 1997.

Chaipat Sahasakul. *Lessons from the World Bank's Experience of Structural Adjustment Loans (SALs): A Case Study of Thailand*. Bangkok: Thailand Development Research Institute, 1992.

Christensen, Scott R., Ammar Siamwalla and Pakorn Vichyanond. "Institutional and Political Bases of Growth-Inducing Policies in Thailand". In *Thailand's Boom and Bust*. Bangkok: Thailand Development Research Institute, 1997.

Dixson, Chris. *The Thai Economy: Uneven Development and Internationalization*. London: Routledge, 1999.

Friedman, David. *The Misunderstood Miracle: Industrial Development and Political Change in Japan*. Ithaca: Cornell University Press, 1988.

Fukagawa, Yukiko. *Kankoku: Aru Sangy? Hatten no Kiseki* [South Korea: A Trajectory of Industrial Development]. Tokyo: JETRO, 1989.

Gomez, Edmund. *Politics in Business: UMNO's Corporate Investments*. Kuala Lumpur: Forum, 1997.

Hashimoto, Juro, Shin Hasegawa and Hideaki Miyajima. *Gendai Nihon Keizai* [The Contemporary Japanese Economy]. Tokyo: Yuhikaku, 1998.

Higashi, Shegeki. "Sangyo Seisaku: Keizai Kozo no Henka to Seifu-Kigyo-kan Kankei" [Industrial Policy: Business and Government in a Changing Economic Structure]. In *Tai no Keizai Seisaku: Seido, Soshiki, Akuta* [Economic Policy in Thailand: Institutions and Actors]. Chiba: Institute of Developing Economies, 2000.

IMD (Institute for Management Development). *World Competitiveness 2001*, Lausanne, Switzerland: IMD, 2001.

JETRO Bangkok Center. "Tai Sangyo Kozo Chosei Jigyo Gaiyo to Wagakuni no Kyoryoku" [Outline of the Thailand's Industrial Restructuring Plans and Japan's Cooperation]. Bangkok, October (mimeo), 1998.

———. "Tai Chusho Kigyo Seisaku no Genjyo to Mondaiten" [Current Situation and Problems of SMEs Policies in Thailand]. Bangkok (mimeo), 1999.

JICA (Japan International Cooperation Agency). *Tai Oukoku Kogyo Bunya Kaihatsu Sinko keikaku Chosa Hokokusho* [Research Reports on Industrial Sector Development in the Kingdom of Thailand, The First Phase]. 3 vols. Tokyo: JICA, 1991.

———. *Tai Oukoku Kogyo Bunya Kaihatsu Sinko keikaku [Susono Sangyo] Chosa Hokokusho* [Research Reports on Industrial Sector Development: Supporting Industries in the Kingdom of Thailand, The Second Phase]. 2 vols. Tokyo: JICA, 1995.

Kimura, Seishi. *The Challenges of Late Industrialization: The Global Economy and the Japanese Commercial Aircraft Industry*. New York: Palgrave Macmillan, 2007.

Lauridsen, Laurids S. "Industrial Policies, Political Institutions and Industrial Development in Thailand 1959–1991". In *Glob Asia: Changing Global and Regional Conditions for Industrial Development and Environment Protection in the Third World*, Vol. 8, n.a., 1991.

Masuyama, Sei'ichi, Donna Vandenbrink and Chia Siow Yue, eds. *Industrial Policies in East Asia*. Singapore: Institute of Southeast Asian Studies, 1997.

Ministry of Industry (Thailand). *Industrial Development and Investment in Thailand*. Bangkok: Ministry of Industry, 1966.

Ministry of Industry, Department of Industrial Promotion (Thailand). *An Overview: Supporting Industries in Thailand*. Bangkok: Ministry of Industry, 1995.

Ministry of Industry (Thailand). *Kan Prap Khrongsang Utsahakam* (Industrial Restructuring). Bangkok: Ministry of Industry, September 1997.

Ministry of Industry (Thailand). *Phaen Maebot Kan Prap Khrongsang Utsahakam* (Master Plan of Industrial Restructuring). Bangkok: Ministry of Industry, January 1998.

Ministry of Industry, Department of Industrial Promotion (Thailand). *Rai-ngan Prajam Pi 1998: SMEs Small is Beautiful* (Annual Report 1998). Bangkok: Ministry of Industry (in Thai), 1999.

Muscat, Robert J. *The Fifth Tiger: A Study of Thai Development Policy*. Helsinki, Finland: United Nations University Press, 1994.

Narongchai Akrasanee. *Thailand Industrial Sector Background Report*, 2 vols. Bangkok: East Asia and Pacific Region Office, 1982.

NESDB. *Yutthasat Kan Khaenkhan khong Thai phai nai Sathanakarn Mai khong Setthakit Lok* [Strategy of Thailand's Competitiveness in Correspondence to New World Economy]. Bangkok: NESDB, November 2002.

———. *Khrongsang Kan Suksa Kan Phatthana chuk Khwam Samart nai Kan Khaenkhan khong Thai* [Research Project on Development of Thai Competitiveness]. Bangkok: NESDB, October 2003a.

———. *Executive Summary of National Competitiveness Plan*. Bangkok: NESDB, November 2003b.

———. *Rai-ngan Kan Tittam Pramoenphon Kan Phatthana Setthakit lae Sangkhom khong Prathet: 3 Pi khong Phaen Phatthana Chabap thi 9* [Evaluation Report on the National Economic and Social Development: Three Years of the Ninth Five-Year Plan]. Bangkok: NESDB, July 2005.

Nippon Kaihatsu Ginko [Japan Development Bank]. *Seisaku Kinyu: Nihon no Keiken* [Policy Finance: From Japan's Experiences]. Tokyo: JDB, 1993.

Oizumi, Kei'ichiro. "Keizai Renkei Jidai niokeru Thai no Sin Kaihatsu Senryaku" [New Development Strategy of Thailand in the Era of Economic Partnership]. In *Higashi Ajia Keizai Renkei no Jidai* [Emerging Economic Partnership in East Asia], edited by Toshio Watanabe. Tokyo: Toyo Keizai Shinpo-sha, 2004.

Oki, Akira. "Tai no Chusho Kigyo no Genjyo to Seisaku: Nihon no Shien" [Situation and Policies for SMEs in Thailand: Special Reference to the Japanese Assistance]. *Shoho* [Japanese Chamber of Commerce in Bangkok] (June 1999): 1–7.

Pasuk Phongpaichit and Chris Baker. *Thaksin: The Business of Politics in Thailand*. Chiang Mai: Silkworm Books, 2004.

Phatcharee Siroros. *Rat Thai kap Thurakit nai Utsahakam Rotyon* [State and Business in the Automobile Industry in Thailand]. Bangkok: Thammasat University Press, 1997.

Porter, Michael E. *The Competitive Advantage of Nations*. New York: The Free Press, 1990.

————. "Clusters and the New Economic Competition". *Harvard Business Review* (November–December 1998): 77–90.

————. *Thailand's Competitiveness: Creating the Foundations for Higher Productivity*. Bangkok: NESDB, May 2003.

Somsak Tambunlertchai. *Import Substitution and Export Expansion: An Analysis of Indusrialization Experience in Thailand*. Bangkok: Thammasat University, 1981.

Sturgeon, Timothy. "How Do We Define Value Chains and Production Networks?". *IDS Bulletin* (University of Sussex), 32, no. 3 (2001): 9–19.

Suehiro, Akira. *Capital Accumulation in Thailand 1885–1985*. Tokyo: UNESCO, The Centre for East Asian Cultural Studies, 1989.

————. *Kyacchi-appu-gata Kogyoka-ron: Ajia Keizai no Kiseki to Tenbo* [Catch-up Industrialization: The Trajectory and Prospects of East Asian Economies]. Nagoya: Nagoya University Press, 2000*a*.

————. "Tai no Keizai Kaikaku: Sangyo Kozo Kaizen Jigyo to Chusho Kigyo Shien" [Economic Reforms in Thailand: Industrial Restructuring Plans and Assistance to Small and Medium-sized Enterprises]. *Shakai Kagaku Kenkyu* 51, no. 4 (March 2000*b*): 25–65.

————. "Asian Crisis and Economic and Social Restructuring: Americanization and Social Governance". In *Developing Economy in the Twenty-First Century: The Challenges of Globalization*, edited by Ippei Yamazawa. Chiba: JETRO, Institute of Developing Economies, 2000*c*.

————. *Famili Bijinesu-ron: Kouhatsu Kogyoka no Ninaite* [Family Business: Agents of Late Industrialization]. Nagoya: Nagoya University Press, 2006.

————. *Catch-up Industrialization: The Trajectory and Prospects of East Asian Economies*. Singapore: National University of Singapore Press, 2008.

————, ed. *Tai: Kezai Bumu, Keizai Kiki, Kouzou Chosei* [Thailand: Economic Boom, Economic Crisis and Structural Adjustment]. Tokyo: Nihon Tai Kyokai, 1998.

————, ed. *Tai no Seido Kaikaku to Kigyo Saihen: Kiki kara Saiken e* [Institutional Reform and Corporate Restructuring in Thailand: From Crisis to Recovery]. Chiba: Institute of Developing Economies, 2002.

Suehiro, Akira and Shigeki Higashi, eds. *Tai no Keizai Seisaku: Seido, Soshiki, Akuta* [Economic Policy in Thailand: Institutions and Actors]. Chiba: Institute of Developing Economies, 2000.

Takayasu, Ken'ichi. "Jidosha Meka no Gurobaru Tenkai to Ajia Senryaku" [Global Activity and Regional Strategy for Asia of the World Auto Manufacturers]. *Kan Taiheiyo Bijinesu Jyoho RIM* 2, no. 4 (2002).

Thai-German Institute. "Your Partner in High Tech Training and Consultancy". Bangkok: TGI, 1999.

Thailand Development Research Institute (TDRI). *Survey Reports on Industrial Development in Thailand*, 2 volumes. Bangkok: TDRI, 1996.

Thailand Productivity Institute. *Annual Report 2000*. Bangkok: TPI, 2001.

Wade, Robert. *Governing the Market: Economic Theory and the Role of Government in East Asian Industrialization*. Princeton: Princeton University Press, 1990.

Warr, Peter and Bhanupong Nidhiprabha eds. *Thailand's Macroeconomic Miracle: Stable Adjustment and Sustainable Growth*. Washington, D.C.: The World Bank, 1996.

Worawan Chandoevwit. "Thailand's Grass Roots Policies". *TDRI Quarterly Review* 18, no. 2 (June 2003): 3–8.

World Bank. *The East Asian Miracle: Economic Growth and Public Policy*. New York: Oxford University Press, 1993.

Yusuf, Shahid and Simon J. Evenett. *Can East Asia Compete? Innovation for Global Markets*. Washington, D.C.: The World Bank, 2002.

5

THE ROLE OF INDUSTRIAL ESTATES IN THAILAND'S INDUSTRIALIZATION
New Challenges for the Future

Natacha Aveline-Dubach

The rapid industrialization in Thailand has strongly relied on the capacity to allocate land resources for industries, and provide high-quality facilities and services in industrial sites. Among these sites, as already pointed out in Chapter 1, Industrial Estates (IEs) have played a key role in shaping Thailand's industrialization. Developed after 1972, together with major transportation and communication infrastructure, they have contributed to fostering growth in Thailand by attracting a large share of FDI and multinational companies while preserving the country from heavy pollution and reducing unwanted industrial "sprawl".

This development has been facing two major challenges briefly mentioned in Chapter 4. The first challenge is the growing regional imbalance in the manufacturing industry, which causes an overconcentration of firms in the region of the national capital, a problem shared by many Asian countries, but particularly worrying in Thailand.

The second challenge is the necessity to upgrade the Thai manufacturing industry by focusing on local capacity building and innovation rather than passive technological learning from foreign firms. In the 1980s, IE development was fully undertaken by private developers, under the strict regulations and guidance of the Industrial Estate Authority of Thailand (IEAT). As a result, services and facilities in IEs were gradually improved to meet the demands of multinational firms, to the extent of transforming some estates into virtual "industrial cities". The present chapter describes this evolution and examines whether it is consistent with the urgent need to restore the regional imbalance and improve local input in the manufacturing sector.

In the first section we describe briefly the distinctive features of Thai IEs. Then we examine the development of the existing IE network, in line with the regional development policy. The third section deals with the role of private involvement in IE development, and its effects on the supply of services and facilities. Finally, we examine to what extent the existing IE framework could be used as a basis for ongoing innovation and cluster-based policies.

1. DISTINCTIVE FEATURES OF THAILAND'S INDUSTRIAL ESTATES

According to the definition given by the United Nations, "Industrial Estates" are distinguished by four key features:

(1) A large-scale area where land is developed in accordance with a comprehensive plan.
(2) An area served by roads, infrastructures, utilities, and services.
(3) Sale and lease of factory buildings for manufacturing purposes.
(4) Controlled development with restrictive covenants for the benefit of both the occupants and the community at large.

The development of IEs has become a widely common practice across Asia. The first IE was established in Singapore in 1951. Japan, Korea, Malaysia, and Thailand started ten years later, followed by the Philippines and Indonesia in the seventies (Ramos and Sazanami 1991). In all the countries, the purpose of introducing IEs was to encourage economic development — in particular rural and regional development — while raising the living standards of the population. Originally, IEs were developed by a public authority, a state body, or a local authority, but private operators have made inroads into this sector throughout Asia.

Malaysia and India have developed the highest number of IEs, and account for half the estates within the zone between them. Malaysia's importance should be put in perspective: out of its 378 estates, 76 (20 per cent) measure less than 20 hectares. China, on the other hand, shows a high degree of concentration, with more than a third of its IE (41 out of 198) exceeding 1,000 hectares (Table 5.1). The gigantism has peaked in South Korea, with the Kwangyang National Industrial Complex of 9,770 ha, recently developed along the south-central coast, 150 km west from Pusan. The industry is also moderately concentrated in Indonesia, the Philippines, and Vietnam, with very few estates measuring less than 100 ha. Thailand stands between these extremes, with majority of its estates varying between 100 and 500 hectares.

Yet the Thai concept of the "industrial estate" has no equivalent in other Asian countries. Amongst the seventy-three industrial grouping areas in Thailand, only thirty-four are officially listed as IE.[1] Apart from these, there are twenty-three industrial zones, seventeen industrial parks

Table 5.1
Industrial Estates in Asia

	Total number of IEs	Known area of the IEs	IEs of areas less than 20 ha	IEs of areas between 20 and 100 ha	IEs of areas between 100 and 500 ha	IEs of areas more than 1000 ha
China	114	108	0	5	36	26
India	254	254	42	63	141	8
Philippines	99	97	1	56	35	3
Indonesia	22	21	1	2	11	6
Malaysia	378	376	76	178	102	16
South Korea	71	70	13	21	15	9
Thailand*	73	72	2	13	46	9
Vietnam	24	23	0	4	16	3
Taiwan	80	Total area: 45,587 ha, an average area of about 569 ha per estate				

Note: *Only thirty-four IEs are officially listed.
Source: Composed by the author using data from Asian Industrial Estates, Taiwan: Taiwan government, 2003, APEC

(private for the most part), ten "industrial communities", and a science park (see Chapter 8). The Thai "IEs" may be distinguished from other types of industrial groupings by five key features.

First, they are all developed or co-developed by the Industrial Estate Authority of Thailand (IEAT), a dedicated body set up in 1972 under the supervision of the Ministry of Industry. IEAT is responsible for constructing basic infrastructure (road, rail, and waterway networks, access routes to the IEs) for which it receives an annual royalty when not acting as the sole project operator (as in the case of private developments). It also monitors polluting emissions strictly in each IE — a permanent team is deputed on site — with special attention paid to waste water. Owing to the existence of a unique body in charge of the IEs, Thailand suffers less from a lack of coordination that impedes the management of IEs in neighbouring countries (Malaysia, Indonesia, and the Philippines).

In return for the strict control by IEAT, the firms operating in IEs enjoy quality infrastructure and resources adapted to their requirements: dedicated on-site power stations (thereby avoiding notorious power cuts experienced in other East Asian countries), efficient telecommunications networks, purification and effluent treatment plants, abundant water resources, transport infrastructure for access to and within the zone. The quality of infrastructure, both inside and outside the estates, is a distinctive feature of Thailand's IEs relative to countries of a similar development level in the region. Furthermore, land and infrastructure are supplied at a relatively low cost compared with neighbouring countries. Shipping cost is substantially lower than in Vietnam and India. Land in industrial estates is supplied at a lower cost than in China, the Philippines, Vietnam, and Laos.[2]

The third feature is a wide array of services such as the IEAT logistical support through the "One Stop Centre" in each estate (providing advisory services to investors and assistance in administrative procedures), training support services (centres for training facilities, testing centres occasionally set up in the estates), as well as banking, postal, commercial services, and various other neighbourhood amenities. This goes in par with the very easily understood system and quick procedures for establishing a company. Thailand requires the lowest number of days to start a business in Asia after Singapore (thirty-three days on average) and ranks fifth in the word for dealing with building permits (World Bank 2009).

Fourth, the IE enables companies to benefit from a number of tax incentives. BOI (Board of Investment) privileges are automatically granted by the IEAT, which also confers special privileges to the EPZ (Export Processing Zone): exemption from registration fees, custom duties, and VAT, on machinery and equipment. This is quite similar to the free zone concept existing elsewhere, but tax privileges are particularly attractive in the Chonburi and Rayong provinces, for example, where BOI zone 3 offers one of the best incentive packages of the region, with quick access to airports and seaports.

Last but not least, significant guarantees are offered in Thailand's IE. Foreign experts and technologists invited into a company can repatriate profits. Foreign investors can enjoy full property rights over land (100 per cent freehold ownership) in private IEs, whereas leasehold or joint ventures with local partners owning 51 per cent of the operation is common in other Asian countries. This is a substantial merit, as land has always appreciated consistently in Thailand. The land title can be used to secure local financing, and property owners have a guarantee that none of their holdings will be expropriated in the future.

Adding to these distinctive features, other factors contribute in drawing companies to Thailand's IEs instead of those in other countries in the region. Intellectual property rights protection and high transparency rules are seen as strong assets by foreign firms. Limited pollution — especially compared with that of major Chinese cities — reasonable housing rents available for expatriates, the easygoing and hospitable nature of the Thai people are assets that converge to attract expatriate managers seeking a good quality of life. Owing to these factors, Thailand ranks thirteenth out of 181 economies for overall ease of doing business, according to the World Bank's 2009 survey. It occupies fourth position in Asia, behind Singapore, Hong Kong, and Japan, and stands far ahead of comparable economies in the region, except for Malaysia (see Figure 5.1).

2. IE FRAMEWORK SETTING AND REGIONAL DEVELOPMENT POLICY

Industrial estates are very unequally distributed across the national territory (see Figure 5.2). Out of thirty-four IEs, twenty-eight are concentrated in the central region (Bangkok and its bordering provinces) and the eastern region. The remaining ones (six IEs, 18 per cent of the total) are in three peripheral regions — six in the north, one in the north-east, and two in the south.

Figure 5.1
Ranking of Countries in Asia on Overall Ease of Doing Business There (2009)
(Out of 181 countries worldwide)

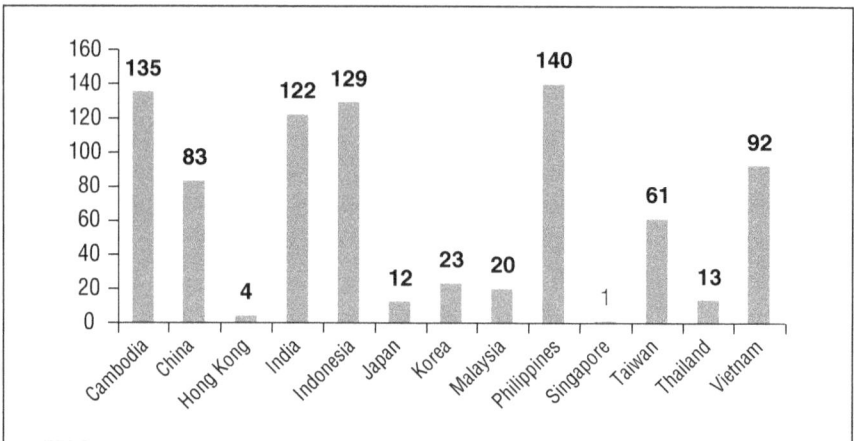

Source: Composed by the author using data from "Doing Business 2009", The International Bank for Construction and Development/The World Bank.

As mentioned above, the foundation of this framework goes back to the 1970s. Thailand had based its growth model on the establishment of foreign companies, in the hope that the outsourcing tie-ups between them and Thai small and medium-scale companies would lead eventually to a diversification of the national industries. Foreign industries had been confined to a few sites to enjoy the full benefits of economies of scale. But the weaknesses of such industrial concentration surfaced quickly. Excessive exploitation of resources (mainly water), various nuisances (olfactory, noise, landscape deterioration), and air and water pollution became worrying. A new agency, IEAT, was formed in 1972, with the mandate to regulate industrial development and integrate respect for environmental protection.

The principle behind the decisions of IEAT was to orient new industrial groupings on suitable sites equipped with infrastructure adapted to the needs of these companies (transport, effluent treatment, waste water treatment, power, telecommunications, and water distribution networks) and offering a wide range of services to facilitate the relocation of foreign companies.

Figure 5.2
Distribution of IEs in Thailand

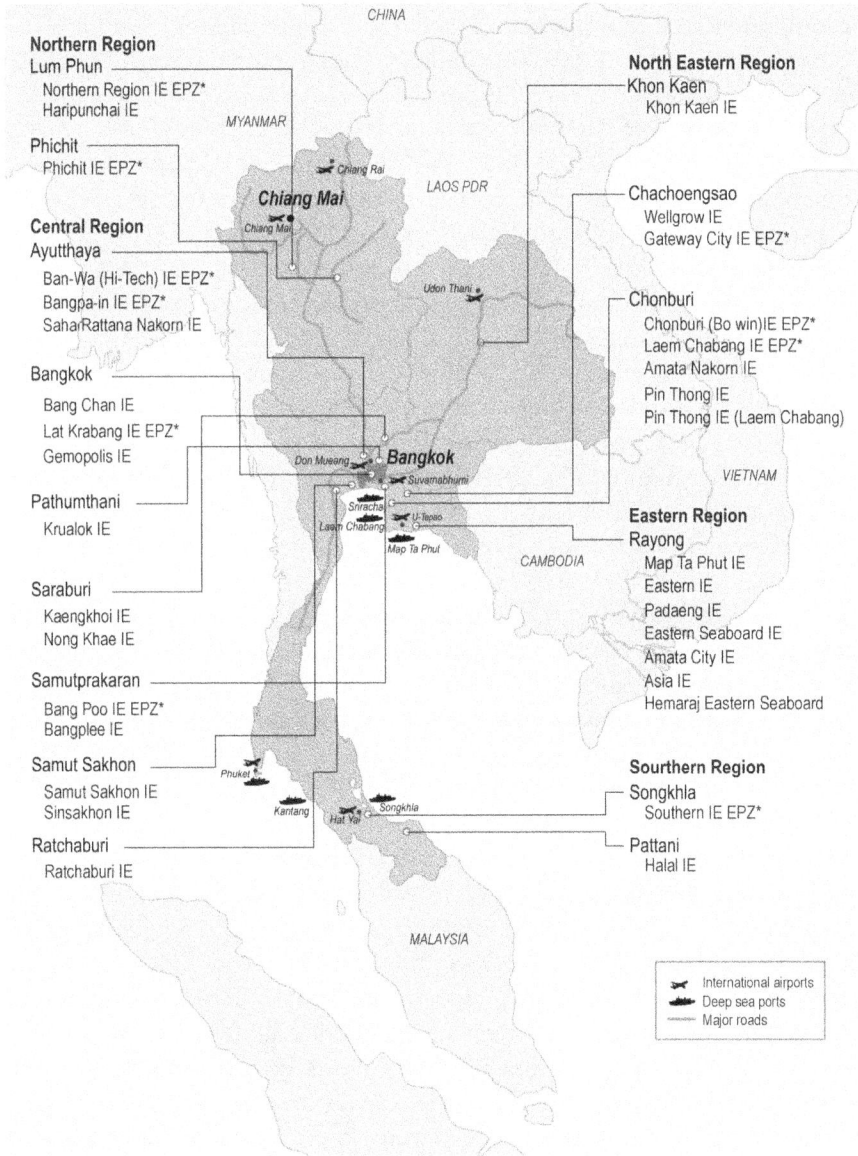

Northern Region
Lum Phun
  Northern Region IE EPZ*
  Haripunchai IE
Phichit
  Phichit IE EPZ*

Central Region
Ayutthaya
  Ban-Wa (Hi-Tech) IE EPZ*
  Bangpa-in IE EPZ*
  Sahar Rattana Nakorn IE

Bangkok
  Bang Chan IE
  Lat Krabang IE EPZ*
  Gemopolis IE

Pathumthani
  Krualok IE

Saraburi
  Kaengkhoi IE
  Nong Khae IE

Samutprakaran
  Bang Poo IE EPZ*
  Bangplee IE

Samut Sakhon
  Samut Sakhon IE
  Sinsakhon IE

Ratchaburi
  Ratchaburi IE

North Eastern Region
Khon Kaen
  Khon Kaen IE

Chachoengsao
  Wellgrow IE
  Gateway City IE EPZ*

Chonburi
  Chonburi (Bo win)IE EPZ*
  Laem Chabang IE EPZ*
  Amata Nakorn IE
  Pin Thong IE
  Pin Thong IE (Laem Chabang)

Eastern Region
Rayong
  Map Ta Phut IE
  Eastern IE
  Padaeng IE
  Eastern Seaboard IE
  Amata City IE
  Asia IE
  Hemaraj Eastern Seaboard

Sourthern Region
Songkhla
  Southern IE EPZ*
Pattani
  Halal IE

Map labels: CHINA, MYANMAR, LAOS PDR, Chiang Rai, Chiang Mai, Chiang Mai, Udon Thani, VIETNAM, Don Mueang, Suvarnabhumi, Bangkok, Snracha, U-Tapao, Laem Chabang, Map Ta Phut, CAMBODIA, Phuket, Kantang, Hat Yai, Songkhla, MALAYSIA

Legend:
✈ International airports
⛴ Deep sea ports
〜 Major roads

Source: Made by the author.

The first two IEs, Bang Chan IE (108 ha completed in 1973) and Lat Krabang IE (407 ha, completed in 1978) were developed by the IEAT about thirty kilometres from Bangkok. Two new development projects were later launched slightly further east, about forty kilometres from Bangkok in the border province of Samut Prakarn. Unlike the two earlier IEs, these new estates were not entirely developed by IEAT. Bang Poo IE, completed in 1977, was the first IEAT–private joint venture. This massive estate of 872 ha was built by the Thailand Industrial Development Company, a company created through a German-Thai government agreement with the objective of promoting development of small and medium-scale companies. As for the second, Bang Plee IE (161 ha), it was integrated with the construction of a new town to provide accommodation for families going to work in these new industrial estates and parks within the region — and consequently assigned to the National Housing Authority,[3] the public developer for social housing.

These new IEs enjoyed considerable success with foreign companies, especially in the automotive and electronics industry, key industrial sectors of Thai production. Nonetheless, they only served to reinforce the primary importance of Bangkok, whose hypertrophy had reached alarming proportions.

In 1981, 70 per cent of national production was concentrated within the capital region (Watanabe 2003). Then IEAT initiated the development of a new IE in the northern region of the country ("Northern Region IE") to serve as an industrial growth pole and alleviate the problem of rapid urbanization in Chiang Mai. However, this IE could not aspire to draw major foreign companies in state-of-the-art industries.

The discovery of natural gas reserves in the Gulf of Siam was to change all perspectives. By galvanizing infrastructure development to open up the eastern coastal zone (Eastern Seaboard), it was thence feasible to plan the redeployment of industry 100 km south-east of Bangkok. Thus the "Eastern Seaboard Development Plan" was launched in the early 1980s, by which the government hoped to achieve its ambition of developing petroleum and chemical industries along the eastern coast, as Chapter 4 already mentioned. Infrastructure projects took off with the construction of two pipelines and a gas processing plant at Map Ta Phut. The region was then opened up with railway access between Sichrea and Laem Chabang (130 km from Bangkok) and from Sattarit to Map Ta Phut (200 km from Bangkok), as well as a highway linking Chonburi to

Pattaya. In order to handle heavy industrial requirements for water resources, a reservoir and water distribution networks were also constructed. These activities had to be regrouped in two new, large-scale industrial estates developed by IEAT at Laem Chabang (569 ha) and Mat Ta Phut (1,634 ha), both flanked by a deep sea port to reorient Thai industries towards exports. In order to attract foreign companies to establish themselves or migrate there, the region was registered in BOI zone 3, which offered the maximum privileges to investors, or as many privileges as the regions 800 km beyond the capital. The government also shifted to financial liberalization by lifting the limitation on external borrowings for Eastern Seaboard industrial projects.

This policy did not take long to bear fruit. The development of the eastern coastal zone was stimulated by the surge of the yen following the Plaza agreement, which drove Japanese firms to the area. Private Thai developers were soon enticed by the idea of developing industrial zones in the region. Once the state had opened up the region, it became less risky to convert agricultural land into industrial land to derive higher capital gains. Many industrial zones flourished along the new axis of Highway 301. Two large private companies were founded, specifically dedicated to industrial estate development: Hemaraj and Amata Public Corporation.

While the development of the petrochemical industry was anticipated along the Eastern Seaboard, it was the automotive industry which was by far the most heavily drawn to the region. Fleeing traffic congestion in Bangkok and attracted by zone 3 privileges, Japanese manufacturer Mitsubishi Motors built an assembling plant in 1996 at Laem Chabang, in Chonburi province. Ford Mazda, General Motors, and BMW soon followed, setting up factories with their outsourcing partners a little further east in the Rayong province, between 1998 and 2000 (Lecler 2002; see also Chapter 6).

In the meantime, IEAT started to launch industrial estate projects in the countryside, in accordance with a new decentralization policy of industrial activities decided by the MOI (Chapter 4). The strategy involved industrial development based on the use of local natural resources. One such case was in South Thailand where IEAT developed an IE of 191 ha for the rubber industry (raw rubber and derived rubber products). Situated in the Songkhla province, 900 km from Bangkok, this public IE was recruited into a vast project to accentuate the importance of this border region, with the construction of a road network providing access to Malaysia, airports (Surat Tani, Chapeau Yai, Phuket), and the Songkhla port.

Central Thailand, another neglected region, was also targeted by the regional development policy. Two public IEs were built here by IEAT: these were the Phichit IE (124 ha, 336 km north of Bangkok) and the Khon Kaen IE in the textile-dominated north-east, 456 km from the capital. Industrial activities relied on the textile tradition of these regions and involved the manufacture of raw materials for textiles, production, and dyeing of fabrics.

During the 1990s, a dozen new public IEs were on the IEAT programme for the peripheral regions. With areas of between 150 to 400 hectares, these projects spread out nationwide, but most of them were concentrated in the southern provinces (Surat Thani, Nakhon Si Thammarat, Krabi, Yala, Trang, and Narathiwat). The regional development initiative in the south was meant to stimulate economic development in the "Growth triangle", linking Indonesia, Malaysia, and Thailand (IMT Growth Triangle[4]), launched in 1993 under the impetus of Malaysian Prime Minister Mahathir Mohamad. But the 1997 crisis dealt a severe blow to these ambitions. None of the public industrial estate projects planned during this period was implemented.

When Thaksin Shinawatra came to power in 2001, he launched the so-called "dual-track policy" (see Chapters 2 and 4), which promoted economic development in rural areas through various funding programmes for small-sized activities, while continuing to support manufacturing industries with government incentives. The cluster concept was the key instrument through which this policy was to be implemented in order to stimulate innovation. In other words, clusters were to replace IEs as a matrix for economic development.

The first axis of the "dual-track policy" related to rural areas was aimed at encouraging new grass roots activities in small districts to generate more value added from projects based on processing, and light manufacturing and trading activities. Clusters had to be planned and implemented at the regional and local levels. This policy did not rely on proactive regional or local governments having a clear vision of desirable measures and capable of coordinating economic development. Instead, it was supervised by provincial governors appointed by the central government to act like provincial Chief Executive Officers (Intarakumnerd 2009).

The second axis, related to the manufacturing and service sectors, focused public effort on five targeted industries for which Thailand possessed comparative advantage, namely the automotive, fashion, software, tourism, and food industries. Here again clusters had to be planned and implemented. However, in these strategic industries, as mentioned in Chapter 2, clusters covering the whole country had been defined — that is, sector-based clusters, rather than territory-based. For example, an automotive cluster, a tourism cluster, and a software cluster had been designated at the national level without involving geographic clustering. Furthermore, investment packages for clusters, regardless of their geographical location had been introduced in 2004. Industrial activities tended consequently to re-concentrate in the region of Bangkok and the eastern coastal provinces.[5]

The present IE framework reflects the double dynamics ushered in by the governmental policy after the Asian crisis well: firstly in redirecting industrial activity towards the central and eastern regions, and secondly, in consolidating local activities around main public estates (or those having a strong public-private tie-up) in a small number of peripheral provinces.

The latter policy consisted of pushing for more specialization — through the cluster framework — and making the best possible use of the frontier locations of the estates. In the case of the Northern Region IE, development plans have been drawn up with border countries (South China and other countries of the Indochina peninsula) so as to draw foreign investments into this region. This IE has been provided with a stocking central and transportation hubs to facilitate exchanges with neighbouring regions of the Mekong. The principal activities include the manufacture of precious stones and jewellery, fabrics and electronic components, with particular emphasis on the use of local resources and technological development.

The southern part of the country continues to draw special attention owing to its relative underdevelopment and separatist movements in the Muslim provinces (Yala, Pattani, Narathiwat, and Satun), annexed in 1902 by the Kingdom of Siam.[6] In 2003, a new IE specializing in halal foods ("Halal Food IE") was created with a view to exporting halal products to Muslim countries. This 144-ha estate is situated in the Pattani province, 1,055 km from Bangkok. Measures have been taken to guarantee the respect of hygiene standards and the halal tradition. Since the project was approved by the OIC (Organisation of Islamic Conference), interest-free loans are now granted by the Islamic Bank to producers of halal foods. Unlike previous initiatives that drove local development, IEAT is not the primary developer of the project. The task was undertaken by a private operator, the food producer, Halal Fattoni Industries. But the state strongly supports the development project since the political stakes are high, with violence escalating within the zone since 2004. Moving beyond economic development, the government seeks to promote moderate Islam in the region. The construction of an Islamic university in synergy with the production of halal food could activate a cluster dynamics and consequently curtail the departure of students to universities in the Middle East, where the doctrine is far more radical.

In a parallel move to the Halal Food Estate, the government plans to consolidate activities around rubber in the public industrial estate of the Songkhla province, also situated in South Thailand (the "Southern IE"). The goal is to reinforce the importance of this industry, largely oriented towards exports (90 per cent of raw rubber and rubber products are being exported), through collaborations with Malaysia and Indonesia. This IE benefits from the proximity of a new deep sea port recently opened in Kantang (Tang Province, see map), which was jointly financed by Thailand, Indonesia, and Malaysia within the framework of the "IMT Growth Triangle".

Despite these attempts to promote regional development, regional city centres have not gained a significant role. Economic activities continue to concentrate in the central and eastern regions, thus exacerbating the regional imbalance. The Bangkok Metropolitan Area has reached a population of 8.1 million inhabitants, dwarfing that of Chiang Mai, the second largest agglomeration (less than 1 million inhabitants). The other regional cities are far smaller even, with populations below 160,000 inhabitants. In contrast, in Malaysia and the Philippines, regional cities stand over 500,000 inhabitants. The figure is much higher in Indonesia, Korea, and Japan, where several regional cities have more than one million inhabitants.

The severe imbalance in the distribution of the population goes hand in hand with a weak local institutional framework. Although the new constitution enforced in 1997 stipulates that the central government must allow autonomy for local governments, decentralization is far from being effective. Many functions at the level of local government are performed by the central government whose departments extend their operations into the provinces. Most resources and revenues generated are drawn into the centre, leaving local governments with inadequate means to meet the growing needs of local communities, especially in urban areas. This lack of resources restricts the capacity of local governments to deliver basic services to the local communities, and impedes their capacity to develop their own projects.

Clearly, Thailand's government has been ineffective in implementing a regional policy based on the IE framework. Amongst various factors, poor local governance and the lack of infrastructure in peripheral regions are to blame. It is widely acknowledged that achieving regional development requires a strong commitment by local government and stakeholders. More recently, the idea that regional economic development might give way to new innovation paths has given rise to the concept of "Regional Innovation Systems" (RIS). Unlike other Asian countries such as Japan and Korea, where the focus has been recently put on regional development though geographical agglomeration of firms or innovative poles (IEs, clusters, etc.), Thailand has chosen to promote an industry-specific policy without consideration for geographical factors. This partly explains why the so-called "cluster policy" has been mostly disconnected from the IE framework. We shall discuss the implications of this choice later (in section 4).

3. PUBLIC-PRIVATE COOPERATION IN IE DEVELOPMENT

The IE framework formed the matrix of Thailand's industrialization, but the very core of this matrix was made up by effective public-private cooperation in IE development. The basic idea was that IEAT will provide large infrastructure projects (especially transport and communication facilities), services (through One Stop Centres), and environmental quality control, while private developers will bear the risk of land development within the estates. In fact, as mentioned earlier, the initial IEs were totally relying on IEAT's development initiative. But private developers soon stepped in. The major impetus was given in the early 1980s by the launching of the "Eastern Seaboard Development Plan". After the advent of the Thaksin administration, the withdrawal of state funding accelerated. Private developers were fully entrusted with the initiative of large-scale IE development and even construction/management of large facilities such as deep seaports (in Sriracha and Chonburi for the eastern region, and more recently, in Kantang for the Southern region).

Of the thirty-four IEs officially listed, only nine are run by public operators (eight by IEAT and one by the National Housing Authority).

The vast majority of IEs hence belong to the private sector. Private developers have very different profiles, but they may be classified into three broad categories: entrepreneurs developing production in the IE; entrepreneurs that become developers to seize an opportunity; land development companies specialized in industrial parks (Table 5.2).

The first category is barely represented, with fewer than ten operators. Two German-Thai initiatives may be cited in this category in the central region: the Bang Poo IE (first private IE launched in 1977) born of a governmental initiative in support of small and medium-scale companies, and the Nong Khan IE, a German-Thai joint-venture in the ceramics industry. Also in this category is the Ban-Wa (Hi Tech) IE, the only estate comprising high-tech companies, developed by a group of petrochemical industrialists associated with a Singaporean specialist in high-tech park development (Jurong Town Corporation). Other estates are highly specialized: Padeang Properties, an estate focused on zinc, constructed close to the zinc mines of Padeang; Gemopolis, specializing in gems and jewellery; Sinsakhon Printing City IE, for printing activity. In the last two cases, the IE tries to bring together different small and medium-scale companies whose activities are related to the industry in question.

The second category also comprises about ten IEs developed by industrialists, but without the objective of specialization. Hence a wide variety of activities may be found on one site. The operators of these estates most often have seized an opportunity to diversify into development. This is the case of Well Grow industries (member of the Taiwanese steel group Hsiung) or subsidiaries of Thai public works such as Bang Pa-In Land Development or MDX Public Corporation. Also in this category is the company Mahachai Land, set up by a Thai plastic manufacturer.

Lastly, it is in the third category that the most important operators may be found. In particular, two major Thai companies specialized in Industrial Estate development towards the end of the 1980s. The first, Hemaraj, was founded in 1988 by the financial firm Thailand Securities, a subsidiary of the Thai Stock Exchange. Within a decade, the operator became the main private industrial developer in the country. Apart from the four large estates completed in the Chonburi and Rayong provinces totalling 4000 ha, the developer also completed two new IEs in the same region, on land obtained through absorption from a subsidiary of the cement manufacturer Siam Cement Public Company Limited (SIL Industrial Land Development) in 2005. In total, the Hemaraj group was flush with

Table 5.2
Developer Types of Thai IEs

Name of IE	Developer	Year established	Year of completion	Area developed by end 2006 (ha)	Developer type
Bang Chan IE	IEAT	1972	1973	124	State enterprise under the control of Ministry for Industry.
Lat Krabang IE	IEAT		1978	407	idem
Laem Chabang IE	IEAT		1982	569	idem
Map Ta Phut IE	IEAT		1989	1,634	idem
Northern region IE	IEAT		1983	201	idem
Bangplee IE	National Housing Authority		1984	161	Public development company for new cities and social housing construction
Phichit IE	IEAT		1994	124	State enterprise under the control of Ministry for Industry
Southern IE	IEAT		1995	191	idem
Khon Kaen IE	IEAT		1999	0,6	idem
Bang Poo IE	Thailand Industrial Development	1977	1994	872	German-Thai governmental agreement. The development of this IE was accompanied by a government policy to promote the development of small and medium-scale companies and industries.
Saha Rattana Nakorn IE	Saha Rattana Na-korn		1993	328	
Well Grow IE	Well Grow Industries	1987	1989	516	Industrial company affiliated to the Taiwanese steel group Hsiung.
Hemaraj Chonburi IE	Hemaraj LDP	1988	1989	655	Land developer, 78% holding subsidiary of the finance firm Thailand Securities Depository Corp, itself 100% owned by the Thai Stock Exchange.

IE	Company		Year	No.	Notes
Eastern IE	Hemaraj LDP		1989	398	Idem
Eastern Seaboard IE	Hemaraj LDP		1994	1,123	Idem
Hemaraj Eastern Seaboard IE	Hemaraj LDP		1999	1,867	Idem
Amata Nakorn IE	Amata Public Corp.	1989	1989	1,059	Land developer, 31% capital held by the Kromadit family, institutional investors and companies established in the IE. Another IE in Vietnam.
Amata city IE	Amata Public Corp.		1996	714	Idem
Bangpa-in IE	Bangpa-in Land Devlpt		1994	314	Subsidiary of the Thai building and public works group Karn-chang
Kaeng Khoi IE	Saraburi industrial park co		1990	94	Thai building and public works company
Gateway City IE	MDX Public Corp.		1990	1,040	Plastic manufacturer
Samut Sakhon IE	Mahachai Land Developmt	1990	1990	233	Idem
Ratchaburi IE	Mahachai Land Developmt		1998	228	
Nong Khae IE	Thai-German Industry Public Co.	1981	1990	327	German-Thai joint-venture in the ceramics industry
Gemopolis IE	IGS Public co		1993	28	Jewellery industry. Shown as a jewellery cluster
Padaeng IE	Padaeng Properties Public Corp.	1981	1992	86	100%-owned subsidiary of the group Padaeng Industry, mining zinc in Padaeng
Pin Thong IE	Pinthong Industrial Park Corp.	1994	1995	81	Jutha Wan Metal Ltd, firm that stocks and distributes stainless steel, 67% held by the Pira family.
Asia IE	Asia Industrial Estate Corp.		2001	398	

continued on next page

Table 5.2 — cont'd

Name of IE	Developer	Year established	Year of completion	Area developed by end 2006 (ha)	Developer type
Sinsakhon Printing City IE	CAS Printing City Corp.		2006	134	Shown as a cluster comprising printing and packaging industries.
Ban-Wa (Hi tech) IE	Thai Industrial Estate Corp.	1986	1992	367	Group of petrochemical industrialists in a tie-up with a Singaporean hi-tech park development specialist, Jurong Town. Corporation. Received the ASEAN Association of Housing and Planning award for this development in 1996.
Halal Food IE	Fattoni Industries				Regional development project with participation of investors from Malaysia, Indonesia, Brunei, and Bangkok.
Krualok IE	Khunchai Corp.				
Hariphunchai IE	Dhevi Spa and Longstay Resort Corp.				
RIL IE	Rayong Industrial Land Corp.	1996			Company affiliated to SIL, recent joint venture tie-up with Hemaraj.
304 IE zone2	304 industrial park Co	1993	2001		Developing company founded by a group of Thai entrepreneurs to build complete "industrial cities". This company built an industrial park at Prachinburi before taking on the multiphase development of a new project near the Laem Chabang port.

Source: Composed by the author based on data from IEAT.

property stocks of close to 5,000 hectares.[7] The second largest private developer is the company Amata, founded in 1989 by the Sino-Thai businessman Vikrom Kromadit, who is among the wealthiest people in the country. With a capital far more modest than Hemaraj (1 million and 13 million baht, respectively), Amata has developed two large IEs of more than 2,000 hectares. Its activity is not confined to Thailand though. It is the first Thai property developer to enter Vietnam (on a site of 700 hectares), owing to the strong relations established by Vikrom Kromadit with Vietnamese authorities. In the last few years, Amata has asserted its position as a market leader in the country for the commercialization of property with a market share of 37 per cent. It places particular emphasis on client services. This is how Kromadit succeeded in drawing one of the most prestigious schools into one of his IEs, the Suankularb Wittayalai International School.

It may be observed that a number of industrial park developers easily exploit the label "Industrial Estates" to serve their commercial strategies. This is the case for the firm Rojana, a Japanese-Thai joint-venture with a 49 per cent stake held by *sôgô shôsha* Sumikin Bussan of the Sumitomo conglomerate, which runs two industrial parks in Ayuttaya and Rayong. The industrial parks offer the same BOI privileges as the IE, and a reasonably wide array of services, including housing (up to 250 units available in the Rojana Park at Rayong) but they lack a "One Stop Centre" and free zone (EPZ). Furthermore, foreign companies cannot acquire full rights over property. This explains why developers here offer turnkey factory rentals and leasehold property. Despite these shortcomings, Rojana is particularly well positioned to attract large Japanese automotive and electronic companies, because of its Japanese-Thai status. This explains the scale of its projects whose areas are comparable with those of the Industrial Estates (672 ha for Rayong Park where the sixth phase is underway). Flush with success, Rojana is now a pioneer among Thai developers, having attempted to penetrate China with a vast industrial park project of 880 ha in the Zhonglou Economic Zone, 160 km from Shanghai.

The advent of specialist operators in IE development may be explained by the enormous opportunities resulting from the opening of the eastern coastal region, but also by the increasing demands of IEAT with respect to the environmental and urban quality of projects.

Obtaining the "Industrial Estate" label entails lengthy administrative procedures. The developer must first present a project to IEAT, which takes sixty days to examine its feasibility, followed by a site study. Subsequently the project is submitted to the Ministry for Industry and the Environmental Agency. The first registers the IE for industrial zoning (official declaration for the creation of an IE) while the second undertakes a study on the environmental impact in collaboration with IEAT. Once the necessary authorization has been granted for establishing an IE on the identified site, the developer must obtain approvals for the layout, equipment, and infrastructure required in the IE. Finally, permission must be obtained to allot land holdings and allocate plots to potential occupants. It should be highlighted here that despite the imposition of strict environmental quality control standards, IEAT can grant permission within short timeframes of barely three months (ninety-seven days for all procedural steps). Development projects are completed in phases, thereby alleviating financial risks (taxes and financial costs for holding properties), since the land acquired is for public purposes by the estate as and when the property is acquired. However, the IE is always enclosed in order to prevent intrusions and protect manufacturing trade secrets. Several developers such as Hemaraj and Amata are implementing their seventh or eighth phase in the eastern coastal region.

In reality, negotiations between the private operator and IEAT commence long before procedures are officially launched. The developer begins by acquiring land in a region suitable for IE development, that is, conforming to the following conditions: registering the site in a BOI zone offering massive privileges (zone 2 or 3), proximity to a port (if possible a deep sea port to attract major firms in automotive or electronics industries) and/or an international airport, highway access within a reasonable distance-timeframe to Bangkok (enabling senior management executives to shuttle daily within timeframes of three-and-a-half and four hours per day). A workforce is not a prerequisite since the rural population, largely from the north-east, migrates readily to the IE. Worker housing needs are addressed by promoters or small-scale local private entrepreneurs, less often by public developers. A number of public IEs have, nonetheless, built new towns, such as Bang Plee (developed by the National Housing Authority) or Laem Chabang (about 100,000 people of whom more than 50 per cent live in social housing). It may not come as a surprise that these urban projects are not a result of local initiatives, but emerged from concerted action among the principal state bodies concerned: IEAT and the ministries for Industry, Environment, and Labour.

Parallel to property acquisition, the developer consults IEAT to examine the nature of industries that may be located on the estate, given the site features. The strategy consists of attracting a large "anchor firm" to help commercialize other lots. Such companies attract not only outsourcing partners, but also confer a positive image to the project, the basis for a marketing strategy. IEAT, supported by the BOI, has a significant role to play in estate promotion, which is then entirely billed to the developer.

As we have seen earlier, IEAT provides major transport infrastructure (ports, roads, highways, and railroads) and networks (telecommunications, water, gas, electricity). In return, the developers pay an annual fee to IEAT, which accounts for 50 per cent of its turnover (57 per cent in 2004[8]). The developer also pays for the maintenance of the IEAT "cell" and a Customs office. Costs are very high since they include the construction and maintenance of the premises, employee housing (up to fifteen employees in some estates, including even the housemaid!).

The IEAT cell provides logistical support services to companies located in the estate ("One Stop Centre") and exercises rigorous control over infrastructure quality and services offered within its boundary. Controls are particularly strict over water and air pollution. Agents in the cell also grant the permission to construct factories on the estate, and manage land records in which all property registrations are entered. Permissions take a little over a month to obtain. Properties are available for sale only in private IEs. Those developed by IEAT are leased to companies for an annual rent that accounts for 25 per cent of the IEAT turnover (27 per cent in 2004[9]). Foreign companies, however, prefer to enjoy absolute ownership rights over the land since property rights are totally secure in Thailand, unlike in China or Vietnam.

As more IEs moved away from the capital and the private sector took over development projects, a broadening of services offered to tenant companies was required. In the first public IEs, services were essentially confined to the industrial domain. The developer did not look into housing needs except in the case of the Bang Plee public estate, undertaken by the National Housing Authority. Moreover, only worker housing requirements were taken into consideration, since executives had the option of travelling to and from Bangkok on a daily basis. With the multiplication of IEs in the eastern coastal region, in the zones reached only by a two-hour car journey from Bangkok, it became necessary to consider executive housing needs, if only to ensure a temporary housing facility during the week (for families preferring to stay in the capital). Luxurious condominiums have been constructed on the new estates alongside more modest house types for middle-management. The workers continue to live outside the IEs, but developers also build housing for these workers close to their workplace.

The introduction of housing on the estates entailed the development of an entire range of connected services: the IE hereafter must have a golf course, neighbourhood amenities such as shopping centres, restaurants, banking services, security, health, and less frequently, educational institutions. This widening of services fits in with the marketing strategy of developers, some of whom virtually transform their estates into live urban projects. This is how the developer Amata Corporation uses the concept of the "Perfect City" to promote its two estates in Chonburi and Rayong. It emphasizes "care for human needs", a large array of facilities available in the neighbourhood, including 24-hour hospitals, ambient surroundings (greenery, bird parks), technology (state-of-the-art communication infrastructure), education (childcare services, Suankularb Wittayala International School), as well as arts and culture (sponsored by the Amata Foundation). Likewise, the Gemopolis developer launched the concept of the "Factory Town", a small urban enclave in a large Bangkok suburb a few kilometres from the new international airport. Manufacturers and traders in the precious stone and jewellery industry may stay here for varying lengths of time and thereby avoid the congestion in metropolitan Bangkok.

Even if these urban projects are enclosed and under close surveillance, they are far removed from the "gated community" model. On the contrary, they are largely open to local communities, and offer the latter access to sports, commercial, and educational facilities. Private developers in fact seek to be like regional developers in providing work opportunities and modern equipment. They also emphasize "sustainability" by providing open spaces with natural landscapes, and adhering to environmental quality standards (ISO 14001 standard for the two estates of the Amata Corporation and the industrial parks of Rojana). They also actively sponsor education and cultural activity in the region in the form of school materials and study grants. The founder of Amata, Vikrom Kromadit, has withdrawn from business activities to dedicate himself to the foundation, to which he donates generously (US$110 million in 2007).

These strategies for regional development earn the support of the authorities, and especially, IEAT, but they also have the irrefutable advantage of facilitating land acquisition ahead of the projects. Even though some zones are far from the urban centres and not always suited to agricultural activity — as is the case of the eastern coastal region, where the high salt content leaves the soil sterile — the purchase of land at low prices is not a simple affair. This is because once farmers are aware of development projects, they raise land prices or refuse to sell them, speculating for better gains. Private operators cannot resort to expropriation; unlike public developers, they must depend on a local agent to facilitate land acquisitions. Hence, they turn to the local functionary, the *puyah*, who alone can convince farmers to sell their land at reasonable prices by demonstrating the beneficial impact of IEs on the local community.

Owing to these skilful strategies, private developers are able to keep land at a reasonable price for incoming firms. This in turn allows for the upgrading of infrastructure and the enhancement of support services within the IE so as to meet client demand. Some developers are trying to promote an "urban life" in their estates, but expatriates are not likely to renounce Bangkok's true vibrant urban atmosphere and highly diversified services. This does not leave much room to locate future IE projects. Industrial land developers have thus invested heavily in the eastern costal region where abundant land reserves can be made. Chonburi and Rayong provinces offer particularly well balanced conditions. They are far enough from Bangkok to avoid traffic congestion and to provide the highest BOI privileges (zone 3), but at the same time close enough to allow expatriates to live with their families in Bangkok. Furthermore, they give close access to the deep sea ports from which manufactured products can be exported.

In fact, the comparative advantages offered by these two provinces are so favourable that even Chinese firms have relocated there. This move is explained by various factors. First, the cost of labour has become lower than in Chinese major cities and coastal regions since 2006. Second, the privileges granted by BOI in zone 3 beat the highest tax exemptions in China. Third, access is offered by Thailand to a large consumer market in the region through numerous FTA agreements. Chinese investors set foot on Thailand's soil after the signing of a bilateral Thailand-China trade agreement, in October 2003. Chinese FDI peaked in 2004, when Thailand became the fifth largest recipient of Chinese FDI on the continent.[10]

Quite obviously, Thai estates are gearing up for expansion. Becoming more sophisticated and inclined to match the requirements of the firms closely as they evolve, they remain the most appropriate instrument for attracting multinational firms to Thailand. However, no matter how well they fulfil clients' needs, private IE are no longer meant to advance the technological content of national production. Fully relying on market forces to accommodate a wide range of local and foreign firms, they do not differ basically from ordinary, profit-oriented land development projects. In this respect, Thailand's recent orientation contrasts with that of other Asian countries. We will now examine more closely evidence from empirical research on industrial grouping and economic growth.

4. THAILAND'S IE FACING THE NEW INNOVATION PARADIGM

Until the 1980s, academic research on economic development mainly concentrated on the national level. As national economies progressively integrated into a globalized economy, the gap between regions widened — especially in emerging countries — and became a source of political concern. Regional economic development therefore gained growing interest in both academic and politic circles. Literature and research in this field can be classified into two main bodies.

The first body deals with city and regional development planning. Questions are raised on how to achieve a more balanced regional growth, increase the participation of the local stakeholders (especially the residents), and what role local governments should play in the development process under very centralized administrative systems of planning and administration. In Asia, particular attention was paid to overconcentration of population and activities in mega-urban regions (see Ramos and Sazanami 1991). In terms of policymaking, these empirical studies usually come out with recommendations for appropriate institutional arrangements and planning procedures to improve the management of mega cities and alleviate the regional imbalance.

The second body, of particular relevance to this chapter, deals with the concept of regional innovation systems (RIS). Originated in the 1990s from modern innovation theory, the RIS concept has recently evolved into a widely used analytical framework and is currently underlying innovation policymaking (Storper, Porter, Doloreux, Cook, among others).

There is no commonly accepted definition of a RIS, but it is usually understood as a set of interacting private and public interests, formal institutions, and other organizations that function according to organizational and institutional arrangements and relationships conductive to the generation, use, and dissemination of knowledge (Doloreux 2003). It would be beyond the scope of this chapter to review the extensive academic literature produced on this issue, but we shall summarize here the major findings.

The RIS concept strongly emphasizes the fact that innovation is a *locally embedded process* (Storper 1997; Malmberg and Maskell 1997). Far from being location-free, RIS are embedded in local networks and communities of firms and support infrastructure operating in research and training institutions, financial intermediaries, government agencies, as well as community and business associations.

The distance between the actors of a RIS may be critical. Thus, geographic proximity is of much importance. Not only does it facilitate knowledge spillovers, but it also generates economies of scale and scope, as well as network externalities. Particularly crucial for innovation is the knowledge transfer between universities and high tech firms, which requires spatial proximity, at least in the early stages. It takes the form of information transmission in local personal networks of university and industry professionals, or formal business relations. Local university knowledge spillovers may also be generated by industrial application of university physical facilities, but it very much depends on the nature of the concerned industry (Lim 2006).

The region is considered the best geographical level for an innovation-based economy because, according to Porter (1998), the enduring competitive advantage in a global economy often arises from a concentration of highly specialized skills and knowledge, institutions, related businesses, and customers in a given region. The success stories of famous "innovative regions" such as the "Third Italy", the Silicon Valley, or the Route 128 in Boston, have given evidence to the relevancy of the regional scale in the innovation process. They have also displayed the strong disparity of local networks of firms and industries prevailing in each region. Some have the characteristics of "Marshallians" districts with predominantly small-scale enterprises, others are "hub and spoke" districts with regional structure and domination by several major corporations, or one satellite "branch plants" districts, or complex state-oriented districts such as military or research centres (Edgington and Fernandez 2001).

Whatever the form taken by the local networks, institutional support from local governments and local quasi-government organizations (such as chambers of commerce, public-private cooperation networks) is considered necessary to secure continuous product innovation in an unstable globalized economy. Small firms in particular are unable to bear the cost of developing new technologies, finding new markets, training skilled engineers and workers, and raising capital. Thus support through "soft" infrastructure (regional organizations, access to low-cost credit, information, and training) tends to be more important than the supply of "hard" infrastructure (Edgington and Fernandez 2001).

Some authors have pointed out the shortcomings in the RIS concept. Doloreux and Parto (2007) argue that there is no clear definition of a "region" in empirical studies referring to RIS. The term "region" encompasses a wide variety of scales, ranging from small-scale industrial districts within cities, to national territories. Also unclear are the boundaries of the region. The authors argue that innovation is not exclusively an endogenously generated process within a given region. Innovative firms are linked to the outside world by various sorts of connections, and their ability to tap into different innovation systems is a source of competitive advantage. Available knowledge that can be drawn from outside the region must, therefore, be integrated into the analytical framework.

Though not a panacea, the RIS concept has gained growing popularity over the past decade, policymakers having enthusiastically adopted it. The European Union has started to implement RIS programmes in its less developed regions. Similar innovation systems are also being experimented in Asia. In Japan, Ministry of Economy, Trade and Industry has launched in 2001 an industrial cluster programme designed to upgrade existing industrial agglomerations, and promote, although not exclusively, symbiotic clusters of SMEs where expertise and skill could accumulate, while Ministry of Education, Culture, Sports, Science and Technology established in 2002 its Knowledge Cluster initiative, using regional industrial, but also, researching potentialities to develop new industries or technologies (Hattori and Lecler 2009).

But South Korea is the only country that has explicitly attempted to experiment with RIS concept so far. As Southeast Asian countries have been constantly learning from the experience of the most mature economies in the region, it is interesting to review Korea's experience with regional policy over the past decades.

Due to its particular recent history (the partition of the country in 1953 and the subsequent massive immigration from North Korea), South Korea has been facing strong spatial polarization in its capital city. The Seoul

National Capital Area — which includes the major port city of Incheon and satellite towns in Gyeonggi Province — has 24.5 million inhabitants, and ranks second in the world after the Tokyo Greater Region. With a national population of 48.85 million inhabitants, its share of the national population reaches the critical figure of 50 per cent. Therefore, regional policy has been a major concern since the early stage of Korea's industrialization.

The basic regulation for regional planning was set in 1963. As in Thailand, the purpose was to decentralize industries from the capital city to alleviate regional imbalance and prevent pollution. Large-scale public investments were provided to expand infrastructure along the Seoul-Pusan expressway axis, and in both the capital and south-east regions. The first IE was developed in the south-east coast in 1962 (Ulsan IE). Furthermore, IE development, undertaken by a devoted public corporation and planned by the government with strict guidelines, was concentrated in major cities, mainly in the capital and south-east regions, in conjunction with roads, railways, power plants, and ports.

To discourage firms establishing in the capital region, heavier taxation and stricter control of pollution applied in Seoul. Construction and expansion of higher education facilities (universities, colleges) were also restricted in the capital city; furthermore, the state proceeded with the relocation of government offices and headquarters of public organizations (Ahn and Ohn 1997). The central government could also act on regional location through the strict control of low-rate industrial loans — both foreign and domestic — granted to Korean large-scale firms. This control did not apply to SMEs and firms with foreign participation (Renaud 1974).

As in Thailand, the regional policy did not achieve much success in its early stage. During the 1970s and 1980s, Seoul continued to dominate the economy, although the momentum for growth spread to adjacent areas (in particular, the five new towns created in 1989) and to the southeast provinces. A common factor with Thailand was the necessity to raise the competitiveness of the capital region against other world cities in a growingly globalized economy. It did not leave much room for reducing regional disparities, and regional development was thus seen as a "byproduct" of national economic plans.

The situation changed after the Asian crisis in 1997. Severely hit by the disaster, South Korea came to question its economic model. Regional development policy was brought back on the agenda, but the approach differed from that of the previous period. Local governments, which had been given more autonomy in 1995, were encouraged to adopt an entrepreneurial approach to promoting value-added and high technology industries. This change culminated in 2003, when Korea adopted the concept of RIS.

The new model went far beyond the purpose of achieving regional balance and mitigating the ill effects of Seoul's over concentration. It relied on the acknowledgment that Korea lacked competitive original technologies and lagged behind other industrialized nations in terms of productivity. As major instruments of the RIS policy, so-called "innovation clusters" were introduced. They were to replace the previous generation of technopolis/innopolis whose purpose had been to bring together industry, research institutes, and universities in a devoted area — to generate proximity effects — but which had failed to come up with innovative products (Japan had a similar experience with the failure of the "Technopolis Plan" launched in the 1980s). The new framework builds on seven large industrial complexes (IEs), accounting for 64 per cent of the output of national industrial complexes and forms a balanced framework throughout the country. They are all specialized in one or two industries: Changwon (machines, mechatronics); Gumi (electronics); Ulsan (automobile); Banwol-Siwha (parts, material); Gwangju (optical electronics industry); Wonju (medical instruments); and Gunsan (motor parts). SMEs are primarily targeted as key players for innovation. This is a major outcome of the 1997 crisis, which revealed the ill effects of an economic model based on gigantic conglomerates.

To enforce this policy, the South Korean government has established a company, KICOX (Korea Industrial Complex Corporation), which is entrusted with the task of upgrading the industrial complexes into "innovation clusters", by creating new industrial space for SMEs, providing apartment-type factories, and offering a variety of services. But the more crucial component of this system is the industrial-academic network consultation body called "mini cluster". It is an integrated group joined by stakeholders in firms, universities, and research institutes, to extend their efforts for promoting innovative technology. Its tasks are typically information exchange and network activities to grasp on-the-spot difficulties, problem settlements and assistance, after-management methods, business planning, and appraisal methods. Each industrial complex contains four to six mini clusters. KICOX has acquired a patent for its mini cluster management, indicating its ambition to standardize the

Korean-type cluster. It is too early to assess the results of this policy, but KICOX has reported a significant increase in the number of innovation-type companies since 2004.[11]

In considering Korea's experience, what lessons can we draw for Thailand? Thailand could also rely on its IE framework to develop new types of industrial grouping, that rely on proximity effects and industrial-academic networks prone to innovation. However, Thailand's capacity to set up such structures is limited by the following factors:

— the weak urban framework across the country. Innovation takes place in (or close to) urban areas where universities concentrate. In South Korea, many regional cities have more than one million inhabitants, whereas Thailand contains only two large urban areas, Bangkok and Chiang Mai. Additionally, the lack of power and resources of local governments impedes the making of a favourable business and innovation climate at the local level. The poor investment in infrastructure and public facilities in the peripheral regions contributes to aggravate the weakness of the urban framework.
— the lack, until recently, of industry-specific policies. In South Korea, policies seeking economic development have continuously targeted specific industries, especially in the manufacturing sector, where the prospects for technology transfer were the highest. Specialized IEs were created to generate proximity effects and to facilitate spillovers. Although these objectives have been far from fully achieved, the current RIS policy can take advantage of the strong potential of sector-specific grouping. In contrast, Thailand has put its priority on the quality of its physical infrastructure and services within the IEs, at least until 2001. The wide industry mix within most of the IEs consequently does not allow for the building of such industry-specific advantages.
— the lack of concern for geographical grouping. The cluster-based innovation policy recently launched in Thailand does not rely on "geographic clusters". There are, however, a few exceptions. The "Gemopolis IE" (gem and jewellery industry) falls in this category and is the only IE to have obtained the label "cluster". The jewellery industry has a long history in Thailand, owing to a tradition of gem mining. Skills have been acquired in the heat treatment of gem stones and synthetic gems (Yusuf and Nabeshima 2006). The Gemopolis has

a good potential to upgrade the jewellery sector, given its complete supply chain, its proximity to Bangkok (and to the new international airport), as well as its global linkages (through the Bangkok Gem and Jewelry Fair). But it still needs to strengthen its linkage with academic institutions.

Looking more closely at the two key sectors of Thailand's industry — the electronic and automotive sectors — the situation seems quite contrasted. The cluster programme of the hard disk industry has been designed on a national scale without any concern for its geographical dimension. Hence the production of hard disks is scattered in various IEs, though concentrated in the central region, as documented in Chapter 8. In the case of the automotive industry, an "automotive cluster" has been created within a 50-km perimeter of Bangkok to support a network of small and medium-scale companies operating around shared infrastructure and services. Production in this sector shows a certain level of specialization in large private IEs, namely in the Rayong and Chonburi regions, owing to the proximity of major port infrastructure. However, it is questionable that an innovation policy could successfully rely on these IEs, given the weak institutional support at the local level, and more importantly, the poor intrafirm and industry-academic linkage in these estates.

CONCLUSION

This chapter has provided an overview of the evolution of industrial estates in Thailand. As in most other countries of the region, IEs were introduced soon after the early stage of industrialization as a major instrument for enhancing economic development across the country. This regional policy was aimed at reducing the ill effects of overconcentration of the population and activities in the Bangkok Metropolitan area, while creating new development poles in peripheral areas. However, these goals came into conflict with the need to promote Bangkok in the global competition of mega cities. The central government accordingly put its priority on industrialization near Bangkok, neglecting infrastructure, and political and economic development in peripheral areas.

The Asian crisis dealt a further blow to Thailand's regional policy. The dozens of IE projects planned in the 1990s in the peripheral regions had to be abandoned due to lack of financial resources. It then turned out that even in the more central IEs, where major foreign manufacturers had located, Thai suppliers did not benefit from the expected technology transfer. As a result, the new policy enforced by the Thaksin administration in 2001 to foster innovation, no longer relied on the IE framework. As was also explained in Chapter 4, the government chose instead to base its innovation policy on "clusters". However, unlike Japan or South Korea, where the term "cluster" explicitly refers to the Regional Innovation Systems (RIS) concept, Thailand has defined a distinctive kind of cluster — that is, a sector-based cluster covering the whole country, rather than a territory-based cluster. Although also referring to Porter's cluster concept, the Thai-type of cluster ignores the essential effects of geographic proximity, in particular, interactive and collective learning, as well as positive externalities for participating actors that have been highlighted in empirical studies on innovation systems.

Yet, the IEs are not about to vanish, far from it. The Thai economy still needs foreign companies to establish themselves in the country and industrial estates entirely fulfil this role. The development of private IEs thus continues to be encouraged by the generous tax exemptions and privileges granted by the BOI, and have expanded in the vicinity of the Bangkok metropolitan area by the enlargement of zone 3. Since regional balance is no longer a state priority, manufacturing activities tend to reconcentrate in the region of Bangkok and the eastern coastal provinces. Private IEs developed in these areas have become highly sophisticated, with services and facilities closely matching the needs of multinational firms and their subcontractors. However, it is clear that they are no longer meant to stimulating innovation through technological transfer, as evidenced by the recent establishment of Chinese factories.

Could Thailand nevertheless try to rely on the existing IE framework to develop future regional poles of innovation, following Korea's example? We have shown in this chapter that it would be difficult for it to do so for three major reasons. First, Thailand's urban framework is one of the weakest in Asia. With a population of a mere 160,000 inhabitants (compared with 500,000 in Malaysia-the Philippines, and 1,000,000 in Indonesia, South Korea, and Japan), a typical Thailand's regional city does not have the critical size to develop innovation poles. Adding to this, the strongly centralized institutional framework does not leave much room to strengthen local governance. Second, unlike many Asian countries, Thailand until 2001 did not implement sector-specific policies since its strategy was to attract the widest range of foreign industries by its low-cost labour and high-quality infrastructure. Thai firms did not, therefore, accumulate the necessary knowledge and skills to shape a competitive domestic industry upon which innovation could take root. Third, innovative poles in South Korea rely on sector-specific industrial groupings, whereas the industry mix in Thailand's IEs is generally too wide to allow a critical concentration of firms in a given industrial sector.

An exception is the Gemopolis IE, which has the ambitious project of becoming a world centre for jewellery. This estate seeks specialization and industrial synergy, building on an old domestic tradition of gem mining and treatment. Strongly supported by the new innovation policy that is fashionable with the five industrial sectors to be promoted, the Gemopolis IE has been granted the "cluster" label. Conditions are favourable for turning this estate into a true innovative pole, but it would require a more proactive policy in education and training, as well as further development of industry-academic linkages.

Notes

1. Based on data released on the IEAT website, updated in September 2005.
2. According to the Asian Industrial Estates database, the most expensive locations in 2009 hit US$60–US$70 per sq. metre in Thailand, compared with US$50–US$100 in similar locations in Shanghai, US$60–US$110 in Vietnam, and US$40–US$110 in the Philippines. Malaysia has similar prices as Thailand, and India stands far below, with peaking locations at US$20/sq.m, <http://www.asianindustrialestates.com/aie/asp/default.asp>.
3. The Bangplee IE is usually included among estates developed by the IEAT, owing to its public character.
4. IMT-GT included the two Indonesian provinces of Sumatra in the north, and Daerah Istimewa (DI) Aceh; the four northern Malaysian states of Kedah, Penang, Perak, and Perlis; and five provinces of Southern Thailand, Narathiwat, Pattani, Satun, Songkhla, and Yala.
5. The fashion industry was dependent, however, on the two public IEs of Phichit and Khon Kan, in central Thailand, where the government wished to concentrate all textile operations.
6. The intensity of these separatist movements may be explained by the fact that these provinces, which were earlier part of the Malaysian Muslim Kingdom of Pattani, were annexed in 1902 by the Kingdom of Siam (present-day Thailand).
7. Statistics of 2005, from the site <www.thailand 4.com/real-estate/hemaraj-in-joint-venture–zith-siam-cement-industrial-park.html>.
8. IEAT Annual report, 2005.
9. Property sales in 2004 made up only 0.8 per cent of IEAT figures.

10. After Hong Kong, the United States, Canada, and Australia. Investments were directed mainly at construction, mining, and electronics. In 2004 there were 235 Chinese industrial projects, totaling US$263 million (Source: Thailand-China links, Kasikorn Research Center).

11. *Korea IT Times*, 31 December 2008. In the seven cluster model estates put forward by KICOX, combined production increased from 198 trillion won in 2004 to 232 trillion won in 2006; the number of companies in the estates rose from 10,036 in 2004 to 11,084 in 2006; the number of employed expanded from 428,000 in 2004 to 448,000 in 2006; and the number of innovation-type companies expanded from 655 in 2004 to 1,644 in 2006. <http://www. kdcstaffs.com/it/main_view.php?mode=view&nNum=4761&parts= Policy&This_Issue=20080>.

References

Adams, D., L. Russel, and C. Taylor-Russel. *Land for Industrial Development*. London: Taylor and Francis, 1994.

Adams, Watkins C. and M. White. *Planning, Public Policy and Property Markets (Real Estate Issues)*. London: Blackwell Publishing, 2005.

Ahn, K. and Y.-T. Ohn. "A Critical Review of Urban Growth Management Policies of Seoul since 1960". *Journal of Korean Planners Association* 32, no. 3 (1997).

Asheinm, B. and J. Vang. "Regional Innovation Systems in Asian Countries: A New Way of Explaining the Benefits of Transnational Corporations". *Innovation: Management, Policy & Practice The International Journal for Innovation Research*, 2006.

Cooke, P., M. Heindereich, and H-Y. Braczyk. *Regional Innovation Systems: The Role of Governance in a Globalized World*. London. New York: Routledge, 2004.

Doloreux, D. "Regional Innovation Systems in the Periphery: The Case of the Beauce in Quebec". *International Journal of Innovation Management* 7, no. 1 (2003): 67–94.

———. "Innovative Networks in Core Manufacturing Firms: Evidence from the Metropolitan area of Ottawa". *European Planning Studies* 12, no. 2 (2004): 173–89.

Doloreux, D. and S. Parto. "Regional Innovation Systems: Current Discourse an Unsolved Issues". *Technology in Society* 27, no. 2 (2005).

Edgington D.W. and H. Fernandez, eds. *New Regional Development Paradigms, volume 2, New Regions-Concepts, Issues, and Practices*. Santa Barbara: Greenwood Press, 2001.

Hattori, A. and Y. Lecler. "Innovation and Clusters: The Japanese Government Policy Framework". In *Shakaikagakukenkyu* (The Journal of Social Science) 60, no. 1 (2009): 117–39.

Intarakumnerd P. "Thailand's National Innovation System (NIS) In the Context of East Asian Economies: Initial Findings". NSTDA, seminar on "Innovation Systems in Asian Economies", 2003.

———. "Thailand's Cluster Initiatives: Successes, Failures and Impacts on National Innovation System". In *Asian Industrial Clusters, Global Competitiveness and New Policy Initiatives*, edited by B. Ganne and Y. Lecler, pp. 467–506. Singapore: World Scientific Publishing, 2009.

Kuchiki A., M. Tsuji. "Industrial Clusters in Asia: Analyses of their Competition and Cooperation". IDE Development Perspective Series No. 6, Institute of Developing Economies, Japan External Trade Organization (JETRO), 2003.

Laurisden L. "Industrial Policies, Political Institutions and Industrial Development in Thailand, 1959–1991". Working Paper No. 21, International Development Studies, Roskilde University, 2000.

Lecler, Y. "The Cluster Role in the Development of the Thai Car Industry: Some Evidence from Empirical Studies". *International Journal of Urban and Regional Research* 26, no. 4 (2002).

Lim, J. D. "Regional Innovation System and Regional Development: Survey and a Korean Case". Working paper series vol. 2006-05, The International Centre for the Study of East Asian Development, Kitakyushu, 2006.

Malmberg, A. and P. Maskell. "Towards an Explanation of Regional Specialization and Industrial Agglomeration". *European Planning Studies* 5, no. 1 (1997).

NSTDA. Seminar on "Innovation Systems in Asian Economies". Mimeographed, 2003.

Porter, M. "Clusters and the New Economics of Competition". *Harvard Business Review* (1998): 77–90.

Ramos, J. and H. Sazanami, eds. *Industrial Estates and Regional Development in Selected Asian Countries: A Review of Experience*. United Nations Centre for Regional Development, Nagoya, 1991.

Renaud Bertrand. "Regional Policy and Industrial Location in South Korea". *Asian Survey* 14, no. 5 (1974): 4566.

Storper, M. *The Regional World*. New York: The Guilford Press, 1997.

Veltz, P. *Mondialisation, villes et territoires, l'économie d'archipel*. Paris: PUF, 1996.

Yamawaki, H. "The Evolution Structure of Industrial Clusters in Japan". The World Bank Institute, Washington, 2001.

Yusuf, S. and K. Nabeshima. *Industrial East Asian Cities, Innovation for Growth*. Washington, D.C.: The World Bank and Stanford University Press, 2006.

Watanabe M. "Official Development Assistance as a Catalyst for Foreign Direct Investment and Industrial Agglomeration". In *External Factors for Asian Development*, edited by H. Kohama, pp. 136–68. Singapore: Institute of Southeast Asian Studies, 2003.

World Bank. *World Bank's Doing Business Report, Country Profile for Thailand 2009*. <http://www.doingbusiness.org/Documents/CountryProfiles/THA.pdf>.

Part III

Firms and Government
New Initiatives:
The Industry Analysis

6

MANUFACTURING AND MANAGEMENT SYSTEMS OF JAPANESE MANUFACTURERS IN SOUTHEAST ASIA
The Case of Automobile Industry in Thailand

Shinya Orihashi

As earlier chapters have shown, the car industry is one of the major engines of growth of Thai industrial development in recent years. Its contribution to exports increased a lot after the Asian crisis of 1997, and the local content achieved is high in comparison with other high-tech industries such as electronics, for example. But, as the literature on this points out, this success is mainly due to the presence of MNCs; pure Thai firms involved in the industry are still quite few in number (Mori 2001; Lecler 2002). The importance of FDI in industrial development was also emphasized in previous chapters. In the car industry, the Japanese were the first and for a long time, the only ones, to invest in Southeast Asia[1] as a whole, and also in Thailand. Unlike for electronics (see Chapter 8), American car makers came in much later.

This chapter will focus on the manufacturing and management strategies of Japanese car makers and their evolution over time, taking the electronics industry as a reference to illustrate specifications of past strategies, and those of American car makers to analyse more recent dynamics. But while speaking of Japanese car makers, we should also distinguish between them as they did not all follow the same strategy all the time. The history of Japanese car makers' implementation in Southeast Asia and in Thailand is already well known,[2] so it will just be briefly mentioned in each section to help position the shift in management strategies within the chronological evolution.

Japanese car makers started overseas operations around 1960, by which time the Japanese economy had managed to recover from the ruins of World War II. While they had not yet acquired a competitive advantage in global competition, they started overseas operations in Southeast Asia. Why did they start their oversea business by entering Southeast Asia? Although its market was too small to attract Western manufacturers, it was near Japan geographically, and there were no strong local competitors there.

However, as Japanese manufacturers acquired global competitive advantage, their focus on global strategy moved to large markets in developed countries, which are located in North America, Western Europe, and so on. But the rapid growth of Japanese exports to developed countries caused trade friction, and it became necessary for Japanese manufacturers to limit their exports voluntarily. So, in order to fulfil demand from the local markets, they established manufacturing subsidiaries one after another, and allocated managerial resources to those subsidiaries.

In recent years, as there has been little chance to make significant market growth in the saturated markets of Japan or other developed countries, Japanese manufacturers are looking at Asia once again. Needless to say, China attracts their attention on both the market and manufacturing side. On the other hand, Southeast Asia also has large market potential. Moreover, many Japanese manufacturers have maintained manufacturing operation in Southeast Asia for many years, as mentioned earlier, and China still carries some country risk, so the importance of Southeast Asia is growing in the global strategies of Japanese manufacturers. Indeed, these fundamental changes in the corporate strategy of Japanese manufacturers have influenced their manufacturing and management systems in Southeast Asia. But such changes in strategies imply new needs whether in terms of human resources, or in terms of supporting industry which might put future evolution into danger.

After having briefly overviewed the past global strategy of Japanese manufacturers after World War II (section 1), this chapter, based on several case studies done at car makers factories in Thailand, will examine the evolution of their manufacturing and management systems centrally, according to strategic changes that occurred due to the Asian crisis of 1997 (sections 2 and 3).[3] But if, as already stated, the Thai car industry achieved a high local content ratio and if subsidiaries could learn enough from the Japanese management system to enhance their international competitiveness, thus changing their position within their parent companies' global strategies, it would then also be true that the future remains uncertain unless present bottlenecks are urgently addressed as will be discussed in the conclusion.

1. ESTABLISHMENT OF MANUFACTURING SUBSIDIARIES IN SOUTHEAST ASIA — 1950s–80s

The overview of the strategic changes of Japanese manufacturers in Southeast Asia, especially those who are in assembly industries, and the detailed observations of the case of the automobile industry in Thailand, show how these changes have influenced the manufacturing and management systems of each Japanese subsidiary.

1.1 Infancy Period: Late 1950s to 1960s

It was in the late 1950s that Japanese manufacturers started exporting to Southeast Asia on a full scale. However, as Southeast Asian countries began introducing import-substitution policies, Japanese manufacturers started to establish small-scale knockdown plants in each country in order to maintain a presence in Southeast Asian markets from the early 1960s.[4] Due to strong restrictions on foreign capital in Southeast Asian countries, almost no manufacturer established a 100 per cent owned subsidiary. Instead, joint ventures with local distributors and/or with Japanese trading companies were established. The lack of financial resources and know-how for managing overseas businesses, as well as their low strategic importance within worldwide strategic plans, also contributed to Japanese manufacturers taking this strategy.

In this period, both in the automobile and electronics industries, Japanese manufacturers established manufacturing companies where they engaged in multiproduct small-volume production solely for local markets. For example, Matsushita Electric Industry established so-called "Mini-Matsushita" subsidiaries in Malaysia, Taiwan and Thailand. At these subsidiaries, they did multiproduct small-volume production solely for each local market.[5] In this period, almost every Japanese manufacturer adopted an "import substitution strategy", regardless of the industry.

1.2 Appreciation of the Yen and Start of Large-scale Offshore Manufacturing: 1970s–80s

It was during the 1970s and 1980s that great differences started to be seen between the automobile and electronics industries. The trigger was the Nixon Shock in 1971 which brought about the appreciation of the yen.

Electronics Industry

The appreciation of the yen pushed Japanese electronics manufacturers to move their labour-intensive production processes for low-end products from Japan to Southeast Asia, as labour cost in Japan jumped. They established many large-scale offshore manufacturing subsidiaries in this region, especially in Malaysia and Thailand, because of their lower labour cost. Their form of establishment differed from that of the 1960s.

First, most of the subsidiaries were 100 per cent owned. Every country in Southeast Asia maintained strong restrictions on incoming foreign capital, however they generally allowed 100 per cent owned subsidiaries if all the products were for export. With this "deregulation", Southeast Asian governments tried to promote industrialization, in addition to keeping their existing import-substituting policy.

Second, as most manufacturers adopted divisional organization and each division established its own subsidiary, subsidiaries producing a single product (or product line) increased. Previously, the management of subsidiaries in Southeast Asia was handled by an export department or overseas operations department. But this time, these subsidiaries were handled by each originating division.

Third, almost all the products were exported to developed countries, such as Japan, the United States, and so on.

The much higher appreciation of the yen after the Plaza Agreement of 1985 accelerated these moves. Intensified international competition and organizational capability building within the subsidiaries also led Japanese manufacturers to transfer more functions and processes to Southeast Asia.

Automobile Industry

In contrast, unlike in the case of the electronics industry, no major move was observed during this period in the automobile industry. Existing knockdown factories gradually expanded as the local markets grew although slowly, but they still were small import-substituting subsidiaries. In spite of the much higher appreciation of the yen, Japanese automobile manufacturers did not start large-scale offshore manufacturing.

Studying the characteristics of both industries may be necessary to explain such a great difference in global strategy between the automobile industry and the electronics industry. An automobile has a relatively "integral architecture" because it consists of many components and delicate coordination between each component is necessary (Fujimoto 2003). So, it was necessary for each subsidiary to acquire strong enough organizational capability to fulfil higher quality standards required by developed countries. As of the early 1980s, however, no overseas subsidiary had acquired such a high standard level. This was mainly because each subsidiary had only done knock-down production solely for its local market. Moreover, industrial clusters in Southeast Asia were still primitive; so many automobile parts, components, and materials had to be imported from Japan. These competitive disadvantagess stemming the advantage coming from lower labour cost.

1.3 Manufacturing and Management System of Japanese Automobile Subsidiaries in Southeast Asia during the "Knockdown Production Period"

As for the characteristic of the manufacturing and management systems of Japanese automobile subsidiaries in Southeast Asia during the "knock-down production period",[6] it is possible to say that Japanese automobile manufacturers were not particularly eager to transfer the so-called Japanese-style manufacturing and management systems that they had adopted in Japan to Southeast Asia.[7]

There may be two reasons that compound the architectural factors stated earlier.

One is the lower strategic importance that subsidiaries in Southeast Asia had. Each Japanese automobile subsidiary in Southeast Asia supplied only its own local markets. During this period, the Southeast Asian automobile market was much smaller than those of Japan and Western countries. Moreover, as Japanese manufacturers were working hard to start their Western manufacturing subsidiaries in their effort to overcome trade friction, they did not have enough resources to strengthen subsidiaries in other regions at the same time.

Another reason lies in the division of labour implemented among Japanese automobile manufacturers. As most of their subsidiaries in Southeast Asia had been started in order to overcome import substitution policies, they were often controlled by the export department in each firm. So, the subsidiaries received technical assistance from headquarters only when it was absolutely necessary because they were not directly controlled by the department which offers technical assistance. This attitude was different from their subsidiaries in Western countries which were often directly managed by the manufacturing division in each firm.

2. RAPID GROWTH OF THE FIRST HALF OF THE 1990s AND JAPANESE AUTOMOBILE MANUFACTURERS' STRATEGY

In the 1990s, the Southeast Asian economy went into orbit and the size of its automobile market started to grow rapidly. On the other hand, automobile markets in developed countries grew slowly, so not only Japanese automobile manufacturers, but also Western ones, became interested in the potential of Southeast Asia. Some manufacturers started to expand their production capacity and/or change the strategic position of their subsidiaries in this region. With these moves, intercompany differences in regional strategies gradually emerged. In Thailand, which is the largest market in Southeast Asia, Japanese brands have dominated the automobile market since 1960s, and there have been no purely local manufacturers. No industrial policy has taken root to promote a local capital automobile manufacturer in contrast to Indonesia, Malaysia, and South Korea. So, we can say that industrial policy for Thai automobile industry has consistently been import substitution since the early 1960s.

Another major characteristic of the Thai automobile industry is the large share of one-ton pickup trucks.[8] From April to November 2008, pick-ups accounts for 54.7 per cent of automobile market in Thailand, passenger cars, 39.9 per cent, and the others, 5.4 per cent are others.[9] One of the major reasons for the dominance of pickups is the taxation rate which is favourable for this type of vehicles. As shown in Table 6.1, the value-added tax for pickups is much lower than that for passenger cars.

Thanks to a high rate of economic growth, the automobile market in Thailand grew rapidly until 1996. It was estimated that market size would reach up to one million by the year 2000.[10]

Most Japanese manufacturers expanded their production capacity in Thailand in order to cope with this growth, and as a stronger supporting industry began to emerge,[11] Western automobile manufacturers such as Ford and GM announced plans to start large-scale production in Thailand.[12]

From this time onwards, some strategic differences started to appear between the Japanese manufacturers. These variations led to differences in their manufacturing and management systems, making it necessary to distinguish between two types.

2.1 Type 1: Expand Production Capacity, but Target only the Growing Local Market

Honda Motor Manufacturing Thailand (HMMT), Siam Nissan Motor, and Toyota Motor Thailand (TMT) adopted the strategy to increase their

Table 6.1
Excise Tax Rates for Automobiles in Thailand

	Category	Tax rates (%)
Passenger cars	2400cc and below	35
	2401cc to 2999cc	41
	3000cc and above	48
Pick-ups	Small truck	3
	Double cab	12
	PPV	18
	Pickups used as public transportation	0
Others	Mid-size and large-size trucks	0
	OPV, SUV	29
	Motorcycles	3

Source: Based on data from *Shukan Thai Keizai*, 18 November 2002, and material from Toyota Motor Thailand.

production capacity, targeting the local Thai market. TMT opened a brand new passenger car plant in Gateway Industrial Estate, located in an eastern suburb of Bangkok, in addition to its existing Samrong Plant. At the new Gateway plant, TMT aimed to produce the Asian car "Soluna" which targeted emerging middle class customers. With this expansion, TMT's annual production capacity was boosted to 240,000 vehicles. HMMT used to manufacture in a plant that it purchased from a local capital knockdown manufacturer, Bangchan General Assembly. However, this plant was too primitive to assure a high enough quality, so HMMT decided to construct a brand new plant in Ayutthaya, located in the north of Bangkok and to relocate most of its automobile manufacturing operations to the brand new factory. In addition, HMMT decided to introduce the Asian car "city" as TMT did. At the same time, Siam Nissan also installed new production equipment and boosted its production capacity.

However these three subsidiaries targeted only the local market and they were not considered to be an offshore production as was the case in the electronics industry. So, in this period, for this type of manufacturers, there was no change in their strategic position of the subsidiaries in Thailand.

Characteristics of Manufacturing and Management System

Even though there was no change in strategy, the manufacturing processes which started in this period were apparently different from the previous ones.

For example, at TMT's Gateway plant, the automation ratio in the body shop was, of course, lower than that in Japan, largely because of the low labour costs in Thailand, but welding robots were installed at critical points to ensure adequate quality and ergonomics. Also, the latest equipment were installed in paint shop and press shop in order to ensure quality standards, which had been set by Toyota's headquarters and were applied to all subsidiaries. On the shop floor, leaders and managers began to meet and discuss quality issues every morning, and the plant aggressively adopted a suggestion system which is common in Japanese plants. Thanks to these attempts, the operating performance of this plant placed it at the highest level among overseas subsidiaries. For example, the direct run ratio in each shop was high; the time that was needed for die change was short.

So, we can say that, in spite of producing mainly for the local market, the new processes which were introduced at TMT widely adopted Japanese manufacturing and management systems. Also, they were designed to achieve high levels of productivity and quality, and to be able to do high volume production. The same tendency can be observed at HMMTs' Ayutthaya plant, and at Siam Nissan.

2.2 Type 2: Expand Production Capacity; New Plant Solely for Export

Mitsubishi Motors also expanded its production capacity in this period, but its strategy and background differed from that of Type 1 firms.[13] In the first half of the 1990s, Mitsubishi Motors' sales performance in Japan was very good, due to the market success of its sport utility vehicle, Pajero, so there was no excess capacity at its manufacturing plants in Japan. Moreover, the market for pickups in Japan is small. In order to utilize effectively its limited managerial resources, Mitsubishi Motors decided to relocate its worldwide production of pickups (including exports to Japan) to Thailand, and make its Thai subsidiary the production base of its pickups (Orihashi 2000b). In 1996, MMC Sittipol, a subsidiary of Mitsubishi Motors, began production at a newly opened, export-oriented plant for pickups which is located next to Laemchabang port, a primary port in Thailand. The plant's first export destination was the Australian market, where right-hand drive vehicles are used, followed by European markets, and general export.

MMC Sittipol continued operating a passenger car plant. This plant is located next to the new plant and started operations in 1992, exported a medium-size passenger car, Lancer, to Chrysler Canada for some years. For this export, MMC Sittipol had already gone through organizational capability building efforts in cooperation with its suppliers to make the export project a success. This experience would clearly seem to have played a major role in making each export project succeed in a relatively short period.

As every export project had met with success, Mitsubishi Motors stopped its pickup production in Japan by the first half of 1997. That is to say, by the mid-1990s, MMC Sittipol had already changed its strategic position from that of a knockdown plant to that of an export-oriented plant.

Characteristics of Manufacturing and Management System

The automation ratio of the production lines at MMC Sittipol is low, much the same as at other plants in Thailand. However, the layout of the production line is different from that of existing knockdown plants in order to ensure a good enough quality for export. Export markets included developed countries where quality requirements are much higher than in developing countries, largely because of their long motorization history. So, it became necessary for MMC Sittipol to ensure quality, and in order to achieve that, it was necessary for the company to build up its organizational capability on the shop floor. Strategic change triggered this capability-building process earlier than for any other competitors.

A remarkable feature of this plant is its aggressive outsourcing. Not only in the press shop, but also in many parts of the body shop, for example, the frame and bed building processes, are outsourced. In order to maintain efficient logistics despite being highly outsourced, MMC Sittipol asked its major suppliers to locate themselves at the same industrial estate (Laemchabang Industrial Estate). Through a computer network, MMC Sittipol shares assembly sequence information with nearby suppliers to try to manufacture synchronously. Moreover, MMC Sittipol is working hard to enhance the organizational capabilities of its suppliers. Originally, Mitsubishi Motors' limited financial capacity for investment led to this aggressive outsourcing, but it has turned out to be an efficient manufacturing system.

3. ASIAN ECONOMIC CRISIS AND EMERGENT STRATEGIC CHANGES: SECOND HALF OF 1990s AND AFTERWARDS

The Asian economic crisis in 1997 hit the Southeast Asian region's economies very seriously. The automobile industry, which had seen booming, and the many manufacturers which had worked hard to expand their production capacity, suffered especially serious damage. On the other hand, the electronics industry, which was mainly doing offshore production, suffered relatively little damage (K. Shimokawa 2002).

In the automobile industry, total production capacity had been remarkably increased to cope with local market growth expectation. But instead of increasing, the market shrank drastically (see Figure 6.1). To survive, manufacturers had no choice but to export. So, whether they were

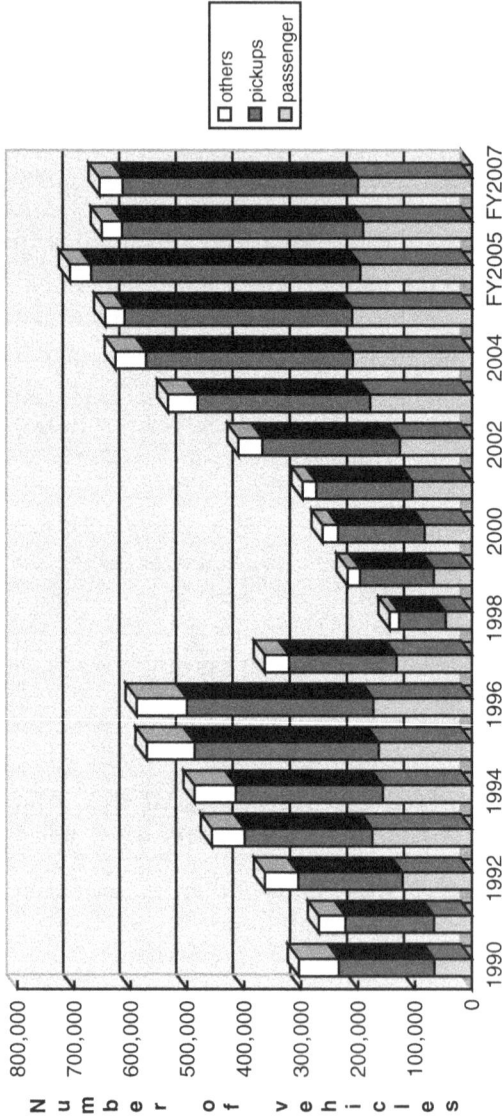

Figure 6.1
Size of Thai Automobile Market

Note: "FY" is from April to the next March.
Source: Based on data obtained from Mitsubishi Motors Thailand, Tri Petch Isuzu (Interviewed in 1999, 2005, and 2008.

willing to or not, each subsidiary had to become an export-oriented plant (Orihashi 2000*a*).

Figure 6.1 shows the change in the size of the Thai automobile market. With such a drastic shrinkage, local Thai suppliers that could not receive relief from their headquarters faced especially hard conditions. Moreover, despite the shrinkage in the local market, Western manufacturers were scheduled to start their operations, which would bring tougher competition. This move would widen gaps between market size and production volume. With the exception of MMC Sittipol, which had already become an export-oriented plant (classified as Type 2 in the previous section.), all the other automobile plants (classified as Type 1 in the previous section.) in Thailand suffered from a low operation ratio. In order to maintain an adequate operating ratio, they had to start exporting.

The depreciation of the Thai baht helped automobile manufacturers' attempts to export. However, they were not able to start exports at once. As mentioned in Orihashi (2000), in order to export to foreign markets, Thai subsidiaries had to improve their quality dramatically, as well as the image of Thai products. Exports hit to 40 per cent of total production at its peak (see Figure 6.2).

Some manufacturers also make personnel cuts, requested large capital infusions from their Japanese headquarters, and obtained support for suppliers. I will use Toyota Motor Thailand, which has the biggest market share (see Figure 6.3) to illustrate the measures taken by Japanese car makers, followed by Western manufacturers' strategy as newcomers in this region.

Toyota Motor Thailand is a company representative of "Type 1", whose strategy as well as manufacturing and management system changed dramatically in this period due to the absolute necessity of integrating exports instead of focusing on the local market only. As Mitsubishi Motors, representative of Type 2 described previously, had already turned to exports before the crisis and did not have to change its strategy or its manufacturing or management system, I have therefore omitted it in this section. But two Western manufacturers which started production in this period have apparently implemented a different strategy or manufacturing and management system to that of Toyota Motor Thailand (representing Japanese car manufacturers), and so a comparison between them is meaningful. However, interestingly enough, the two Western manufacturers did not adopt the same strategy as well as manufacturing and management system either. Of course, as AAT is a joint venture of

Figure 6.2
Export Volume of Thai Automobile Industry

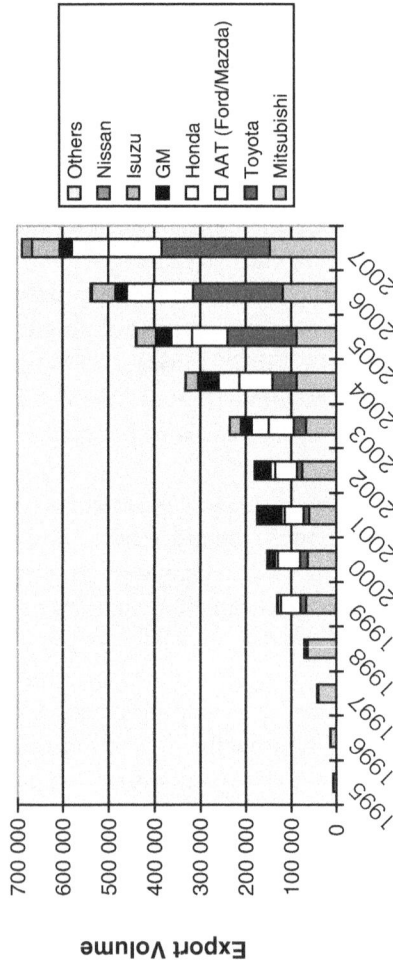

Legend:
- Others
- Nissan
- Isuzu
- GM
- Honda
- AAT (Ford/Mazda)
- Toyota
- Mitsubishi

Source: Based on data obtained from Mitsubishi Motors Thailand.

Figure 6.3
Major Brands in Thailand (April 2008–Nov 2008, sales)

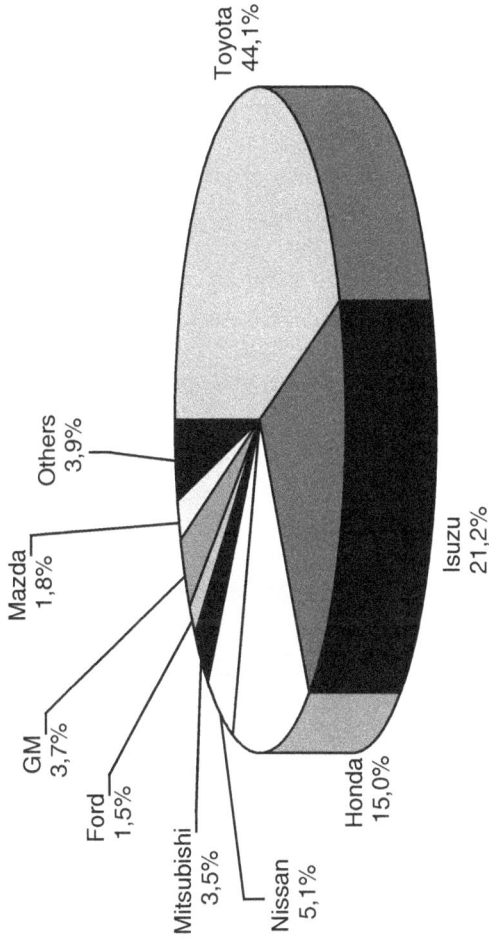

Toyota
44,1%

Others
3,9%

Mazda
1,8%

GM
3,7%

Ford
1,5%

Mitsubishi
3,5%

Nissan
5,1%

Honda
15,0%

Isuzu
21,2%

Source: Based on data obtained from Mitsubishi Motors Thailand.

Ford and Mazda, one could easily think that it is a hybrid factory explaining why its strategy is different from that of GM. But as will be discussed below, GM also appears to have a hybrid one. Whatever the case, as both strategies were decided at their U.S. headquarters (Ford and GM), they could be considered representative of Western car manufacturers.

3.1 Moves by Toyota Motor Thailand (TMT)

As TMT faced the crisis just after its brand new Gateway plant had started its operations, it had a very hard time. TMT took measures to deal with the crisis, doing almost everything it could possibly do to overcome the hardship, without laying off its permanent employees. In order to retain its permanent employees, TMT sent many employees to Japan under various schemes, and at the same time, decided to start exports from Thailand. In September 1998, TMT started to export pickups to Australia, which had previously been supplied by Hino, a Toyota affiliated truck manufacturer. Moreover, TMT tried to export the Asian car, Soluna, and engine parts.

TMT's Manufacturing and Management System: To Become a Global Plant[14]

With its exports strategy starting, TMT's positioning within Toyota's global strategy changed dramatically. It became a centre base of IMV (Innovative International Multipurpose Vehicle). This strategic move brought large changes to TMT.

The IMV project aimed to create an optimized global manufacturing and supply system for pickup trucks and multipurpose vehicles to satisfy market demand in more than 140 countries worldwide (Toyota 2004). Previously, Toyota had several types of pickup trucks and multi-purpose vehicles each on distinct platform according to countries. With this project, Toyota tried to integrate all of them in a common platform to raise its operational efficiency dramatically. The IMV project is being conducted almost entirely outside Japan, including its purchasing, manufacturing, and logistics. One of the project's ultimate goals was to procure nearly 100 per cent of its vehicle components from sources outside Japan (Toyota 2004). From TMT, 140,000 units would be exported and knock-down parts and equipment would be supplied to nine countries including Indonesia, India, Argentina, and South Africa. On the other hand, TMT also would receive knock-down parts and equipment from AFTA countries, as well as India and South Africa, in order to prevent trade imbalances. This was the first time for Toyota to introduce a major vehicle to the global market which was not at all manufactured in Japan. The reasons TMT was chosen as the basis of this important project may not only be due to TMT's history of more than forty years. It was surely more because Toyota headquarters recognized that TMT's capability had been enhanced through its attempt to make its Australian exports project a success.

Starting up the IMV project brought increased complexity to the shop floor. In order to overcome this issue, TMT introduced the "Jiritsuka project" (a project aimed at making subsidiaries self-standing) and the "Working Life Plan" (an effort to make the career path of team members clear and raised their motivation levels) in order to enhance organizational capability building at the shop floor. As a result of these attempts, according to TMT, the plant achieved one of the highest quality level in the world (Result from the audit by Toyota headquarters).

However, at the same time, TMT introduced quality checkpoints ("Quality gates") within the production line, in order to cope with the increased complexity on the shop floor as well as a great number of newly hired workers for increasing production capacity. Quality checkpoints would seem to be inconsistent with the Toyota Production System (TPS). Yet, from another perspective, quality gates ensure that problems are discovered at an early stage, so, in this way, it enhances "built-in quality" as well as promotes organizational capability building on the shop floor.

Incidentally, in November 2002, TMT introduced the Soluna VIOS, which is the next generation of the Asian car Soluna. Soluna VIOS is using a common platform with Vitz (Yaris), Platz (Xiali 2000 in China), and so on. It is one of the "NBC (New Basic Car) series" vehicles and was developed as an Asian strategic car (compact sedan). It is now being produced in China (Tianjin FAW Toyota Automobile Co., Ltd.) and Taiwan (Kuozui Motor, Ltd.) as well.[15] The vehicle is completely different from the former Asian car, Soluna, which was developed from an older version of the Tercel. Introducing Soluna VIOS also symbolized the change of Toyota's strategy in East Asia.[16]

3.2 Moves by Western Manufacturers: The Case of Auto Alliance Thailand (AAT)

In the middle of the 1990s, Ford and Mazda announced that they would jointly establish a manufacturing venture with an annual production capacity of 135,000 vehicles in Thailand. For Ford, this plant would allow the firm to strengthen its level of sales in the Southeast Asian market which had growth potential while for Mazda, which was lacking financial resources, it was a means to increase overseas production while minimizing capital investment. So, a joint venture with Ford would be favourable for Mazda. This congruence of interests pushed the JV project forward. Facing the economic crisis in 1997, AAT decided to export pickups worldwide (excluding North America) from its inception. Products are sold under both the Ford and Mazda brands. Now, AAT produces pickup based SUVs as well.

Characteristics of Manufacturing and Management System at AAT

As Mazda has a relatively strong capability in production and product development, Mazda has been in charge of manufacturing at the joint venture plant. Excluding the purchasing division which is headed by a dispatch team from Ford, every division related to the manufacturing function, is under the supervision of those sent from Mazda. As a result, there are many aspects at AAT in common with Mazda. The layout of the plant is similar to that of Mazda's Hofu plant in the way that production office is surrounded by every workshop. Also, there is a very clear physical demarcation within the plant between an "automated zone" and a "manual zone," which also can be observed at Mazda's Hofu plant. On the shop floor, there are many elements that came from the Japanese production system, such as utilizing *pokayoke* (mistake-proofing)[17] to avoid mis-assembly, minimizing inventories on production sidelines in order to promote visualization (*mieruka*), and so on. Of course, as the majority of its employees were new hires who were not familiar with the automotive assembly itself, AAT installed a parts synchronization line ("picking") which is not usual in Japan.[18] In addition to manufacturing, Mazda also handles the R&D function at AAT, with Mazda's R&D centre in Japan handles most of the product development processes related to AAT. Now AAT has started to introduce the so-called kit supply that Toyota Motor Corporation is introducing to its plants worldwide.

On the other hand, managerial functions, such as human resource management (HRM), finance, and so on, are handled by those dispatched by Ford, because Ford has relatively strong capability in these functions. For example, the number of hierarchical layers has been kept low to be similar to that of other Ford production sites worldwide. AAT has adopted a wage system which has much in common with other Ford production sites. It is largely based on ability and a "performance review" which is carried out at Ford plants worldwide every year, and which is also done at AAT. In this review, employees are asked about various plant satisfaction issues, and so on. Results are directly linked to managerial bonuses. Supervisors evaluate shop floor workers according to measures such as, level of cooperation, quality achievement, attendance, and so on. Results from these evaluations are linked to bonus levels. Managers are evaluated by their immediate bosses and through the yearly reviews described above. There was little influence from Mazda in these managerial functions, despite Mazda's past experience in running a joint venture plant with a local partner company in Thailand.[19]

3.3 Moves by Western Manufacturers:
The Case of General Motors Thailand

General Motors (GM) moved to Thailand[20] together with its affiliated companies: Opel, Isuzu, Fuji Heavy Industry, and GM Daewoo. General Motor Thailand is a 100 per cent owned subsidiary of GM. Because of the Asian economic crisis, GM's projected investment in Thailand was reduced, but it was still double the amount AAT initially invested. Also, originally GM planned to produce a small passenger car, Astra, to be sold in Thailand, but after the crisis, the proposed plant changed to an export-oriented plant.

GM Thailand finally started operations in 2000. Zafira, a minivan developed by Opel, was assembled at the plant and exported to Europe as the Opel Zafira. At the same time, it was sold in Thailand as the Chevrolet Zafira. Fuji Heavy Industry also sold the vehicle as the Subaru Traviq, after making minor changes for the Japanese market.

In 2003, receiving Isuzu's full technical support, a new production line for pickups started operations at the GM Thailand plant, and all the export production of Isuzu's pickups (D-MAX) moved from existing Isuzu Motor Manufacturing Thailand (IMMT) to GM Thailand. Now, pickups produced at GM Thailand are exported worldwide, as well as sold domestically as the Chevrolet Colorado. At present, the passenger car line has ceased producing the Zafira and is doing knock-down production of the Chevrolet Optra that was developed by GM Daewoo in South Korea.

Characteristics of Manufacturing and Management System at GM Thailand

The manufacturing system at the passenger car line (at least at the time it was doing full production) can be called "Hybrid of Europe and Japan".[21]

As the line's first product was developed by Opel, there were many European elements, for example, module production. But, while it is usual that module parts were completed and checked by suppliers in Europe, final assembly of the module was done by GM Thailand. Moreover, the production line was quite ergonomically friendly, which was a rare case in Thailand, then.

On the other hand, many elements from the Japanese production system could also be observed. There may be several reasons for this. First, managers who were in charge of the plant's start-up had been hired from a Japanese automobile subsidiary in North America. They tried to put into practice what they had learned from Japanese colleagues dispatched to North America. For example, standardized operation sheets are completed by team leaders and are always subject to change by continuous improvement activity (*kaizen*). Also, a *kanban* system[22] is used in the process in order to minimize inventory levels on production sidelines.

Second, the production process was designed and constructed by Chiyoda Corporation,[23] a famous plant constructor in Japan. The final assembly line is designed to be a "T" shape. According to a GM manager, it is a common layout of GM's overseas plants that started after 1990, such as those in Argentina, Brazil, China (Shanghai), and Poland.

Third, the result of organizational learning from New United Motor Manufacturing Inc. (NUMMI), a joint venture plant in the United States between GM and Toyota, could also be observed. GMS (Global Manufacturing System), which is a GM version of the Toyota Production System (TPS), was promoted at GM Thailand, as well.

With regard to the pickup production line, Isuzu was in charge of its layout and many workers dispatched from Japan were working for it. On this line, the Japanese production system was fully adopted.

On the management side, GM Thailand was equipped with the most elaborate welfare centre in Thailand. Also, the administration process for visitors was observed to be much the same as that found in GM plants in the United States. In this area, it seems that American elements were largely adopted.

3.4 Lessons from Case Studies

Case studies have clearly shown that the Asian economic crisis gave each subsidiary a trial and forced them to do structural reform. It played out that subsidiaries could use the opportunity to enhance their international competitiveness, and furthermore, change their strategic position within their respective parent company's global strategy.

During the crisis, as already mentioned, Japanese car manufacturers, not willing to fire their surplus permanent employees and qualified workers, used to send many of them to Japan for training. Also, the crisis eliminated most of the opportunities for middle-managers and engineers to job hop from one subsidiary to another as they often used to do before, due to their scarcity in the labour market (see Chapter 3). This permitted subsidiaries to invest in human development with less anxiety. So, although the Asian economic crisis led manufacturers into hard times, it was a great chance for the Thai automobile industry to advance its position in the world. Most manufacturers including Type 1 ones made the most of this chance and transformed themselves from knock-down plants into strategically important production bases.

But after the economic recovery, the production volume of Thai automobile industry grew rapidly again as most automobile manufacturers in Thailand had started large-scale export. This trend has gradually revealed some shortages again. Technological universities in Thailand do not educate and train enough engineers to help Thailand cover needs to expand its higher quality automobile production and other high-tech industries (see Chapter 8). Car manufacturers tend to invest in training, but the shortage in the labour market has led to the revival of "job-hopping" (switching from one job to another). This shortage of engineers also makes it very difficult for local Thai suppliers to hire them. Their workforce remained composed mainly of shop floor workers of whom a surplus still exists in the labour market, especially in northern Thailand,[24] and their average wage remains low, much lower than those in China.

This situation also does not help solve the other major problem car manufacturers have to deal with: the shortage of supporting industries in Thailand, especially supplier in the second tier and lower.

Thai supporting industries also lack organizational capability. This has pushed many local suppliers down from first tier to second tier. As production volume of automobile manufacturers increased and, as strategic importance moved up in the value chain as more functions were transferred from Japan to Thailand, the required quality level for first-tier suppliers has become much higher. Participation in product development, in particular, became required, which it was not in the knock-down production stage. This, and the higher quality requirement pushed Thai suppliers down. In their place, many multinational suppliers moved in.

Adding to that the recent appreciation of the Thai baht which is causing a competitive disadvantage to the Thai automobile industry, multinational automobile manufacturers that have production operation in Thailand might have to reconsider their strategy of continuing to make their Thai manufacturing subsidiaries export oriented. As mentioned before, the Asian economic crisis brought about the depreciation of the Thai baht. That raised the profitability of exports and induced almost every automotive manufacturer in Thailand to start exporting. But, the recent appreciation of the Thai baht undermines that crucial assumption, which is also threatened by the emerging excess production capacity in the Chinese automobile industry and the commencement of the China-ASEAN FTA. This will bring tougher competition to the export operations of Thai automobile manufacturers. Also, the Thai-India FTA will bring the same threat to them. But, of course, the China-ASEAN FTA does not have to be a threat only, but could also become a great opportunity for the Thai automobile industry in much the same way as the Asian economic crisis was, provided the country is able to solve its twofold shortages. Recent higher oil prices and the political uncertainty in the country which forced the domestic market to shrink again are, of course, not positive signs for car manufacturers.

CONCLUSION

In the past years, Japanese automobile manufacturers had operated import-substituting knock-down plants in Southeast Asia. There might have been oligopolistic interdependence. However, in the Thai automobile industry, for example, which is facing harsh conditions, we can currently observe larger differences among the companies.

When comparing the "knock-down period" with recent conditions, we can observe that the increased strategic importance of Japanese subsidiaries in Southeast Asia promoted Japanese manufacturing and management systems. The degree to which this observation made in the case of Thailand will also hold true for other countries remains an interesting area for further research.

Related to this, the chapter also delineates the factors that enabled Thai subsidiaries to build up their capabilities when faced with a severe crisis. It does not seem that the Thai government, or even manufacturers, had a clear vision of positioning Thai subsidiaries as strategically important production bases at the beginning of the industry development. However, the automobile industry in Thailand experienced capacity expansion during an economic boom followed by a severe crisis. As a result it happened that these Thai subsidiaries became strategically important production bases. In that sense, the developments could be called an "emergent strategy"[25] (Mintzberg and Waters 1985; Fujimoto 1998).

Of course, this does not mean that during the development process, the government did not support the evolution by taking some measures to promote the industry. This occurred with the local content requirement in the earlier period,[26] or with the taxation policy to promote pickups. As these vehicles to some extent are less complex, and require a quality level lower than passenger cars, the policy worked very well. Pickups being acceptable in worldwide markets, certainly helped Thailand to turn to an export-oriented strategy rather rapidly.

But today, as we have seen in the former section, and as some other chapters of this book show, the further industrial development of the country is reaching some limits. The lack of education of the nation's workforce, especially the limited number of good quality technicians and engineers, is not new indeed. The poor capabilities of pure Thai SMEs that could have worked as subcontractors (second tier and below suppliers) in segments such as mould and die, precision engineering services, machine tools, testing, and others, is not a recent issue either.

But the problem deepened for car manufacturers since they turned to export-oriented strategies as explained in previous sections.

Indeed, in this context, they focused not only on assembly, but also on activities which require higher technological capabilities, such as design, engineering, and new product development. These kinds of activities do require different types of engineers and technicians. What is needed now are not only "production engineer" but also "research engineers", for example, and as was argued in Chapter 3, the country does not seem prepared for such an evolution.

And it also needs strong and innovative supporting industries that are able to keep up with the technological progress of their clients, as Japanese SMEs did in the past. The existing and would-be Thai suppliers need to develop their capabilities in order to take advantages of the new production and management techniques introduced by their Japanese and American manufacturers. This means that a huge upgrading of Thai suppliers is needed to avoid a reconsideration of the international division of labour. It is necessary for the Thai government to change the education curriculum, and the training of engineers and technicians to absorb these new techniques. Furthermore the government should continuously support and further develop such initiatives as the Thai Automotive Institute (TAI) which is providing technical assistance and training for parts manufacturers receiving aid from the Japanese government.

In the present difficult economic situation that sees a huge decline in car markets worldwide, reinforced in Thailand by its political crisis, it is an important challenge for Thailand's policymakers to find a way urgently to produce the kind of human resources and supporting industries that car manufacturers need to develop more qualitatively their future activities and bring them to global standards.

Notes

1. In this chapter, "Southeast Asia" is considered to comprise ASEAN countries and Taiwan
2. On the historical development of Japanese multinational manufacturers in Southeast Asia, several authors such as among others, Yoshihara (1997), Yoshihara (2001), Yoshihara, Itagaki, and Morogami (2003), Shimokawa (2002), and Higashi (1995) have already discussed the issue extensively.
3. I surveyed Thai automobile manufacturers in June 1999, December 2000, September 2002, January and December 2003, September 2004, February and September 2005, March 2006, and January and December 2007.
4. These countries, including Indonesia, Malaysia, the Philippines and Thailand, introduced import-substitution policies, in order to industrialize their countries, by replacing imported industrial products with domestic products.
5. As of 1 October 2008, Matsushita Electric Industry changed its name to Panasonic Corporation.
6. The knock-down period includes both the infancy and the yen appreciation periods.
7. Literature on the "Japanese-style manufacturing and management system" is abundant. For further details, please refer among others to Abo (1994) who discusses the competitive advantage against the manufacturing and management system in the United States; Fujimoto (1999) who discusses the evolution of manufacturing and management system at Toyota; Womack, Jones, and Roos (1990) who point out the competitive advantage of Japanese

automobile manufacturers, based on their international comparison survey, and call the Japanese production system, a "lean production system".

8. Hereafter called "pickups".
9. Source: Mitsubishi Motors Thailand.
10. On the market growth and further expectations at that time, see, for example, and Guiheux Lecler (2000).
11. Ishizaki (1996); Mori (2001).
12. On that issue, sees also Takayasu and Toyama (1997), Mori (2000).
13. Mitsubishi Motors (Thailand) Co., Ltd. was called MMC Sittipol Co., Ltd. until November 2003.
14. Please refer to Toyota Motor Corporation (2004) as well.
15. In China and Taiwan, it is produced as VIOS.
16. Now the new generation VIOS has started to be produced at TMT's Gateway plant.
17. A *pokayoke* is any mechanism in a lean manufacturing process that helps an equipment operator avoid (*yokeru*) mistakes (*poka*); cf. Wikipedia, <http://en.wikipedia.org/wiki/Poka-yoke>.
18. Recently, due to the increasing number of non-permanent workers, many automobile assembly plants in Japan have installed similar lines.
19. This plant was gradually closed with the opening of AAT.
20. For the reason they chose Thailand, see, for example, Takayasu and Toyama (1997), Lecler (2002).
21. For details about the Japanese manufacturing and management system in comparison with the American one, refer to Abo (1994). For details about the European manufacturing and management system in comparison with the Japanese one, refer to Kumon and Abo (2004).
22. A *kanban* system is a Toyota-born production system related to lean production and Just-In-Time. It improve efficiency in eliminating waste, vizualizing problems and so on.
23. Called "Chiyoda Kako Kensetsu" in Japanese.
24. However, among plants located more than approximately 100 kilometres from Bangkok, shop floor workers tend to seek the chance to move to plants that are closer to Bangkok because wage levels in the Bangkok area are higher.
25. In the field of strategic management, the notion of "strategy as plan", in which strategic intent precedes strategic implementation has been a prevalent idea for many years (Andrews 1980; Hofer and Schendel 1978, etc.). However, there has also been another strategy concept which assumes the possibility that competitive strategy may be formed even without a competitively rational prior intention. Mintzberg and his colleagues call a strategy that was unintended but realized "emergent strategy" (Mintzberg and Waters 1985).
26. See Higashi (1995), Guiheux and Lecler (2000).

References

Abo, Tetsuo, ed. *Hybrid Factory*. New York: Oxford University Press, 1994.

Andrews, K.R. *The Concept of Corporate Strategy*. Dow Jones-Irwin, 1971.

Fourin. *Fourin's Monthly Report on the Asian Automotive Industry*. Fourin, 2007.

Fujimoto, Takahiro. "Toyota Motor Manufacturing Australia in 1995: An Emergent Global Strategy". Discussion Paper, Faculty of Economics, The University of Tokyo, 1998.

———. *The Evolution of a Manufacturing System at Toyota*. New York: Oxford University Press, 1999.

———. *Noryoku kochiku kyoso* [Competition in Capability Building]. Tokyo: Chuokoronshinsha, 2003.

Guiheux, Gilles and Yveline Lecler. "Japanese Car Manufacturers and Parts Makers in the ASEAN Region: A Case of Expatriation under Duress — or Regionally Integrated Production?". In *Global Strategies and Local Realities: The Auto Industry in Emerging Markets*, edited by J. Humphrey, Y. Lecler, M. Salerno, pp. 207–33. London: Macmillan, 2000.

Heller, D.A. and S. Orihashi. "Pooling Capabilities Abroad for Global Competitive Advantage: Investigating Ford-Mazda Cooperation in Southeast Asia". *International Journal of Automotive Technology and Management* 3, no. 1 (2003).

Higashi, Shigeki. "The Automotive Industry in Thailand: From Prospective Promotion to Liberalization". IDE Spot Survey on The Automotive Industry in Asia: The Great Leap Forward?, Institute of Developing Economies, 16–25 October 1995.

Hofer, C.W. and D. Schendel. *Strategy Formation: Analytical Concepts*. West, 1978.

Ishizaki, Yukiko. "New Phase in Asia Strategies of Japanese-affiliated Automobile and Parts Manufacturers". *RIM Pacific Business and Industries* 1, no. 31 (1996): 17–32.

Kumon, Hiroshi and Abo Tetsuo. *The Hybrid Factory in Europe*. Palgrave Macmillan, 2004.

Lecler, Yveline. "The Cluster Role in the Development of Thai Car Industry: Some Evidence from Empirical Studies". In *International Journal of Urban and Regional Studies* 26, no. 4 (December 2002): 799–814.

Mintzberg H. and J. Waters. "Of Strategies, Deliberate and Emergent". *Strategic Management Journal* 6 (1985): 257–72.

Mori, Minako. "New Trends in ASEAN Strategies of Japanese-affiliated Automobile Parts Manufacturers — The Role of Exporting and Priorities for the Future". *RIM Pacific Business and Industries* 1, no. 43 (1999): 12–27.

———. "The Formation and Development of the Automobile Industrial Cluster in Thailand". *RIM Pacific Business and Industries* 1, no. 50 (2001): 54–67.

Orihashi, Shinya. "Breaking from Import-Substituting Plant to Export-Oriented Plant, The Case of Japanese Automotive Makers in Australia and Thailand".

The Journal of Asian Management Studies (in Japanese), Vol. 6, Japan Scholarly Association for Asian Management (2000*a*): 97–102.

―――. "Plural patterns of international strategy in the same industry, the case of Toyota and Mitsubishi Motors in Thailand and Australia". *The Annual Bulletin Japan Academy of International Business Studies*, No. 6, 2000*b*, pp. 238–49 (in Japanese).

―――. *Kaigai Kyoten no Souhatsuteki Jigyoutenkai* [Emergent Business Evolution of Overseas Operations]. Tokyo: Hakuto Shobo, 2008.

Shimokawa, Koichi. "Reevaluation of the International Division of Labor in Japan's Automobile Industry in Asia". In *Japanese Foreign Direct Investment and the East Asian Industrial System*, edited by H. Horaguchi and K. Shimokawa. Berlin: Springer Verlag, 2002.

Takayasu, K. and A. Toyama. "Business Development of the Big Three US Auto-makers in Asia Accelerating their Global Strategies". *RIM Pacific Business and Industries* 3, no. 37 (1997): 22–33.

Toyota Motor Corporation. "IMV Project Shifts into Production Gear: Toyota Introduces its Optimized Global Manufacturing and Supply System". Special Report, Toyota Motor Corporation, 2004.

Womack, J.P., D.T. Jones and D. Roos. *The Machine that Changed the World*. New York: Rawson Associates, 1990.

Yoshihara, Hideki. *Kokusai keiei* [International Business]. Tokyo: Yuhikaku, 1997.

―――, ed. *Kokusai keieiron heno shotai* [Introduction to International Business]. Tokyo: Yuhikaku, 2001.

Yoshihara, Hideki, Hiroshi Itagaki and Shigeto Morogami. *Case Book kokusai keiei* [Case Book International Business]. Tokyo: Yuhikaku, 2003.

7

THE TEXTILE AND GARMENT INDUSTRY IN THAILAND
The Technology and Education Upgrading Challenge

Audrey Baron-Gutty

At the beginning of the twentieth century, and despite in-depth reforms implemented by King Chulalongkorn, Siam, as the country was named at the time, was still very traditional in its political, social and economic structures. Economic life in the country was dominated by Royal patronage and an elite linked to the Royal Family. This started to change with the surge in Chinese migration, urbanization, and internationalization of the kingdom. The society, as a consequence, evolved more complex and diverse; governing and trading patterns reshuffled with the rise of a market economy and the involvement of various foreign partners. The absolute monarchy, unable to adapt, fell in 1932 and the following decades witnessed an alternation between "strong-state" and "state for the well-being of people" governing patterns, with the "strong state" tradition being dominant (Baker and Phongpaichit 2005).

Different actors have fuelled the mutation and their agency is relevant for pointing out the mechanisms and forces at stake in the various steps undertaken. Indeed, the textile[1] industry, which is a bridge between the past and the future, epitomizes Thailand's transformation well. In that sense it is a relevant example for emphasizing not only where Thailand comes from, but also what the current threats and needs are to ensure its sustainability.

Surveying the industry's long history clearly shows a move from production based in the villages and anchored in tradition and self-reliant living, to manufacturing oriented towards exports and relying on plants in which foreign investors have had an important role. The insight into Thai textile industry is, therefore, a way to stress the role played by different actors, namely the government, domestic entrepreneurs, banks, and foreign investors, in the build-up of the Thai market economy (part 1).

But, for the last two decades, the textile industry's weight in the national economy (contribution to GDP, exports, employment) has started to fall. This is to some extent due to the rise of other industries such as electronics or automotive, but this positive explanation is not the whole story. The relative decline of the Thai textile industry also reveals some inherent weaknesses that the industry, as well as the country as a whole, needs to overcome to ensure its sustainability.

The emergence of new competitors on the global market (Vietnam, China, or Indonesia) makes it necessary for Thailand to address several issues, the least of which is not cost efficiency. The concentration of the industry around Bangkok has contributed to the Thai textile industry's loss of competitiveness, while the industry structure and the lack of financial support did not easily allow for it to update technologies, innovate new products, or develop an efficient supply chain. All these issues are on the agenda and government policies now tend to take a new step by encouraging investment outside the Bangkok area where manpower cost is still lower and by favouring linkages between firms, research and financial institutions (section 2).

1. A CHANGING THAILAND

A historical study of the development of the textile sector in Thailand is required in order to account for what has brought this industry to the position it currently holds, but also to outline the elaboration of modern

Thailand and to underscore the role played by several actors in this transformation.

1.1 From Tradition to Modernity

The traditional economy was characterized by self-sufficient agriculture whose exchanges with the outer world were scarce, and based on the surpluses it generated and on barter trade. There was no market economy and relations between the countryside and the (small) cities were limited, as were the exchanges between the different parts of what would later be known as the kingdom of Siam.

Textiles fitted in with that traditional pattern. Production was cottage-based, the cottage industry being defined as a small business that is run from someone's home (especially one that involves a craft). This involved a pattern of villages outside Bangkok: Textile production was carried out among other activities; simple peasants knitted and wove their own clothes during the off-season. They were self-sufficient and part of a small community, which meant that textiles were also in the middle of counter trade deals: When a surplus in textile production was generated, it was usually directed to tailors or peasants in exchange for other goods.

With the beginning of urbanization, and the growing importance of the Central Plain, patterns changed to adapt to the new situation. Not all urban dwellers could be involved in multiple activities: Agriculture, for instance, was mainly carried out in the peripheral areas of Bangkok, where the environment was favourable and fields were big enough for a living.

Specialized districts appeared quickly in the capital city, based on craft or ethnic origin, with both being intertwined. These "villages" were characterized by a multiple urban function, with residential, commercial and production features (Boontharm 2005, p. 149). This phenomenon of district specialization is a common feature in Southeast Asia (for example, nowadays the Bobae district in Bangkok specializes in the production and retailing of textile/garments). It can mainly be explained by two factors:

- As urban living was growing and Bangkok as a urban centre developing, self-sufficiency was not possible and people had to specialize in a craft or an activity.
- It was necessary for craftsmen to settle close to one another to

enhance know-how through daily exchanges (this is because of the importance of tacit or implicit knowledge, especially in craft-related activities).

Moreover, a growing number of exchanges was done in market places, and the merchant community began structuring itself, leading to the rise of a market economy and the decline of traditional forms.

Things were not meant to stay traditional: Siam's turning point was the signing of the Bowring treaty in 1855.[2] The outer world was in those days getting into Siam gradually. The kingdom used to have historical trading links with China mainly, but also with India. But its partners, at the end of the nineteenth century, changed from those from the East to the ones from the West and their grasp was more and more fierce, impacting on the Siamese society. Though it did not submit directly to a colonial power, Siam had to handle colonial appetites and was taking part in the colonial economy: Some imports came from Western economies and the importance of exports to Europe was increasingly important. All of this affected the Siamese economy.

Siam's village-based textile industry managed at first to resist the surge in imports from Britain. However, the share of imported cloth in the local market started to increase from the 1880s due to two interrelated factors:

- The advantages shown by "Manchester imports" in terms of quality, quantity, and availability.
- The predominance of rice: the Chaophraya Plain concentrated its energies on promoting the rice economy, therefore, neglecting other activities.

Western textiles became more and more present in Siam, but not equally in every region. In remote areas, local production remained strong, carried out in the off-season. People favoured locally woven goods, but eventually the railways reached distant areas in the 1920s, and this, combined with the possibility to trade paddy and other produces for cash, meant that imported textiles were given improved reception (Baker and Phongpaichit 2002, p. 105).

However, foreign countries' influence on the textile industry remained relatively limited. Western business was not backed by a colonial government and "without access to political power, Western firms were unable to structure the economy of Siam to suit colonial aims" (Baker and

Phongpaichit 2002, p. 106). The political control from European powers was indeed not direct and not the entire Siamese economy was dedicated to achieving colonial aims. This explains to some extent why Siam, for instance, kept domestic textile industry unlike to India, which struggled afterwards to bring back domestic cotton spinning. Through exchanges with the West, raw materials were more easily available for Thai textile production. Still, at that time, the Thai textile industry was not able to compete with other major nations in the international textile and garment trade, as it was entrenched in a limited local market with insufficient funding, using simple technology, facing competition from foreign protected textile companies, and had poor relevant experience (Lehman 2004, p. 124).

At the beginning of the twentieth century, textile production was on a small scale and trade was carried out by domestic entrepreneurs, usually of Chinese descent. Foreign entrepreneurs were playing a limited, but growing, role in a more and more internationalized environment. Thai textiles at the beginning of the twentieth century were not pre-eminent in a mainly agrarian economy: Before the late 1950s, there were practically no textile plants in Thailand, except for a few cotton firms. Manufacturing was limited and so were textiles. Attempts to create a real textile industry started before the Second World War from both public and private actors.

From the mid-1930s to the late 1940s, the Thai state played an important role by helping to start a wide range of industrial enterprises, with full or partial public ownership. That was the case, for instance, for public utilities companies, or consumer goods industries such as textiles, or paper.[3] They filled the space created by European powers retreating from the country, because of the Depression and then the war. Fundraising and allowances were progressively institutionalized, through the Thai Industrial Development Agency (1942), a public institution designed to be the government's investment arm in industry (Baker and Phongpaichit 2002, pp. 123–24).

With regard to private actions, manufacturing was backed by the new economic structure in which trading played a major role. Businesses usually started in retailing and trading (mostly in primary goods), and then progressively found new opportunities to move to manufacturing. This was the onset of Thai conglomerates, such as the one founded by Sukree Potiratanangkun, who started as a cloth importer and became a textile magnate. Most of the domestic entrepreneurs were actually Chinese, sometimes from the first generation of immigrants, but mainly the second.

This all happened in an international context characterized by the Great Depression, the early beginnings of the Second World War, and the Japanese occupation of the country. Through these political and economic upheavals, both domestic and international, a new political and entrepreneurial environment began to form; Thai manufacturers seized new chances opened up by the disruption of European trade and the withdrawal of Western entrepreneurs.

1.2 The Import-Substitution Strategy (1950s–late 1980s)

From the nascent manufacturing opportunities started in wartime, the next crucial step taken was induced by an import-substitution strategy, implemented from the 1950s. Scholars place the beginning of the changes with the ascension to power of General Sarit Thanarat in 1958 via a military coup, a period that differed from the past in political and economic terms.[4] Thailand's nascent textile industry was then boosted by private investments and governmental incentives.

Sustained paddy exports provided funds for industrial development. Banking played a major role in channelling investment into manufacturing. Household savings, accumulated through paddy trade and saved in the banks, were transferred into industrial enterprises. Agricultural development contributed to manufacturing development through the transfer of generated surpluses to consumption and investment. The Bangkok Bank played a particularly prominent role. "Among all the banks, Bangkok Bank reigned supreme.... Bangkok Bank was *involved* with just about *everybody*". This was especially true in the textile industry as Bangkok Bank helped family-owned businesses involved in rice trade to get into textile (Baker and Phongpaichit 2002, p. 137).

Sarit implemented public measures to promote import-substitution industrialization (ISI). Through ISI, the country aimed at replacing imports progressively by national products, beginning with the most simple industries and spinning off to more complex sectors (such as machinery): Cloth merchants spun off into textile manufacture, primary exporters, into agro-processing, consumer goods importers, into assembly. Figure 7.1 presents the textile and garment production cycle. The R&D stage impacts on all stages of the textile and garment production cycles. For instance, the synthetic industry can be improved through R&D research for the process of fibre production; the weaving and knitting industry is directly linked to innovation in weaving procedures and machinery.

Figure 7.1
The Textile and Garment Production Cycle

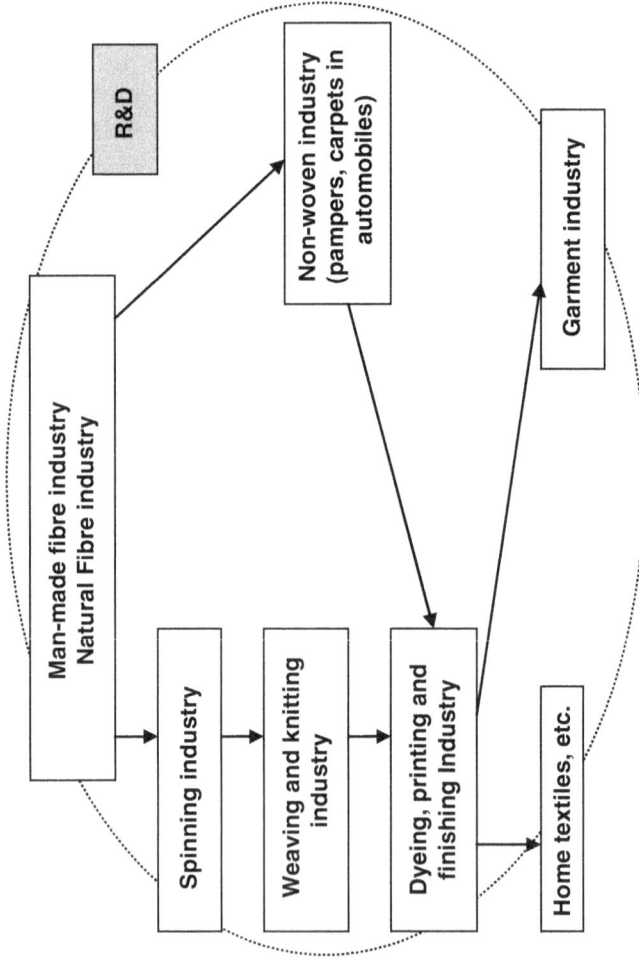

Source: Adapted from *L'industrie textile en mutation — des ambitions nouvelles*, No. 154, September 2001, available at <www.industrie.gouv.fr>; Chalumpon Lotharukpong (2004).

Protectionist measures were implemented by the Thai government. Being a latecomer, Thailand needed protection from products coming from more developed countries (at the beginning of the import-substitution strategy, products from developed countries were much more competitive). High tariffs exemplified this protection. The tariff structure implemented in the 1960s relied on a differential structure, favouring the imports of parts and components, and discouraging those of finished goods. The aim was to boost domestic manufacturing and meet national needs with local goods. Table 7.1 presents the evolution of tariffs in Thai textiles between 1960 and 1985.

When calculating the "effective protection rate" of the Thai textile industry, by "adjusting tariffs on output net of those on input and expressing them in terms of the rate of increase in value-added of domestic activity in producing goods competitive with the import concerned", it appears that the effective protection rate proved much higher than nominal tariff rates (Hirose 1996).

In the mid-1970s, the Thai textile industry completed import substitution in cotton and synthetic fabrics, as can be seen by the evolution of the import/domestic demand (M/D) ratio and the export/domestic production (X/S) ratio.

The M/D ratio started declining in the early 1960s for cotton fabrics, and in the mid-1960s for man-made fabrics. In contrast to this decline the early 1970s witnessed a rise in the X/S ratio, both in cotton and man-made fabrics. In the mid-1970s, the X/S ratio exceeded the M/S ratio (Hirose

Table 7.1
Import Tariff of Thai Textile Goods, 1960–80s (%)

	1960–62	1962–65	1965–68	1968–71	1971–78	1978–82	1982–85	1985
Yarn	20.0	20.0	20.0	21.7	21.7	21.7	23.7	30.0
Fabrics	32.0	36.3	38.3	60.0	60.0	80.0	66.0	60.0
Clothing	27.5	27.5	30.0	60.0	60.0	80.0	66.0	60.0

Notes: The value "Yarn" is the average value of tariffs applied on cotton yarn, polyester cotton yarn and polyester rayon yarn. The value "Fabrics" is the average value of tariffs applies on cotton fabrics, polyester cotton fabrics and polyester rayon fabrics.
Source: Table made by the author based on data mentioned in Tambunlertchai and Yamazawa, 1981.

1996). In 1959, more than 80 per cent of domestic demand for cotton fabrics was satisfied by imports; in 1972, this share fell to 10 per cent.

Foreign influence eased, and in many ways, shaped Thai import-substitution-oriented development. Starting in the 1960s, U.S. involvement kept on growing with the Vietnam War and the use of Thailand as a military base. Glassman (2004, p. 37) referred to this period as the one of "U.S. hegemony", and argued that this had numerous repercussions on the Thai state apparatus: It allowed authoritarian figures such as Sarit to stay in power; it shaped Thai bureaucracy through training that "facilitated cooperation with international development agencies", and it developed Thai infrastructure. The U.S. involvement was, therefore, political, ideological, and economic, and was achieved through foreign aid, huge allowances to targeted departments, and direct investments.

All actors were intertwined. Akira Suehiro (1989, p. 282) described the development alliances as "a tripod formation" with one leg composed of state firms in which the military was involved, a second leg comprising Sino-Thai business groups and financial conglomerates, and a third leg constituted by transnational corporations (TNCs). The three pillars of capital accumulation were interconnected through joint ventures, and the whole structure was maintained together via the military dictatorship and its U.S. backers.

Japan also played an important role in Thailand. Japanese aims were essentially economic whereas U.S. strategies were motivated by the fight against communism. Japan did not want to appear as though it was imposing a hegemonic domination reminiscent of the Japanese occupation. Therefore Japanese investors were careful to involve (but sometimes only on paper) Thai partners in their investments. In textiles, the Japanese impact was strong: "Between 1963 and 1971, Japanese textile groups including Toray, Teijin, and Kanebo established twelve major projects, helping to increase the spinning capacity eight times and cloth production six times in just nine years" (Baker and Phongpaichit 2002, p. 142).

Though not actively promoting FDI development at first, the Thai government turned a kind eye to Japanese manufacturers moving labour-intensive tasks to Thailand, as they were pulled away from their home base by increasing production costs, rising wages, and the need for cheaper goods. This was then supported by the Investment Promotion Act (1962) that eased up on FDI through tax incentives and relocation packages. TNC investments were of two kinds: Tariff-jumping assembly operations that gave access to the local market, and circumvened potential harsher measures that would stop foreigners from having access to the domestic market;[5] and investment in manufacturing to build a strong export base, enjoy available resources and infrastructure in place.

As a consequence, by the mid-1970s, the situation with textiles was complex. Because of the heavy presence of TNCs, a dual structure appeared in labour productivity, with TNCs ranking much higher than Thai-owned companies. Labour productivity of TNCs in Thailand was lower than that of Japanese weaving firms in Japan. The capital-output ratio was high, pointing out a lack of efficiency in using capital for production (Figures 7.2 and 7.3).

The products needed from outside became more and more complex, and, therefore, increasingly expensive, whereas main exports from Thailand were simple manufactured goods, and paddy, which, therefore, meant relative low revenues. Through FDI and on-site manufacturing, Thailand admittedly accessed higher technology content, but new technology brought by foreign investors was limited: It did not boost genuine Thai manufacturing content, because most of the relocated tasks were highly labour intensive. Capital and investments focused on specific geographical areas, causing "maldevelopment", with isolated growth poles and deserts elsewhere, and only a few people benefiting from the economic growth.

At the same time, Thai textile domestic opportunities were growing, but the situation was still fragile. The cottage industry, described earlier, decreased because peasants had been offered new opportunities in the off-season for planting. Attracted by better paid urban jobs, they only returned to their villages for the harvest or the planting seasons and, therefore, did not have time for spinning or weaving as they used to, and they turned instead to trade to get the clothes they needed.

Locally made "technical" textiles[6] were assigned to assembly firms set up through FDI. Thai-based textile manufacturing rose parallel to the growing number of car manufacturing companies. This is explained by the fact that technical textiles are used in the automotive industry to produce items such as air bags or car seats and that measures were implemented by the Thai government to ensure that the development of local production would go on a par with the construction of car assembly units in Thailand (Lecler 2002). Local textile suppliers benefited from the partnership with foreign car assembly companies, especially those from Japan, through (limited) technology transfer, but also from their involvement in new processes, such as just-in-time manufacturing.

Figure 7.2
Labour Productivity of Firms in the Early 1970s (1,000 baht)

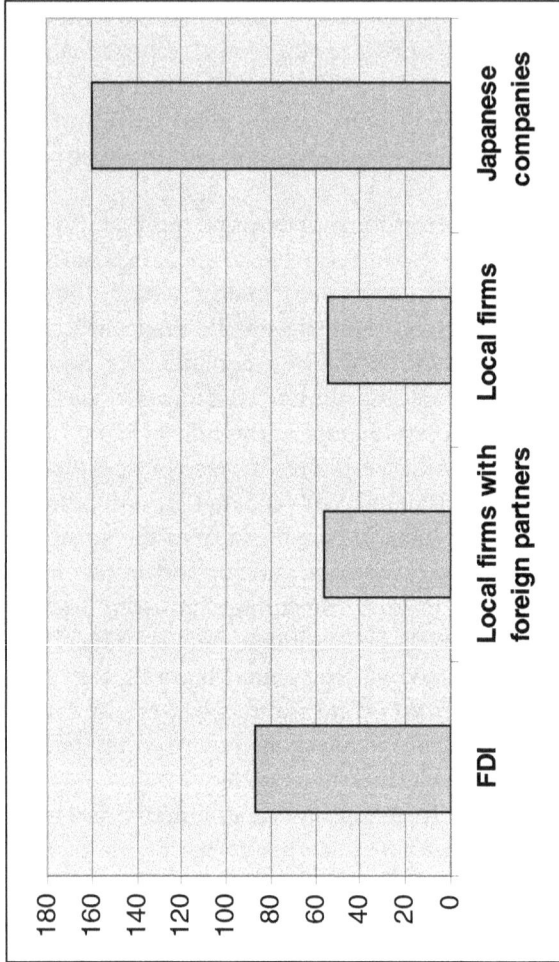

Note: FDI: TNCs stock share represents more than 50 per cent; Local firms with foreign partners: foreign partners hold less than 50 per cent of total stock share; Local firms: 100 per cent of stock share is held by Thai partners; Japanese companies: Japanese firms involved in weaving and located in Japan.

Source: The figures was made from data collected by R. Buddhikarant (1973); MITI, Industrial Statistics, Japanese Long-term Statistics (as presented in Hirose 1996).

Figure 7.3
Y/K: Capital Output Ratio of Firms in the Early 1970s (1,000 bahts)

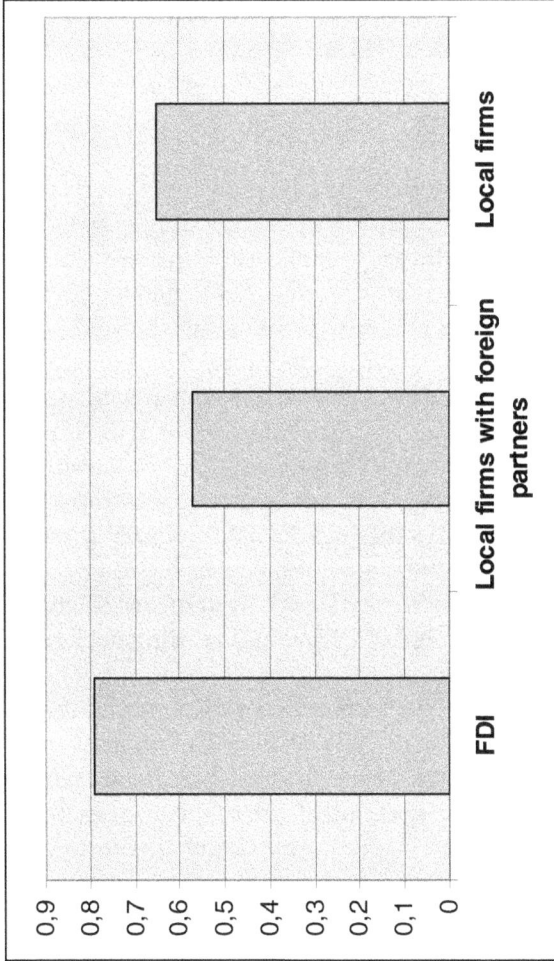

Note: FDI: TNCs stock share represents more than 50 per cent; Local firms with foreign partners: foreign partners hold less than 50 per cent of total stock share; Local firms: 100 per cent of stock share is held by Thai partners. Y/K: capital output ratio; K = gross value of land + building + machinery, equipment & improvement plus other fixed assets.

Source: The figure was made from data collected from R. Buddhikarant (1973); MITI, Industrial Statistics, Japanese Long-term Statistics (as presented in Hirose 1996).

Thai production met domestic needs, and even exceeded them. Producers searched for new outcomes and succeeded in tapping border markets, such as Laos, Cambodia, and Vietnam with domestically produced items. But by the end of the 1970s, domestic suppliers were faced with increasing stocks and oversupply. This was due to many intertwining factors, not the least being border countries becoming socialist and closing up businesses with Thailand (Hirose 1996).

1.3 Export-oriented Industrialization

The import-substitution period in Thailand was characterized by the better exploitation of primary resources (rise in agricultural exports), success in mobilizing capital through the banking system (the accumulated savings of the trading community were channelled into new opportunities), links with partners able to bring in new technology (through joint ventures), but also a competition troubled by inappropriate government policies. The textile industry was one of the key sectors of this changing environment. Rapidly, constraints appeared and the limited size of the domestic market did not favour furthering the import substitution strategy, while the measures implemented had induced capital concentration. Along with these domestic features, by the mid-1970s, trouble had occurred in the international arena. The 1970s spelt the end of the long post-war boom; with the breakdown of the Bretton Woods system, instability was hanging over a more "open to the outside" Thailand. Leading businesses and bank managers pressed for changes.

Beginning in the late 1960s in Latin America, the criticism of import-substitution regimes led to the rise of a new paradigm: the Heckscher-Ohlin-Samuelson theorem and a neoclassical interpretation of comparative advantage. If a country specializes in what it does best, this will automatically be beneficial. This requires full integration and liberalization of world markets.[7] This conceptual shift was symbolized by export-led growth strategies, especially in Asia, with countries such as Singapore, Hong Kong, Taiwan, and South Korea turning to exports to grow their economies. In the academic field, this was further reinforced by works on commercial openness (Balassa 1977; Krueger 1978; Bhagwati 1978), promoting free exchanges and opposing tariff protection.

Export promotion regimes, however, do not mean a no-state intervention environment. If an export promotion policy is, by nature, more liberal than import substitution, it does not eradicate government export incentives (Treillet 2002). To be competitive at the international level, Thai producers had to improve their knowledge and increase the quality of their outputs. It was not only product quality that was required, but also "sophisticated sales technology", such as appropriate product packaging (Tambunlertchai and Yamazawa 1981). This needed to be done without hampering Thai competitiveness and could only be achieved with government support. The BOI (Board of Investment) favoured investments in new machinery and promoted technology transfers with multinational companies. The Foreigners' Occupation Control Law restricted the number of working visas issued to foreign personnel to promote the hiring of Thai personnel (Hirose 1996).

Export orientation was supported by the signing of the Multi Fibre Agreements (MFAs) that set up quotas in international textile trade. At first, they impacted badly on Thai textile export volumes, but when at the end of 1970s, South Korea and Taiwan became internationally competitive, their exports were also restricted under MFAs. As a consequence, the United States and the European Community countries increased their textile trade with Thailand (Suphachalasai 1990; Hirose 1996). This was supported by the establishment of multinational companies in Thailand that increased export capacities. When the quota for Thai fabrics was nearly filled, it encouraged the Thai textile industry (and its foreign partners) to move to the clothing and garment industry and increase the production of garments, to the detriment of yarns and fibres (Hirose 1996). Consequently, exports in textile rose, boosted by the garment industry.

In the 1980s, the export-oriented strategy was pushing Thai economic growth and it seemed that it would go on for a long time. Export promotion was fostered by the need for Japanese (and then Taiwanese and South Korean) manufacturers to relocate their production more intensively in lower-cost countries, especially after the Plaza Agreements (1985) that dramatically appreciated the Japanese yen. However, signs appeared that started to warn Thai officials that the situation was not as good as it seemed: New, fierce competition had appeared from countries not constrained by quotas (such as China, Indonesia).

On the top of that, the 1997 crisis had a tremendous impact on the Thai structure, and the textile industry was impacted the same way. Changes in the financial system (mainly bankruptcies of banks and financial institutions afflicted with bad debts) altered access to funds, reduced lending, and therefore, the ability to invest in new machinery. Foreign investors often bought the shares of their Thai partner to prevent their bankruptcy and ownership changed hands and nationality. Because of the crisis, the textile industry restructuring was significant, with the fall of combines, such as the Sukree textile empire, SMEs facing major difficulties, and the economy starting to turn to more technology-based export industries (Baker and Phongpaichit 2002, pp. 179–83).

Thailand has recovered progressively from the 1997 crisis, but is still fragile. Its textile industry is now facing a specific challenge with the ending of MFAs and the Agreement on Textiles and Clothing (ATC). The ATC was implemented in 1995 to allow a ten-year transition period for participating countries to obey the GATT (General Agreement on Tariffs and Trade) principles. The ATC was, therefore, the extension of the MFAs and ended in 2005. We saw earlier that though MFAs were a constraint, it allowed the Thai textile and garment industry to develop its exports. The end of the ATC in January 2005 has, therefore, been a threat to the Thai textile industry, and as we shall see later in this chapter, competition among exporters for post-ATC market shares has become fiercer across the globe.

2. THAI TEXTILE AND THE CHALLENGE OF COMPETITIVENESS

Textile and garment industry has been a relevant contributor to the Thai economy in terms of production, exports, and employment. But today the industry is facing many threats, which, if not overcome, could lead it into a dangerous situation.

2.1 The Situation of the Thai Textile Industry

In 1993, which means before the 1997 crisis, and in the golden days of export promotion, textiles accounted for 23.2 per cent of manufacturing GDP and for 6.88 per cent of total GDP. Manufacturing in the same year represented 29.65 per cent of total GDP (see Table 7.2). In 1993, 12.3 per cent of total employment was in manufacturing. Employment in the textile and garment subsector represented 3.4 per cent of total employment, and 27.8 per cent of employment in manufacturing, meaning that more than 1.1 million persons were employed in that sector.[8] In 1990, textile and

Table 7.2
Share of Selected Sectors in Total GDP (%) for Years 1993, 2000 and 2005

Industry or subsector	Share of GDP (%)			
	1993	1998	2000	2005
Agriculture	8.66	10.78	9.02	10.18
Non-agriculture	91.34	89.22	90.98	89.82
Hotels and Restaurant	5.39	4.99	5.59	4.89
Motorcycles, Personal and Household Goods	17.76	17.22	14.64	14.64
Transport. Storage and Communications	7.51	7.80	8.04	7.37
Manufacturing	29.65	30.87	33.59	34.80
Textiles, wearing apparel, leather products, footwear	6.88	6.72	6.79	5.27
Share of manufacturing in non-agriculture	32.46	34.60	36.92	38.74
Share of motor vehicles in manufacturing	7.31	1.83	4.83	9.66
Share of textiles, wearing apparel, leather products, footwear, in manufacturing	23.20	21.76	20.21	15.15
Share of office, accounting and computing machinery in manufacturing	2.30	5.40	6.03	6.93

Note: The item "agriculture" includes agriculture, hunting, forestry, and fishing.
Original data were in baht at current market prices.
Source: Data compiled by the author based on NESDB statistics on National Income.

garment exports represented 4.1 per cent of total Thai merchandise exports; the highest share noted for the clothing industry between 1980 and 2006 was achieved in 1991, when clothing amounted to more than 13 per cent of total merchandise exports.[9]

Today, the textile industry employs about 20 per cent of total workers in manufacturing, which is about 3 per cent of total employment and more than 1 million persons (Mission Economique 2006). As for the contribution of textiles to GDP and exports, Tables 7.2 and 7.3 compare it with other relevant industries or subsectors.

Non-agricultural production prevails in Thailand. Manufacturing ranks first in terms of the contribution to the non-agriculture share of GDP (Table 7.2). The next positions are taken by sectors involved in the tourism industry and the production of consumer goods. Not every manufacturing sector performs equally. As will be seen in the next chapter (Chapter 8), the share of computer components, such as HDD, rose to 6.93 per cent of manufacturing production in 2005. The automotive industry, after a sharp fall in 1998, recovered and accounted in 2005 for 9.66 per cent of manufacturing.

The textile sector still holds a strong position, but its share in total GDP and in manufacturing is decreasing. Its share in manufacturing fell from 23.20 per cent in 1993 to 15.15 per cent in 2005, whereas at the same time, manufacturing contribution to the Thai GDP rose from 29.65 per cent in 1993 to 34.80 per cent in 2005.

The structure of Thai exports has changed dramatically over the last decades (Table 7.3), buttressed by government incentives to promote exports of manufactured goods as it was explained in the first section of this

Table 7.3
Share of Selected Industries and Subsectors in Total Merchandise Export from Thailand in Selected Years

Industry or subsector	Share in Total Merchandise Export (%)					
	1980	1993	1998	2000	2005	2006
Agricultural products	59.42	26.20	22.06	18.27	16.46	16.80
Fuels and mining products	14.52	1.62	2.66	4.49	5.67	6.56
Manufactured goods	26.05	72.19	75.29	77.24	77.87	76.64
Textiles	5.28	3.74	3.37	2.93	2.55	2.24
Clothing	4.27	11.42	6.78	5.62	3.77	3.31
Total Textiles+Clothing	9.55	15.16	10.14	8.55	6.33	5.55
Automotive products	0.20	1.45	1.99	3.61	7.37	7.71
Electronic data processing and office equipment	0.05	7.71	15.39	13.11	10.68	11.43
Integrated circuits and electronic components	0.00	4.67	6.07	8.79	6.04	6.47
Share of Textile+Clothing in Manufactured Exports	36.66	21.01	13.47	11.07	8.13	7.25
Share of Automotive products in Manufactured Exports	0.78	2.01	2.65	4.68	9.47	10.06
Share of Electronic data processing and office equipment in Manufactured Exports	0.20	10.68	20.45	16.98	13.71	14.91
Share of integrated circuits and electronic components in Manufactured Exports	0.00	6.47	8.06	11.38	7.76	8.44

Note: Original data were in U.S. dollar at current prices.
Source: Data compiled by the author based on WTO Time Series.

chapter. Whereas agricultural products still accounted for 59.42 per cent of Thai merchandise exports in 1980, it only represented 16.80 per cent in 2006. This trend has been beneficial to manufacturing, which moved from 26.05 per cent in 1980 to 76.64 per cent in 2006.

The situation has evolved differently according to industrial activities. Some sectors which barely existed in 1980 now hold a good position (electronics), but textiles' lion's share has dramatically decreased. In 1980, 36.66 per cent of manufacturing exports were textiles and clothing; in 1998, it fell to 13.47 per cent, and in 2006 it only represented 7.25 per cent.

In 2006, Thailand was twelfth in rank for both textile and clothing world exports. Some Asian countries have risen quickly from a very low position as is the case with Indonesia: In 1980, its contribution to world exports was close to zero, and in 2006 it accounted for 1.6 per cent of textile world exports and for 1.8 per cent of clothing world exports (see Table 7.4). Vietnam was tenth in rank in 2006 in clothing exports whereas its position in 1980 and 1990 had been irrelevant.

Though it has doubled since 1980, the Thai textile and clothing's share in world exports remains weak. It peaked in 1990 (3.5 per cent) and fell to 2.7 per cent in 2006. Sixty per cent of Thai exports are clothing, in particular labour-intensive items, such as cotton garments, brassieres, and corsets.[10] The share in world clothing, after peaking in 1990 (2.6 per cent), is on the decrease (1.4 per cent in 2006). The share in world textiles has risen from 0.6 per cent in 1980 to 1.3 per cent in 2006, and this is mainly due to the increase in synthetic fibre exports (Chalumpon 2004).

As Figure 7.4 shows, although China is increasingly important, along with other Asian partners, the structure of Thai exports of garments and textile is still related to the MFAs era, with nearly half of the production heading to the United States and the European Union.

The United States is the major destination for Thai textiles and we will focus on this market and more precisely on garments, as 80 per cent of U.S. total imports of textiles consists of garments. Thailand is still in top fifteen in terms of clothing importers to the United States but the situation has changed in a few years. Table 7.5 shows the change in U.S. garment supplying sources.

Asia is the United States' major supplier. China takes the lead and accounts for nearly 30 per cent of all clothing imports to the United States. Positions in Asia changed between 2000 and 2006. The most striking breakthrough was Vietnam, whose exports to the United States rose by 100 per cent taking this country to the fifth rank. Indonesian exports

Table 7.4

Top Textile and Clothing Exporters in 2006 and Share in World Exports in Selected Years

	TEXTILES						CLOTHING					
	Value	Share in world exports					Value	Share in world exports				
Exporters	2006	1980	1990	2000	2006	Exporters	2006	1980	1990	2000	2006	
1 The European Union (25)	71.21	–	–	35.6	32.6	China[a]	95.4	4.0	8.9	18.2	30.6	
2 China[a]	48.68	4.6	6.9	10.2	22.3	The European Union (25)	83.4	–	–	26.9	26.8	
3 Hong Kong, China	13.91	3.2	7.9	8.5	6.4	Hong Kong, China	28.4	12.3	14.2	12.2	9.1	
4 United States	12.67	6.8	4.8	6.9	5.8	Turkey[b]	11.9	0.3	3.1	3.3	3.8	
5 Korea, Rep.	10.11	4.0	5.8	8.0	4.6	India[b,c]	10.2	1.7	2.3	3.1	3.3	
6 Taipei, Chinese	9.76	3.2	5.9	7.5	4.5	Bangladesh[b,c,d]	7.8	0.0	0.6	2.1	2.8	
7 India[b,c]	9.33	2.4	2.1	3.8	4.3	Mexico[a]	6.3	0.0	0.5	4.4	2.0	
8 Turkey[c]	7.59	0.6	1.4	2.3	3.5	Indonesia	5.7	0.2	1.5	2.4	1.8	
9 Pakistan	7.47	1.6	2.6	2.9	3.4	United States	4.9	3.1	2.4	4.4	1.6	
10 Japan	6.93	9.3	5.6	4.4	3.2	Vietnam	4.8	...	...	0.9	1.7	
11 Indonesia	3.61	0.1	1.2	2.2	1.6	Romania	4.4	...	0.3	1.2	1.4	
12 Thailand	2.88	0.6	0.9	1.2	1.3	Thailand	4.3	0.7	2.6	1.9	1.4	
13 Canada	2.37	0.6	0.7	1.4	1.1	Pakistan	3.9	0.3	0.9	1.1	1.3	
14 Mexico[a]	2.19	0.2	0.7	1.6	1.0	Morocco[a]	3.2	0.3	0.7	1.2	1.0	
15 U.A.E.[c,d]	1.89	0.1	0.0	0.8	0.9	Tunisia[b]	3.2	0.8	1.0	1.1	1.0	
Above 15	197.22	–	–	89.6	90.2	Above 15	256.1	–	–	77.1	82.2	

Notes: a. Includes significant shipments through processing zones;
 b. Includes Secretariat estimates;
 c. Figures refer to fiscal year;
 d. 2005 instead of 2006.
 Value in US$ billion; share in %.
Sources: WTO, International Trade Statistics 2007, Table II.58 and II.53.

Figure 7.4
Thai Textile and Clothing Exports by Destination
(Country or group of countries), 2006

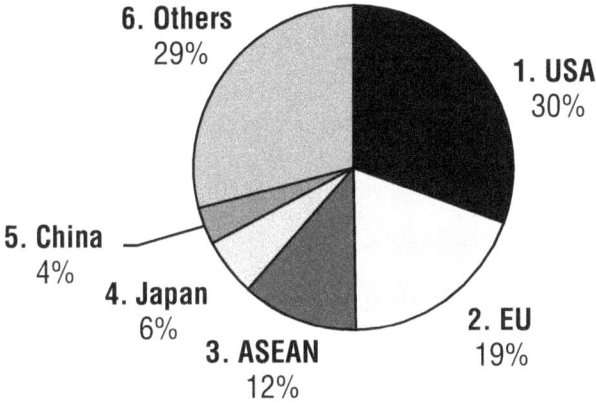

Source: Made by author based on data from Information and Communication Technology Center with
        Cooperation of The Customs Department; compiled by Textile Information Center, Thailand
        Textile Institute.

increased by 9 per cent between 2000 and 2006, and ranked third in 2006.
At the same time, Thailand's exports remained stagnant (+1 per cent);
Taiwan's and South Korea's positions dramatically decreased and they are
now at the bottom of the table.

To summarize the Thai situation, the textile industry is still a good
contributor to Thai manufacturing GDP, exports, and employment: 10
per cent of its exports to the United States are in textiles. However its
position is declining, especially as far as garments are concerned. The
problem is that garments represent most of the Thai textile industry as
shown in the following table (Table 7.6) which presents the structure of
Thai textile industry.

This table does not take into account production units with fewer than
twenty sewing machines. However, parts of garments are made in very
small units, with fewer than twenty sewing machines, sometimes based at
the worker's home itself, and then garment parts are assembled in bigger
units, usually located around Bangkok. Therefore the textile industry
employs more workers than what is shown in these statistics and the

Table 7.5
U.S. Clothing Imports by World Region (Share and value in 2006, percentage change 2000–06) and suppliers
(Value in 2006 and percentage change 2000–06)

	Share in 2006	Value in 2006	2000–06		Suppliers	Value in 2006	2000–06
World	**100.00**	**82,972**	**4**	1	China	24,403	18
Asia	68.90	57,169	7	2	Mexico	5,574	–7
South and Central America	13.13	10,891	0	3	Indonesia	4,003	9
North America	8.34	6,916	–7	4	India	3,560	9
Europe	4.46	3,700	–3	5	Vietnam	3,430	100
Africa	2.64	2,193	8	6	Bangladesh	3,121	5
Middle East	2.29	1,903	4	7	Hong Kong, China	2,968	–8
CIS (Commonwealth of Independent States)	0.24	197	–13	8	Honduras	2,579	1
				9	The European Union (25)	2,571	–2
				10	**Thailand**	**2,395**	**1**
				11	Cambodia	2,271	18
				12	The Philippines	2,127	1
				13	Sri Lanka	1,836	2
				15	Pakistan	1,628	7
				18	Malaysia	1,397	0
				21	Macau, China	1,220	0
				22	Taipei, Chinese	1,129	–11
				23	Korea, Republic of	1,053	–14

Note: Value in million USD; share in %
Source: Data compiled by the author from WTO, International Trade Statistics, table II.62

Table 7.6
Structure of Thai Textile Industry

Type of establishment/Year	Number of factories		Number of employees	
	2002	2005	2002	2005
Clothing factory/Garment firm	2,648	2,541	840,850	825,650
Weaving and knitting firms	1,345	1,320	118,910	116,040
Dyeing, printing and finishing mills	409	409	46,930	46,770
Spinning mills	150	153	60,580	61,100
Synthetic fibre mills	18	17	15,600	14,430
TOTAL	4,570	4,440	1,082,870	1,063,990

Note: Only factories with more than twenty sewing machines are counted in the item "clothing factory/garment firm".
Source: Thailand Textile Institute.

weight of the garment and clothing firms in the overall textile industry is also much bigger than what these figures tell at first glance.

Small and very small garment firms are indeed in subcontracted for tasks involving very high manual skills (manual embroidery, for instance). The garment industry has the ability to fragment part of its production, but then the full-package assembler needs to coordinate all steps carefully. Larger firms undertake every step of the process at the same location, to avoid time and distance constraints. The industry is, therefore, hierarchical, but few links exist between all its components: The supply chain in the Thai textile industry is not integrated.

Garment and weaving industries are labour intensive and involve a large number of firms, whereas spinning, dyeing, finishing, and synthetic fibre firms are capital intensive. Thai resource endowment focused on labour intensive tasks and this gave the country a competitive advantage, for example, in weaving. Though Thailand had old technology, it was able to compete on the world market because its cheap labour costs counterbalanced this.

2.2 Losing Competitiveness: A Major Issue for Thai Textile

The decrease of Thai textiles is relative and caused by the rise of other industries, as we demonstrated earlier. But its loss of competitiveness and productivity should not be overlooked. Many factors account for the competitiveness of the textile industry.

First is the exchange rate of the local currency to international currencies, such as the U.S. dollar or the euro. As the main export market for Thai textiles is the United States, the exchange rate of the baht with the U.S. dollar affects the value of exports, and also its volume. For several years now, the strong baht, combined with a low U.S. dollar, has had a bad impact on the level and volume of Thai textile exports.

A second factor to discuss are the domestic costs of non-tradable inputs, such as utilities and labour. The following table (Table 7.7) presents textile labour costs in different countries.

Thailand used to be one of the cheapest places to produce textiles. But its labour costs (mainly wages) have constantly increased for twenty years. On 1 January 2007, the minimum wage in Thailand was again marked up. Now other places such as Vietnam or Indonesia can produce more cheaply.

More than 70 per cent of textile companies are located in Bangkok and its vicinity (Tait 2005), whereas about 30 per cent of Thai total manufacturing is located in that area. Increasing land costs and constrained infrastructure

Table 7.7
Textile Labour Costs Comparison, in 1980, 1990, 1994, 2001, and 2007
(Unit: US$/hour)

	1980	1990	1994	2001	2007
Japan	4.35	13.96	25.6		22.69
Taiwan	1.26	4.56	n/a	7.15	7.64
Hong Kong	1.91	3.05	4.40	6.15	6.21
South Korea	0.78	3.22	4.00	5.73	7.77
Thailand	**0.33**	**0.92**	**1.40**	**1.18**	**1.75**
China	n/a	0.37	0.50	0.41	
*Coastal					0.85
*Inland					0.55
India	n/a	n/a	0.60	0.57	0.69
Indonesia	n/a	0.25	0.50	0.50	0.65
Vietnam	n/a	n/a	0.40	0.39	0.46

Sources: Table compiled by the author from Hirose (1996) based, for year 1980, on JICA (1989) and, for year 1990, on Textile Industry Division, Ministry of Industry in Thailand; from Werner International Primary Textile Labor Cost Comparisons 1994 and 2007; year 2001 from Chalumpon Lotharukpong (2004).

in the capital city, such as huge traffic jams, have, therefore, affected textile companies in particular, and these have tended to relocate further and further from the city centre so as to enjoy cheaper land and better utilities.

Relocating to the regions has been considered by entrepreneurs as a way of reducing costs. By doing so, Thailand will be following the same path as China to some extent: Entrepreneurs in China have moved away from coastal areas to inland locations, in the search for cheaper labour. The trend is now strong enough for figures about textile labour costs to be divided into costs for coastal and inland China (see Table 7.7).

Inner regions in Thailand enjoy cheaper land, looser environmental controls, and local sources of raw materials. In Thailand, the minimum wage is managed in a decentralized way: It is different for a worker in Bangkok (191 baht in 2007) than in Chaiyaphum (146 baht in 2007).[11] In remote areas, it is even more difficult to check whether minimum wages are applied or not, and the wages are even lower than what is officially published. This is reinforced by the weakness of trade unions and worker organizations in these areas (Glassman 2004). All this counterbalances disadvantages such as higher transportation costs, "difficulties in enticing managers to locate in comparatively remote and undesirable areas" and "the inevitable dislocation from key centre(s) of financial and bureaucratic decision-making (that is, the capital city)" (Rigg 2003, pp. 226–28).

This shift away from Bangkok has been supported by the BOI (Board of Investment) which divided the country into three zones and granted different benefits according to the zone criterion (the further from Bangkok, the better) and the industrial estate criterion. If a company decides to relocate its activity to zone 3 and in an industrial estate, it will be granted full benefits.[12]

Third, the country's competitiveness in textile also depends on the overall business environment, comprising the government regulatory regime, property rights, judicial, or tax system. Though Thailand ranked rather well (twenty-eighth out of 131 countries) in the Global Competitiveness Index 2007/2008 set up by the World Economic Forum, as is also discussed in Chapter 3 and Chapter 8, the report points out the following factors as problematic.

Doing business in Thailand is not always easy, especially due to corruption and the inefficient bureaucracy, but also some political instability. In 2006, a military-led coup overthrew the Thaksin government and the military soon afterwards enforced a law restraining foreign

Table 7.8
Ten Most Problematic Factors towards Thai Competitiveness

1. Policy instability
2. Inefficient government bureaucracy
3. Government instability/coups
4. Corruption
5. Inadequately educated workforce
6. Foreign currency regulations
7. Access to financing
8. Inadequate supply of infrastructure
9. Tax regulations
10. Poor work ethic in national labour force

Source: Based on data from World Economic Forum, The Global Competitiveness Report 2007–2008.

investments. This had a cooling effect on foreign investors, but the law was rapidly put on the backburner and the military then tried to calm things down. Despite the minimum effective impact of the above, it shows, however, that the business environment can change quickly through political decisions or turbulences.

Table 7.8 indicates that access to financing is a problematic factor for Thai competitiveness. To conduct business efficiently, it is essential to have a functioning financial system, but Thai textile manufacturers have suffered from the 1997 financial crisis and have had less access to lending and financing. Thai textile officials regularly call for banks to support their investment in new machinery. This issue of finding appropriate funds is reinforced by the lack of an integrated textile industry, which hampers the implementation of overall industrial programmes, thus impacting badly on investment and supply-chain efficiency.

The fourth and last point we will discuss is the country's policies towards international economic integration. This can be assessed, but not only through FDI flows (Hill 1998). FDI can be an asset: In labour-intensive, export-oriented industries such as textile, FDI transfer knowledge from international markets to the home country. Then, when it moves on to more technology-intensive content, the country can benefit from the transfer of production and management technology. But FDI in textile are decreasing as Table 7.9 shows.

The share of textiles in industry FDI has continually decreased since the 1990s, whereas at the same time, industry FDI were increasing. This is

Table 7.9
Net Flows of FDI to Thailand (Share in % of total FDI)

	1970–1995	1996	2001
Industry	37.2	31.2	57.3
Trade	17.4	24.0	23.7
Real Estate	18.6	33.2	4.3
Share of textiles in industry FDI	7.5	6.9	2.6
Share of electrical applicances in industry FDI	35.1	34.0	30.7
Share of machinery/transport equipment in industry FDI	8.9	15.4	20.0

Source: Based on data from Bank of Thailand, Economic Research Department. Data quoted in
    Brooker Group Plc (2002).

relevant to show Thai textiles' loss of attractiveness. Another interesting
data would be the strategy and choices of international buying groups,
but unfortunately we do not have precise data on that. However, we can
assume that they have turned a kind eye to countries with cheap labour
costs, such as Vietnam or Indonesia.

Thailand's loss of competitiveness in textiles is due to different factors:
a high baht, rising labour costs, increasing utility costs especially in Bangkok
where most of the industry is located,[13] an overall low-ranking business
environment, a non-supportive financial system, a lack of industrial
strategy, and international actors that are interested in moving to other
places where comparative advantages have become better.

But these are not the only factors that explain Thai textiles' ailing
position. The experience of South Korea is of a great help in understanding
where the main challenge for Thailand lies. Lynn Krieger Mytelka (1995)
demonstrated that if the competitiveness of South Korea in textile
decreased, it was not because of increasing labour costs, or the won
appreciation, but because of its backwardness in terms of technology.
The trend in international markets towards more technology-intensive
goods should have led South Korean textile producers to invest in new
technology, but this was not done in time. Big conglomerates were
favoured at the expense of SMEs, which eventually proved to be far
more innovative and competitive.

Thailand's textile machinery is outdated: As labour was particularly
cheap, there was no need to substitute capital for labour, and entrepreneurs
relied on labour-intensive tasks and postponed investments. This was

reinforced by the difficulties in getting access to loans. Now that labour is more expensive, the industry has lost its competitiveness. This is particularly the case in weaving and garment firms.

In the garment industry, only basic sewing machines are used and the import of state-of-the-art machines, such as the Computer Cutter System, is at its very early stage (Chalumpon 2004), hindering the move towards capital-intensive production. Moreover, the weaving machines are still all imported and about 80 per cent of the machines in use have shuttles and are more than ten years old. All this is still happening although the efficiency and productivity of shuttleless weaving machines are much higher than their shuttle counterparts.

Differences between the two have been very important (Chalumpon 2004) in terms of:

- investment cost (50,000 baht for a shuttle weaving maching and 700,000 to 2,000,000 for a shuttleless one);
- speed (calculated in rank per minute): 150 to 220 for machines with shuttles and 600 to 800 for shuttleless machines;
- and efficiency: low-medium for shuttle weaving machines and over 2 to 3 times higher for shuttleless weaving machines.

In addition to the productivity issue, when there are no technological improvements, work becomes routine and there is no upgrading momentum that leads to innovation or quality enhancements. This might have worked for a long time, but now international markets have found other sources for such products. To be able to keep on playing a role in the textile arena, Thailand should reorient its textile strategy towards new technology, innovation, and quality.

2.3 Supporting the Thai Textile Industry: A Role for Public Institutions?

Collaborative actions have to be taken in order to achieve these goals, namely, improving production processes, innovation in design and fabrics, and enhanced quality, both of the products and the supply chain. The Thai textile industry is organized hierarchically, but is highly fragmented: The industry alone cannot succeed in implementing a coordinated strategy involving every actor. Thai public institutions have been involved in different schemes to overcome these hurdles by playing the role of coordination and supervision.

First, to acquire new technology, the Thai Textile Institute has listed areas where foreign assistance is needed most because they require expertise that cannot be found in Thailand yet (BOI 2005). The Thai Textile Institute argues that this can only be achieved through FDI or joint venture (JV) projects. Though it is a way to save on R&D, it also shows that Thailand does not yet have the skills to produce all the modern materials itself.

The areas identified as essential by the Thai Textile Institute are the following:

- Advanced dyeing and finishing technology;
- State-of-the-art printing technology;
- R&D activities and technology to produce innovative fibres;
- Supply chain management technology and software;
- Commercial-scale fashion designers;
- Expertise in fashion branding and marketing for international markets.

Investment in those areas has not been "instinctively" done so far, therefore, it has appeared necessary to attract foreign investors by offering them specific incentive packages. This has been done by the BOI (Board of Investment/Ministry of Industry) which has offered promotional privileges specifically targeting these areas.

Second, innovation efforts need to focus both on the fabric characteristics and the design of Thai products. Supportive measures have been taken in these two directions.

The Thailand Textile Institute has teamed up with the National Nanotechnology Centre to find innovative solutions.[14] The first step will be to develop technology to give conventional textiles new functions and properties, for example, clothes with anti-bacterial or self-cleaning properties. The same institute has also planned to set up a plant where new textile technology concepts can be tested.[15] The Institute applied for governmental funds, presenting the plant as a place where researchers or local textile manufacturers can do experimental production.

The Thai textile industry needs to move from being an OEM industry (Original Equipment Manufacturing) to an OBM industry (Original Brand Manufacturing). Some firms are at an intermediate stage, the ODM stage (Original Design Manufacturing), as some domestic research and designing tasks are included in their production (e.g. the domestic labels Pena House, or Greyhound). To succeed, the Thai textile industry needs an integrated supply chain and trained engineers dedicated to innovative textiles.

The Bangkok Fashion City project was launched by the government in 2000. Its aim was to have Thailand become the "fashion hub" of the region, encompassing all aspects of Thailand's fashion trade covering textiles, garments, jewellery and ornaments, footwear, and leather industries on a grand scale.[16] BOI officials explained the Bangkok Fashion City project: "[o]ur goals in targeting Bangkok as a World Fashion City are clear. First, we are looking to create 6,000 'fashion people,' consisting of 3,000 designers, 2,000 merchandisers, and 1,000 production specialists. Second, we must transition from cut, make, and trim to higher-value-added production. Third, we want to achieve a synergy in the textile and apparel industry, with no broken links in the supply chain. Fourth, we want to secure 1.2 million jobs for the Thai textile and garment industry".[17]

The third point that needs to be enhanced is quality. It can be achieved through adequate training of managers and employees. The textile industry relies on the educational system to provide the industry with an appropriate labour force, able to enhance its technological, innovative, and quality content. The Thai educational system is burdened with learning methods that have proven to be inappropriate in encouraging critical thinking and initiative necessary to generate creativity in the industry. Rote learning and a general consensus on a low-quality education have prevailed and have hampered the Thai educational system from providing society with appropriate students and workers. Research is not appropriately valued in academic arenas, and, therefore, is not a top priority for the university community. Moreover, the ongoing process towards decentralization and privatization is not leading to more quality and coordination: The "current reform [of the educational system] proves itself unable to improve the weak quality of education, to forge the skills needed by the productive system, to develop research capacities and to build an efficient system of innovation" (Mounier 2006). The lack of long-term policy, coupled with political instability, has inhibited improvements in education. Chapter 3 of this book provides further hindsight on the education and industrial upgrading issue.

If we compare the current situation in Thailand with the one experienced by some of its main competitors in textiles, such as Vietnam and China, we can see the urgency. In Vietnam, the educational system is more selective, and higher vocational training, needed for textile engineers, for instance, attract some of the best students, whereas in Thailand higher vocational training is an extension of secondary technical education that does not attract the best students to say the least (CELS 2008). China has invested massively in education both to improve its educational system and to attract more students (Mok 1997, 2000, 2002). Some programmes have specifically targeted technological and scientific upgrading, such as Project 211 that aims to propel Chinese universities into the top-class world arena (Collins and Rhoads 2008).

The Thai textile industry is facing an uphill battle. As we have learnt from the first part of this chapter, the Thai economy best succeeds when all actors involved in the shaping of the industry work together and in the same direction. Today the situation is not different. More links between all its actors seem necessary to ensure an optimistic future for the Thai textile. The theory of cluster has, in that sense, appeared as the panacea to governmental agencies, further to Michael Porter's visit to Thailand in the early 2000s (see Chapter 4). Clusters, as a means of promoting innovation, technology, and quality, were seen as the best way to cope with problems that the Thai textile industry has been facing. It could especially promote linkages between SMEs and other components of the business environment by creating active networks between companies, research and training centres, and financial and supporting institutions. It could also help match the labour force (human capital) with the needed skills in the labour market.

The Chaiyaphum Cluster

Let's take the example of a cluster programme implemented by the DIP (Department of Industrial Promotion/Ministry of Industry) in Chaiyaphum province (northeast), traditionally well known for its silk industry.

Cluster programmes in Thailand stem from the collaboration between public (for example, NESDB) and private (for example, KiAsia) institutions that conducted preliminary mapping prior to the launching of the cluster scheme. The implementation of targeted clusters has then been passed onto various institutions, such as the DIP. Cluster programmes shall be considered as part of a wider trend aimed at strengthening the national innovation system of the country (see Chapter 2 for more details about NIS in Thailand).

Indeed the main aim of clusters is to enhance innovation by bringing together different actors that otherwise would be apart. Companies, either competitors or those on the same supply chain, are located in the same place (or nearby) and this proximity is meant to improve innovation as tacit and explicit knowledge are easily transmitted from one company to another. For instance, if one company efficiently implements new patterns, it will have an impact on its supply chain and the word will spread quickly: related partners will then copy it, apply it and benefit from it.

Clusters are, in theory, also supposed to promote increased linkages between companies and financial institutions. Sometimes banks are a bit wary when they hear about investment in new technology. They would be more willing to invest in it if they knew their partners well. Locating the different components of the national innovation system geographically close together and tightening the relationships among them through cluster structures can, therefore, be a good way to increase the Thai innovative potential.

The cluster programme of Chaiyaphum[18] (see Figure 7.5) is aimed at strengthening links between local garment companies themselves, and between them and the "outer" world (universities, R&D institutes, public supporting institutions, financial organizations) and at creating common structures (for example, training centres, shipping platforms). The DIP structured its programme in different steps, starting from building entrepreneur awareness on clusters, gathering cluster participants, continuing with the signing of a MOU (Memorandum of Understanding) between the province governor, DIP officials, and company managers.

Starting with nineteen companies in 2003, which represented 5,000 employees, the cluster programme involved twenty-nine companies (9,000 employees) in 2006 and this figure was expected to grow to about forty.[19] The motives are numerous, such as common use of machine tools, knowledge sharing with better skilled staff, common purchasing of raw materials, order sharing, technology transfer, sharing of R&D costs. An adviser of High Progress Chaiyaphum Knitting Co. Ltd., a member of the cluster, said "the concept of clusters was good as it helped lower the production costs for the entrepreneurs as they together bought raw materials and took purchasing orders".[20] Another incentive was the possibility for cluster participants to visit one another's plants, and this has been desired by entrepreneurs, who were eager to do so, but did not want to be suspected of industrial spying.

One key point of the DIP-cluster programme is the implementation of a CDA (Cluster Development Agent) that will coordinate actions between all the cluster actors and give the cluster its inner impetus. In the literature

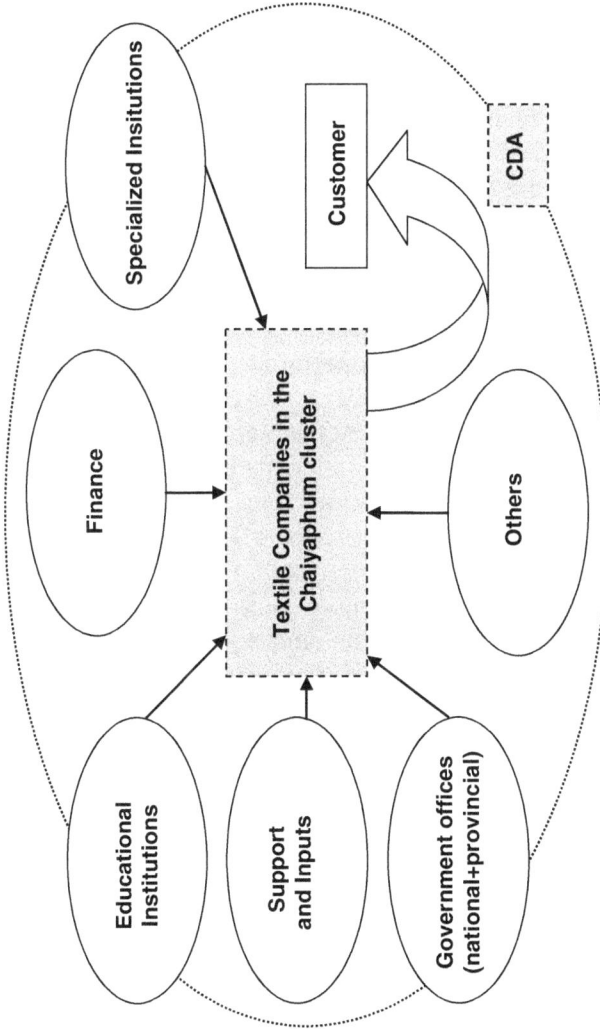

Figure 7.5
Structure of the Chaiyaphum Cluster (2006)

Source: Adapted from a presentation of the Chaiyaphum Cluster by the Department of Industrial Promotion (DIP 2006).

on this (Anderson et al. 2004), it is often referred to as an IFC (Institute for Collaboration). As far as the DIP is concerned, the CDA does not emanate from the cluster itself, but comes from the outside. In Chaiyaphum, during the first year, it was a group from Chulalongkorn University that took on the responsibility of cluster coordination. Then the CDA responsibilities moved to the local agency of the Federation of Thai Industries. The CDA has organized collective activities to let participants know one another better and to enhance collaboration among members (monthly meetings among managers, common "road shows" in Bangkok, overseas factory visits). According to DIP officials, the cluster also benefits from common structures, such as training and order sharing, and this seems to have worked pretty well.

Cluster programmes in the case of Thailand show the role taken by public institutions in organizing a suitable framework for further development and for the cooperation among varied actors (see Table 7.10). Though it is still too early to assess the results of that cluster on textile productivity and efficiency, it seems that this kind of programmes, if conducted carefully, can be a means for facing rising competition as it should allow companies to meet the deadlines and boost the technological content of their products through cooperation and suitable training and research.

With the BOI incentives, more companies are expected to relocate to regions such as Chaiyaphum, and foreign investors are especially welcomed. Still, the fact that an increasing number of firms is involved in the programme does not automatically mean that it is working: Quantity does not mean quality; and some clusters just look like a peer club, nothing more. Moreover, through training programmes only dedicated to matching workers' skills with the cluster needs, there is a threat of favouring sole vocational dimension at the expense of the cognitive mission of education, but this is another debate.

CONCLUDING REMARKS

The Thai textile and garment industry has experienced tremendous changes in parallel with the evolution of Thailand since the mid-twentieth century. Evolving from a cottage-based industry, it has undergone a real metamorphosis through import-substitution strategies and then export-led reorganization. Nowadays the Thai textile and garment industry

Table 7.10
Actors in Chaiyaphum Cluster (2006)

Educational Institutions
– Polytechnic College
– Provincial Vocational Education
– University of Khon Khaen
– Faculty of Economics/Chulalongkorn
– Industrial and Community Education College/Kaeng Kro
– Technical College/Chaiyaphum
– Technical and Vocational College/Bamnet Narong

Support and Inputs
– Packing/Packaging
– Machinery
– Raw Material
– Transportation/Logistics

Specialized Institutions
– Thai Textile Institute
– Foundation for Clothing

Others
– Housewives' Association
– Chaiyaphum Industrial Council
– Chaiyaphum Chamber of Commerce

Textile companies
– Knitting (11 companies)

Government offices
– Department of Industrial Promotion (DIP)
– NESDB
– Provincial Office of Employment Provision
– Provincial Centre for labour and skills development
– Provincial Centre for Non-Formal Education
– Provincial office for industry
– Provincial office for land administration
– Provincial office for agriculture and cooperation
– Provincial office for labour force
– Provincial office for commerce
– Provincial office for urban planning and construction
– Telephone, electricity, water (provincial level)
– Public relations office for provincial administration
– Centre for economic investment in North-East 1

Finance
– Industrial Finance Corportation of Thailand
– Banker Club
– SME Bank

– Weaving (13 companies)
– Spinning (5 companies)

Source: Adapted from a presentation of the Chaiyaphum Cluster by DIP (2006).

needs once again to reorganize itself to overcome uphill challenges, mainly the competition from lower-cost countries. Like in the previous stages of its evolution, the industry will find strength in the coordinated agency of the actors that shape it: companies, banks, foreign investors, and public institutions.

But a new component plays a stronger role than ever before: knowledge. Chapter 3 of this book has underlined the challenges raised by the industrial and education upgrading in Thailand; and the comments raised then are highlighted further through the analysis of the garment and textile industry in Thailand.

The Thai textile industry needs to focus on technology upgrading, innovation and quality, of both the products and the supply chain. It is only by guaranteeing the on-time delivery of innovative and high-tech textiles that Thailand will be able to maintain its textile industry. The challenge is worth it, in particular, because of the importance of textiles in the manufacturing labour market.

Programmes such as clusters emphasize the need for strong linkages between companies, research and training centres, public institutions, and financial institutions. Strengthening their relationship while aiming to acquire more technology and undertake innovation will enable the Thai textile industry to overcome the difficulties discussed.

But cluster programmes, even if fully and efficiently implemented, cannot succeed in this battle on their own. This type of plans must be backed up by an appropriate educational system, which promotes research and enhances workers' ability to adapt to an ever changing environment.

Steps to be undertaken are in-depth, and presuppose long-term policies, especially because they deal with a core component of society. The Educational Reform, which started in Thailand in 1999, has so far proved incapable of raising the standard and quality of education. Defining what an efficient educational system is and what an education of quality is, though not an easy task, is necessary, prior to any further reform plans. An overall strategy encompassing and articulating quality education and skilled labour is needed for Thailand to achieve sustainable development. For the textile and garment industry in particular, creativity, especially in design and customized production, as mentioned above, is absolutely important for achieving the target of a World Fashion City. Rote learning and a low-quality education have so far hampered such needed creativity. It would be too late to train fashion designers when they are adults, creativity should be institutionalized in the education curriculum and teaching methods from the kindergarten level.

Notes

1. When talking about textiles, we usually refer to textile and garments: the textile industry provides the garment sector with the fabrics needed. But fabrics may also be used in other sectors, such as the automotive industry. Textiles can, therefore, be described as involving every process from fibre production to finished goods, that is fibre production, spinning, weaving and knitting, dyeing, printing, finishing, and garment production.
2. This agreement signed between Siam, represented by King Mongkut, and Britain, opened up the country to Western trade and influence. Other Bowring-like treaties followed, signed with other powers such as France, the United States, or Japan. These treaties lifted many restrictions on foreign trade, abolishing the royal monopoly over external trade. Foreign traders were allowed to deal directly with local trading houses. It signed away the legal power of the king of Siam over foreign subjects by creating extraterritorial laws which foreigners were subject to. Foreign traders were, therefore, not tried by Thai courts, but by their consuls.
3. See Chapter 4 (Suehiro).
4. For information on the political side, refer to James Ockey (2004).
5. See Chapter 1 (Hoyrup and Simon).
6. We can distinguish three categories in textiles: fashion, home furnishing, and technical textiles.
7. If this theory refers to the neoclassical thesis, it brings, however, a new aspect as it is based on dynamic comparative advantages: resource allocation in one country may vary with time and a country will see, for example, its manufacturing sector spinning off into other activities. The comparative advantage will in that case move to more sophisticated goods.
8. Source: Taiwan Institute of Economic Research, Survey of Thai Textile Industry, 1999; available at <http://moeaitc.tier.org.tw>.
9. Source: WTO.
10. See the Thai Textile Institute website for a more detailed breakdown.
11. Minimum daily wage rates in 2007; source: Ministry of Labour, <www.mol.go.th>.
12. Source: <www.boi.go.th/english/about/boi_privileges_by_location.asp>.
13. Utility costs also need to be compared with those of other relevant places, such as Vietnam, China, or Indonesia. See Chapter 8 (Lecler) for a comparison of utility costs in electronics.

14. Pongpen Sutharoj, "Researchers Add value to Thai Fabrics", *The Nation*, 25 September 2006

15. "Plant to Help Research to be Proposed", *The Nation*, 25 September 2006.

16. Presentation to UNESCAP of Phongsak Assakul, President of the Federation of Thai Textiles Industries, Thai Textiles Manufacturing Association; available at <http://www.unescap.org/tid/mtg/tradenv_s6thai.pdf>.

17. BOI speech, "Fashion Industry in Thailand", November 2003; available at <http://www.boi.go.th/english/download/business_sectors/4/November_Fashion_speech_2003.pdf>.

18. For further information, see A. Baron-Gutty (2006).

19. Interview by the author with a DIP official, 2006.

20. Quoted in Industrial Cluster Boosts Thai SME Potential, <http://www.smethai.net/en/>.

References

Anderson, T., S. Schwaag Serger, J. Sörvick, E. Wise Hansson. *The Cluster Policies Whitebook*. IKED (International Organisation for Knowledge Economy and Enterprise Development). Malmö, Sweden: Holmbergs, 2004.

Baker, Chris and Pasuk Phongpaichit. *A History of Thailand*. New York: Cambridge University Press, 2005.

———. *Thailand: Economy and Politics*. New York: Oxford University Press, 2002.

Balassa, Bela. *Stages Approach to Comparative Advantages*. Fifth World Congress of International Economic Association, Tokyo, 1977.

Baron-Gutty, Audrey. "Agglomérations d'entreprises et clusters en Thaïlande — théorie et études de cas" [Firm agglomerations and clusters in Thailand: theory and study cases]. Master's dissertation, MA in East Asian Studies, Department of Political Sciences, Université Lumière-Lyon 2/IAO Lyon, 2006.

Bhagwati, Jagdish. *Anatomy and Consequences of Trade Control Regimes*. New York: National Bureau of Economic Research (NBER), 1978.

BOI. *Thailand Investment Review* 17, no. 6 (July 2005). Available at <http://www.boi.go.th:8080/issue_content.php?issueid=6;page=5>.

Boontharm, Davisi. *Bangkok — Formes du commerce et évolution urbaine*. Bangkok: Archithèses, Editions Recherches/Ipraus, Paris, 2005.

Brooker Group Plc (The). *Foreign Direct Investment — Performance and Attraction. The Case of Thailand*. Presented at Workshop on Foreign Direct Investment: Opportunities and Challenges for Cambodia, Laos and Vietnam, in Hanoi, 16–17 August 2002. Available at <www.imf.org/external/pubs/ft/seminar/2002/fdi/eng/pdf/brimble.pdf>.

Buddhikarant, R. "A Case Study on the Economic Contribution of Private Direct Foreign Investment in the Textile Industry". Master's thesis, Thammasat University, Bangkok, June 1973.

CELS (Center of Education and Labour Studies). "Labour Capacity Preparation: Comparative Analysis of Thailand and Vietnam 1980–2025". Abstract of final report submitted to Thai Research Fund, Chiang Mai, Thailand, 2008.

Chalumpon, Lotharukpong. *The Future of Thailand's Textile and Garment Industry — The Challenge, Opportunity and Threats in the Post-quota Period*. International Chamber of Commerce Thailand, <http://www.iccthailand.or.th/file_download/TheFuture.pdf>. 2004.

Collins, C.S. and R.A. Rhoads. "The World Bank and Higher Education in the Developing World: The Cases of Uganda and Thailand". In *International Perspectives on Education and Society*, volume 9 (2008): 177–221.

DIP. Study Meeting on the Cluster Approach for Industrial Development. Bureau of Supporting Industries Development, Department of Industrial Promotion, Ministry of Industry, Bangkok, 2006.

Glassman, Jim. *Thailand at the Margins. Internationalization of the State and the Transformation of Labour*. Oxford Geographical and Environmental Studies, New York, 2004.

Hill, Hal. "Vietnam Textile and Garment Industry: Notable Achievements, Future Challenges". Appendix II of the Industrial Competitiveness Review, Ministry of Planning and Investment Vietnam, UNIDO, 1998.

Hirose, Yayoi. "Did FDI Replace the Role of the Government, or the Government Supported the FDI in the Process of Industrial Development? A Case Study of the Thai Textile Industry". MSc thesis in Urban Studies and Planning, Massachusetts Institute of Technology, 1996.

Krueger, A.O. *Liberalisation Attempts and Consequences*. National Bureau of Economic Research (NBER), New York, 1978.

Lecler, Yveline. "The Cluster Role in the Development of the Thai Car Industry: Some Evidence from Empirical Studies". *International Journal of Urban and Regional Research* 26, no. 4 (December 2002): 799–814.

Lehman, Sanne. "Learning in Global Networks? Industrial Restructuring of Thai Manufacturers in the Automotive and Garment Commodity Chains". PhD thesis, International Development Studies, Roskilde University, Denmark, May 2004.

Mission Economique. "La filière textile-habillement en Thaïlande". *Fiche de Synthèse*, August 2006.

Mok, K.H. "Retreat of the State: Marketization of Education in the Pearl River Delta". *Comparative Education Review* 41, no. 3 (1997): 260–76.

———. "Marketizing Higher Education in Post-Mao China". *International Journal of Educational Development* 20, no. 2 (2000): 109–26.

———. "Policy of Decentralization and Changing Governance of Higher Education in Post-Mao China". *Public Administration and Development* 22 (2002): 261–73.

Mounier, Alain. "The Education-work Controversy". *Journal of Education* (Chiang Mai University) 33, nos. 1–2 (January–December 2006).

Mytelka, Lynn Krieger. "L'industrie du textile et de l'habillement: le modeèle coréen en difficulté". In *Economie Internationale*, No. 61, 1st trimestre, 1995.

Ockey, James. *Making Democracy: Leadership, Class, Gender, and Political Participation in Thailand*. Honolulu: University of Hawaii Press, 2004.

Rigg, Jonathan. *Southeast Asia: The Human Landscape of Modernization and Development* 2nd ed. New York: Routledge, 2003.

Suehiro, Akira. *Capital Accumulation in Thailand 1855–1985*. Centre for East Asian Cultural Studies, Tokyo Bunkko, 1989.

Suphachalasai, S. "Export Growth of Thai Clothing and Textiles". *The World Economy* 13, no. 1 (March 1990).

Tait, Niki. *An Overview of Thailand's Clothing Industry — Management Briefing*. Bromsgrove, UK: Aroq Limited, 2005.

Tambunlertchai, S. and I. Yamazawa. *Manufactured Exports and Foreign Direct Investment: A Case Study of the Textile Industry in Thailand*. Bangkok: Thammasat University, May 1981.

Treillet, Stéphanie. *L'économie du développement*. Collection CIRCA. Paris: Nathan/VUEF, 2002.

Relevant Websites

ASEAN: <www.aseansec.org>.
BOI of Thailand: <www.boi.go.th>.
Chaiyaphum Cluster: <www.clusterchaiyaphum.com>.
Fibre 2 Fashion: <www.fibre2fashion.com>.
National Economic and Social Development Board: <www.nesdb.go.th>.
Thai clusters: <www.thaicluster.com>.
Thai SMEs website: <www.smethai.net/en/>.
Thailand Textile Institute: <www.thaitextile.org>.
The Nation (newspaper): <www.nationmultimedia.com>.
UNESCAP: <www.unescap.org>.
UNIDO: <www.unido.org>.
World Economic Forum: <www.weforum.org>.
World Trade Organisation WTO: <www.wto.org>.

8

FROM GROWTH BASED ON LOW COST TO CAPABILITY UPGRADING POLICIES
The Thai Hard Disk Drive Industry

Yveline Lecler

As previous chapters have shown, Thailand has to upgrade its capabilities in various areas to make its industrial development sustainable for the future. The hard disk drive (HDD) industry, which is a high tech industry, is a good example for illustrating the challenges the country is now facing to keep or improve its position in the global value chain.

It started in Thailand in the early 1980s as a spinoff from Singapore, and developed continuously during the past two decades, making the country the top world producer and exporter in 2005–06. This apparent success story, is however, hiding weaknesses that might put the industry's future growth in danger. Indeed, the Thai HDD industry's past and further development cannot be isolated from the regional agglomerations that took place over time in various countries, nor from the network implemented by foreign HDD assemblers and major global suppliers. It cannot be evaluated either without taking into account a broad variety of national factors, including public policies, education and manpower training, technology upgrading resources, etc., that gave the country some comparative advantage over its Asian neighbours. But while this is eroding today, these factors also constitute new challenges for the future.

The HDD which is one of the major segments of the electric and electronic (EE) industries accounts for a significant part of the whole exports of the country and, although this has not always been the case, it is now one of the industries benefiting from government attention.

After presenting Thailand's past and present positions in the industry's global and regional division of labour (section 1), the chapter will address the issue of the sustainability of the industry in the future, focusing on the policies implemented to take up the new challenges and remain attractive (section 2). It will finally introduce the HDD cluster programme which appears to be the most achieved initiative to address altogether the different challenges the Thai HDD industry has to face to remain globally competitive (section 3).

Unless other sources are noted, the information is based on a survey done by the author in January 2007 through interviews with officials of two HDD manufacturers[1] (company "A" and "B"), members of relevant Thai public authorities (National Science and Technology Development Agency, National Electronics and Computer Technology Center, Board of Investment, Electrical and Electronics Institute), including the cluster managing staff, and some academic or consulting people concerned with HDD and the cluster activities (Chulalongkorn, Asian Institute of Technology, Asia Policy Research). For confidentiality reasons, the names of persons met cannot be given.

1. THE GLOBAL HDD INDUSTRY: THE ASIAN RELOCATION OF FIRMS AND THE THAI POSITION

In 1983, when the HDD industry started to be moved to Asia, the production was concentrated in the United States (72.3 per cent of world shipments) followed by Japan (12 per cent) and Europe (5 per cent). Asian shipments (Japan excluded) were almost non-existent. In 1990–95, a little more than a decade later, U.S. firms were assembling 67 per cent of their HDD in Southeast Asia, compared with 4 per cent in 1983 (McKendrick 1997). The region took up 60 per cent of global HDD employment, including upstream activities. By 2006–07, Thailand had become the world number one producer and exporter of HDD accounting for some 50 per cent of world shipments.

The Progressive Shift to Southeast Asia

The HDD industry is quite sensitive to costs as the reduction in price per storage capacity unit continuously dropped over time from more than US$2,000 per megabyte in 1965 to US$0.005 in 2003 (Coughlin, Wait, Porter 2004). At the beginning of the 1980s, several factors acted together to trigger the move to low-cost countries. As Amano (2006) explains, the industry experienced a radical technological change in the 1980s leading to the modularization of HDD and freeing to some extent HDD manufacturers from computer manufacturers. At that time, the 3.5 inches disks were developed and the growth expectations of this market induced fierce competition with many new firms entering into the business. From about fifteen HDD manufacturing firms in the 1960s, some 105 (Amano 2006) to 136 (Coughlin, Wait, Porter 2004) competing companies emerged in the 1980s. In such a context, lowering prices through extended production volumes and production cost reduction was a matter of survival. As modularization made the distance between computer assembling units and HDD ones less important, the relocation of production to lower-cost countries became the main strategy.

But the HDD industry is a high-tech industry and while low production costs were needed, qualified labour was also requested. In the 1970s, U.S. firms already tended to reduce production costs by relocating some parts and component manufacturing units to South America, but these were rather unsuccessful.

Singapore, whose labour force was well educated and where American firms had already experimented with semiconductor production, was offering capital incentives for plant construction and tax exemption for about five years to attract foreign investors. The city state, which had the additional advantage of using English rather extensively, was targeted by most firms, starting up with Seagate, an American Silicon Valley innovative start-up.

The experience of the first comers, and, moreover, the decisive competitive advantage that Asian production gave to Seagate, which became the world leading firm in the HDD segment, led other U.S.

independent manufacturers (Maxtor, Miniscribe, Micropolis, Conner Peripherals, Cybernex) to follow suit in the mid and end of the 1980s. Almost all established plants in Singapore, which rapidly became an HDD assembly hub from which activities progressively spread over to Thailand, Malaysia, the Philippines, and more recently China, according to their respective comparative advantages.

The elements generally recognized by the investment theory literature as explaining investors' agglomeration in a specific area, region, or country, are:

- costs (labour, land and taxes, etc.),
- infrastructure or labour availability or quality,
- incentives from governments (taxes, grants, etc.),
- proximity of clients, presence of suppliers or eventually raw materials,
- follow-the-leader behaviour.

In the case of the HDD industry, all these elements have played a role in the relocation of firms albeit not all at the same time and in the same place, and progressively built up a vertical intraregional production network (Hiratsuka 2006), allowing firms to benefit from the comparative advantage of each country involved.

As already mentioned regarding the choice of Singapore, the low costs, combined with government incentives and availability of qualified workers, constituted the starting point. In the 1980s, the city state became the core of HDD assembly production, although at the beginning, most of the industry's specific components were imported from manufacturers' home country, or integrated by manufacturers.[2]

In 1983 and afterwards, Thailand started to implement liberalization measures and incentives to attract foreign investors while creating industrial estates (see Chapter 5) to provide modern infrastructure. Thanks to its export-oriented fiscal incentives, Thailand, whose labour force appeared to be rather skilled, while being less expensive than Singapore's, and whose currency was appreciating less than that of Singapore, was targeted as early as 1983. First entrants,[3] of which Seagate was the pioneer in opening a factory of head-stack assembly (HSA), also chose Thailand as a complementary location for less value-added parts because of its proximity to Singapore, to which the whole production was shipped for final assembly.

Progressively, suppliers of which the Japanese were among the first, were attracted by growing market expectations. They also opened factories in Singapore or Thailand, depending on the location advantages that were suitable for their production. Soon afterwards a follow-the-leader behaviour kicked in, explaining the agglomeration in these countries, and adding for the latecomers the advantage of the presence of numerous suppliers.

A shift also occurred from Singapore to Malaysia,[4] in the late 1980s and 1990s. Malaysia also combined cost advantage with an experienced labour force in semiconductors, since American firms had already been outsourcing precision engineering to local suppliers (in Penang) from the 1970s. This led to a new agglomeration of firms engaged in HDD head assembly at first. Malaysia, while benefiting from the proximity to Singapore, and a government incentive system not far different from that of the city state, also had the merit of having attracted computer manufacturers, giving the country a local market for HDD. But over time, the tightening of the labour market made it more difficult to hire workers. Wages increased and Malaysia lost part of its competitiveness, especially for low value-added parts. Also the numerous mergers and acquisitions (M and A) that took place at that time led to a higher concentration in the HDD industry. As a result, the surviving small number of stronger manufacturers implemented a more extensive cross-border division of labour in the region. Malaysia turned to more value-added components such as disk media, which is a key component of the hardware on which electronic data are written in the data recording process, with the arrival of Komag in 1995. For Kumagai (2006), Malaysia shares with Singapore a decisive advantage due to their common history of having been British colonies. The broad use of English led to special linkages with American firms and explains, the author believes, why, not only HDD but also other electronics industries, developed so extensively and remained located in these countries although wages increased dramatically. Easy communication, thanks to the understanding of English eased the working climate within firms, and the technology transfer between MNCs and local firms, enabling the progressive relocation of design and R&D activities, and constituting a non-cost advantage difficult to measure.

The Japanese HDD manufacturers, mainly internal divisions of computer subsidiaries of electric/electronic appliances groups, waited a decade more before following their American competitors.[5] Firms such as Matsushita or Hitachi still continued to invest in capacity increases in

Japan at the end of the 1980s, betting on the hope that more automation applied to drive assembly would override Japanese higher costs (McKendrick 1997).

During the bubble economy of the second half of the 1980s, the high yen should have pushed Japanese firms to play the card of low-cost countries though. But following the strategy that succeeded before, and that was also experienced in other high-tech EE industry segments,[6] which meant,

(1) producing and exporting from Japan to overseas markets
(2) starting production locally to be close to consumers when exports to a specific market have become important enough,

their first overseas location was in fact the United States, which is the biggest computer market. Fujitsu, NEC, Toshiba, opened plants in the United States during the second half of the 1980s and early 1990s, just at the time when American HDD firms were relocating volume production (assembly) to Southeast Asia. So in 1990, Japanese firms were still assembling as much as 95 per cent of their HDD in Japan and only 2 per cent in Southeast Asia (McKendrick 1997, p. 17, and Amano 2006, p. 19).

The domination of U.S. manufacturers for high volume, low-to-medium capacity drive, led Japanese manufacturers to be confined to small-volume, high capacity segments. The burst of the bubble and the continued yen appreciation in the first half of the 1990s finally made them decide to reconsider their past strategy. All Japanese major HDD manufacturers finally invested in Southeast Asia around 1994/1995.[7] As opposed to American firms, they located mainly in the Philippines.[8] This gave birth to a second wave of supplier (mostly Japanese) relocation to the Philippines where a new agglomeration took place progressively (see Tecson 1998).

According to Japanese firms (related by Tecson 1998), the Philippines where cheap labour force was still in abundance had, as an advantage over Thailand for example, a rather highly educated workforce and a number of technicians and engineers trained every year, as well as widespread English language knowledge. Also, government incentives gave the possibility of benefiting extensively from full tax exemption.[9] But the political instability associated with terrorism appears to have, at least until recently, limited the expansion of the industry in the country despite its comparative advantages.

So, by 1995, the HDD assembly landscape had completely changed. Production in the United States fell below 5 per cent of world shipments, and in Japan, 15.7 per cent. Japanese firms had rapidly caught up with their U.S. competitors, and were producing nearly 55 per cent of their HDD in Southeast Asia (McKendrick 1997). Singapore was the core of the Asian production network, accounting at that time for some 40 to 50 per cent of global HDD shipments (McKendrick, Doner, and Haggard 2000) even though Singapore costs were not so low anymore due to wage increases alongside economic development. As we have seen above, Singapore's position was complemented by neighbouring lower-cost countries also involved in the industry, in a vertically integrated intraregional production network using each country's specific comparative advantages.

China as a New HDD Production Hub

It is the existence of a broad market that led HDD manufacturers to expand recently in China, where major computer manufacturers have assembly facilities. In 1995, Seagate, once again a pioneer, opened a factory in Shenzhen that became the third largest, final assembly site for the company (Hiratsuka 2006) which had transferred its low-end drive assembly.

It was followed by IBM/Hitachi which started with components assembly, namely head gimbals (HGA) in 1996.[10] In 2006, ten years after its creation, the joint venture firm was shipping 125 million head gimbals annually to all assembly plants in Asia (China, Singapore, Thailand, and the Philippines). In 2003, HGST (Hitachi Global Storage Technology) announced its plan to relocate progressively its disk media production from the United States and Japan to a new factory in China's Shenzhen, before deciding in 2004 to implement the big project of creating in Shenzhen a "mega manufacturing centre" called Hitachi Global Storage Products (HGSP), representing an investment of up to US$500 million, and complementing its two component factories with a HDD final assembly plant. The first media made in China were shipped to Thailand in 2006. HGST invested several hundred million U.S. dollar to enable the Shenzhen facility to manufacture media. Also in 2006, HGSP had already achieved one million shipments of HDD from the "mega manufacturing's" hub of Shenzhen, which placed the entire supply chain of HDD production in a central location, with component manufacturing, supplier network, product assembly, and final delivery within a sixty-km radius of Shenzhen.

In 2005, Maxtor also entered the country, but located itself in Suzhou. Its recent acquisition by Seagate might lead to restructuring of the Shenzhen Seagate's location and Suzhou, even though it is still too early to know. Finally, in 2006, Samsung joined the others by opening its first factory in the country.

All this, of course, led to a broad supplier agglomeration, creating in China an additional large final assembly and component production hub.

Thailand Hard Disk Drive Industry: Global and Regional Position

As mentioned before, the story started in Thailand in 1983–84 when Seagate, having obtained privileges from the Board of Investment (BOI), opened a component manufacturing unit (parts manufacturing and assembly of heads), just one year after opening its Singapore assembly facilities. Seagate was followed by other HDD manufacturers and components suppliers at the end of the 1980s, then during the 1990s, as mentioned above.

According to McKendrick, Doner, and Haggard (2000), the HDD exports grew from roughly US$2.6 million in 1985 to US$1.3 billion in 1990 and US$5.3 billion in 1998. After the Asian crisis and the currency fall, though stagnating at a rather high level until 2002–03, exports grew again at a sustained pace to reach US$15.4 billion finally in 2006 (see Table 8.1). With more than 100,000 employees (approximately 118,000), Thailand was producing some 150 million units in 2006, and had already taken over the position of world number one exporter and producer from Singapore in 2005.

Table 8.1
Production and Exports of HDD, Thailand 2003–06

	Production volume (million)	Exports in value (US$ billion)
2003	54	10.38
2004	73	11.27
2005	111	14.23
2006	150	15.40

Source: Made by the author based on *Electrical and Electronics Industrial Economics Situation Report*, January 2006 for 2003–05; interviews (January 2007) for 2006.

Today, four of the six HDD world main assemblers[11] are operating in Thailand:

- Seagate which absorbed Maxtor in 2006,
- Western Digital which first located in Singapore, then opened a factory in Malaysia before buying a Fujitsu 3.5 inch-disk factory in Thailand in 2001,
- Hitachi Global Storage Technology (HGST) after Hitachi bought IBM HDD division in 2003,[12]
- Fujitsu which was the first among Japanese assemblers to be located in Southeast Asia and chose Thailand.

To these main global players it is necessary to add Union Technology, a Thai listed company of the Saha Union group which manufactures HDD and components under contract with IBM/HGST. But as previously mentioned, assemblers are not the whole of the landscape, major suppliers[13] of the industry also have factories in Thailand.

Both assemblers and suppliers are still expanding their activities in the country. For example, Fujitsu opened a second factory in mid-2007 which, at full capacity, will allow it to double the present production volume to reach five to six million units a month. It is part of a 15.8 billion baht project approved by the BOI which should lead the company to produce approximately seventy million units per year by 2011, and double its labour force from 5,500 currently to some 13,000 people. At the end of 2006, Western Digital (WD) submitted to the BOI a US$1 billion project for the expansion of its Bang Pa-in factory, while Nidec, a major supplier of spindle motors, supplying all HDD manufacturers, announced its expansion project over five years for an investment amount of US$0.5 billion (*Thailand Investment Review*, BOI June 2007).

Indeed, although Thailand industrial classification does not allow for the differentiation of HDD from the computers and parts statistical category, this industrial segment which, according to McKinsey estimates (2000), represents some 60 per cent of the category, appears to be a very important one for the country's economy and exports.[14] HDD employs some 100,000 persons, a small number compared with the textile industry, but contributes more than textiles to GDP (see Chapter 7). EE industries are dominating Thailand exports, and sharing with automobiles and parts the top position (*Thailand Investment Review*, BOI June 2007).

The Vertically Integrated Intraregional Production Network

The position reached by the Thai HDD industry, or the growing trend of production in China, does not mean that Singapore or other locations such as Malaysia and the Philippines are losing their HDD industries.

The HDD world market is a fast growing one, estimated at some 640 million units in 2010, compared with 383 million in 2005. The market is largely fragmented according to the product application divided into several categories:

- enterprise group and desktop PCs, both using 3.5-inch drives
- notebook PCs and a new products group, both using 2.5-inch drives[15]

Of these market segments, new products category referring to consumer electronics goods, including personal video recorders, audio appliances, games, GPS, car computers, etc., is the one growing most rapidly. It is expected to represent 40 per cent of the whole HDD market in 2010 (Business-in-Asia.com).

These market growth estimates explain why HDD manufacturers continuously expand their production capacities. In doing so, new locations appear while former ones are not abandoned, contributing to the fragmentation of production. As stated by Kimura (2006), this fragmentation is two-dimensional, including intra- and interfirm transactions both within the location country, and across the border. Indeed, the comparative advantages of countries evolved over time and firms eventually shift activities from one country to another according to these evolutions, but also according to technological concerns (product innovations, new technologies, or products).

Through this process, Singapore lost its number one position as final product assembler, a position taken over by Thailand as we have seen above. Some major HDD manufacturers reduced the number of workers like Seagate did, cutting its staff from 20,000 to 8,000 in 2002 (Brimble, KRC report); WD closed its assembly factory in 1999. But those did not leave the country and Singapore remains at the top of the value chain, often housing regional headquarters, technological R&D centres, and getting progressively involved in design activities (research still remains in assemblers' home country though), while suppliers originating in Singapore started to invest abroad, following their clients to new locations.

Malaysia too, though to a lesser extent than Singapore, tends to specialize in highest value-added components such as disk media and some designing activities. Also Malaysia has remained active, thanks to its supporting industry pool of suppliers that emerged as a result of government measures and the concentration of the electronics industry in Penang namely.

The Philippines for its part is assembling final products and manufacturing some components, but does not attain the volumes manufactured by Thailand, nor the same variety of components. So, in the Philippines and Thailand, firms tend to specialize their plants, according to their product range. For example, Fujitsu assembles drives for enterprise group products in the Philippines, while assembling the notebooks ones in Thailand.

Fragmentation has, therefore, led to a kind of specialization according to each location's comparative advantage. Some strategic differences might exist according to the firms with manufacturers either buying media and heads from outside or making them at home; and between American and Japanese manufacturers too. Japanese manufacturers still rely more on their home country than their American competitors do on the United States. Perhaps because of the distance from their home country, U.S. manufacturers appear more willing to purchase key components from their Asian bases, and to locate some designing activities where possible, as we shall see later on.

But, if specialization exists, it clearly appears that duplication is also the rule. The same parts tend to be purchased from several geographical origins as well as from intrafirm and interfirm procurements.[16]

According to Doner and Richie (2001), the network built by manufacturers and major suppliers allows firms to create a geographic redundancy in their production and thus avoid any type of risks. Manufacturers can increase or lower production in specific locations depending on the changing market or technology related needs. This redundancy also introduces a global competition between suppliers (Hiratsuka 2006) in the way to lower costs, increase quality, etc. According to Hiratsuka (2006, p. 195) it means that location advantages across involved countries are not as large for the assemblers as initially assumed. This might be true, but even though redundancy exists, as we have discussed before, specialization also matters, depending on human resource and supporting industry technological capability, availability and cost, as evidenced by the progressive shift of activities from Singapore to Thailand,

Malaysia, then China.[17] Governments of involved or possibly targeted countries also compete through incentive packages to attract investors. In that sense, the redundancy might also be explained by continuous and sustained market growth, making it possible for manufacturers and global suppliers, using their bargaining power, to take advantage of opportunities offered, including continuous tax exemptions, for example. Service link cost, including transportation costs, well developed logistic services costs, must be low enough though to offset the disadvantage of procuring from overseas suppliers, and obtain overall total cost reduction (Hiratsuka 2006, p. 195; Kimura 2006, p. 20). This is the case in the Asian area and in the HDD industry, in particular, with most parts being very small.

But all this means that positions within the intraregional network cannot be taken for granted. Of course, investments are heavy enough to prevent firms abandoning one location just to benefit from short-term advantages, but unless capabilities grow along with development and its correlated cost increases, enabling a country to engage in higher value-added production, its future might be at risk. This is the situation Thailand is now facing as its former comparative advantages are eroding progressively while too little has been done in the past for it to enter higher knowledge-based segments currently occupied by Singapore or Malaysia.[18]

2. THE CHALLENGE OF THE HDD INDUSTRY'S SUSTAINABILITY AND NEW POLICIES IMPLEMENTATION

Even though EE industries have been rather neglected in the past decade, Thailand's government and institutions now feel concerned about the HDD industry's future due to its importance for the country's export potential as we have seen before.

The Thai HDD industry is centred on disk assembly and consists of five product groups, including heads (assembly, slider fabrication, suspensions, and components), PCBA, motors, media substrates, and bases/covers. Thailand became a major player in disk assembly as well as the manufacturing hub of motors and heads. The emphasis is now put on the coverage of the whole value chain and, therefore, the integration of the most sophisticated components that Thailand is not manufacturing yet: disk media and wafers. To reach this goal, the country has to act in several correlated directions: manpower, technology, and supporting industries.

The Eroding Cost Advantage

Even though comparative general statistics still position Thailand rather well in comparison to its Southeast Asian neighbours, namely Malaysia, and to some extent, the Philippines, the country cannot compete with China on most costs items.

Labour costs are increasing in Thailand and the mid-1990s can be considered the end of the "cheap labour era".[19] Although for unskilled as well as skilled labour, Thailand still has a strong advantage over Malaysia where labour costs have also increased drastically, the gap is important with China (and Vietnam) as Figure 8.1 shows for the case of electrical and electronics sector. Due to the high-tech nature of the industry, HDD manufacturers are experiencing wage increases that are above the average.

For example, according to company "A", in only two years, hourly wage averages in the company grew from 170 baht in 2005 to 194 in 2007. The situation is even worse for technicians and engineers the number of whom is far from covering firms' needs. The strong growth of both the HDD and automotive industries in recent years has largely drained the skilled workers and engineers market and meeting future needs is far from guaranteed. Company "B" estimates that if the Thai government continues to attract more firms all the time, the competition to hire engineers will become so strong that it could lead to a situation where firms have to pay some US$6,000 a month to attract some of them. In that case assembly in Thailand would not be sustainable. Of course, this extreme estimate is not reflecting the present wage situation, where the average wage for an engineer is about US$1,000 a month, but it puts into question the government's past strategy of attracting FDI, and developing human resources, based exclusively on fiscal incentives without linking these to any kind of more qualitative requests, as, for example, Singapore did.

In terms of infrastructure and facilities, the situation is more contrasted, with the position changing depending on costs items, as Figure 8.2 shows. When all of them are aggregated, it appears that Thailand still has a small advantage over Malaysia, while both countries remain cheaper than China where the cost of office leasing is particularly high, and also the Philippines, where building construction cost is largely exceeding other countries' average.

Apart from this, the baht is also appreciating strongly and faster than currencies of neighbouring countries (40.22 baht/US$ on average in 2005,

Unit: US$/month

Figure 8.1
Cost of Labour in the Electronics Sector by Category and Countries in October 2003
Unit: US$/month

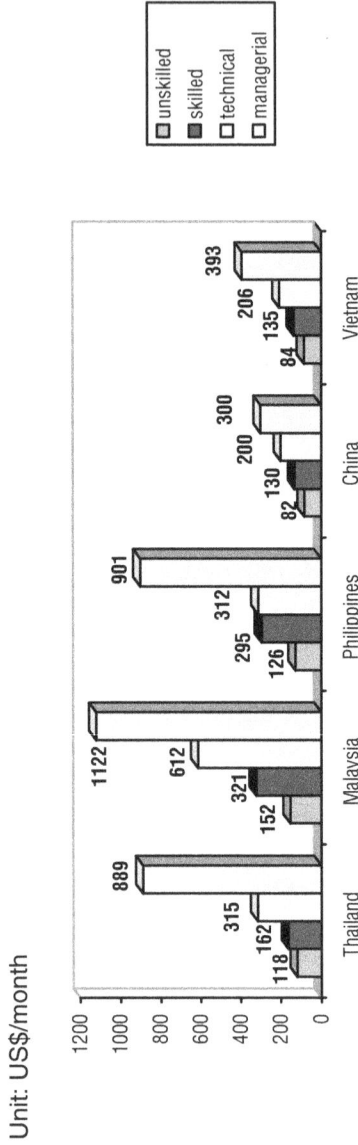

Legend:
- □ unskilled
- ■ skilled
- □ technical
- □ managerial

	Thailand	Malaysia	Philippines	China	Vietnam
	889	1122	901	300	393
	315	612	312	200	206
	162	321	295	130	135
	118	152	126	82	84

Source: Made by the author based on BOI: Thailand investment opportunities in electrical and electronics, October 2005, available at <http://www.boi.go.th>.

Figure 8.2
Real Estate and Utility Costs in Electronics, Comparison in October 2003

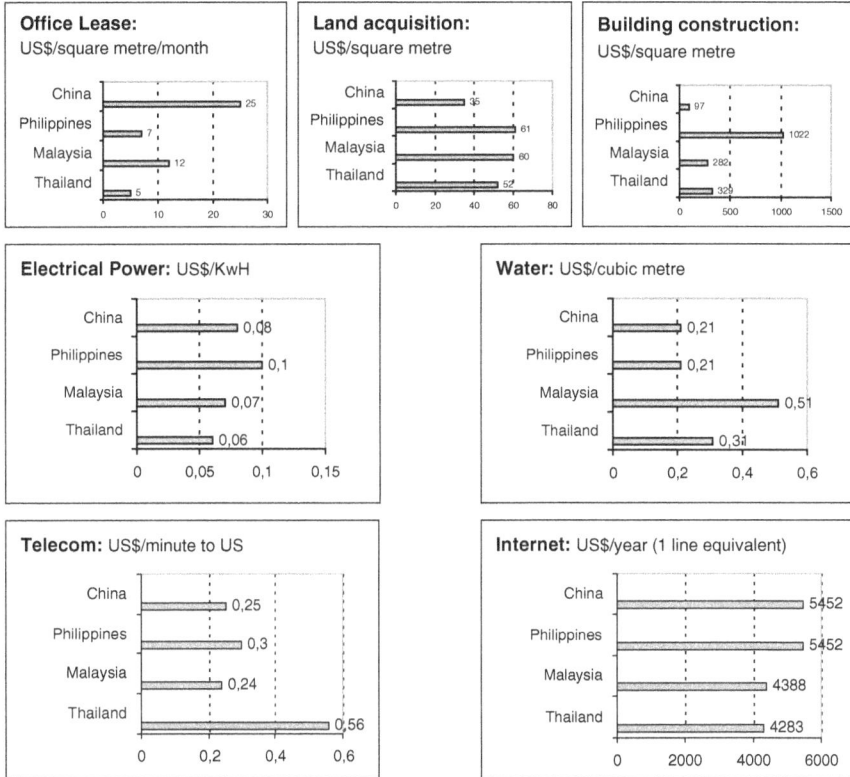

| Office Lease: US$/square metre/month |
| Land acquisition: US$/square metre |
| Building construction: US$/square metre |
| Electrical Power: US$/KwH |
| Water: US$/cubic metre |
| Telecom: US$/minute to US |
| Internet: US$/year (1 line equivalent) |

Source: Adapted from BOI: Thailand investment opportunities in electrical and electronics, October 2005, available at <http://www.boi.go.th>.

32.47 in 2007)[20] and plays a significant role in the cost increase as almost 100 per cent of the production is exported.

The country, which is successful, thanks to its comparative cost advantage, seems to have to some extent failed in preparing for the future or the post-low-cost era, especially as far as manpower is concerned. But labour cost is indeed not the whole story. Availability (or number) and quality are also very important as confirmed by an executive of the BOI who related that today, the first question firms ask the BOI before choosing their location is: "Are you able to guarantee xx number of workers or xx engineers? Will it be possible to increase the number by xx% after five years?" Even though implementing programmes for training workers for a specific industry as HDD does not seem easy for Thai authorities nor easily acceptable by universities whose mission is to train for industry in general, manpower development and education are now key in making Thailand's position sustainable in a high-tech industry such as HDD.

The Thai Technological Competitiveness and Upgrading Challenge

As was shown in Chapter 3, competitiveness indicators give Thailand an intermediate position in world ranking, whether by IMD or the World Economic Forum (WEF).

Compared with neighbouring Asian countries, Thailand does not do very well. It is ranked the seventh out of ten countries[21] by IMD, except in 2005 when it came fourth, and the sixth out of eleven Asian countries by WEF, behind Taiwan, Singapore, Korea, Malaysia, but ahead of China, India, Indonesia, the Philippines, and Vietnam.

As far as the technological issue is concerned, Thailand's ranking during the period 1997–2006 is not better. IMD indicators measuring technological and scientific capabilities point to a decline from the thirty-second (1997) to the forty-eighth (2006) position in terms of technological infrastructure, and from the thirty-second to the fifty-third in terms of scientific infrastructure (Termpitayapaisit 2006). In terms of innovation or technological readiness which appears important for the HDD industry needs, Thailand lags far behind Singapore, according to WEF, and is also below Malaysia as Table 8.2 shows.

According to IMD, Thailand's strength lies in the employment and labour market, cost of living, tourism receipts and high-tech exports, monetary conditions, fiscal policy, basic infrastructure, while the weaknesses are its political instability, inefficient competition legislation, low transparency of government policies, investment risks, inefficient SMEs, low expenditure on technological and scientific infrastructure, R&D, health and education, low productivity and efficiency (Patrawimolpon and Pongsaparn 2006[22]).

In fact, compared with Malaysia for example, Thailand appears inferior in terms of educational attainment, R&D expenditure (0.26 for Thailand and 0.69 for Malaysia, 2003) or patents (0.07 for Thailand and

Table 8.2
Ranking of Innovation, Technological Readiness and Technology Transfer

	Innovation index (1)	Technology readiness index (2)
Singapore	13	7
Malaysia	40	15
Thailand	43	39
China	75	68

Note: 1. the index deals with the country's ability to innovate;
         2. the index deals with the capability of the country in technology adoption, transfer, copy, and imitation.
Source: Made by the author using data from Termpitayapaisit (2006).

0.28 for Malaysia, 2001–04) (Termpitayapaisit 2006[23]). The contribution of the private sector to Malaysia's R&D expenditure is much higher than in Thailand, also reflecting the higher level of the Science and Technology Development of Malaysia. While the Malaysian population is only 22.7 million compared with Thailand's 62 million inhabitants, the former has 3,500 R&D workers in the private sector with a per capita ratio of 0.16 (full-time equivalent per 1,000 people) while Thailand has 5,300, with a ratio of 0.086.[24]

In Thailand, the development of the capabilities of firms and manpower is still largely limited to the needed production technologies. As related by Intarakumnerd and Panthavi (2003, pp. 94–95), a study of the World Bank has shown that a majority of firms nationwide were still struggling with increasing their design and engineering capabilities, while a very large number of SMEs, were mostly concerned with building up operational capabilities to upgrade fairly standard technologies incrementally. Also, most sample firms of the R&D/innovation survey of 2000 had no design capabilities (more than half). Only one third had reverse engineering capabilities and less than 15 per cent had R&D knowledge. Thai firms have few links with R&D, universities or RTO organizations, and public policies did not really give any incentives in this sense. Even though some firms tended to work from time to time with researchers, they did it on a personal basis, and so did not contribute to the building of a National System of Innovation (see Intarakumnerd and Panthavi 2003; Intarakumnerd 2005, 2006; Brimble and Doner 2007). A survey from the NSTDA in 2005 shows that 70 per cent of firms surveyed identified their client as their external information source with whom they have intensively cooperated. But until recently, FDI attraction policies were not linked to technology transfer, leading to low technological spillover from MNCs' subsidiaries. Those used to train their workers (or sometimes their suppliers[25]) just enough to give them the needed capabilities to produce the required goods efficiently, but the acquisition of knowledge for designing, and innovation were often kept outside the relationship.

This does not mean that during its long experience in the industry Thailand did not upgrade its capabilities. For example, while at the beginning production ramp up and debugging were done in the HDD manufacturers' home countries (the United States and Japan) before launching production in Thailand, these activities were later relocated in the country. Also Thailand (like Malaysia) was in charge of these functions before production launching in China. Of the seven steps in an HDD production, company "B" admits that it was doing about five in the United States and only two in Thailand, while now five steps are taking place in Thailand and only two are done elsewhere (the United States or Singapore). To do so, firms had to invest heavily in the training first of their workers, then of their technicians and engineers. For example, Seagate used to train its manpower on an informal basis during the initial periods, sending engineers to the United States for training when needed to learn some elements of the production process. But later the training system was formalized. As explained by M. Hobday and H. Rush (2007), a training department was established, employing between 100 and 300 persons,[26] to give each employee four weeks of training per year. Training for operators includes initial training in a classroom, then on the job.[27]

American manufacturers now tend to transfer some designing activities as much as possible to Asia, namely Singapore, Malaysia, but also Thailand, where process engineering is already occurring. In that sense it is may be not surprising that U.S. firms, and especially Seagate, were also the first to initiate linkages with universities such as, for example, the Asian Institute of Technology that developed a certificate in storage technologies. Japanese manufacturers, whose Thai subsidiaries are less distant from headquarters and R&D centres in their home country, are less advanced in this domain. Company "A", for instance, even though it opened an R&D centre in Thailand recently, is still doing all its R&D in Japan.[28]

But for the whole HDD value-chain to be located in Thailand, including sophisticated components, or designing and R&D activities, as the Thai government would like, it will be necessary for Thailand to educate many more engineers and science and technology staff. Also, to anchor the industry in the country and increase the local content, it will be necessary for the government to favour MNCs that do technology transfers in a way that upgrades the technological capabilities of Thai firms too.

The Supporting Industry Challenge

All the major players of the industry are foreign-owned companies, mostly American and Japanese. According to the manufacturers, without the presence of Japanese suppliers in Thailand (or Thai-Japanese joint ventures), the manufacturing of HDD would not be possible. The Thai success story has, therefore, to be nuanced to some extent. Even though Thailand counts some 130,000 SMEs of which about 85,000 are working in industrial sectors,[29] pure Thai firms acting as subcontractors for HDD industry are very limited in number and mostly engaged in annex production such as packaging, etc., or in the sub-assembly of parts. Assemblers purchase most of their procurements inside Thailand as is the case in company "A" whose procurements are almost 80 per cent Thai originated.[30] But first-tier suppliers, mostly foreign owned, rely much more on imported parts, components, or material than manufacturers do (see Sukhpisarn 2002, pp. 93–101). This shows that Thailand is lacking supporting industries able to conduct processes or produce parts with the required quality. In 1992, the BOI implemented the BUILD programme that aimed at bringing together foreign clients and Thai SMEs to generate transactions. This programme, which seems to have generated new transactions every year, may of course be used by HDD manufacturers, but the local content, estimated at around 30 per cent, has remained low.

Countries such as Singapore or Malaysia have benefited from some twenty years of experience in the industry to develop knowledge, upgrade their technologies, and build a local supporting industry. Kumagai (2006) gives some examples such as the Eng Technology Group, a Malaysian small firm that started business in 1974 in parts for the machine industry, and could then develop a precision machining activity. Working with major HDD manufacturers (Seagate, Maxtor, Fujitsu, Minebea, HGST), the company grew and now has subsidiaries in Singapore, Taiwan, China, the Philippines, and Thailand.

If Singapore remains at the top of the network, it is also because it has the biggest suppliers agglomeration of which foreign-owned companies form the majority, but local firms involved are also quite significant. But the strength of the Singapore suppliers agglomeration is not only a question of numbers. It lies in its specialization in the highest technologies, such as clean room designing, printed circuit board assembly, disk media, complex heads, etc. or in related industries such as machining, die casting, etc. — specialization that led them to invest abroad to follow their clients (see Wong 1999).

Although it was never linked to any industry specificities, but just general policies, Thailand also used to implement measures for local SME development, or technology upgrading with some results,[31] but due to political changes each time accompanied by policy changes (see Chapter 4), the measures appear to have been less successful than in Singapore or even Malaysia.[32]

Very low-rate loans or subsidies, capital grants, were never available in Thailand as they were in Singapore or for example, Japan during the development stages of the modern industry. This might at least partially explain the relative weakness of pure Thai firms that had difficulties in upgrading or starting new businesses. They lacked the funds to do so, but the problem might also have some cultural basis:[33] Thai people are risk averse and not prone to taking risky initiatives.

Making the Thai position sustainable in the global HDD industry implies an increase in the local content though. This is already high for assemblers, but what is really key now is to get the industry better established in the country so parts manufacturers too (first- or second-tier suppliers) have the possibility to purchase from, or subcontract to, Thai firms, most of the parts or processes they need, including the downstream activities of the value-chain, such as metal finishing, clean room, heat treatment, and so on.

A Qualitative Change in the BOI Policy Packages

To address all these issues, and make the HDD industry sustainable, changes are needed. The priority given to FDI attraction and tax holidays as the only leverage for industrial development seem to have reached their limits. Taxes incentives are, of course, welcomed by foreign investors, including HDD ones, and as already mentioned, they played their part in the location decision of firms. But on their own, they do not necessarily constitute a comparative advantage anymore. Fiscal incentives exist in all countries, and depending on the period of time, some might have been more interesting for firms than the Thai packages. For example, in China, after a complete eight-year tax holiday, firms only had to pay 50 per cent of the taxes for additional years. In the Philippines, as we have seen, simply introducing a new technology was enough for a firm to benefit from the exemption package again, etc.

Fiscal incentives are not the whole of the possible incentives though. Some countries might add to the fiscal packages some other kind of support. It happens, for instance, that to attract an investor, the Singapore or Chinese government decide to construct the buildings themselves and rent them out at a very low rate. As already mentioned, Thailand is willing to cover the whole value chain of HDD production. According to some government sources, the battle for locating disk media production is probably lost as Malaysia and China are already engaged in it. Wafers that are still imported from the manufacturers' home country would be a possibility, but Thailand does not have the capability for producing it yet. Company "B" suggested that it could think about locating wafer production if the government decided to give subsidies for it to do so. A huge training programme would be necessary as well as the hiring of foreign engineers. This would be very costly and surely not cost efficient for the company, as producing wafers in Thailand does not appear to be strategic. Unless financially aided (and not just through tax exemption), no company will be interested to invest in this. As confirmed by our interviews, it appears, however, that it would be difficult for the Thai authorities to use such grants to attract firms, or to favour the start-up of new business or activities due to the Thai political culture that will not easily accept it. It would be judged unfair for all other firms not benefiting from such privilege. Capital grants would be considered as opening the door to corruption or favouritism. Therefore, when in 2003–04, with the aim of becoming the largest HDD manufacturing base worldwide, the BOI announced the implementation of a new policy package dedicated to HDD industry as its top priority, this package was again based on tax exemption. But for the first time, it was also linked to other criteria aimed at addressing the new challenges facing the country through the Skill, Technology, Innovation (STI) programme (see Box 8.1).[34]

The new customized incentives for the HDD industry implemented in 2004 include HDD parts suppliers in addition to HDD manufacturers. While increasing the way to qualify for certain privileges, it allows both to receive up to eight years of income tax holiday depending on the location

---

Box 8.1
The STI Policy

In December 2003, the Skill, Technology and Innovation (STI) new policy was approved for starting in March 2004. This BOI new incentive package is a cross-sector approach to promote investments aimed at increasing the international competitiveness of Thailand's industries while supporting the country's drive to become a knowledge-based economy. The policy is designed to enhance the country's share in R&D, improve human resource development and the supply chain through the development of subcontractors. Specific programmes include developing the technological skill of the Thai workforce and encouraging the manufacture of higher value-added products.

Companies must qualify in at least one of the four following elements to be eligible:

(1) Average R&D or design expenses for the first three years of operations are not less than 1–2 per cent of annual sales.
(2) Employees with at least a Bachelor's degree in science, R&D, design, or other technology-related field, make up not less than 1–5 per cent of the project's total workforce for the first three years of operations.
(3) Average training expenses for the first three years of operations are not less than 1 per cent of total payroll costs.
(4) Average expenses for developing Thai vendors or subcontractors or for supporting related educational institutes are not less than 1 per cent of annual sales for the first three years of operations.

Companies which fulfil these requirements after three years of operations will receive an additional year of corporate income tax exemption for each of the four requirements fulfilled with a maximum tax exemption of eight years. They will be treated as being engaged in priority activities, and the corporate tax holiday will not be limited to the amount of investment. In addition, these projects will be exempt from duties on imported machinery.

Source: Summarized from various sources; for more details, see, for example, *BOI investment Review* 13, no. 2 (March 2004).

---

zone: four years in zone 1, six in zone 2 and eight in zone 3, but without limit based on the investment amount. To ensure that the HDD companies promoted by the BOI in all zones remain competitive in light of the rapidly changing technology of the industry, they became eligible to import upgraded or replacement machinery duty-free for the life of the promotion period. Approved HDD projects were receiving an additional year's corporate income tax holiday for meeting criteria based on the new implemented STI policy:

- Average R&D or design expenditure for the first three years must be:
  - Not less than 1–2 per cent of annual total sales or
  - Not less than 50 million baht for HDD manufacturers
  - Not less than 15 million baht for HDD parts manufacturers.
- At least 5 per cent of the total workforce in the three years should consist of science and technology personnel with a minimum of a Bachelor's degree in science, engineering or other fields related to technology, R&D, or design.
- Average cost of training Thai staff for the three years are at least 1 per cent of total payroll costs.

HDD projects also receive an additional two years of corporate income tax holiday for meeting each of the following criteria:

- cost of developing vendors or costs of supporting related educational institutes for the first three years must be at least:
  - 1 per cent of total sales or
  - 150 million baht for HDD manufacturers
  - 15 million baht for HDD parts manufacturers.
- Establish an R&D centre in Thailand within three years.

To qualify, companies must submit to the BOI an action plan which identifies the way in which the company will interact with Thai entrepreneurs, Thai R&D facilities, or Thai educational institutions.[35]

In December 2005, the HDD special package was revised and extended to all the EE industries to consolidate Thailand as an electronics hub. Compared with its rival countries, Thailand has no national market, almost all its production being exported.[36] Creating a market implies a better link between the HDD segment and the upstream supply chain such as the ICT industry and electronics consumer goods.

Corporate income tax exemptions according to location were revised a little (Table 8.3) while other incentives such as duty exemption for machinery upgrading or replacement were maintained and just extended to all EE industries.

Table 8.3
Corporate Income Tax Exemption: 2005–06 Revision

In number of years	Zone 1		Zone 2		Zone 3	
	Outside IE	Inside IE	Outside IE	Inside IE	Outside IE	Inside IE
Previous priviledges (HDD only)	4	4	6	6	8	8
New priviledges (EE, including HDD)	5	5	6	7	8	8

Note: Priority activities, such as wafers and solar cells, maintain eight year exemption, regardless of location. IE= Industrial Estate, EE = Electrical and Electronic Industries, HDD = Hard Disk Drive.
Source: Adapted by the author from *BOI Investment Review* 14, no. 12 (December 2005): 1.

The major change is that new incentives allow EE industries to combine earlier projects with follow-on projects, automatically extending the corporate income tax exemption period for operation begun in earlier phases. As a result, projects from earlier phases are able to receive more than the eight years' exemption that constituted the limit in the previous package. The condition for qualifying is to submit a plan of additional investment of at least 15 billion baht (US$375 million) before the operation of the first project starts. All projects in the plan must lie within the EE industry's supply chain. Companies also have to participate to the STI programme which was also revised. Projects must make investments in at least one of the three activities to develop skills, technology, and innovation: R&D, or design, advanced technology training, support for educational or research institutions. Minimum STI investments required are calculated according to the location zone, ranging from 1–2 per cent of total sales generated. (*BOI Investment Review* 14, no. 12, December 2005).

Attracting new investors is still on the agenda, but differs from the past policies, which gave the impression that number was more important for policymakers and executives than quality or concern for the country's needs. The recent revisions to the package show that the Thai government now intends to favour investment extensions by companies already located in the country. As far as the HDD industry is concerned, the main global players are already there so what is needed to go up in the value chain is to attract complementary investments in R&D and/or more value-added products. As an executive of the BOI confirms, what is now needed is to attract new technologies rather than new firms. But as we have discussed before, attracting new technologies might not be enough to ensure the industry's sustainability. Developing technologies locally and upgrading the manpower and supporting industries capabilities are challenges that are at least as important to take up urgently.

Government and industry actors have joined to point out the needs that led to the HDD cluster initiative which can also be seen as an attempt to find transversal and enlarged solutions complementing the BOI fiscal policy packages.

3. THE THAI CLUSTER INITIATIVE: THE HDD CLUSTER PROGRAMME

The HDD cluster programme came about from two parallel moves and was officially initiated in October 2005.

First, and as already mentioned, at the national level, after the re-election of Thaksin, the new government launched its dual track policy. For the first time, and as explained in previous chapters, sector specific policies were implemented instead of the traditional general policies that prevailed until then. Competitiveness became the core issue and the National Competitiveness Committee chaired by the prime minister was established (see Intarakumnerd 2005). Until that time, the whole research organization was based exclusively on a vertical structure with NSTDA at the top and National Institutes such as NECTEC below. Funds were shared among small groups of researchers, with each receiving small amounts leading to patents sometimes. To reach the new competitiveness goal, the assumption was that something more transversal was needed to allow Thailand to enter the knowledge-based economy era. A cluster initiative[37] was considered the right approach for responding to the new needs of a large transversal structure relating research with industries and six clusters were eventually formed[38] (see Chapter 2). But NSTDA, whose role is to promote industrial sectors, developed supporting programmes that are also called clusters even though those are not concerned with geographical proximity. These NSTDA cluster programmes are not clusters labelled by the government even if there is some overlapping, making understanding unclear sometimes. The NSTDA cluster programmes are: transportation and automotive industry, agriculture and food, textiles, medical/public health, environment/ energy, electronics/software. Under the main cluster programmes, NSTDA defined some sub programmes, such as the HDD, to simplify the HDD cluster.

Second, in 2004 HDD manufacturers, under the auspices of the newly created Thai branch of IDEMA (Disk Drive Equipment and Material Association) proposed jointly with the NSTDA and the government, seven projects considered vital for the further development of their industry (see Box 8.2).

Before the end of the year, these projects were approved and launched for a one-year pilot run (*BOI Thailand Investment Report*, June 2007, p. 9). In October 2005, these projects served as basis for the launching of the HDD cluster programme.

The HDD Cluster Objectives

As already discussed, for the moment, Thailand is the hub for mechanical parts and assembly, but, as stated by the HDD cluster manager, keeping this position while comparative advantages are eroding will be difficult if more value added components are not integrated. Most sophisticated components such as disk media and wafers are imported to Thailand for assembly on HDD. These parts are difficult for Thai firms to make, so to locate their production in Thailand, it would be necessary first to attract foreign firms having the knowledge in the domain. As already said, media which are purchased from Singapore, Malaysia, and more recently, China, are probably lost to Thailand, since Seagate, after approaching the BOI recently, judged that Thailand does not have enough qualified manpower and chose to invest in Malaysia.

Wafers still mainly purchased from HDD manufacturers' home countries would be a possibility for the future, and according to our interviewees, discussions are taking place with companies even though nothing has been decided yet, as the country is still unable to develop such high value-added components. Technology upgrading, which depends on manpower training/education, and on R&D (or, at least, designing) capabilities are the key issues for the country's HDD industry and, therefore, for the cluster programme.

Based on today's key factors of success for attracting foreign companies or motivating existing ones to expand their activities further, clusters must rely on:

Box 8.2
The IDEMA and its role in the HDD cluster creation

IDEMA is an international not-for-profit trade association founded in 1986 representing 500 corporate and individual members worldwide, and active in Singapore, Malaysia, the Philippines, and since 1999, Thailand. A workshop was then organized by the NSTDA, NECTEC, FTI, BOI, the University of California San Diego, and the Brooker Group. IDEMA presented a paper on addressing the training needs for HDD industry. Government and industry participants identified the HDD industry's workforce training as one of their leading issues. The idea of forming a branch of IDEMA in Thailand was born and a few months later, IDEMA Asia-Pacific Thailand was created. Seagate, WD, Hitachi, Fujitsu, KR precision, Magnecomp, and Gem City Engineering were on the Advisory Committee, in which representatives of the BOI, AIT, NECTEC, and Asia Policy Research Co. Ltd also sat. Two sub-committees were formed: Human Resource Development sub-committee and Automation Infrastructure Development Sub-committee.

AIT-IDEMA jointly offered a Certificate of Competence in Storage Technology, recognized by both institutions. IDEMA organized international HDD symposiums in Thailand which attracted a lot of participants. IDEMA also produced a white paper to lay out key directions required to meet the significant competitive challenges facing the HDD industry. From this the following vision was developed for Thailand in 2007:

– to be a global manufacturing centre of excellence with key global players based there
– to have developed numerous local suppliers at the global frontier
– to be characterized by greater outsourcing at all levels, leading to higher levels of skilled employment
– to have Thai storage industry suppliers serving all precision manufacturing activities
– to be implementing strategic policies and measures jointly formulated by government/industry, vision, HRD, automation, linkage development
– to be home of the Thailand Data Storage Institute (a joint public-private sector agency) carrying out frontier design, research and development in manufacturing, design and applications.

To implement these visions, seven projects were defined:

– Training programme for advanced manufacturing
– Revitalize the Certificate of Competence in Storage Technology (at AIT)
– Establish a precision engineering part of the proposed Thailand Tool and Die Institute
– Implement the IDEMA Automation project
– Establish a Disk Storage Institute in Thailand
– Develop a new investment package for the HDD industry
– HDD Technology road mapping

Note: For more details on the projects, see <http://www3.easywebtime.com/hdd_eng/plan.html> (accessed May 2007).
Source: Summarized from various sources, including: Intarakumnerd 2005, pp. 35–36; Brimble Peter, draft documents kindly given by author during interview on January 2007.

(1)*Creating availability of high-tech facilities and mastering complex processes*
As a qualified manpower is absolutely needed, the cluster programme must focus on supporting training and education first as this is a long process where results are only seen later. Training is costly and firms ask for support. SMEs, in particular, need help since due to both limited financial means and capabilities, they would not be able to engage in the training of their employees on their own.

(2)*Taking the real needs of firms into account to promote more customized incentives*
Even though R&D increased in Thailand recently, the level achieved still remains far from adequate to allow for the complete value chain of HDD manufacturing to be located in the country. Supporting the acquisition of equipment for R&D (not for production) to help firms engaging in such activities is, therefore, on the agenda.

To address these issues, the cluster programme promotes a strategy using four road maps covering a five-year period from 2005:

(i)   Human resources development
(ii) Technology development
(iii) Supply chain development
(iv) Policy incentives and infrastructure development dedicated to the HDD industry with the goal to make the other three road maps achievable.

The year 2007 is the third year since the programme was implemented, but in fact it is only the second one in financial terms as it started only in October 2005.

To pursue these road maps, the cluster was awarded 800 million baht for the then-current five-year plan and, at the time of surveys, a supplemental budget of 1.4 billion baht was expected to be approved before the end of the year (*BOI Investment Review*, June 2007, p. 9).[39] To these public funds, private support (from HDD industries) has to be added as the industry manifested a strong interest in providing support (financial and non-financial) to the projects.

The Management Structure of HDD Cluster Development

The cluster notion used for this programme is not based on geographical dimension, but concerns the whole industry wherever the firms might be located. However, HDD companies are relatively grouped together in the country, even if assemblers are scattered in several industrial estates (IE): Nava Nakorn (Fujitsu), Bang Pa-in (WD), and numerous component manufacturers are in the high-tech and Rojana IE of Ayuthaya. Only Seagate (Korat) and HGST (Prachinburi) are located in other provinces, but they are still at an acceptable distance of no more than three hours' drive from the cluster centre: The Thailand Science Park (TSP) where NECTEC, acting as coordinator, is located. TSP is close to Nava Nakorn, Bang Pa-in, and Ayuthaya. Also, the academic and research network of the cluster, comprising fourteen universities: one private, the others public, is located in the Bangkok area. Two institutions are very close to the TSP: the Thammassat Rangsit campus, and AIT.

The main actors of the cluster at the firms' level are the five HDD assemblers: Seagate, Western Digital, Fujitsu, HGST, and Union Technology. To this leaders group, about sixty companies working as suppliers must be added. Among these suppliers, one or two only are pure Thai firms.[40] All others are completely foreign owned, or JVs between American or Japanese and Thai firms.

The management of the cluster is placed under NSTDA/NECTEC authority. It is chaired by a steering committee which is divided into several sub-committees: Scholarship, training, curricula, technology, development (see Figure 8.1).

The steering committee is composed of representatives of:

- The private sector:
  - HDD manufacturers (generally presidents or vice-presidents),
  - The IDEMA representatives
  - One supplier
- The public sector:
  - NSTDA/NECTEC, MTEC
  - the BOI
  - Ministry of Industry (Industrial Economic Development department),
  - EEI (Electrical and Electronics Institute)
  - iTAP (Industrial Technology Assistance Program[41])
- The academic network:
  - Thammassat University represented by professors
  - AIT, represented by professors

Three centres of excellence — Khon Kaen, King Mongkut's University of Technology Thonburi, and King Mongkut's University of Technology Ladkrabang — are participating in the cluster, but as they are funded (scholarships, and R&D projects with the industry), they cannot be members of the steering committee.

Surprisingly, the Ministry of Education is not involved in the cluster, but in Thailand, the Ministry of Education only establishes standards while universities are independent and may develop their curricula freely. According to public authorities interviewed, the Ministry of Education seems rather reluctant to intervene even though reforms should be implemented in teaching methods, etc. as was already mentioned in Chapter 7 in the case of the textile industry.

The steering committee defines the strategy, the correlated measures, or action to be taken. The cluster manager,[42] based at NECTEC, is in charge of the executive.

The Cluster's Main Actions and Achievements

Main actions taken during the first two years since the creation of the HDD cluster programme concern human resources development and technology development, mainly through research.

– Training of industry employees, mainly technical training of technician and engineers;
Forty-nine curricula were developed in four domains of study: Advanced manufacturing; Data storage technology; Industrial management; and Manufacturing process technology.

Training occurs in cooperation with companies. In the first year, 2,500 persons have been trained through these forty-nine curricula.

In March 2006, the WD HDD Technology Training Institute (HTTI) was established within the NECTEC building at the TSP. It is dedicated to developing technical resources for WD, NECTEC, and HDD components suppliers in Thailand. Seventy-one subjects are taught that are related to seven fields of study.

– Education of future technicians and engineers
Apart from the Certificate of Competencies in Storage Technology of the AIT, a programme of scholarships was established. It allows

Figure 8.3
The Management Structure of the HDD Cluster Development in Thailand

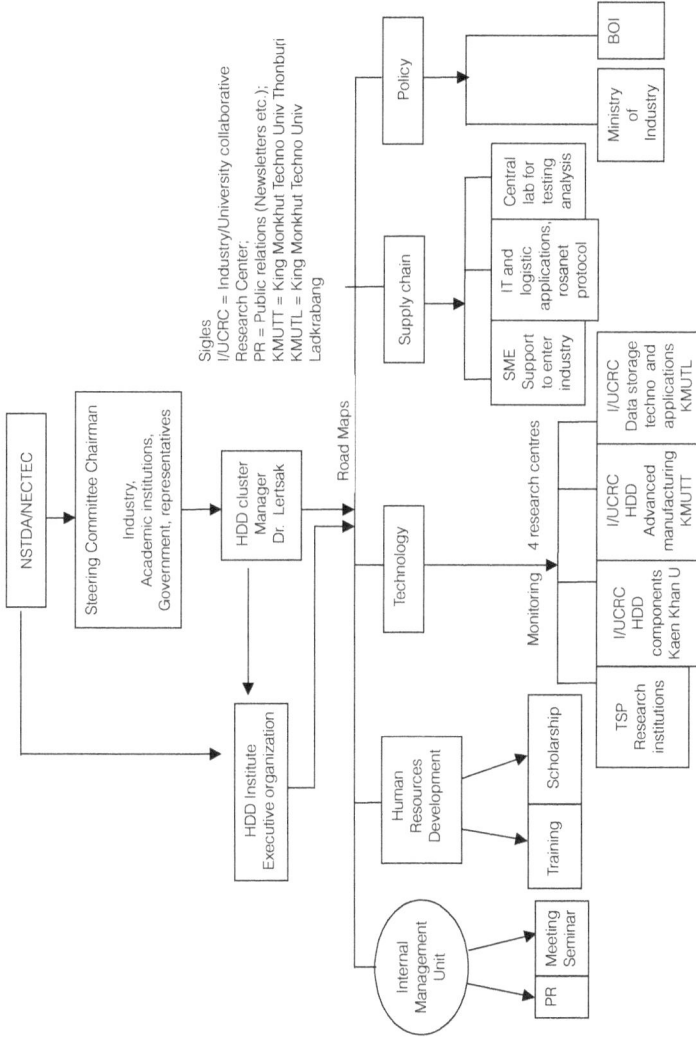

Sigles
I/UCRC = Industry/University collaborative Research Center;
PR = Public relations (Newsletters etc.);
KMUTT = King Monkhut Techno Univ Thonburi
KMUTL = King Monkhut Techno Univ Ladkrabang

Source: Composed from interviews with cluster management, January 2007.

undergraduates (104), Master's (33 projected but due to the many applicants, 57 were granted) and doctoral students (6) to be granted scholarships. To be eligible, a doctoral student must find a subject proposed by a company with which he/she is working (internship) during his/her thesis preparation. It is, of course, expected that the student will then be hired by the company after completing his/her doctorate.

For the Master's students and undergraduates, scholarships are granted to any of the fourteen collaborating universities, but the principle is the same. Students have to start working with a company providing the subject.

The selection of applicants is first done by universities, but the final decision is taken by the HDD cluster steering committee. These scholarships might be granted to employees of firms that go back to study during their scholarship length.

– Investments are also placed in technology development.
HDD manufacturers may apply for grants for R&D projects to be developed with the above mentioned fourteen universities or institutions. If approved, NECTEC would provide 30 per cent of the anticipated cost and the company provides the remaining 70 per cent.

To encourage technology transfer, financial support is provided to companies that need to send engineers abroad to be trained in the use of high-tech equipment, before they start to be used in Thailand.

In 2006, three research centres were established as I/UCRCs (Industry/ University Collaborative Research Centres) in advanced manufacturing, data storage and HDD components.

As already mentioned, the core of the HDD cluster is inside the TSP where NECTEC and other research institutes have been relocated. This structure, created in 2002 to be a fully integrated hub for R&D in science and technology is not dedicated to the HDD industry, but firms can, of course, benefit from its facilities (see Box 8.3).

They might also benefit from other institutions such as, for instance, the Thai MicroElectronic Centre (TMEC), which was created for research but also provides technical services to firms having a problem with specimens for instance. Before its creation, firms had to send the specimens to Singapore for testing and problem diagnostics, but thanks to this service opening, the job can be done in Thailand. The Electric and Electronic Institute, which is also represented in the HDD cluster steering committee,

Box 8.3
The Thailand Science Park's Privileges and Facilities

The Thailand Science Park (TSP) was established with a total investment budget of about US$175 million under the management of the NSTDA. Its mission is to promote innovation and R&D activities in the private sector, and develop a critical mass of R&D human resource for Thailand.

Incentives and Privileges
BOI zone 3 privileges are available for firms locating their research activities in the TSP while it is geographically situated in zone 1: exemption of import duty on machinery; corporate income tax exemption for a period of eight years and 50 per cent reduction on taxes for a period of five years from the expiry of the eight-year exemption; tax deduction for research expenditures at 200 per cent.

Research Grant
Research grants of up to 5 million baht for each project are available for high-risk industrial research and development projects aimed at activating human resource development in R&D both quantitatively and qualitatively in the private sector to enhance capability in research development and engineering.

Soft Loan
Provides up to 30 million baht for applied research and development projects, including product or production process development and the building or refurbishing of laboratories through financial institution (not more than 75 per cent of project investment).

Consultation
Provides financial support for consultancy projects, sources local and international experts to investigate and solve technical problems for firms to help in the upgrading of products and processes, and assists in recruiting human resource in science and technology and engineering areas through network and educational institutions. Technical and technological, financial, human resource, and business or juristic types of support are also provided.

Facilities (other than research centres)
– Technology Licensing Office (TLO).
– Convention centre with more than 2,000 square metres of exhibition areas.
– 350-seat auditorium, meeting rooms with teleconferencing and video conferencing capabilities, research database in actual and virtual libraries.
– High speed telecommunication network.

Source: Summarized by the author from Thailand Science Park homepage at <http://www. sciencepark.or.th/profile-atglance.html>.

provides services such as testing facilities at rather low rates. It seems, however, more concerned about the electrical industries segment where 100 per cent Thai SMEs are more represented, than with high-tech electronics where foreign MNCs cover almost the whole landscape. Indeed, the survey (interviews in January 2007) did not allow us to understand fully how these organizations' respective roles were coordinated with cluster actions.

As mentioned before, human resource development is the most urgent issue both because skilled engineers, etc., are already lacking, and because it takes time to see the results. In that sense, the cluster initiative seems to have already yielded some results. But another important issue for the sustainability of the industry, namely the development of a 100 per cent Thai supporting industry, although on the agenda, seems to have made much less progress. Taking measures to help existing SMEs upgrade their technology is one way to deal with the problem. At the national level, some financial institutions have been created in the past years to provide long and medium-term loans to firms. But they are not well known to SMEs and the application is complicated due to bureaucratic red tape and evaluation procedures. Intarakumnerd (2006) explains that even though those encourage an "innovation culture" to take place progressively in Thailand, their impact remains rather low.

Another way to solve the problem would be to favour the development of innovative start-ups in the country. But Thailand still has very few incubation centres. Altenburg et al. (2004) relates the case of two incubation centres, the Software Park Thailand and the Thailand IC Design Incubator, whose results seem quite contrasted. An incubation centre was also created in the TSP, but it is not dedicated to the HDD industry. According to the chairman of the HDD cluster (interviewed in January 2007), incubation is an objective for the industry with researchers invited to work with firms on projects. SMEs are, for instance, invited to join collective projects in the hope that they would develop with the researchers help. But it appears that identifying SMEs that would be able or willing to engage in such a development process is not easy. Therefore, even if encouraging linkages between big and small companies, and between companies and universities, is one of the cluster's objectives, it will take time to see results. For the moment, linkages between big companies and universities are progressing (Brimble 2007). But as far as SMEs or start-ups are concerned, things are going slowly. It appears that Thailand is lacking entrepreneurial spirit and this might be attributed to an important sector of the population from rural origins. But to this cultural element, a more economical one has to be added. Loans are not easily available, and most of the people, even researchers, do not have the necessary guaranties to get a loan, so they cannot start a business. A venture capital association has existed in Thailand since 1994 and the Thai government has already supported several funds while considering incentives to promote venture capital investments in the country. But, venture capital funds are still too limited in number, and too careful, tending to finance firms at an expansion stage and not at the early start-up phase (Chapter 2).[43] So in the absence of angels, the main source for borrowing remains the banks. But banks do not like risky start-ups business. In such a context, even though incubation as a means of developing start-ups or SMEs for the HDD industry is on the agenda, achieving this goal is not an easy task. As a first step in this direction, a training programme to promote firms creation was launched by NSTDA and AIT.[44] About 1,000 people, mostly students, are trained every year under this programme aimed at building entrepreneurial spirit in parallel with competencies in management, etc. It is too early though to know if it will contribute to the creation of enough innovative SMEs.

Nevertheless, addressing the issue of linkages between the various players of the development, particularly the university industry ones, whose weakness was emphasized by numerous authors in the past years (Altenburg et al. 2004; Intarakumnerd 2005; Brimble 2007), we note that the recent policies implemented, especially the cluster initiative, show progress compared with past measures. Even though the process of change seems slow and difficult in Thailand, it is now underway. It is, however, still too early to conclude if the cluster will succeed fully in making HDD industry sustainable in the long run.

CONCLUDING REMARKS

From a situation in which Thailand's comparative advantage in attracting FDI was merely its abundant low-cost but rather skilled workforce plus the availability of modern infrastructure (IE) and general fiscal incentive packages, the country is now turning to the building of more competitiveness-based advantages to make its position within the global industry sustainable for the next decade. The evidence for this may be seen:

- Through the changes in the policy set that is now correlated to more qualitative criteria (STI programme) and sector-specific to address the needs of both the country's champion industries such as HDD, and the foreign manufacturers involved better.
- Through the creation of cluster which tends to address transversally the diverse issues that HDD industry is now facing, focusing first on human resources development, which appears to be the key factor for improvements in other domains such as technology upgrading, local supporting industry development, design capabilities building, and so on.

According to firms, the business climate in Thailand is good and the country is well ranked among the countries where doing business is easy. Interviews with firms confirm that with the new policy and the cluster, the framework for the further development of the HDD industry is much better than a few years before and is, in fact, rather adequate. This positive statement has to be nuanced though. While firms consider that forming the cluster was a good idea, they also notice that few results have appeared yet, except in human training to some extent. Even though the existing policy appears to be appreciated, problems remain in its execution which is considered to be too slow by firms, at least compared with Singapore that seems able to react very fast. Let's take an example from company interviews.

At the cluster launch, a special subsidy of US$1 million was obtained to acquire sophisticated equipment. Enterprises agreed to buy highly sophisticated equipment for material analysis. The equipment was expected, at the time of interview, to be delivered in August 2007, meaning that it would have taken two years between demand and equipment arrival.

The point here concerns the bureaucratic behaviour of Thai authorities, which makes implementation of approved actions slow. The threat of being accused of corruption seems to be making government executives very cautious in fund utilization. But the weight of bureaucracy is also apparent across the number of institutions that deal with industrial development. This sometimes makes it unclear what exactly respective roles are, even though the cluster initiative which coordinates all actors had, to some extent, the merit of clarifying the situation to participating firms.

The other limit in the development pace of the HDD cluster is probably linked to fund availability. A lot has to be done, but the HDD industry is, of course, not the only one to be aided. Public funds are, therefore, fragmented among the six clusters and their sub-programmes, making the necessary financial means too scarce for implementing all actions at the same time. But Thailand needs to go fast whether in training and educating a large number of technicians and engineers the industry absolutely needs to stay competitive, or in implementing other measures dedicated to SMEs and autochthon supporting industry to achieve its objective of locating the whole value-chain, and increasing the local content while reducing the import ratio.

As long as the Thai business climate allows firms to remain competitive, they will, of course, stay in Thailand, but as we have seen before, Thailand has rivals in the Asian area. These rivals (Singapore, Malaysia, China, Vietnam), whether concerned with the upstream or downstream of the value-chain, are not staying static either. The expected growth of the HDD global market implies that additional investments will still be needed in the coming years. The relative stability in average sale prices of HDD since 2004 — due to heavy consolidation in the sector making price competition between the few remaining assemblers smoother, but also to a certain shortage of components such as media,[45] — keeps inventories small, giving manufacturers or global suppliers the means and the will to invest heavily to cope with the increasing demand. Also, because of new opportunities opening, and as long as transportation, logistics, etc. costs remain low, firms could integrate more locations or enlarge the redundancy of their procurements in their vertically integrated intraregional production network.

Actions taken by Thailand since around 2004 are going in the right direction and the country has expectations of seeing the HDD cluster employing more than 150,000 people and contributing for 4 to 4.5 per cent of the total GDP in 2010.[46] The success will depend on a lot of factors peculiar to the HDD industry as this study has shown, but also on the way the country is able to catch up with its rivals by reforming its education system (Chapter 3), improving its infrastructure (Chapter 5), linking industry and research institutions, and enhancing its national system of innovation (Chapter 2), without forgetting the upgrading of Thai SMEs (Chapter 4).

Notes

1. One is Japanese, the other American. Due to confidentiality requirements it is impossible to give more information about these two manufacturers. The HDD assemblers in Thailand are not numerous enough to prevent easy identification of these two if main characteristics are given.

2. For the history of the HDD industry in Singapore, see Wong (1999); or McKendrick, Doner, and Haggard (2000).

3. For the history of the HDD industry development in Thailand, see Doner, Brimble (1998) or McKendrick, Doner and Haggard (2000).

4. For more details on the Malaysian HHD industry, see Haggard (1998).

5. In fact, American big computer manufacturers did not initiate the move to Asian low-cost countries. Pushed by innovative start-ups of the Silicon Valley (such as Seagate), they had no choice but to compete on price; they were simply quicker to follow to low-cost countries than were Japanese manufacturers, which did not have young start-ups competing with them at home. See McKendrick, Doner and Haggard (2000).

6. See Lecler (2003).

7. With the exception of Fujitsu, which in 1991 located its first HDD assembly-line extension for low-capacity 3.5-inch drives in Thailand where it had already invested in 1988 for the production of communication and electronic components and a few HDD heads components.

8. Where Fujitsu also joined them in 1995 with a second Southeast Asia plant opening.

9. A five-year exemption was given to projects employing new technologies. Firms expected to avoid taxes by introducing new technologies successively (Hiratsuka 2006).

10. Through a contract manufacturing agreement with Excelstore, a subsidiary of Great Wall (Hiratsuka 2006).

11. The two others, ranking below these four leading ones, are Toshiba and Samsung.

12. The new company is 70 per cent owned by Hitachi and 30 per cent by IBM. Hitachi assumes full ownership from the end of 2005. IBM has no involvement in HGST management, but has an agreement on contract for the supply of HDD (HGST home page).

13. Nidec, Magnecomp, KR precision, Donaldson, Innovex, Mektec, to name only few. For more detailed information on suppliers, see McKendrick, Doner and Haggard (2000), or Sukhpisarn (2002).

14. See Chapter 7 for some comparisons between industrial sectors, namely textile.

15. The iPod uses 1.8 inch and mobile phones, 0.85 inch. According to interviews (January 2007), the market for products with under 1-inch drives, does not

have a great future as competition with flash memory technology is not to the HDD's advantage.

16. See, for example, the case of HGST in Hiratsuka (2006), p. 194.

17. Vietnam seems to be recently targeted by some component manufacturers and could become a new location for low-end parts.

18. For a detailed analysis of this issue on all EE industries, see Altenburg et al. (2004).

19. After growing at a 2 per cent annual rate from 1982 to 1990, wages rose at an annual rate of over 9 per cent till 1994 which marked the end of the low-labour cost era (Brimble, Doner 2007, p. 4). Recently wages are increasing by about 6.5 per cent a year (Altenburg et al. 2004, p. 17).

20. It is especially in 2006 that the baht appreciated greatly due to the current account surplus and net capital inflow, which in 2006, was greater than for any other country in the region except Korea (% change of the baht to US$ between 2005 and 2006 = −5.81 (Worl Bank Office 2007, p. 12).

21. The ten countries are: China, Hong Kong, India, Indonesia, Korea, Malaysia, the Philippines, Singapore, Taiwan, and Thailand.

22. Also see Chapter 7 for weaknesses, according to WEF.

23. For more details, see Chapter 3.

24. See Brimble, "Innovation and R and D in the Private Sector", in Lorlowhakard and Teth-Uthepak (2003), Ch. 3.

25. This occurred more in the car industry than in the HDD industry because of local content regulation.

26. 300 when launching a new product, with production staff becoming teachers when needed.

27. This training is attested by a certificate if the operators succeed in the final test.

28. For more details on the question of technology transfer, design capability building, and comparisons between U.S. and Japanese multinationals, see Hobday and Rush (2007).

29. See Thajchayapong Pairash, "Science and Technology in Thailand: An Economic Perspective", in Lorlowhakard and Teth-Uthepak (2003), Ch. 2.

30. Among the remaining 20–25 per cent, more than half comes from Japan (54 per cent, media mainly), then Singapore (18 per cent), Philippines (9 per cent including few parts from China), Indonesia (9 per cent), Vietnam, and the United States (10 per cent; printed circuit from the United States, assembled in Vietnam).

31. See Thajchayapong Pairash, "Science and Technology in Thailand: An Economic Perspective", in Lorlowhakard and Teth-Uthepak (2003), Ch. 2.

32. The situation seems a little bit different in the case of the automotive industry even though the weakness of the supporting industry is also reported by firms. But, as proximity was more important in the industry due to higher transportation costs, production that is mostly dedicated to the domestic

market, and a less developed intraregional procurement network, global suppliers used to train some local subcontractors more extensively (Lecler 2002).

33. On this cultural issue, see Sheehan Brian, "Thailand on the March", in Emery, Ellis, Chulavatnatol (2005), Ch. 2.

34. Also see Chapter 2.

35. Following this new policy, three main HDD manufacturers announced new investments in Thailand for a total amount of over US$600 million and creating thousands of jobs (Brimble, from Afzulpurkar and Brimble 2004).

36. As import-duty exemptions were linked to exports, the whole production is first exported then reimported for local market needs, which are very small in fact (interviews). The main export market in 2005 for parts and accessories (in export value) were China followed by ASEAN then the European Union, the United States, and Japan, attesting to the importance of the intra-Asia production network, which now includes China, where production is fast growing.

37. After Michael Porter's visit to Thailand, see Chapter 4.

38. More recently a seventh one was added which is not really industrial-sector oriented: activities to support community and underprivileged people. The aim of this new cluster is not clear.

39. It was approved in Fall 2007 (from company sources).

40. Thai firms are not engaged in HDD components even though some might supply the HDD industry with packaging or other annex activities.

41. iTAP is an industrial support programme designed to encourage the application of technology to industries in Thailand. It is a department of Technology Management Center (TMC), of the NSTDA, and is managed by Hemaraj Land and Development.

42. He was hired in mid-2004 to prepare for the launch and was still working there at the survey time (2007).

43. For more details, see also Intarakumnerd (2006).

44. In 2002, the New Entrepreneurship Creation (NEC) Programme was launched as a general tool (not dedicated to HDD) to promote the creation of 50,000 new firms. The selection of candidates, the delayed budget attribution, etc., led to poor results in terms of the number of successful enterprise created (see Altenburg et al. 2004).

45. For more details, see Coughlin Associates (2006), executive summary.

46. See NECTEC, <http://tpt.nectec.or.th/nac2006/NAC2006-HDD-1.pdf>.

References

Afzulpurkar, Nitin and Peter Brimble. "Building a World Class Industry: Strengthening the Hard Disk Drive Cluster in Thailand — A Blueprint from Industry/Government/Academia". Report at the NSTDA, Bangkok, 2004.

Altenburg, Tilman, et al. "Strengthening Knowledge-based Competitive Advantages in Thailand". German Development Institute (GDI) Report and Working Papers 1/2004 available online at <se1.isn.ch/serviceengine/FileContent?serviceID=PublishingHouse&fileid=450BF1F1-6B5E-A0FB-3D89-8C93F4C>, 2004.

Amano, Tomofumi. "Competitive Strategy of Global Firms and Industrial Clusters — Case Study on the Hard Disk Drive (HDD) Industry". MMRC Discussion Paper No. 99, September 2006. Available <http://www.ut-mmrc.jp/36 p>.

Berger, Martin. "Upgrading the System of Innovation in Late-Industrialising Countries: The Role of Transnational Corporation in Thailand's Manufacturing Sector". Doctoral Dissertation, Matematisch-Naturewissenschaftlichen Fakultät derChristian-Albrechts Universität zu Kiel (17 March 2005, p. 278). Available at <http://deposit.ddb.de/cgi-bin/dokserv?idn=980863430&dok_var=d1&dok_ext= pdf&filename=980863430.pdf>. Accessed April 2007.

Brimble, Peter. "Harddisk Drives: Industrial Clusters Needed". Kasikorn Research Center (KRC) HDD report (Kindly offered by the author).

Brimble, Peter and Richard Doner. "University-Industry Linkages and Economic Development: The Case of Thailand". World Development 35, issue 6 (June 2007): 1021–36.

BOI (Board of Investment). Thailand Investment Review (online newsletter) 13, no. 2 (March 2004).

———. Thailand Investment Review 14 no. 12 (December 2005).

———. Thailand Investment Review 17, no. 6 (June 2007).

———. "Thailand Investment Opportunities in Electrical and Electronics". October 2005. Available at <http://www.boi.go.th>.

Business-in-Asia.com. Online newsletter. <www.business-in-asia.com/harddisk drive_industry. html>. Accessed 8 December 2006.

Coughlin Associates. "Hard Disk Drive Capital Equipment Market and Technology Report". Executive Summary, available at <http://www.tomcoughlin.com/Techpapers/Capital%20Spending% 20Brochure,%20062606.pdf>.

Coughlin Tom, Dennis Wait, and Jim Porter. "The Disk Drive: 50 Years of Progress and Technology Innovation". Computer Technology Review, April 2004. Available at <http://www.tom coughlin.com/Techpapers/DISK%20DRIVE% 20HISTORY,%20TC%20Edits,%20050504.pdf>. Accessed 8 December 2008.

Doner, Richard F. and Peter Brimble. "Thailand's Hard Disk Drive Industry". The Information Storage Industry Center, Graduate School of International Relations and Pacific Studies, University of California. Available at <http://isic.ucsd.edu/>.

Doner, Rick and Bryan Richie. "Economic Crisis and Technological Trajectories: Hard Disk Drive Production in Southeast Asia". MIT Japan Program, Working paper 01-06, available at <http://mit.edu/mit-japan/outreach/working-papers/WP0106.pdf>. Accessed 8 December 2006.

Electrical and Electronics Institute. Industrial Economics Situation Report. *Electrical and Electronics* (January 2006), p. 27. Available at <http://www.thaieei.com/ GuruPortal/Guru/engineName/ filemanager/site/ensite/pid/886/monthly-janv06.pdf;jsessionid=10C12484C636 F1785843049466F345A4?actionreq= actionFileDownload&fileItem=1062>.

Emery, Silvio L., Wyn Ellis, Montri Chulavatnatol (ed.). *Thailand: Competitive Innovation Strategies*. National Innovation Agency, Amlarin Publishing (2005), p. 199.

EUSEA. *ICT Development in Thailand: Infrastructure, Research and Industry*. Available at <http://www.eusea2006.org/Website/programme/file.2006-07-14.9623885989> (accessed March 2007).

Haggard, Stephan. *The Hard Disk Drive Industry in the Northern Region of Malaysia*. The Information Storage Industry Center, Graduate School of International Relations and Pacific Studies, University of California. Available at <http:// isic.ucsd.edu/ papers/malaysiahdd.shtml> (accessed 8 December 2006).

Hiratsuka, Daisuke. "Vertical Intra-Regional Production Network in East Asia: A Case Study of the Hard Disc Drive Industry". In *East Asia's De Facto Economic Integration*, edited by D. Hiratsuka, pp. 181–99. IDE-JETRO: Palgrave Macmillan, 2006.

Hobday, Michael and Howard Rush. "Upgrading the Technological Capabilities of Foreign Transnational Subsidiaries in Developing Countries: The Case of Electronics in Thailand". *Research Policy*, <doi:10.1016/j.respol.2007.05.004, 2007>.

Intarakumnerd, Patarapong. "The Roles of Intermediaries in Clusters: The Thai Experiences in High-tech and Community-based Clusters". *Asian Journal of Technology Innovation* 13, no. 2 (2005): 23–43.

———. "Thailand National System of Innovation in Transition". In *Asia's Innovation Systems in Transition*, edited by B. Lundvall, P. Intarakumnerd, J. Vang, pp. 100–22. Edward Elgar, 2006.

Intarakumnerd, Patarapong and Pituma Panthavi. "Science and Technology Development Toward A Knowledge-Based Economy". In *Human Resource Development Toward A Knowledge-Based Economy: The Case of Thailand*, edited by M. Makishima and Somchai Suksiriserekul, pp. 89–132. IDE-JETRO: ASEDP, 2003.

Inthaiwong, Sudjit, Deputy Secretary General of BOI. Presentation at the Europe Asia forum, Lyon, 3 April 2007 (from JETRO survey, March 2006).

Kimura, Fukunari. "The Development of Fragmentation in East Asia and its Implication for FTAs". In *East Asia's De Facto Economic Integration*, edited by D. Hiratsuka. IDE-JETRO: Palgrave Macmillan, pp. 16–31.

Kumagai, Satoru. "Sinpaporu Mareshia no PC Kanren Sangyo no Seisui: Takokusekikigyo Chushingata Hatten no Kisu" [The Rise and Fall of PC related Industries in Singapore and Malaysia: A Consequence of MNCs-driven Industrial Development]. In *Higashi Ajia no IT Kiki Sangyo: Bungyo, Kyoso, Sumiwake no Dainamikusu* [The Information Technology Equipment Industry in East Asia: The Dynamics of Specialization, Competition and Symbiosis], edited by Ken Imai, Momoko Kawakami. IDE-JETRO, Kenkyu Sosho (IDE Research Series), No. 556 (2006): 171–216.

Lecler, Yveline. "Pénétration du marché ou plateforme d'exportation? La division du travail dans les firmes japonaises en Asie". In *Après la crise, Les économies asiatiques face aux défis de la mondialisation*, edited by Bouissou, Hochraich and Milelli, pp. 203–33. Paris: Karthala, 2003.

———. "The Cluster Role in the Development of Thai Car Industry: Some Evidence from Empirical Studies". *International Journal of Urban and Regional Studies* 26, no. 4 (December 2002): 799–814.

Lorlowhakarn Supachai and Sasithorn Teth-Uthapak, eds. *Science and Technology in Thailand*. Bangkok: NSTDA, 2003.

McKendrick, David. *Sustaining Competitive Advantage in Global Industries: Technological Change and Foreign Assembly in the Hard Disk Drive Industry*. The Information Storage Industry Center, Graduate School of International Relations and Pacific Studies, University of California, 1997. Available at <http://isic.ucsd.edu/competitivedynamics.html>. Accessed 8 December 2006.

McKendrick David G., Richard E. Doner and Stephan Haggard. *From Silicon Valley to Singapore: Location and Competitive Advantage in the Hard Disk Drive Industry*. Stanford University Press, 2000.

McKinsey. "Computer and Electronics". Available at <http://www. mckinsey.com/ mgi/reports/pdfs/thailand/09Computer_electronics.pdf>. Accessed March 2006.

Patrawimolpon, Pichit and Runchana Pongsaparn. "Thailand in the New Asian Economy: The Current State and Way Forward". In Discussion Paper, DP/ 04/2006, Bank of Thailand, December 2006. Available online.

Sukhpisarn, Narumon. "Analysis of Component Procurement System in Hard Disk Drive Industry in Thailand". Master Thesis of Economics, Faculty of Economics, Thammasat University, Bangkok, 24 May 2002, p. 146.

Tecson, Gwendolyn R. "The Hard Disk Drive Industry in the Philippines". The Information Storage Industry Center, Graduate School of International Relations and Pacific Studies, University of California, 1998. Available at <http://isic.ucsd.edu/philippineshdd.html>. Accessed 22 December 2006.

Termpitayapaisit, Arkhom. *Thailand and its Knowledge Economy*. Available at <http://info.worldbank.org/etools/docs/library/233823/PWThailandIts% 20Knowledge%20EconomyPaper06.pdf>. Accessed on May 2007.

Wong, Poh-Kam. "The Dynamics of HDD Industry Development in Singapore". Paper ISICReport 99'03, p. 67. Information Storage Industry Center,

Globalization of the Storage Industry". University of California San Diego, 1999. Available at <http:// repositories.cdlib.org/isic/gsi/ISICReport-99-03>.

World Bank Office. *Thailand Economic Monitor*. April 2007. Available at <http://www. worldbank.or.th>. Accessed June 2007.

Useful Websites

Hard Disk Drive Institute (HDDI) home page: <http://www3.easywebtime.com/hdd_eng/plan.html>.

Thailand Science Park (TSP) home page: <http://www.sciencepark.or.th/profile-atglance.html>.

National Electronic and Computer Technology Centre (NECTEC) home page: <http://service.nectec.or.th>.

Board of Investment (BOI) home page: <http://www.boi.go.th>.

National Science and Technology Development Agency (NSTDA) home page: <http://www.nstda.or.th/en/>.

Interviews

In addition to the above sources, the information comes from eleven interviews done by the author on 8–20 January 2007.

Index

www.ingramcontent.com/pod-product-compliance
Lightning Source LLC
Chambersburg PA
CBHW021849020426
42334CB00013B/248